A Town In-Between

EARLY AMERICAN STUDIES

Series editors

Daniel K. Richter, Kathleen M. Brown,
and David Waldstreicher

Exploring neglected aspects of our colonial, revolutionary,
and early national history and culture, Early American
Studies reinterprets familiar themes and events in fresh ways.
Interdisciplinary in character, and with a special emphasis
on the period from about 1600 to 1850, the series is published
in partnership with the McNeil Center for Early American
Studies.

A complete list of books in the series is available
from the publisher.

A Town In-Between

Carlisle, Pennsylvania, and the Early Mid-Atlantic Interior

Judith Ridner

PENN

UNIVERSITY OF PENNSYLVANIA PRESS

PHILADELPHIA · OXFORD

Published by
University of Pennsylvania Press
Philadelphia, Pennsylvania 19104-4112

Printed in the United States of America on acid-free paper
10 9 8 7 6 5 4 3 2 1

Library of Congress Cataloging-in-Publication Data
Ridner, Judith E.
    A town in-between : Carlisle, Pennsylvania, and the early
Mid-Atlantic interior / Judith E. Ridner.
        p. cm. — (Early American studies)
    Includes bibliographical references and index.
    ISBN 978-0-8122-4236-2 (hardcover : alk. paper)
    1. Carlisle (Pa.)—History—18th century. I. Title.
F159.C2R536 2010
974.8'43—dc22   2009044903

CONTENTS

MAPS AND ILLUSTRATIONS

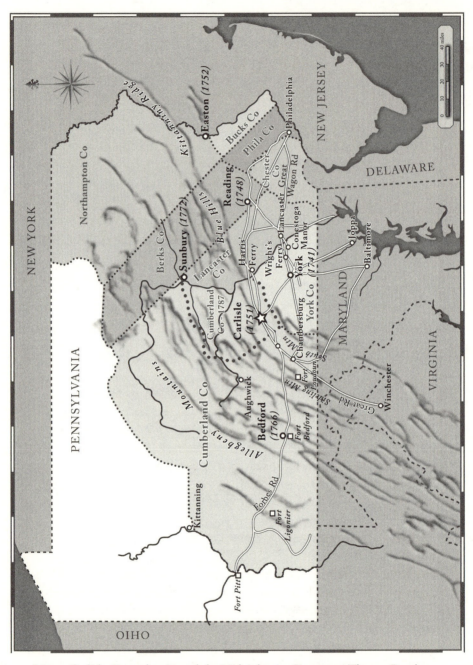

Map 1. Carlisle, Pennsylvania, and the Mid-Atlantic, Circa 1770. Thomas Penn's six proprietary towns (including Carlisle) are listed with their dates of founding. County boundaries are indicated by dotted lines. Large dots outline Cumberland's smaller size by 1787. Drawn by Gerry Krieg.

Introduction

WHY CARLISLE? IS a question I was asked frequently while I worked on this project. Some people have never heard of Carlisle. Others know it only as a place where Interstate 81 and the Pennsylvania Turnpike nearly meet, or they have heard of the Carlisle Barracks, home to the U.S. Army War College and former site of the Carlisle Indian Industrial School. Still others actually know the town from having sent children to college or going to law school there, and have seen it firsthand. They recall its quaint downtown, historic Dickinson College, and the many eighteenth- and nineteenth-century row homes that line its streets. Yet they wonder about the significance of its history; what larger stories could this charming place possibly reveal about America's past?

Twenty-first-century Carlisle is a county seat (of Cumberland County) with a population of 18,000.[1] It is a small place. Aside from the cities of Philadelphia and Pittsburgh, which dwarf it in size, many other towns in the state, including Allentown (where I now live), Erie, and Harrisburg eclipse it, even though they were just hamlets in the eighteenth century.[2] Carlisle also lacks the gritty urbanism of Pennsylvania's larger cities. To be sure, it suffers from the effects of urban poverty, but it does so on a smaller scale—one that rarely claims headlines.

As I also know from my years of living in Carlisle while a student at Dickinson College, if Carlisle is known for anything today, it is for its nonurban qualities. Visitors and even some residents do not pay much attention to the poverty tucked among the streets and alleys of the northern parts of town or the suburban sprawl on its outskirts. Instead, they notice its charms. Carlisle is a pleasant town in which to stroll, attend college, or settle and raise a family away from the big city.[3] Today's Carlisle is not really an urban place at all, therefore, but a quaint throwback to a simpler, more serene time. And thus people continue to ask me: why Carlisle? because the town's early, turbulent, and profoundly interesting history as a key urban place in the mid-Atlantic interior has been either obscured by modern developments or forgotten.

A Town In-Between is my attempt to reclaim Carlisle's overlooked legacy in all its forms. At its most basic, the book is a corrective. It tells the story of eighteenth-century Carlisle so that readers will know it as a place with a dynamic history in the early mid-Atlantic. In this way, it is a microhistory of one of the most significant interior towns of the eighteenth century. My goal, like that of other recent works of this type, is to write Carlisle back into our collective historical consciousness. To do so, I intensively study specific features of this town's history and the activities of its early Scots-Irish inhabitants. This history and their experiences, I argue, are a means to uncover hitherto unknown or understudied aspects of the big events and broader patterns of American experience, particularly in the mid-Atlantic interior.[4]

Eighteenth-century Carlisle has a fascinating history, which deserves to be told on its own terms by moving forward through time, rather than backward from today. By eighteenth-century standards, Carlisle was a sizable and significant place. At a time when most Americans lived on rural farmsteads and urban centers like Philadelphia and New York were only a fraction of the size they are today, Carlisle, as a town, stood out on the landscape; its urbanness made it unique, especially in the interior. So, too, did its rapid growth. From the time of its founding in 1751, Carlisle quickly assumed its place as one of the five strongest and fastest-growing county seats in Pennsylvania.[5] Only two years after its founding, the town already had 105 taxpayers, and total population of perhaps 500, and maybe even 600. Such growth, although variable, continued over the next fifty years. By 1800, when Philadelphia—Pennsylvania's largest and America's second largest city—had 41,000 inhabitants (62,000 including the area surrounding), Carlisle's nearly 2,000 residents (some three to four times its population in 1753) made it the fifth largest town in the state. In addition, it was proportionally larger relative to Philadelphia than it is today. Carlisle was even sizable compared to other interior towns of the time. Although Lancaster, the twenty-fifth largest town in America in 1800, was slightly more than double Carlisle's size, Reading and York were only barely larger. Easton and Pittsburgh were smaller, as were all of the towns heading southward down the Great Valley. Winchester, Virginia, the most significant town at the northern end of the Valley, had just over 1,500 residents, while farther south Staunton and Mecklenberg had only 1,000 inhabitants each.[6]

But size was not the only measure of its significance. Carlisle's history deserves to be known because it was a town that mattered in the eighteenth century. Early Americans, especially those in the mid-Atlantic, did not ask *why Carlisle?* because they knew it as a place. Many had visited, migrated through, worked in, or heard about it. As a town planned by Pennsylvania's principal proprietor, Thomas Penn, Carlisle was a place where things happened: it was a migration gateway to the southern and western interiors, hub of the colonial fur trade, military staging and supply ground during the Seven Years' and Revolutionary Wars, and home to one of the United States' earliest printing presses and colleges. As such, it drew diverse and ambitious groups of planners, speculators, traders, and migrants to its borders, many of whom hoped to harness the town and its resources to advance their economic or political ambitions or personal interests. Yet people of the time also knew Carlisle because it had an infamous reputation as a disorderly place. In fact, as competition among the many divergent interests at work in Carlisle generated tensions, they produced conflicts, including repeated uprisings, jailbreaks, and one of the most publicized Anti-Federalist riots during constitutional ratification. Eighteenth-century Carlisle was thus a contradictory place. For those early Americans who migrated or had commercial dealings there, it offered the possibility of advancement through the abundant opportunities available within or near its borders; Carlisle seemed a place where aspirations could be transformed into realities. But the effects of two wars, one Native uprising, several violent political protests, and ongoing tensions among various class, ethnic, and religious interests generated enough disorder to temper any gains one made, much to the frustration of those who lived or did business there. In this book, I detail these two opposing and irreconcilable aspects of the town's early history. Readers should not only know Carlisle, they must recognize it for what it was—a town of tremendous promise but many thwarted ambitions. It was neither the quaint nor serene place it likes to sell itself as today.

Yet there is more. As this book's title suggests, my work moves beyond an interesting story of an important place in early America. Rather, it has the more ambitious goal of reconceptualizing how we think about the histories of early American towns like Carlisle and the role they played in developing the early American interior. Towns, after all, were what historian Richard C. Wade once called "spearheads of the frontier." Planted by entrepreneurial proprietors mostly in advance of Euro-American colonization, these planned urban places, typically characterized by their grid-patterned streets, were defined by their utility and potential for growth. Those that prospered, like

Carlisle, did so by attracting colonists eager for commercial opportunities. These towns became centers of interior commerce and speculation because new transport and trade networks forged by their first inhabitants linked them to their developing agricultural hinterlands as well as established market centers near the coast.[7]

Carlisle exemplifies these patterns. Like interior towns founded by other colonial-minded entrepreneurs in seventeenth-century New England, the eighteenth-century mid-Atlantic and South, and nineteenth-century West, it was an ambitiously designed urban settlement meant to reap profits for its planners by attracting a hard-working group of residents to build and sustain it. It grew and prospered because townspeople took the initiative—despite the obstacles and constraints they faced—to make it a key midpoint in a chain of commerce and culture stretching from Europe to eastern cities like Philadelphia and Baltimore, and across the mid-Atlantic interior into the American West.[8] Its history, like that of other towns, thus confirms the critical role town founding played in colonizing the interior. In fact, Carlisle reminds us that urban and commercial interests—and the many proprietors, speculators, traders, merchants, shopkeepers, artisans, and laborers who advanced them—are just as central to the story of early America's conquest of the interior as were the agricultural concerns of farmers and planters.

Yet Carlisle's history also adds vital new dimensions to this story. Richard C. Wade conceptualized nineteenth-century America's western cities as "spearheads" of an *urban frontier* that swept triumphantly westward to claim the interior. Studying Carlisle, by contrast, reveals different patterns of spatial orientation and motion that tell a more nuanced, and sometimes even tragic, story of American development. Carlisle sat in-between regions and cultures, not at the edge. The town occupied a contested space between east and west, north and south, Europe and America, and Euro-American and Native American. Its history, in short, was shaped not just by single-minded, westward-moving Americans, but by a complex mix of peoples and colonizers, each with their own myriad interests and agendas, that moved to and through the town from Europe, the Delaware Valley, the Chesapeake Bay, and the deepest reaches of the early American West. In this way, Carlisle's settlement and political-economic patterns model how other interior towns functioned and how their inhabitants experienced a life in-between others.

To be sure, urban life in-between was complicated. As Carlisle's history demonstrates, betweenness had multiple dimensions. Geographically, Carlisle's central location in the mid-Atlantic, and at a pivot point along routes into the southern and western interiors, made it a crucial crossroads for the shifting streams of migration, commerce, and culture flowing between regions and the diverse peoples who populated them. Such physical betweenness affected the shape of Carlisle's landscape and the scope of its economic development, often in dramatic ways. Indeed, the town belonged simultaneously to a west populated by multiethnic Native villages and an east dominated by growing early American cities like Philadelphia and Baltimore. Then, too, in a town settled mostly by immigrants, there were also European influences, particularly from Ireland. Carlisle's history, therefore, was shaped by the interplay among these regions, the multiple interests and influences they represented, and their interactions with local circumstances. During the colonial period, the time when most of the town's immigrant settlers arrived, Carlisle's western ties were strong. At its founding, Carlisle thus stood amid the shifting and sometimes overlapping cultural and territorial spaces between Native American and Euro-American communities in the mid-Atlantic, and the real and metaphorical ties townspeople had to Europe. On the one hand, its development was framed by the Native settlement patterns that predated it, while its colonial economy was fueled by the furs and skins that Native hunters and trappers of the Ohio Valley offered in trade. Yet as a town planned by Pennsylvania's principal proprietor, targeted by Philadelphia merchants as a way station in their cross-colony trade networks, and settled by mostly Scots-Irish immigrants, Carlisle was also a product of the metropolitan east and western Europe. Its town plan, warehouses, and churches stood as tangible symbols of these connections.

Following the American Revolution, the balance of influence shifted, however, and Carlisle leaned more heavily toward the East. The town's new college, newspaper, and its expanding built environment were evidence of this trend. Yet in the early republic, these institutions and structures embodied not just the ways Carlisle's inhabitants reached out to participate in the wider cultural worlds and markets of the eighteenth century, but how they shaped a new, American brand of cosmopolitanism. Independence was won, after all. Native communities whose trade spurred colonial Carlisle's commercial sector were being pushed farther west by an aggressive tide of warfare, settlement, and speculation unleashed at the close of the war. At the same time, many of Carlisle's Scots-Irish inhabitants, some of whom had fought hard for the American cause, were eager to assume new American political and social identities in the nation. Encouraged by Philadelphia reformers who were keen to incorporate the Pennsylvania interior into the cultural and political orbits of the metropole, some town leaders pushed to align their town more closely with Philadelphia. But they did so at their peril; not everyone agreed. And in a republic in which men were conditioned to resist what they defined as arbitrary authority, some townspeople were willing to fight to preserve their vision of what their town was and should be. Some townspeople still looked to look to the West, however distant, for economic gain. Some even migrated there or sent their children to make new lives there. To them, the American interior remained a powerful lure; it represented opportunity. Carlisle thus remained a town in-between.

Betweenness also made Carlisle a contested place. Straddling the ill-defined territory between Native American villages of the interior and Euro-American cities of the Delaware Valley and Chesapeake Bay, Carlisle was a place where east met west in the mid-Atlantic. Its expanding built landscape, commerce, and politics over the second half of the eighteenth century attest to the powerful influences these regions had on its development. Yet Carlisle's betweenness had equally important cultural dimensions. Carlisle was not just a town between regions, but between the cultures those regions encompassed. The eighteenth-century mid-Atlantic, and especially Pennsylvania, was noted for its ethnic plurality. The region was populated by a diverse collection of peoples who represented a variety of ethnic, racial, religious, and cultural backgrounds—including Native American, European, and African. Once settled together in the mid-Atlantic, these groups invented new identities for themselves by adapting traditional cultural practices to suit new circumstances and peoples. The new identities that resulted fostered group cohesiveness and distinguished them from others.[9] Yet such reinvention, I argue, was also intimately connected to space and place. A common regional background typically sets the stage for the shared cultural experiences that shape a group's identity, after all. In the mid-Atlantic, and particularly Pennsylvania, where the colony's plural population was not settled evenly over the region's vast landscape but tended to cluster together in residentially segregated enclaves, the connection between location and identity was especially strong. Certain cultural groups were more closely associated with specific areas than others.[10]

By mid-century, for example, Native American peoples like the Shawnee and Delaware had mostly relocated to the Ohio country. They made their homes on the western side of the Susquehanna near the site of Carlisle for a time, but moved west in response to colonial settlement and imperial politics. Although some members of these communities persisted in the Susquehanna

Valley, their interests and identities as native peoples were aligned more closely with lands and commerce on the western and northern reaches of the mid-Atlantic interior. The British and American colonists recognized them as the "Ohio Indians." Although they were really multiethnic communities representing multiple tribal affiliations, their common Algonquian language and the geographic space they occupied on the margins of British North America united them—especially in the minds of the British and their colonists.[11]

Similar regional affiliations linked settlement patterns and ethnic identity among the mid-Atlantic's Euro-American colonists. At first glance, English Anglicans seem to defy the connection between place and identity. But that was not so. Although they settled across the colony in town and countryside and were among the groups least effective at ethno-religious coalition building in politics, they were nonetheless Britons. As such, they laid claim to an identity that connected them to the institutions of British authority that carried across the Atlantic. For many in Pennsylvania at mid-century, that identity translated into an alliance with the colony's proprietary establishment under the leadership of Penn's sons, particularly Thomas. And with the proprietary leadership taking an Anglican turn in the eighteenth century, many of the most powerful Anglican colonists remade themselves into loyal proprietors' men. They closely associated themselves with the colony's seat of power, the provincial capital of Philadelphia, and its hinterlands in the Delaware Valley.[12] Even more important in shaping the Anglo character of the Delaware Valley were the Quakers—whether of English, Welsh, or Irish origin. The Quakers' numerical predominance in this region, their identity as founding colonists under William Penn, and their long-standing claims to political authority closely connected them to the colony's center of power, Philadelphia. This was the region where Quakers fashioned what one scholar calls "a distinctive regional public culture."[13]

There were also Pennsylvania's many German colonists, particularly of the Lutheran and Reformed faiths. They were among the most recent arrivals to the mid-Atlantic in the eighteenth century and soon became the largest group of non-English immigrants in Pennsylvania. Just as important, as Germans—with language and cultural traditions distinct from those of their fellow Anglo colonists—they were outsiders, which encouraged them to carve out an especially distinct, Euro-American identity in the eighteenth century. Although this German, or "Pennsylvania Dutch," ethnic culture was found throughout the colony, it was most fully articulated in rural Lancaster, Berks, Northampton, and York counties, where they were most numerous. Without doubt, their presence in these outer counties lent a decidedly German cultural tone to the fringes of southeastern Pennsylvania that fast became one of the cultural hallmarks of the colony's interior.[14]

That left the Scots-Irish, or Ulster Irish. They were the other major European ethnic group of the eighteenth-century mid-Atlantic and the single largest group of immigrants, other than Africans, to make their way across the Atlantic to British North America in the eighteenth century. Like their German neighbors, they were mostly recent immigrants who had arrived in the colony after 1718. Virtually all of them were Protestants—overwhelmingly Presbyterians—who had migrated from Ulster, the area of northern Ireland where their Lowland Scots ancestors had migrated as part of the British colonization scheme for Ireland in the seventeenth century. Although their geographic mobility and cultural flexibility in Ireland and America earned them a reputation as a "people with no name," this was mostly a misnomer. For the Scots-Irish, however adaptable they were as a people, nonetheless expressed a distinct cultural identity in America through their shared experiences as immigrants, Protestants, and British citizens.[15] In Pennsylvania, their identity was also intimately connected to their experiences as inhabitants of the colony's interior. Although they settled across the colony, the Scots-Irish at mid-century were particularly concentrated in the newly founded farming communities and towns cut just east and especially west of the Susquehanna River. Most important to this book, they were the predominant ethnic group in Cumberland County and its seat, Carlisle.[16]

Living in Pennsylvania's interior placed the Scots-Irish in a precarious position. It also offered them opportunities by situating them to be a people in-between. And to fill that critical role, they interacted with the multiethnic Native and Euro-American communities to their west and east. Those inhabiting western Cumberland County, for example, lived near and among diverse Native communities. Those living in and near Carlisle, by contrast, the people who are the focus of this book, found themselves living near and among pluralistic, Euro-American Pennsylvania. Living on the eastern side of their county, these colonists traded with more distant Native peoples while forging enduring but sometimes tense contacts with other English and German colonists. Pennsylvania's Scots-Irish, therefore, were not people on the margins of British North America. Rather, occupying a pivotal area of the mid-Atlantic interior, they were at one of its centers. This assured that they would be players in the shifting cultural spaces between the myriad racial, ethnic, and religious interest groups in the eighteenth-century mid-Atlantic.

Of course, inhabiting this real and metaphorical space between regions did not come without challenges. When peaceful relations with the Ohio Valley's Native Americans fractured, as they did during the Seven Years' War and Pontiac's Uprising, Cumberland County's Scots-Irish colonists were among the first to suffer the violent consequences. Likewise, during these wars and then the American Revolution, British and American leaders called on many of these same colonists to assist them in defending the borders of the empire or nation. But not all facets of life in the interior were negative or threatening. Being a people in-between also had advantages; it accorded them a significant measure of cultural power within the mid-Atlantic. As Carlisle's Scots-Irish colonists discovered, occupying a contested space between the Native American communities of the Ohio Valley and English-Anglican, Quaker, and German areas of southeastern Pennsylvania and the Delaware Valley positioned them to act as informal cultural brokers. And as Pennsylvania colonists of European ancestry, this meant that the choices they made about the direction of their lives and that of their community affected how Euro-American cultural practices and values were transmitted and adapted. In this book, I explain some of the mechanisms through which these Scots-Irish colonists translated their European-derived culture into the American interior; I also discuss the implications of their actions. As a people in-between, the Scots-Irish claimed an identity as key actors in the mid-Atlantic interior.

Finally, Carlisle's betweenness rested on its status as an urban place amid the farms and agrarian interests of the interior. As a town and the planned seat of government for Pennsylvania's most sprawling and sparsely populated western county, Carlisle represented a concentration of people and authority in the interior. It was a focal point of its region. As such, Carlisle drew a host of powerful outsiders to its borders. They envisioned the town as a hub for their far-flung ventures intended to link west to east in Pennsylvania. To enact their vision, they planned the town's streets, founded its college, and attempted to guide its economic and political workings. To these men, Carlisle represented opportunity; it was a place where they could focus their ambitions.

At the same time, townspeople and county residents—a collection of entrepreneurial, fiercely independent, and mostly Scots-Irish colonists—had their own, plural visions of this town and its functions. They also aspired to make Carlisle their own, for much was at stake. As the county seat, Carlisle offered them security in a region marked by warfare and other forms of

inter-ethnic violence. As a market in the interior, Carlisle was also an important commercial center that connected them to the markets of Philadelphia,
Baltimore, and the Atlantic world. As home to many churches and taverns,
the town was also a social hub. Yet Carlisle served other functions. As the
center of law, commerce, and culture in Cumberland County, it was a place
of community and confrontation. Local inhabitants congregated there to express their displeasure with colony, state, and national officials. On the town's
streets, in the courthouse, and in the informal setting of taverns or stores
locals challenged outsiders whose activities threatened their community. Finally, locals also confronted each other over the personal, class, or ethno-
religious disputes dividing their community. As an interior town, Carlisle was
thus a stage for public expressions of tension rooted in the competing class,
ethnic, and religious identities of Pennsylvania's interior inhabitants. In this
book, I trace the cooperation and clashes between these groups so that readers might better understand not just Carlisle, but the multilayered human
dynamics at work in other urban places in the mid-Atlantic interior in the
eighteenth century.

So, to tell Carlisle's story as one of eighteenth-century Pennsylvania's
most important interior towns accomplishes several historical goals. It shifts
our historical lens west, away from the oft-studied Delaware Valley, to reveal
the understudied workings of the colony's and state's interior settlements,
particularly those populated by the Scots-Irish. It also refocuses our view by
demonstrating how towns acted as forces of change and continuity in the
eighteenth-century mid-Atlantic interior. In these ways, Carlisle was both
unique and representative. It was a place populated by its own "endless pro-
cession of characters," in the words of a contemporary, whose personalities
and interests lent distinctiveness to the town's experience.[17] Thus, it has its
own interesting story as an early American community. But Carlisle's history
is something more. This is not simply a traditional community study that
examines a local place and people in minute detail in isolation from others. Rather, by situating Carlisle in a wider, regional context, and focusing
exclusively on those individuals and interest groups that most affected the
way it functioned in its region, I uncover larger patterns of early American
experience that are broadly applicable to other urban places of the eighteenth-
century mid-Atlantic.

As a town in-between, Carlisle possessed a malleability and sense of dynamic promise that was prototypically American. It was not isolated, but
connected. It drew people to its borders from all over the Atlantic world. It

encouraged them to think big and act on their ambitions. When disputes arose, these same people took to the courtroom, streets, or marketplace to express their frustrations. In these ways, Carlisle, like early America more generally, was a place where residents found themselves constantly negotiating, and sometimes even fighting between the extremes of continuity and change, consensus and conflict, homogeneity and diversity, prosperity and poverty, optimism and despair, and the often differing interests of insiders and outsiders. Because the outcomes of these negotiations varied over time and space, Carlisle's story is an especially intriguing and quintessentially American one, worthy of not just telling but also remembering for some time to come. So, *why Carlisle*, you ask? Because Carlisle's history mattered in the eighteenth century and still matters now. Its story is a microcosm of America's history as a place and people.

CHAPTER ONE

Creating a Town In-Between

IN 1751, PENNSYLVANIA governor James Hamilton journeyed westward to Carlisle, the recently founded seat of the sprawling new interior county of Cumberland. Upon his return to Philadelphia he admitted with surprise that this interior village, which he had assisted the colony's principal proprietor, Thomas Penn, in planning, had "exceeded my Expectations in all respects." Two years later, Hamilton extended his accolades by boldly advancing that "if any" town of interior Pennsylvania "ever comes to be considerable, . . . Carlisle stands the best chance."[1]

Hamilton saw potential in Carlisle. But why? In certain respects, Carlisle existed more in theory than reality in the early 1750s. There was not much there. The lots of its recently surveyed sixteen-square-block radius were mostly vacant. Its population of at least several hundred, most of them colonists with Scots-Irish surnames, was too "poor" to "think of building a Court House or Market for some time." But Hamilton was optimistic nonetheless. With "near fifty Houses built, and building" during the town's first year of existence, a town, however crude, was taking shape in eastern Cumberland County.[2] And to him, such activity, especially so soon after survey, was indicative of the pivotal role the town might play in the colony's future.

Hamilton, of course, was no ordinary observer. As the proprietor of Lancaster Town, a position that he inherited from his father, Hamilton knew that town founding was an art that required careful planning and some luck.[3] To survive and thrive, new interior towns like Carlisle had to attract colonists who would advance Euro-American settlement, extend social and political connections from the metropolis, and forge networks of commerce and credit; these towns had to become hubs of collection, manufacture, exchange, and law for their regions. More significant, successful towns were also colonial spaces. Indeed, as the colony's governor, Hamilton knew well that town founding was an indispensable tool of British colonization. To British colony builders like himself and his proprietor, founding towns was like drawing borders on a map; towns enabled their proprietors to lay formal claim to disputed lands. New towns also encouraged land sales, from which their founders often profited. And in an empire built on entrepreneurial spirit rather than central regulation, towns set the bounds of human behavior for their inhabitants. Colonial American town founders thus expected these urban spaces to advance the British conquest of the American interior and its Native peoples. By functioning as interior links within expanding colonies, towns narrowed the distance between the early American West and the metropolitan culture, markets, and political institutions of the British Atlantic world. This was especially true in the proprietary colony of Pennsylvania, where Thomas Penn established towns like Carlisle to serve the interests of his colony and empire.[4]

Hamilton thus viewed Carlisle's progress through a wide-angle lens, and by his measure, Carlisle's prospects looked good. As the third of six county seats Thomas Penn founded before 1775, he knew experience went into its planning (map 1).[5] Penn intended Carlisle to be a significant place in-between in the interior. Its carefully selected location was ideally suited to serve Pennsylvania's interests. Although situated on the eastern edge of its county, the town site was central to the growing colony. Located some 120 miles west of Philadelphia, "about fifty miles from the Town of Lancaster," and about twenty miles southwest of what would become Harrisburg, "on a route which leads over the mountains to the western regions, and very near the Susquehanna," Carlisle stood nearly midway between Philadelphia and the Ohio country.[6] This advantageous site also stood at the intersection of several important east-west pathways across the colony. Carlisle thus occupied a longstanding interior nexus between regions and cultures in the mid-Atlantic. To Governor Hamilton, it was this location—particularly its betweenness—that led him to conclude that the town had great potential. Carlisle would foster landed development in the interior, while also modeling social and political order for colonists. Most important, it would be an interior center of commerce for the expanding colony. As Hamilton asserted confidently, Carlisle "must allways be a great thorough fare" from Philadelphia "to the back Countries," as well as "the Depositary of the Indian Trade."[7]

Carlisle's founding as a town in-between in 1751 was not simply a reflection of the ambitious plans of Pennsylvania's leaders or the broader workings of Atlantic world colonization and commerce, however. It was also a product of its location and how this region west of the Susquehanna and south of North, Blue, or Kittatinny Mountain was interpreted by a succession of human inhabitants. James Hamilton and Thomas Penn were not the first people to take interest in this area west of the river, nor were they the first to interpret this location as an especially advantageous and central one. Rather, first for Native Americans, and then for Euro-American traders and colonists of French, English, German, and especially Scots-Irish descent, this region was a significant intersection in the mid-Atlantic. It offered access to settlements to the east and west, north and south, and old and new homelands; it stood between coastal communities populated by increasing numbers of Euro-American colonists and multiethnic Native villagers. In short, this area of the interior was, and had long been, what scholar John Stilgoe calls "shaped land."[8] It was a dynamic space in-between. As such, its contours were engaged, reworked, and contested by different peoples through time. For Hamilton and Penn— the human shapers of this region west of the river in the early 1750s—locating Carlisle where they did offered them the opportunity to build on earlier Native American and Euro-American landscapes, while also reconfiguring them in ways that suited their goals for the colony. Carlisle thus stood as an artifact of the shared perceptions that Indians and Euro-Americans had of the centralness of its geography and the uses they could make of it.[9]

Water, not land, was the natural feature that initially anchored Native American use of the region. The Susquehanna River was one of the region's most conspicuous geographic features. Indeed, the lower Susquehanna was the "mile-wide, foot deep river" that split open the "Ocean of Woods" on its way from Lake Otsego to the Chesapeake Bay. Because it offered access to the coast and interior, it affected Native American settlement patterns in the region in profound ways.[10]

In the immediate precontact period, it was the Iroquoian-speaking Susquehannocks who shaped the lower Susquehanna Valley into a landscape suitable to their needs. John Smith and his entourage met these Native peoples in 1608, and they "seemed like Giants" to him.[11] Although exaggerated, Smith's use of the word "giant" was not wholly inaccurate. In the early seventeenth century the Susquehannocks were the metaphorical giants of region; their identity was shaped by their reciprocal association with the river. The name "Susquehannock," for example, which was first used to describe them by Smith's Algonquian interpreter, translates to the "people at the falls" or "roily water people"; literally, they were the people of the river.[12] But the river also took its human meaning from their presence along its banks. "Susquehanna" was an Algonquian translation of "Sisku," or "Andastes," the Iroquois-French name for the Susquehannock, and "hanne," or stream, making it the "River of the Andastes."[13] The river was central to their lives, but they were central to the way others perceived the river.

Archaeologists confirm the Susquehannocks' presence along the river in the sixteenth and seventeenth centuries. At least nine, and possibly twelve, Susquehannock villages dotted the upper and lower Susquehanna Valley; they housed an estimated 3,000 to 4,000 inhabitants, and perhaps more than 6,000 by the 1640s. Before 1550 the Susquehannocks were most closely identified with the river's North Branch, but by 1570 or so, this pattern changed. Pushed by mounting pressure from their Iroquois neighbors to the north, and likely pulled by new opportunities for trade, they migrated southward into what became Lancaster County where they established villages on both river banks. There, in their palisaded villages of wooden longhouses, these agriculturalists and hunters used the rich soils of the Susquehanna Valley to produce maize, beans, squash, and tobacco, while taking advantage of the sea of woods surrounding them to hunt game and gather edible plants.[14]

The centrality of the river and its valley to other Native and Euro-American communities in the mid-Atlantic also lent strategic importance to the Susquehannocks' new homelands. The Susquehanna was a major highway for Indian canoe traffic during the pre- and early-contact periods, serving as an artery of trade for the exchange of pelts and goods. It was also an important warrior's path between Iroquoia and native territories to the south. As the people who occupied the crossroads of this water-based network of trade and transport, the Susquehannocks commanded considerable authority. Their location on the river offered them access to many people and places in the mid-Atlantic. From their villages they could travel by canoe, with only short portages, to the Finger Lakes and Mohawk River in the north, the Delaware River in the east, tributaries of the Ohio River in the west, and the Chesapeake Bay in the south.[15]

Life along lower Susquehanna had other advantages as well. An extensive network of footpaths cut through the region, offering the Susquehan-

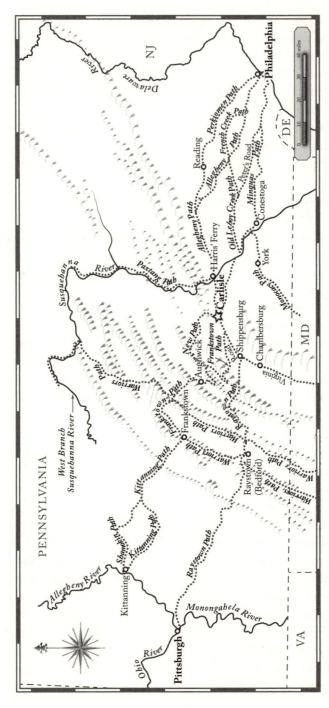

Map 2. Native American Paths of Pennsylvania. In the precontact and colonial periods, the Susquehannocks, then the Iroquois, Shawnee, and Delaware peoples, used these paths for travel, trade, migration, and warfare. After many Native peoples relocated to the Ohio Valley in the 1720s, these routes became important trading paths linking Euro-Americans with Native trappers and hunters. Many later became roads. Drawn by Gerry Krieg.

nocks overland access to places near and far. Some of these trails followed the river valley on a predominantly north-south course; others cut across it. One of the primary Iroquois war trails ran southwest from the Susquehanna to the Potomac and then down into the Catawba and Cherokee territories of the Carolinas. Other trails linked Native settlements on the Susquehanna to the Delaware Valley or led westward toward the Ohio (map 2). As the primary occupants of what one archaeologist characterizes as "the largest intersection of prehistoric travel routes in Pennsylvania," the Susquehannocks enjoyed important strategic advantages.[16] They used them to shape the lower Susquehanna Valley into a hub of migration, trade, war, and social contact in the 1500s and 1600s.

The Susquehannocks enjoyed their privileged position as the people at the crossroads for at least a generation. Yet as the seventeenth century progressed, they found their territory contested by European colonists in the mid-Atlantic and New France. For the Susquehannocks, European contact brought trade while simultaneously accelerating the pace of cultural and demographic change. In particular, contact intensified rivalries and hostilities with the Iroquois, during the Beaver Wars of the mid-seventeenth century, and the Delawares or Lenni Lenapes as each group competed to preserve its influence over interior hunting grounds. By the 1670s, ravaged by disease, and embattled by Iroquois assaults from the north and uprisings of colonists during Bacon's Rebellion to the south, the Susquehannocks gradually lost their authority over this pivotal region. Most dispersed in response, abandoning their villages. Those who remained found themselves settled amid new Native migrant communities arriving in the region. In an ironic way, the river that made the Susquehannocks the giants John Smith encountered in 1608 had also unmade them by offering access to those of their rivals who could take that power away.[17]

Although the lower Valley had fewer Native inhabitants for a time, new groups of Indian migrants relocated there beginning in the 1690s. Shawnees, Delawares, Conoys, and Nanticokes converged in this area, joining those remaining Susquehannocks and some Senecas at Conestoga, the best known of several multiethnic Indian villages that dotted the eastern bank of the river by 1700.[18] Like other peoples of the eastern woodlands, the Shawnees and Delawares were fragmented groups by the eighteenth century. Their communities had been ravaged by European diseases. They had been displaced by intertribal warfare triggered by competition over commerce with Euro-Americans. Both groups also shared a tense tributary relationship with the

Five and later Six Nations who sanctioned their settlements in the region as a way to preserve their influence over this territory. To these Native peoples on the move, the lower Susquehanna Valley was a refuge between Euro-American encroachers and Native American overseers. Although it was not free from the influence of either, the region offered them a new homeland and some promise of greater independence in their trade and diplomatic relations with others.

It did not take long for these new arrivals to make the lower Susquehanna Valley into a major Indian population center again. By the first quarter of the eighteenth century, other multiethnic Indian villages—composed mostly of Shawnees and Delawares, but including Susquehannocks, Senecas, Conoys, Nanticokes, Tuscaroras, and Tutelos—clustered along both sides of the river, creating what historian Francis Jennings calls "a veritable united nations of Indians" along the Susquehanna.[19] Although Conestoga remained the largest settlement, by 1700, Delaware migrants from eastern Pennsylvania and Delaware also built a sizable village at Paxtang, near present-day Harrisburg.[20] Other evidence suggests that between 1720 and 1730 there were at least two predominantly Shawnee towns on the western bank of the river, each located about twenty miles east of where Carlisle would stand. The first of these villages was situated on Conodoguinet Creek. The Conodoguinet, or "Geneptukhanne" as the Indians knew it, translated as "long, crooked creek," an especially appropriate name for a creek that cut a sharply winding course through the northern Cumberland Valley to the Susquehanna. The second was a village established by the French-Shawnee trader Peter Chartier who had led a band of Shawnee east for trade; it was located at the present town of New Cumberland along the more southerly Yellow Breeches Creek, a cold-water stream fed by springs that also flowed to the Susquehanna. Indians knew the Yellow Breeches as "Callapatscink," or "where it returns," referring to the frequent bends in the stream (map 3).[21]

These settlements were centers of new networks that built on older patterns of land and resource use. Once again by the early 1700s, there were Native peoples farming, fishing, hunting, and trading in the lower Valley. Yet there were also important contrasts. These settlements were not Susquehannock-style villages of longhouses surrounded by a stockade. Instead, some were compactly settled villages, others more sprawling. None were stockaded. And their built landscapes were marked by Indian-style huts and European-style cabins, structures that exemplified the hybrid nature of these settlements and their multiethnic inhabitants. The Shawnees espe-

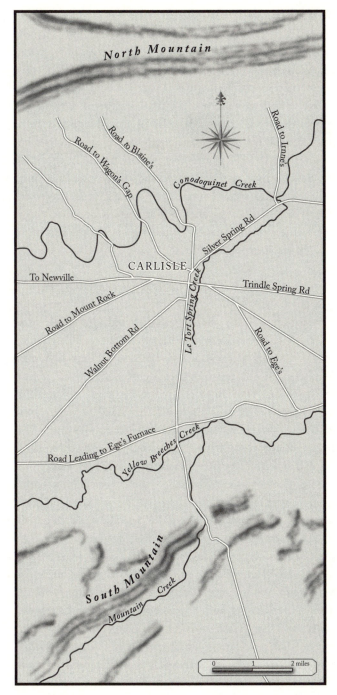

Map 3. Carlisle and Its Environs, Circa 1810. Local roads converged on Carlisle, the seat of Cumberland County. Key geographic features include LeTort Spring, Conodoguinet and Yellow Breeches Creeks, as well as North (or Blue or Kittatinny) and South Mountains. Drawn by Gerry Krieg.

cially, but the Delawares too, had long histories as migrants. To survive, they learned to adapt by accommodating to other Native cultures when needed. They also learned to interact with Europeans, whose commerce and culture loomed large in their communities. They were hybrid cultures. Yet that did not diminish their impact on the Valley. Rather, being able to respond to the multiethnic Native peoples around them, the growing presence of Europeans, and the influence of the Five Nations Iroquois, the Shawnees and Delawares reshaped the lower Susquehanna Valley into a new kind of place in-between. Only this time, as the region became an increasingly contested cultural space between a variety of Native and European cultures trying to claim it, it was not so much the river but the land and its pathways that assumed the geographic foreground.[22]

Native Americans were not alone in shaping the landscape of the lower Susquehanna Valley. Europeans were also interested in this crossroads in the interior. In the seventeenth century, Swedish and Dutch colonists from the Delaware Valley spearheaded European involvement in the region by establishing trade relations with the Susquehannocks. They were followed after Pennsylvania's establishment in 1682 by a group of French and English traders and their patrons, who were drawn to the region as a potentially lucrative outlet for speculation in trade and land. Provincial Secretary James Logan, the Penn family's representative in the colony from 1699 until the 1730s, was especially important in directing their activities. As secretary, the Irish-born Logan, a Quaker, had the power to shape trade and settlement in the interior. He did so to challenge Pennsylvania's trade rivals in New York and New France, and to dispute Maryland's claims to the colony's southern border. At the same time, as an ambitious man of the Atlantic world, Logan also sought to benefit the proprietors and himself by offering goods and credit to traders while offering English merchants markets and pelts. Under his leadership, traders working for Pennsylvania established posts in the interior where they could cultivate Indian hunters as trade partners and allies, while also acting as interpreters, messengers, and information sources for the colony.[23]

On the west side of the river, in the vicinity of Carlisle, the French-born James LeTort developed a landscape geared to suit European, particularly Pennsylvanian, interests. LeTort was the son of trader Jacques LeTort, a Huguenot refugee who had migrated from France to London and then Pennsylvania, where he established a trade post on the Schuylkill River in the 1680s. By 1703, James, following in his father's footsteps, was a trader for

English, and mostly Quaker, interests. He was a close associate of Logan and a licensed trader for the colony. In 1719, in a show of favor, Logan awarded him an extensive tract of land along the Susquehanna. There, among the Shawnee settlements on the west side of river, along what came to be known as LeTort's Spring—a small, spring-fed creek flowing to the Conodoguinet that connected with the Susquehanna—LeTort established a trading post. He maintained this post, trading and farming alongside his Native neighbors, until about 1727, when he left to follow his Shawnee trade partners on their migration west (see map 3).[24] Local historians hail James LeTort as Cumberland County's pioneer; the spring bearing his name forms the town's eastern boundary. More significant, LeTort was one of a handful of Euro-American traders whose connections to the multiethnic peoples of the lower Susquehanna and Ohio River Valleys reoriented the region's landscape along an east-west axis, one more favorable to Pennsylvania's interests. He did so, with Logan's guidance, by strategically positioning his post at a midpoint in an extensive trade network that linked Native hunters and trappers of the mid-Atlantic interior with Philadelphia and London merchants. LeTort's contacts with the Shawnees encouraged Pennsylvania colonists, particularly those connected to the proprietors, to define the colony's commercial interests more expansively by directing trade first to the lower Susquehanna Valley and then farther west, toward the Ohio Valley and Great Lakes regions. Consequently, the focus of the trade shifted from beaver to deerskins, making it a fur *and* skin trade. Trade with the Shawnees thus marked a significant economic shift, as Eric Hinderaker notes, because it "opened the rich game populations of western Pennsylvania and the upper Ohio Valley to the English market for the first time."[25] Such developments had ramifications. Specifically, several decades before Carlisle's founding, this region of the lower Susquehanna Valley had gained notoriety in Euro-American minds as a contested space that stood between Indian hunters, European trade goods, and the colonial traders and interpreters who linked them together. As a proving ground for trade and cultural contacts between Indians and Europeans in Pennsylvania, this site was indeed a place in-between.

It was also a region in flux. By the 1720s, the Shawnees and Delawares, like the Susquehannocks, found that preserving their hold on these spaces west of the river was difficult. As more Native migrants arrived, there were more claimants to the land, which equaled more competition. Then there were the Europeans. LeTort's presence heralded the arrival of other traders, some of them unlicensed dealers who were eager to peddle liquor to their native neighbors. He also paved the way for the arrival of the first Euro-American colonists west of the river by the mid-1720s. Many of them were squatters who were drawn not by the river, but by the Cumberland Valley, a twelve- to fifteen-mile-wide lowland of wide valleys and small rolling hills nestled between North, or Blue or Kittatinny Mountain, and South Mountain.[26] The Valley, as Native peoples knew, possessed abundant natural resources. But the land where "lime-stone rocks everywhere protrude" that swept across its southeastern floor was the feature that drew Euro-Americans. These fertile limestone soils, which were near equal to the best lands in southeastern Pennsylvania, promised the growth of a rich agricultural economy. Simply put, the Cumberland Valley, a region that observers later characterized as "the finest country, as to scenery, fertility, and situation, in the United States," boasted enough "good soil, good air and water" to attract many colonists.[27]

Some of these colonists stayed only a short time on their way west or down into the southern interior.[28] Others, many of whom were recent Scots-Irish arrivals from Ulster, put down firmer roots. Among the first to settle in the immediate vicinity of Carlisle were a cluster of Scots-Irishmen including Richard Parker, who established his farm by 1725, and Andrew McFarlane and Andrew Ralston, who claimed lands near Parker in 1726. These men may have formed the core of Newtown, a hamlet that one historian claims preceded Carlisle by some fifteen years. There was also the Dutchman Tobias Hendricks, likely of Sephardic Jewish ancestry, who claimed lands two miles west of the river by 1727 in present-day Camp Hill. The tavern that he and later his son maintained on the site became an important landmark on the path from the river to Carlisle. In fact, when lands north of Carlisle were re-surveyed in the 1760s, his two-story house was the most prominent feature on the road coming from Harris's Ferry.[29] Together, these colonists were among the estimated 400 Euro-American families living west of the Susquehanna by 1731. Many of them, like Parker, McFarlane, and Ralston, were Scots-Irish men and women who had come to Pennsylvania seeking religious toleration and economic opportunity, including access to land and commerce. But once here, they found that their own, often limited economic resources, coupled with anti-Irish prejudice and incentives offered by proprietary officials like James Logan, pushed them to the outermost reaches of Pennsylvania's expanding interior, particularly the Cumberland Valley. These border peoples of Ireland thus found themselves occupying the fertile lands of this dynamic region in-between.[30]

There in the Valley, these colonists constructed their own landscape amid the Native settlements already in the region. Theirs was initially a rough-hewn, "open-country neighborhood" of dispersed farmsteads and kin networks symbolized by crudely constructed cabins and partly cleared farm-lands.[31] Indeed, as late as the 1790s, one observer noted that the "wretched log houses without windows, and with chimneys of sticks and clay" that housed the "new farmers" of the Valley, were among the most distinct and depressing features of Pennsylvania's rural landscape.[32] But set amid the existing landscapes of Native villages and trade posts, and isolated from the Euro-American settlements of the Delaware Valley, it was also a hybrid landscape. Populated mostly by humble squatters, these settlements depended on Indian goodwill for their existence. Moreover, because these mostly Scots-Irish colonists possessed little more than linen and liquor, they had to live much like Indians to survive. They practiced subsistence agriculture and hunted. They drank, caroused, and sometimes fought with each other and their Indian and trader neighbors. And because markets were distant, they relied on bartering with the local Native peoples for needed goods in a frontier exchange economy. This was a harsh world, one marked by hard work and considerable brutality.[33] It was also an increasingly Euro-American one. Farmsteads—even if scattered and crudely constructed—and the taverns, stores, shops, and meeting houses that followed, hailed the birth of a Euro-American colonial landscape. Even the region's Scots-Irish, whom many in the colony saw as outsiders and ruffians, were colonists who carried European culture and religion with them. By the 1730s, the Valley was becoming a Euro-American place.[34]

For the Shawnees, Delawares, and other Native peoples of the Valley, the arrival of traders and colonists had consequences. They suddenly had to defend their communities against the multiple effects of European diseases, depleted supplies of game, liquor, and land-hungry colonists who did not always respect Native territories. For these Native peoples, the bounds of their recently established territories were contracting rapidly by the 1720s. Iroquois influence in the region compounded these effects. The Five Nations turned their attention increasingly southward after 1701. They staged long-distance raids against their Catawba and Cherokee enemies to the south, which meant passing through the Susquehanna Valley. They also developed diplomatic alliances with Pennsylvania's leaders, which simultaneously strengthened and undermined their claims over the lands of the Susquehanna Valley. For the multiethnic Indian villagers of the lower Valley, Iroquois assertions of authority, even if disputed, created additional pressures in communities already stressed to their limits. By the 1720s, these Native peoples were pushed and pulled to relocate. Some moved north into the upper Susquehanna and Juniata Valleys. Most, however, moved westward toward the Ohio. By the early 1730s, they, along with traders like LeTort who lived and worked among them, founded more than six towns in the Ohio Valley.[35]

With few Indians left along the lower Susquehanna by the 1730s, the influence of the north-south aligned river diminished. It no longer fulfilled the trade and transport needs of Native communities. Instead, with Pennsylvania's primary Indian trade partners having moved west, the colony's commercial visions fixed on an east-west course extending from Philadelphia toward the Ohio Valley. Meanwhile, Valley colonists were eager to connect their interior farmsteads and congregations to the commerce and culture of the Delaware Valley. For these reasons, the river became an obstacle rather than an advantage.[36] Traders hauling goods and pelts and migrants carrying their belongings were painfully aware of the Susquehanna's limitations; the river was not only, as one traveler reported, "a mile wide," but was also "so shallow that the boat would scrape across the large stones so as almost to prevent it from proceeding."[37] Pennsylvanians thus redefined what they saw increasingly as *their* landscape. To do so, they gave new precedence to the overland pathways that crossed the Valley on a mostly east-west trajectory. They made these routes, rather than the river, the conduits of Euro-American commerce, migration, and cultural contact. This shift had important ramifications for Carlisle's future as a town of the interior.

Such profound reorientation of the landscape did not happen by accident. Human agents, in the guise of a new group of colonial proprietors and their officials, took new interest in the area west of the Susquehanna by 1730; they hoped to shape the land and its inhabitants to suit their interests. Pennsylvania at this time was no longer the colony of William Penn, but his sons. For these new proprietors—Penn's sons John, Richard, and particularly Thomas, an Anglican convert who possessed three-fourths of the proprietary rights by 1746—attaining formal possession and greater control of this region west of the Susquehanna offered significant opportunity. In a colony that was increasingly diverse, politically contentious, and economically prosperous, the Penns reasoned that a tighter hold on the interior might increase their family's dwindling fortunes while boosting their political authority in their colony and the Atlantic world. As one of Thomas Penn's provincial surveyors put it, it was in "thy Interest to keep fooling on the west Side of Sasquehanah."[38]

"Fooling" is an intriguing term. It has several layers of meaning, all of which shed insight into the motives of Pennsylvania's proprietary establishment. In one respect, "fooling" expressed the Penn family's willingness to take risks to claim lands and control settlement in the interior. Thomas Penn wished to manage the Cumberland Valley's emerging Euro-American landscape as part of a broader effort to collect profits from land surveys, sales, and quitrents by regulating the land office. For this reason, the Valley had to be made a formal part of his colony. But land was not the only resource he wished to oversee. Important trade interests were at stake there as well. By the 1730s, following the westward migration of many of its Native peoples, the Cumberland Valley had become a nexus in a trade network stretching between Europe, Philadelphia, and the Ohio Valley. Thus, the speculative "foolings" of Thomas Penn and his provincial officials—particularly provincial secretaries James Logan and then Richard Peters, his proxies in the colony—were also carefully calculated commercial moves. Each action they took west of the river was intended to exploit the region's strategic potential in trade to gain commercial advantages over their colonial rivals. Coming at a time when the long-standing border dispute with Maryland over Pennsylvania's southern boundary was intensifying, and the colonial fur and skin trade was competitive, the Penn family had powerful incentives to strengthen their claim to this contested interior region in-between. Their "fooling" therefore was not folly, but a purposeful attempt to direct the landscape and trade networks taking shape there in ways conducive to their multiple interests.[39]

Yet what they did to pursue these goals demonstrated the manipulative connotations of this "fooling." The Cumberland Valley was no virgin land. Native peoples remained there, while Euro-American colonists had just arrived. If these residents were to be "fooled" with, it would have to be done indirectly. What is more, in a politically contentious colony where Quakers still held much sway, Penn's authority as an Anglican was circumscribed; he exercised his power through patronage and the limited prerogatives he claimed as proprietor. Attempts to carry out his proprietary ambitions west of the river would have to be partly covert. Penn and his officials did not plan to march in an armed force and take over; they had neither the power nor desire to do so. Rather, following the lead of his father and other English Atlantic world entrepreneurs, Thomas Penn's "conquest" of this region would be carried out through a series of calculated maneuvers by his officials that were intended to engineer local colonists into peace and prosperity.[40] But this approach had consequences. It made his goals dependent on Indians' willingness to negotiate, traders' eagerness for skins and furs, and colonists' enthusiasm for land. Penn had to convince others to do his bidding.

By the 1730s, Penn's plans were under way. Traders like James LeTort and the squatters settled west of the river were the first colonists to assert, in knowing and unknowing ways, the Penn family's claim to this contested region. In fact, by negotiating their own land deals with local Indian peoples, squatters inadvertently wrested control of the land from local Native inhabitants to Pennsylvania's advantage.[41] What is more, by constructing trade posts, farmhouses, and retail establishments, they refocused the Valley's landscape for trade and agricultural commerce linked to Philadelphia.

These actions were not enough, however. Penn had not purchased formal title to these lands from the Indians. Thus, the Penn family's interests in the region took on new urgency when the longtime border dispute with Maryland escalated in the 1730s. Maryland colonists, encouraged by their proprietors, the Calverts, began to wage an often violent settlement offensive in the area. When Pennsylvanians returned the violence, Thomas Penn knew that he had to establish formal rights of proprietorship immediately in order to defend his family's claim. To do so, in 1734, Penn sanctioned the establishment of technically illegal settlements in the region when he authorized one of his surveyors, Samuel Blunston, to grant "Licenses"—a temporary title—to squatters west of the river. His goal was to impose provincial management atop the settlement processes already underway by using settlers, particularly the Scots-Irish colonists whom Blunston characterized disdainfully as "Idle trash," to preserve "the frontiers of an Improveing Colony." In this way, colonists were to act as unwitting tools to assert his claims.[42] Although this policy contradicted his father's practice of purchasing lands from the Indians before authorizing settlement, Penn and his officials shrewdly reasoned that only an interior inhabited by colonists loyal to Pennsylvania would give his family the leverage needed to secure the border. Although one official recognized that it would likely "be Necessary by all Civill means to protect and Encourage those [settlers] who are brought into trouble by maintaining it [the colony's southern boundary]," providing some measure of defense and issuing licenses for land were small prices to pay for a potential victory over their Maryland rivals.[43]

Colonists were not the only unwitting participants in this process of conquest, however. To finalize his family's claim, Penn needed legal title from the Indians. To win it, Penn abandoned another of his father's practices: negotiating land deals with individual tribes and chiefs. Instead, he and his officials targeted the Six Nations, chief claimants to the lands west of the river. Their goal was to secure possession of this key region by extinguishing the remaining Shawnee and Delaware claims and pressuring the Six Nations to negotiate a sale. The sale finally happened in October 1736 in a treaty at Philadelphia when Thomas Penn, accompanied by his advisors and interpreters, met with twenty-three chiefs of the Six Nations. They exchanged a vast assortment of trade goods for title to an estimated two million acres of land (approximately 41,000 square miles), including much of the lower Susquehanna Valley. More important to Carlisle's future, this purchase included "all the lands lying on the west side of the said River to the setting of the Sun, . . . from the mouth of the said River Northward" to the North or Blue Mountain.[44]

With this treaty, the Penns won formal control of the Cumberland Valley. They also had the formal claim required to secure the southern border of their colony. It seemed like the Penns' takeover was near complete in 1737 when the Calverts agreed to a temporary boundary line between Maryland and Pennsylvania (to be confirmed with the surveying of the Mason-Dixon line in the 1760s). The Penns had made substantial gains; they had acquired a sizable chunk of territory west of the river, won a major political victory over a colonial rival, and moved one step closer toward redirecting the region's landscape in ways that better suited their interests. Their victory was secured in 1750, when the founding of Pennsylvania's sixth county, Cumberland, extended provincial government into the Cumberland Valley; it was only the second county situated west of the river.[45]

Winning formal title to the lower Susquehanna and Cumberland Valleys was an important victory for Thomas Penn. But he and his officials had other interests in the region, and controlling the mid-Atlantic fur trade was paramount among them. At the time of the 1736 purchase, Pennsylvania officials knew well that "the Indians cannot live without being supplied with our goods; they must have Powder and Lead to hunt, & Cloaths to keep them warm." Yet these same officials were worried. Native peoples, they knew, were not powerless; they had a choice of trade partners. Their fear, as one official warned, was that "if our People do not carry them [goods], others will from Maryland, Virginia, [the] Jerseys, or other places." The challenge, therefore, was how to engineer circumstances so that the Indians would "not desire" to "trade with those People rather than with ours?"[46]

To gain advantage over his rivals, Penn, a man historians have described unflatteringly as having a "grasping nature" and being "uncompromising in his pursuit of wealth," had to obtain tighter control over the economic development of his colony's interior.[47] The west side of the Susquehanna thus became a proving ground. He assumed that founding roads, market centers, storage facilities, and especially towns in this area would generate order and revenue for his colony. Therefore, Penn, working from England where he resided after a stint in the colony during the 1730s, appended a more ambitious management plan onto his schemes for the interior. Taking advantage of his prerogative powers as proprietor, which designated the founding of towns a proprietary (or private) and not a legislative function, he began establishing a network of small urban centers (county seats) situated strategically across Pennsylvania's interior.[48]

Founding county towns was central to advancing Penn's interests because they extended proprietary government. They also served significant commercial functions. Penn's county towns were planned as important market and service centers for their agricultural hinterlands; the hope was that the growth of an orderly and profitable economy would result. As regional collection and distribution points connected to others across the colony, these towns were also intended as dynamic places in-between linking the peoples and products of the interior to the commercial orbits of Philadelphia and the Atlantic world. New county towns would thus bolster Pennsylvania's role in the fur and skin trade while expanding its grain trade. What is more, because town life represented a distinct urban experience, county towns were also to be vehicles for cultural assimilation. They would help socialize colonists to a landscape conducive to Penn's interests. In the Cumberland Valley, where Scots-Irish colonists predominated, town life was also a model to encourage immigrant squatters to settle down and become sober, productive, and surplus-minded farmers, or town-dwelling retailers or licensed traders. In all these ways, Penn's towns were the hallmarks of a new, integrated, and overtly commercial geography in Pennsylvania. They were designed to carry political authority west, generate revenue, anchor export trades critical to the colony's economic well-being, and spread a civilization that was to the liking of the proprietors. Thomas Penn had established a framework for a new, more pragmatic peaceable kingdom. His model was built on the same economic shrewdness that motivated his father, but without the idealism.[49]

The founding of Carlisle, Cumberland's county seat, was integral to this process. Plans for the town began shortly after the county's establishment when Thomas Cookson, deputy surveyor of Lancaster County, was directed to recommend an appropriate site for the new seat. Cookson complied and "viewed several Places spoke of as commodious Situations for the Town." In a letter to Governor James Hamilton, Cookson outlined several possible locations, but most heartily endorsed the "Situation . . . on Le Torts Spring," an area just north of James LeTort's former trading cabin. His choice was a logical one. Natural resources drew Cookson, like LeTort, to the location. This site was distinguished by its "fine Stream of Water and a Body of good Land on each side, from the Head [of the Spring] down to Conedogwainet [Conodoguinet] Creek."[50] There were also "good meadows" and "a good body of well Timber'd Land" nearby.[51] A town there, Cookson reasoned, would have sufficient resources to attract and sustain town dwellers (see map 3). Signs of prior and current habitation also made this the best location. That the nearby lands were "thick settled" with farmsteads was affirmation that others read the land as he had.[52] It was better to displace a few farmers, he implied, than to pick a site without sufficient resources for a town. Settled land also implied cleared land, which made surveying a town easier. Existing settlements assured that a Euro-American agricultural landscape was already taking root on site. A town there would thus serve multiple functions. It would become the market and service center Penn sought. It would also likely increase land values, which would benefit the proprietors and officials like Richard Peters who owned "an abundance" of land nearby.[53] Yet the area was not so densely settled as to make acquiring the town site difficult. Cookson estimated that there were about "Five or Six Thousand Acres about that Water [LeTort Spring] of good Land all vacant."[54] Without doubt, LeTort Spring was the most "commodious" location. Cookson was "sure [that] if the Proprietaries were on the spot they would chuse that place themselves."[55]

More important, as Cookson's use of the word "commodious" suggests, LeTort Spring possessed strategic advantages other sites lacked. Of particular interest was its "most convenient" location.[56] The site, he noted with an eye to trade, had ready access to points west. "This place," as Cookson explained, was "convenient to the New Path to Alleghenny, now mostly used, being at the Distance of four miles from the Gap in the . . . Mountain."[57] In fact, in selecting the site, he viewed "the several passes thro' the . . . Mountains for the conveniency of the Traders."[58] He favored the LeTort Spring site because it was accessible to one of the two principal pathways that traders used to reach their Native American partners in the Ohio Valley. Traders were already accustomed to passing in and near the site, ensuring that the fur and skin trade would be central to the town's economy.

Cookson's assessments were correct. The site for Carlisle stood at the convergence of five Indian pathways across the region. Two of the most frequently traveled pathways that merged at the fording spot along LeTort Spring, the Allegheny and Conoy Paths, originated in eastern Pennsylvania. The other three, the New, Frankstown, and Raystown Paths, headed west from the site.[59] All were important conduits of trade and migration. Two of them connected to the Delaware Valley, but the site's western connections most caught Cookson's attention. The New Path, of which Cookson spoke, was actually an old shortcut between Paxton (Harris's Ferry) and Aughwick (Shirleysburg); by 1749, it was a favorite of Pennsylvania's traders. This path headed northward from LeTort Spring and crossed North Mountain at Croghan's Gap, which was "thought by the Traders to be the best in the Ridge." Then it continued on and after 1752 headed past Andrew Montour's homestead along Sherman's Creek (Landisburg).[60] From there, it wended northwest to Aughwick, where it connected with other paths leading toward the forks of the Ohio (Pittsburgh) and beyond. The second path, the Frankstown Path, although not mentioned by Cookson, was actually, according to one scholar, the "most important and frequently traveled" westward path for traders hauling packhorse trains of goods and furs because it passed through some of the most important Native trading villages.[61] This path began at Paxton (Harris's Ferry), headed past LeTort Spring, turned west toward Frankstown, and then went on to the Indian village of Kittanning on the Allegheny River. Of equal importance to Carlisle, the colony, and the British empire was the Raystown Path. It led down the Cumberland Valley from Harris's Ferry, through LeTort Spring, and on to the small village of Shippensburg. It then turned westward, leading to Raystown (Bedford), Loyalhanna (Ligonier), and eventually to the forks of the Ohio (Pittsburgh). The Frankstown Path was the foundation of the Forbes Road built to take British troops to Fort Duquesne during the Seven Years' War (see map 2).[62]

These paths made LeTort Spring an especially advantageous location for a town. They offered ready access to the coast and interior, which guaranteed a steady stream of migrants, traders, and travelers to the town. Just as important, this site stood nearly midway between the Delaware and Ohio Valleys, making it for Euro-Americans what it had been for Native Americans, a place that stood geographically in-between. At a time when the colonial fur trade was more distant and competitive, centralness was an important quality. A town on this site might serve as a hub of this Atlantic world enterprise because it could house warehouses to store goods and pelts and inns to lodge travelers and traders; resident craftsmen and haulers could also offer vital services to sustain the trade. There was even forage and water nearby for packhorses. The LeTort Spring site, in short, was the "most convenient" location that "answers best to the paths over the Blue Hills." Because it was also situated along one of the main routes from Philadelphia, provincial officials were sure that "most of their Trade will be carried on with Philadelphia."[63] How could a town at this location not flourish?

But not everyone in Cumberland County agreed with Cookson's recommendation of the LeTort Spring site; colonists had their own opinions about the location of the county town. Despite all efforts to keep the site selection "secret," controversy erupted.[64] County seats were guaranteed a steady flow of residents coming to do business in the courts. Locals often disputed their locations because these towns often made or broke local economies by reconfiguring settlement patterns and transport networks.[65] In the case of Cumberland County, colony officials knew that "the Inhabitants of the different Parts of the County are generally partial from the Advantages that would arise from a County Town in their own neighbourhood."[66] It thus came as no surprise when some county residents who were "most exceedingly anxious for the Town" discredited Cookson's choice and promoted their own sites for the seat.[67] Their objections are interesting for the way they focused on the town's betweenness by questioning whose definition of between would prevail— the proprietor's or the people's. Would the county seat be located at LeTort Spring, a convenient place in-between in the colony? Or would another site be chosen, perhaps an established settlement situated closer to the middle of this sprawling county, as many residents wanted?

Debate over the seat's location began in 1750, when some western residents petitioned with their concerns about the proposed site. They contended that "if the county town [wa]s not some place near the Center of the County," then "it wo[ul]d have been much better for us . . . to [have] continu[e]d in Lancaster County;" otherwise they would miss out on "all the benefits . . . the Assembly Intended Us by being Made a County." Living on the far edge of Lancaster County, they had few responsibilities. By contrast, as residents of a new county they would be expected to participate in local affairs. Yet they would still have "near as fare [far] to travel to Courts as we had in Lancaster without aney [any] hopes left us of its ever being better."[68] The county seat was meant to serve their needs by providing them the benefits of law and government, and so it should be situated in a locale convenient to the majority—and truly central to the county.

More interesting, their protest, like Penn's plans, transcended local concerns. In their petition, these semiliterate colonists astutely acknowledged the proprietor's interest in this proposed town. To convey their recognition, they phrased their protest to play on Penn's fears and challenge his plans for the interior. The location of a county seat, they suggested, might well influence their political loyalties and economic activities. Reminding the governor that this was still a contested region, these petitioners feared that many of their frustrated neighbors were "in danger of leaveing and Joining themselves to the Provance [province] of Maryland." Others, meanwhile, might take "advantage" to "Cariey [carry] away our tread [trade]. . . . Espacally the Indian tread" to another colony. Even those who remained loyal to Pennsylvania, they warned, would be "much discouraged from improveing in the town and our part of the Countey," because money spent at the county seat would be at "too great a distance to Circulate back to us again."[69] Penn's development scheme, in other words, was at risk, for it depended in large part on the cooperation of colonists like them. By locating the town at a site inconvenient to the majority, they implied that Penn reduced their incentives to comply with his plans. These petitioners showed their savvy. They would cooperate with provincial authorities, but not without reward. Their position set a precedent that later residents would build upon in their own struggles with authorities.

While western residents raised provincial anxieties, other colonists proposed alternative locales. Shippensburg was the first. It was the oldest town in the Valley, first settled in 1730, then transformed into Edward Shippen's proprietary town by 1738. Located about sixteen miles southwest of LeTort Spring, it was said to be "the most central place and properest Situation for the County Town."[70] Yet this site was dismissed by Penn and his agents for its "Want of Water."[71] Others in the county favored another settlement located at the far southwestern end of the Valley along Conococheague Creek (the soon-to-be town of Chambersburg) pioneered by the brothers Benjamin and Joseph Chambers in the early 1730s. It, too, was deemed "not so proper a Place" by Penn for a more significant reason that reiterates the essential role he expected this town to play in the colony's commercial development. A county seat at Chambersburg was too likely to upset the tenuous balance of competition in the colonial fur and skin trade. As Penn reasoned it: "I cannot think it will be of any advantage to have the Town so near those . . . to be Laid out by Mr[.] Dulany [in Maryland] and my Lord Fairfax [along the Potomac in Virginia]."[72] Cookson concurred. As he saw it, if Chambersburg were the county town, it would pose a real threat to Pennsylvania's "Indian

Trade," as "it wou'd be no Advantage to our Philadelphia Merchants too have their seat of Trade too near that of their neighbours." This situation would "only give the People concern'd the Choice of two Markets, . . . in which we cannot possibly be any Gainers." "Having already the Bulk of the Trade in our Hands," Cookson feared the "risque . . . [of] loosing some Part of it."[73]

Despite objections, the LeTort Spring site was the only viable location for the county seat, according to Penn's officials. It had the necessary resources to support a town. It was "the nearest Situation to the Centre of the County on the East side" that would "admit proper Supplys of good Water, Meadows, Pasture, Timber, Stone, Lime and other necessaries and conveniences for such a Town." More important, it was centrally located, which assured its commercial potential. The LeTort Spring site had a "commodiousness to the great Road leading from Harris's Ferry to Patowmec [Potomac] and to other necessary Roads." This meant that its location, which "answers best to the paths over the Blue Hills," was most likely to advance the economic interests of the proprietor by answering "to the Trade, both with the Indians and with the City of Philadelphia."[74]

With the site "determined," Thomas Cookson purchased 1,200 to 1,300 acres from the six Scots-Irishmen and one widow settled on the site. Cumberland's new county seat, "the Town . . . to be called Carlisle," was ready for survey.[75] The acquisition of these lands presented Thomas Penn with another opportunity to design a county town for his colony's expanding interior. By 1751, Penn was an experienced town planner. He founded York and Reading in the 1740s. After Carlisle, he planned Easton in 1752, Bedford in 1766, and Sunbury in 1772 (see map 1).[76] Carlisle's founding thus was part of a broader colonial enterprise. In planning the town, his goal, like other town planners, was to create a visible landscape of roads, buildings, and structured spaces, as well as an invisible landscape of values, attitudes, and behaviors. Carefully planned urban spaces were to act as vehicles through which he and his officials would wield indirect authority over their inhabitants.[77] For Penn, the grid survey was the plan that best fit these goals. This long-established urban design, which dated back to Roman times, was closely associated with Britain's colonial enterprises in Europe and America. This gave Penn plenty of examples to follow in designing his towns; they included his father's design for Philadelphia and British town plans in seventeenth-century Ireland. Both influenced his plans for Carlisle.[78]

Penn planned Carlisle working mostly from his residence in London

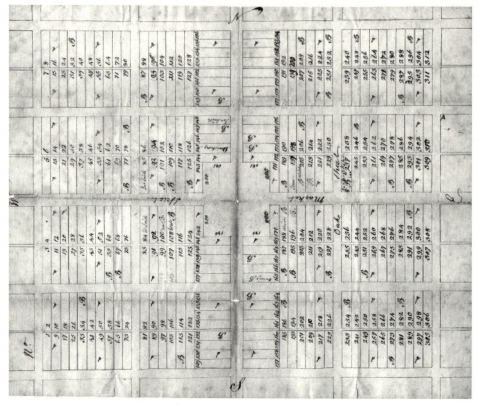

Figure 1. *Draught of Carlisle, May 17, 1751.* This plan map, likely drawn by surveyor Thomas Cookson, is the earliest extant map of the town as it was finally surveyed. It was used to distribute lots to the town's first purchasers and coordinates with a list of "Lot Applyers." The "B's" designate lots that were already built upon in some way, while the "P's" indicate proprietary lots that were to be reserved for later speculative sales. Note the street names of Market and Oak. These did not conform to the instructions Thomas Penn gave for naming. Market Street was soon changed to High and Oak to Bedford. Other street names soon included Pomfret, Pitt, Louther, and Bedford. (From the Cadwalader Papers, courtesy of the Historical Society of Pennsylvania, Philadelphia.)

with input from his officials in the colony. His design called for the survey of a compact gridiron pattern of streets and alleys punctuated by a central square. Within this rectilinear design, two eighty-foot-wide main streets predominated: the north-south Hanover (or York, originally unnamed on the first complete map) and the east-west High (or Main, originally named Market). They ushered residents and visitors toward the political, commercial, and spiritual structures to be situated prominently on the town's central square. From there, what one traveler later termed the "wide and well laid out" streets of Carlisle extended only two blocks in each direction, bound by the descriptively named North, South, East, and West Streets. (The use of Oak on the first town map, was likely in imitation of the use of names of trees in Philadelphia.) Town space was subdivided into 312 lots—each measuring a narrow 60 by 240 feet. Even the outlots surrounding the town, plots for pastureland or planting, were surveyed on an orderly grid pattern of rectangles and oriented so that "the Roads to the Town pass thro' them in the most advantageous manner" (figure 1).[79]

Although the regular spaces and ninety-degree angles of Carlisle's grid were irrefutably orderly, Penn's design for Carlisle was neither especially creative nor original. Many town proprietors, especially those working in America's interior, adopted the grid as their preferred urban plan. Town plans, though not identical, varied little in the eighteenth century. Indeed, examples of grid-patterned towns with central squares abounded. Aside from his father's town of Philadelphia, they included Lancaster and Allentown in Pennsylvania, Winchester in Virginia, William Cooper's town in New York, and a host of other interior towns in the backcountries of Virginia, North Carolina, and nineteenth-century Tennessee. Carlisle's plan thus was not exceptional, especially for Pennsylvania. In fact, it followed what geographers call a typical "Pennsylvania" or "Philadelphia" plan, one that mimicked Philadelphia, the first sizable North American city laid out on a grid.[80]

But Philadelphia was not wholly original either. William Penn envisioned his town as a new and "unorthodox" urban place. Large house lots surrounded by gardens would offer serene backdrops for a utopian colony where persecuted Quakers and other immigrants pursued religious freedom and opportunity. But the design he and his surveyor general Thomas Holme devised ultimately built on distinctively European precedents. Philadelphia was a grid, and thus imitative. Penn and Holme borrowed from ancient models and Renaissance ideals of city planning expressed in London following

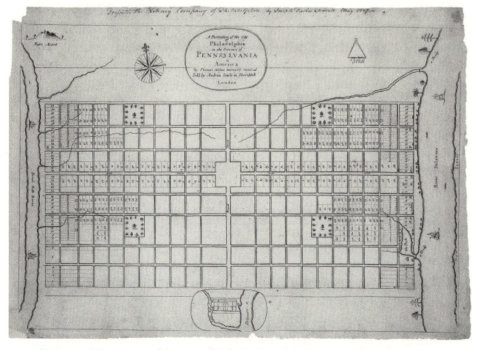

Figure 2. *A Portraiture of the City of Philadelphia in the Province of Pennsylvania in America*. This 1683 map, drawn by William Penn's surveyor, Thomas Holme, was the original plan for Philadelphia. As one of the first American cities planned on a grid, Philadelphia has been long hailed by scholars for its Renaissance-inspired symmetry that became a model for American frontier town planning, including Carlisle, planned by William's son Thomas. Yet Holme's design also borrowed from English-founded towns in Ulster, Ireland (Figure 3), making it an explicitly colonial design as well. (Courtesy of the Library Company of Philadelphia.)

the Great Fire of 1666. Philadelphia's only design novelties were its large-size, open, park-like squares, wide streets, and sprawling lots—features that did not manifest themselves until a century of development had pushed growth away from the Delaware riverfront (figure 2).[81]

Philadelphia never became the green country town Penn planned. But it did serve as a model city for British North America, one his son Thomas borrowed from when planning his own towns some sixty years later. Carlisle's grid, along with Thomas Penn's other towns, illustrates the continuities in the urban visions of father and son. The grid was an urban vision imposed on the land by its planner; it was a highly conscious plan that took no account of topography. It ordered space in advance of colonization. In these ways, the design was a tool for development that was quickly associated with the American interior. In addition, rectangular town lots were easily divisible into half or quarter parcels for faster disposal, which encouraged speculation and promoted urban density.[82] In Carlisle, where Thomas Penn wanted his lots to sell quickly, he suggested that those around the square, lots likely to be in high demand, might be redrawn to "accommodate a far greater number of Houses."[83] Grid plans thus presumed future growth. Penn, for example, was "well pleased" to find that so much Land had been surveyed about Carlisle, "for although not valuable in itself," it would "become so by its situation if the Town encreases."[84]

Grid-patterned towns were also symbols of colonialism. In the British Atlantic, colonial proprietors had already made extensive use of such plans in Ireland, England's first colony. In fact, town planning was an integral component of the seventeenth-century English conquest of Ireland. This was especially so in Ulster, where the plantation scheme was the strongest. "Towns," as historian T. C. Barnard notes, were "designed for a pivotal role in the new Ireland."[85] They were to be centers for defense, government, commerce, and Protestantism by imposing a rationality that Ireland's native landscape lacked in the eyes of English colonizers. Carefully planned, English-style towns, built on Roman and Renaissance ideals, were meant to help civilize Catholic Ireland. Populated by merchants, professionals, and artisans from England and Scotland, these towns were intended to establish patterns of urban commercial life especially beneficial to England.[86]

Carlisle's plan bore close resemblance to the north Irish town of Londonderry, planned in 1609. Londonderry was a walled, grid-patterned town. It featured two main streets that intersected at a center square where a building stood that housed a market, town hall, and prison. Tightly packed row houses with gardens behind lined its streets. As a highly ordered and enclosed space, derived in part from the grid system long used in military camps, it was designed with defense in mind. English and Scots colonists wanted protection from the oft-rebellious Irish natives surrounding them.[87] As the government, commercial, and service center for its region, the town, with public structures placed prominently on the square, extended English authority into the region. Londonderry's artificiality and uniformity reflected the goals of its colonizers. As historian Anthony Garvan notes, aside from America, the grid prevailed only in Ireland, Wales, and small sections of the European continent, places "where the English had found themselves in a minority and

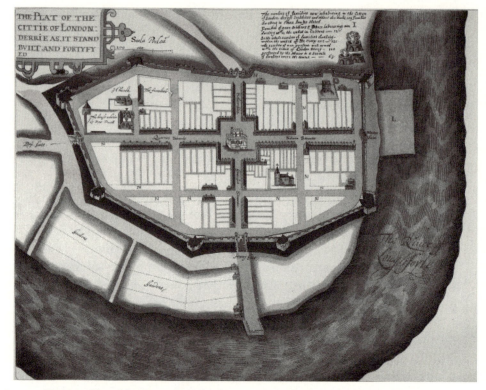

Figure 3. *Plat of the Cittie of Londonderrie as it Stand, Built, and Fortified.* With its center square, containing a building that housed a market, town hall, and prison, seventeenth-century Londonderry's walled, grid-patterned plan was one inspiration for Carlisle. (Part of the Carew Papers, courtesy of Lambeth Palace Library, London.)

feared the native inhabitants," and where such adversity created "universal agreement as to the ideal town plan (figure 3).[88]

That William and Thomas Penn used grids for their towns sheds light on their colonial ambitions. The Pennsylvania- or Philadelphia-style plan was not just convenient, nor was it an innocuous adaptation of English Renaissance design derived from London, as most scholars assume. It was instead an explicitly colonial design that this father-son pair borrowed in planning the urban spaces of their colony. There were distinct differences in the way these plans were implemented in Ireland and America, however. In Pennsylvania, for example, a colony founded on toleration, there seemed little need for defensive walls, especially before the outbreak of Native American hostilities in the mid-1750s. But such adaptations do not detract from the Penns' goals to assert their authority over the land and colonists they claimed as their own. Surely, they recognized the implications of their design choices. William, especially, knew Ireland well. His father had been rewarded with confiscated land in the south of Ireland for assisting in the Cromwellian conquest. Moreover, William had spent time in the 1660s managing his family's Irish lands.[89] It thus was no accident that when William selected a surveyor for Philadelphia he chose Thomas Holme, a man who had surveyed in northern Ireland. According to one historian, Holme's design for Philadelphia was likely inspired by the 1609 plan for Londonderry as well as the 1666 plan for London's rebuilding.[90] English towns in Ireland offered the Penns a powerful model of how urban design might be used to claim land, direct commerce, and order colonists and natives.

Yet the continuities between father and son end there. Carlisle's plan was meant to address circumstances specific to eighteenth-century Pennsylvania, including planning a town in the less-accessible geography of the colony's interior and managing the actions of the colony's particular population of new immigrant colonists. Unlike the Delaware Valley, with its large populations of Quakers and Anglicans, or other interior counties like Lancaster, York, or Berks, with their many Germans, Cumberland County was an especially Irish place at mid-century, as well as a highly contentious one. Squatters continued to settle illegally on unpurchased lands. In fact, it seemed to many close to the proprietors that "the County of Cumberland [was] in great Disorder," with "numbers in Defyance [defiance] of Law . . . gone or going over the Blue Hills." With Native leaders pressing the colony to keep unruly colonists off their lands to the north of the Cumberland Valley, Penn and others knew that issuing licenses for the land would not suffice.[91] Squatters threatened the peace. As the majority of these squatters, the Scots-Irish, whom one official characterized as "the most stubborn and perverse People" in the colony, merited particular concern.[92] Penn needed to control them. Creating orderly space in the county seat was one way to achieve this goal. Indeed, Gov. Hamilton and others hoped that with guidance Carlisle might "flourish" even "under the management of the Irish."[93]

The planning of Carlisle's central square best exemplifies Penn's quest for control. Carlisle's square "was intended," as Penn explained, "to be Like the Squares in Philadelphia." As he first sketched it, it was also a replica of the English town square in Londonderry.[94] In lengthy explanations to those executing his plans, Penn made clear that the square was to be the central feature

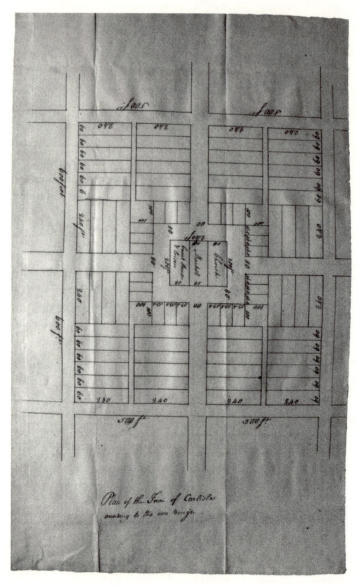

Figure 4. *Plan of the Town of Carlisle According to the New Design.* Although this undated map is not the first of Thomas Penn's designs for Carlisle's center square, it is the clearest. As he conceived it, the square was to be Carlisle's focal point. The two main streets, Hanover and High, were to frame a square that would house a courthouse and prison, a market, and an Anglican Church. Due to miscommunications and the actions of the town's colonists, however, this square was never built. Instead, the town's main roads were surveyed through it by 1765, thus splitting it into four equal quadrants. (From the Penn Papers, Land Grants, courtesy of Historical Society of Pennsylvania, Philadelphia.)

of the town. This "inverted Square of about the size of the common ones" (a rectangle), as he described it, was to be home to a "Court House . . . in the middle of one side," a "Gaol . . . any place near," and a "Market," in the "Middle of the Center." As discussions continued, the Anglican convert Penn innovated the design by also adding a spot for an Anglican Church.[95] With spaces designated for the public buildings of law, order, commerce, and religion, built symbols of authority in British colonial America, Penn hoped that Carlisle's square would unify townspeople, thereby remedying the troublesome actions of its seemingly lawless hinterlands (figure 4).[96]

Thomas Penn also ordered space through naming. Naming, or renaming, was another mechanism European colonizers had long used to order colonial peoples and spaces. In a county where there were townships named Antrim, Derry, and Donegal, in homage to the Ulster origins of many colonists, Thomas Penn stated forthrightly that he "would not have Indian[,] Dutch[,] or Irish names given" for streets in any of his county towns; instead, he instructed surveyors to give English, and particularly London, names preference.[97] Furthermore, unlike his father, whose Quaker beliefs discouraged glorifying individuals by naming streets for them, Thomas Penn embraced traditional English naming patterns. Having severed his association with the Quakers and embraced the Anglo-centered world of the Church of England that he shared with his new wife, he celebrated English royal and aristocratic authority in his colony.[98] His father's town, Philadelphia, had streets named for local trees—Cedar, Pine, Spruce, etc.—or they were numbered. Carlisle, by contrast, had Hanover, Pitt, and Lowther Streets—names explicitly associated with English authority. In addition, like Easton, another of his proprietary towns, street names honored the family of his new bride, Lady Juliana Fermor, the daughter of Lord Pomfret. Both Carlisle and Easton had Pomfret Streets, for example. Easton, which he named for "my Lord Pomfret's House," also had Juliana and Fermor Streets.[99]

More telling of his motives and models, Thomas Penn celebrated English imperial and military authority in other names he chose. The county name Cumberland, town name Carlisle, and street (and later town) name Bedford all referenced the war that Scottish Jacobite rebels, who supported restoration of the Stuart line, waged against Britain's Hanoverian monarchy on the British borderlands in the 1740s. Specifically, these names celebrated the rebels' defeat by the Duke of Cumberland, King George II's second son, at the bloody battle of Culloden in 1746. These were well-known events in the British Isles and America. Depending on one's perspective and ethnic identity, the outcome either confirmed or raised anxieties about the sometimes brutal authority of Britain's monarchy. Thomas Penn's wish to associate place names with this rebellion conveyed important messages to colonists, particularly the Scots-Irish, about the authority and righteousness of the English state, and by extension his enterprise in Pennsylvania.

This was especially clear in his choice of name for Carlisle. Its namesake, the ancient English fortress town of Carlisle that stood on the borderlands between England and Scotland, was the site where the Duke of Cumberland fought and won one of his most decisive victories. There he reclaimed the city from rebel control and then charged many town leaders with treason. The name Carlisle thus evoked powerful images of an English nation that took a violent and uncompromisingly aggressive approach to asserting and defending its authority. There was no fooling, idealism, or harmonious images of a peaceable kingdom here, but an implicitly serious warning from Thomas Penn that he controlled and might defend his town. In a region where so many Scots-Irish peoples resided and looked to settle, this model of authority and the threat of punishment to dissenters it implied had poignant meaning to them. British imperialism was something that caused them and their ancestors to be wary.[100] Some colonists resisted its imposition on their lives. Carlisle, like other settlements that had stood on and near it before, thus remained a contested space. Despite Penn's bold plans and assertions of authority, Carlisle's future was up for grabs.

In these ways, the story of Carlisle's founding not only occupies a central chapter in the history of the lower Susquehanna and Cumberland Valleys, it is also part of a larger chronicle of British imperialism in the Atlantic world. As an urban landscape derived from European models, Carlisle's founding symbolized a Euro-American and specifically British-style claim over the land, peoples, and resources of the mid-Atlantic interior. At the same time, Thomas Penn's imperial interest in the site was no accident. Penn's motives for founding Carlisle demonstrate important continuities in the way various peoples interpreted the land and resources of this region. Carlisle was built in part on the Native peoples' understanding of the land they occupied for generations. Then, Euro-American traders and colonists, along with Penn and his officials, altered these readings. Their territorial and commercial ambitions shifted the region's geographic orientation. Making use of the land, its resources, and its strategic potential in their own way, and bolstered by the force of England's colonial experiences in Ireland and Scotland, Penn and his supporters fashioned Carlisle into their own place in-between. Much like its English namesake, which was also a border town, Carlisle, Pennsylvania was to be a beacon of civilization in the woods and a transitional point for colonists from one cultural world, the British Atlantic, into another, potentially profitable, but more distant interior world of Indian villagers, warriors, and traders.

CHAPTER TWO

Negotiating the Boundaries

AS THE 1750S progressed, it was clear that creating Carlisle would be neither the simple nor predictable process Thomas Penn anticipated. Surveying a town determined its borders and asserted provincial authority over contested territory, but these were only first steps. To control this new town and its first inhabitants, survey lines had to be made meaningful and preserved over time. These tasks posed challenges, as Penn and his officials quickly discovered. Because town building was a dynamic process, function did not necessarily follow form in even the most meticulously planned places. Therefore, Penn found himself dependent on colonists to implement his plans. It was the town's first inhabitants—not Penn's officials—who would construct the town's buildings and forge its social, economic, and cultural networks. But there was a catch; these colonists had their own agendas, ones that were not always compatible with Penn's interests. And for Penn, a proprietor who carefully planned Carlisle to serve as the defacto "capital" of nearly two-thirds of his colony's interior, mediating his way through colonists' myriad agendas was a vexing matter.[1]

Carlisle's first inhabitants had their own ethno-religious identities, economic interests, and personal ambitions, which they expressed in building their town. They built log and stone homes to live in and Presbyterian, Anglican, and Lutheran meetinghouses for worship. These structures symbolized the diverse community they, not Penn, were creating in Carlisle. Then, too, they constructed businesses, particularly the many retail establishments that formed the core of Carlisle's commercial sector. These taverns, stores, and warehouses confirmed Carlisle's role as a crossroads place in the interior. Finally, they built roads, which were the basis of a transportation and communications infrastructure within and beyond the Valley. Some roads, aligned on an east-west axis, linked Carlisle to its hinterlands, to Philadelphia, and the Ohio country, much as Penn planned. Other roads, built on a north-south axis by contrast, connected Carlisle to the growing markets of Baltimore, Philadelphia's rival; these pathways exemplified the disconnect between colonists' ambitions and Penn's vision for his colony.

Through these actions, the town's first inhabitants made critical choices about how to make Carlisle their own. In doing so, they expressed *their* interpretation of Carlisle as a place in-between in the mid-Atlantic interior. Equally significant, they demonstrated the extent to which building this town would entail more than simply superimposing a proprietor's interests, or Philadelphia- or Ulster-based ideals, onto Pennsylvania's interior. Carlisle was a dynamic place. Its evolving built urban landscape, or townscape, was far more complex than any Penn and his advisors had envisioned in 1751, and far less predictable than any they wanted.

Carlisle did not take shape the way Penn had planned. Rather, unanticipated obstacles kept hindering its progress in the early 1750s. Colony officials grew wary in response. It was "necessary to move there [in Carlisle] with abundance of caution," said provincial secretary Richard Peters to Thomas Penn in 1752, "as so many discouragements have from time to time been there thrown in our way."[2] It seemed as if each time Penn attempted to advance his interests in the Cumberland Valley, a host of circumstances stymied his plans. These "discouragements," as Peters termed them, originated from a variety of sources, some from inside the provincial establishment and others from local colonists. In consequence, caution, rather than confidence, became the watchword of Carlisle's planners.

Inefficient work by surveyor Thomas Cookson caused the first complications. Cookson's delay in purchasing the townsite from colonists already settled there postponed the survey of the grid. Had Cookson acted more quickly, Penn and others believed, the prices paid for these lands would have been cheaper, and as Governor Hamilton conjectured, "by this time [April 1751] the Town might have been pretty forward in its Buildings." Instead, the town's progress was stalled; lots were not laid out until a month later.[3]

Carlisle's founding also came at a time of heightened tension between proprietors' agents and Cumberland County colonists. Residents' deep suspicions of the proprietors and their agents prompted them to dispute the location of the new county seat. To these colonists, some of whom had lived in the area since the 1730s and remembered the border struggles Pennsylvania had waged with Maryland, Penn and his officials were outsiders more interested in advancing their own economic interests than protecting colonists' welfare. But that was not all. Colonists were equally cautious of the Native Americans among whom they resided. Although many colonists traded with these local Native peoples and sometimes even worked cooperatively with them to undercut proprietary authority, they also feared them as potential threats to their security.[4]

Their suspicions came to a head when provincial officials attempted to push forward several overlapping ends by enforcing the boundary lines of the newly formed Cumberland County. Specifically, they hoped to bolster proprietary authority by controlling the squatter population and to establish Carlisle, the new seat, as the westernmost locus of provincial authority in the colony's interior. Simultaneously, to ensure the colony's continued role in the fur and skin trade, officials also hoped that policing the lines between colonial and Native American settlements would preserve peace with the Native peoples of Iroquoia, Pennsylvania, and the Ohio Valley. The 1736 treaty had fixed Cumberland County's northern boundary at North Mountain. Yet few Pennsylvania colonists paid much attention to this border. Instead, they squatted on lands, sometimes even negotiating their own settlement boundaries with local Indians.[5]

The outcome was a pattern of escalating tensions by the 1740s. Colony officials grew angry as they watched as squatters—those "vile people" as one official called them—"seized" lands in the valleys north and west of the 1736 purchase. These settlements were disorderly; officials also feared that these colonists might "become tributary to the Indians."[6] Native Americans complained publicly about these squatters. At a treaty in 1749, several Ohio Senecas charged that "bad People" were "spoil[ing]" their "Hunting" and "insist[ed]" that Pennsylvania remove them "instantly."[7] To remedy this "breach," Pennsylvania officials acted. They warned "Delinquent" settlers to "remove themselves."[8] When they persisted, provincial secretary Richard Peters took action. "Severity," he said, would be "exercised on the first people," while the "rest" would likely "be intimidated & go off voluntarily." In cases of "Resistance," he knew "no way . . . but to get the Indians to burn the Log houses."[9] And that was what he did. In the spring of 1750, Peters, accompanied by a party of local officials that included the well-known fur trader, go-between, and newly appointed Cumberland County justice George Croghan, five other justices, and the sheriff, and joined by a small group of Oneidas and several other Native peoples from the Ohio country, ventured over North Mountain and "effected the work there" by "destroying & burning small Houses & laying all [of their occupants] under Recognizances & Bonds." Although some of these settlements, Peters admitted, "were many, & valuable," their residents "saw no help & so submitted to the same fate as the rest."[10] Even so, at least one squatter, Andrew Lycon, resisted. This Scots-Irishman presented "a loaded Gun" and threatened to "shoot the first man that dar'd to come nigher." After subduing him, a group of Indians, who "by Accident" had been camped nearby, "insisted" that this settler's cabin be burnt, or "they would burn it themselves." The cabin was set on fire. The Scots-Irishman went to jail.[11]

Although only Lycon resisted, his actions put Peters on the defensive, especially after critics raised questions about the legality of his expedition. Peters responded by altering his telling of these events. He admitted that he had forced these squatters to "give" him "Possession of their Houses." Yet they "did not refuse." And as he rationalized it, with "the House being mine for the Proprietaries, and on the Principle that a Man cou'd do what he pleases with his own, I order'd it to be burn't."[12] Peters was immensely pleased with himself. Once these squatters were evicted, "there was no Kindness in my Power which I did not do for the Offenders," he claimed. He gave them money; he pointed them toward purchased lands for resettlement; he even offered to let several of the most needy families stay rent free on some of his own "vacant" farmland, serving his own interests.[13] To his friend Penn, he reported proudly that: "My Success pleases me not only because the Indians & these wild people must inevitably have fallen into Quarrels but because a very valuable Country is reserved from being cut to pieces by a Rabble." By his reckoning, little of substance had been lost and much gained. The cabins burned "were of no considerable value, being such as the country people erect in a day or two."[14] Peters had saved the day. He had protected the colony's interests by averting a possible war with the Iroquois and readied the land "over the hills" for future purchase and more "orderly" forms of development; Penn agreed.[15]

The response from outside proprietary ranks was mixed. Ohio Senecas offered their "Thanks for their Care of our Lands."[16] Cumberland County colonists, by contrast, were furious. They were shocked by these evictions, which confirmed their suspicions of the proprietors and their agents as set against them. Colonists were particularly troubled by the alliance among proprietary officials, county magistrates, and Native Americans. These deeds were "done at the Instance of the Indians and in the Presence of some of them." In their view, succumbing to pressure from the Iroquois, confiscating and destroying property, imprisoning trespassers, and allowing Native peoples to assist in the process were ominous precedents. Colonists refused to "go away" in response. Those remaining squatters stubbornly declined to vacate their lands and were "said" to be "confederated together to resist the Government." Meanwhile, new colonial settlements appeared beyond the 1736 boundary. By Peters's assessment, "the disorderly & low part of these foolish Settlers" had "overpowered the people of better Judgement & disposition."[17]

Peters was correct in part. Although those resisting proprietary authority were not necessarily disorderly, low, or foolish, as he asserted, there were indeed two distinct groups at work in Cumberland County, each with its own interests—one commercial, one agricultural—that worked against the other. Equally significant, their differing responses to Native and proprietary interests highlighted tensions that separated Carlisle from its county and divided Scots-Irish colonists among themselves. Colonists like Croghan and the magistrates who accompanied Peters were closely aligned with proprietary authority. These mostly Scots-Irish traders, merchants, and officials had strong commercial interests that they wished to ground in the new county town. Those who opposed them, by contrast, although mostly Scots-Irish also, aligned themselves with the agricultural interests of the county; they were deeply suspicious of the new county town because of its close connections to the proprietors and the fur and skin trade. And they were willing to defend their interests by resisting these unjust actions. Peters hoped that the Governor would react "with Spirit" and "not suffer such an Indignity & open Defyance [defiance]" among these squatters, but Hamilton could do little; he needed support for the county town.[18] Thus, with the two sides poised for continued confrontation, Carlisle's prospects looked dim. Even after another, controversial land purchase in 1754 added all lands between North Mountain and the Alleghenies to the county, divisions among colonists persisted.[19] As evidence, surveyor John Armstrong of Carlisle reported that he "thought it absolutely necessary to bring three or four Indians along" with him for protection when surveying part of this new purchase for the proprietors. This Scots-Irishman feared that he would be "Stopt by the Irish with guns" as he had been "Stopt by them" in the past.[20] Economic and political concerns, fueled by fear and resentment of Native peoples, trumped colonists' shared ethnic identity and pitted them against one another. These were tense times.

Then came the "unexpected" bankruptcy of George Croghan and his partner William Trent, the second and third people to apply for lots in Carlisle after its survey. Croghan and Trent were among Pennsylvania's most experienced fur traders, interpreters, and middlemen at mid-century. Colony officials had hoped they would smooth over these heated conflicts between interest groups while promoting proprietary interests. The Irishman Croghan, who farmed and traded several miles northeast of Carlisle, was one of Pennsylvania's most controversial backwoodsmen. After emigrating from Ireland in 1741, Croghan quickly established himself as a trader and land speculator. Soon, he was playing a leading role in the conduct of Pennsylvania's Indian affairs. By 1750, he was named one of Cumberland County's first justices and helped Peters evict the squatters over North Mountain. His house was the setting for an Indian treaty conference. Even Thomas Penn's protégé, Richard Hockley, was linked to him; he was Croghan's largest creditor. Croghan's and the proprietors' interests were deeply intertwined.[21]

More important to Carlisle were Croghan's extensive contacts in the fur and skin trade. From his farm, tanyard, and warehouse complex on Conodoguinet Creek, just south of the mountain gap that bore his name, it was said that Croghan "drew a great Trade to that part of the Country."[22] But in the wake of the failure of his partnership with Trent and Hockley, in 1751, Croghan abandoned this home and took up residence farther west at Aughwick. His sudden relocation was a blow to the proprietors' interests. The governor feared that his loss would have devastating effects on the town. As Hamilton reported to Penn, the sudden collapse of these "Principal dealers, had made every body desirous of Withdrawing their effects from that Precarious Trade as soon as Possible." This was a frightening prospect to officials like Hamilton, whose desire to make Carlisle an economic crossroads in the colony depended on town residents' continued participation in this trade. Landed interests were also at stake. Croghan and Trent's failure, Hamilton believed, "must necessarily occasion a great scarcity of Money in those remote parts, and will, I fear, retard the progress of the town, as well as lessen the Value of the Lands for the Prop[rietors]."[23]

This bankruptcy was also "unfortunate on another account." While Croghan and Trent were "in Credit," as Hamilton explained, "they had obtain[e]d a great influence in the County," which he believed they would have used to have a prison built long "before this Time." Instead, because "their Interest and reputation with the People is now utterly sunk and come to nothing," Trent, but especially Croghan, could no longer assist in translating Penn's ideals into action.[24] They could not smooth over the tensions about the eviction of squatters, mediate the disputes over the location of the county seat, or ensure order. And in a colonial world in which patronage was paramount and spreading proprietary authority depended on establishing networks of influence among people of the interior, men like Croghan and Trent were essential links in a chain of association stretching from Cumberland County to Philadelphia and London. Penn had lost not just allies, but two important mediators whose reputations as men of the interior with connections to the east would have bridged the gap between the proprietor's wishes and the needs and aspirations of colonists and Native peoples. Without these men to broker his interests, it would be difficult to translate his vision onto what his officials perceived as the unruly contours of the colony's interior.[25] Penn's plans were in jeopardy.

As the proprietor and his agents struggled to reconcile these conflicts and regain authority, Carlisle's founding came to rest on the shoulders of its first inhabitants to a greater extent than anyone involved in its planning anticipated. In certain respects, this shift was a predictable part of the town building process. All town planners, especially absentee proprietors such as Penn, depended on colonists to build their towns. But in Carlisle, where controversy raged and patronage channels were interrupted, the proprietor's dependence on the town's first inhabitants was especially pronounced. To what extent would Carlisle's first colonists respond to the cues imbedded in Penn's grid plan and put his ideas into action? The answer was uncertain. In response, some officials worried that his plans might fail.

But Penn was not the only one who faced obstacles. Establishing a town in the interior was tough work that presented Carlisle's first colonists with challenges. As they arrived in 1751, they confronted a place bearing only limited resemblance to a town. The grid was surveyed; town colonists had tickets for their lots from surveyor Cookson. These tickets, the first step to obtaining full legal title, obligated holders to erect a structure on their lot within five years.[26] This required them to get to work quickly, and they did. They cleared lots, dug cellars, and built houses. Taking advantage of "the nearness of All materials for building," Carlisle's first inhabitants began constructing their town.[27] Their work showed quick returns. As the first map of Carlisle's lots depicts, as early as the spring of 1751, only months after the town's survey, forty-six of the town's 312 lots, over half of them on the north and east sides of town closest to the Great Road and the LeTort, were already built upon in some way. With 177 applicants for town lots and 105 householders on the first sketchy tax list of 1753, many more townspaces were also likely under construction (see figure 1).[28]

Yet Carlisle was also a place of contrasts in its first years. Despite the construction underway, the town was sparsely settled. With the exception of a string of contiguously occupied lots along High Street just east of the square, few townspeople had immediate neighbors. Some houses stood alone on their blocks; other blocks were devoid of structures (see figure 1). Furthermore, with overgrown vacant farmland covering many lots, some kind of dilapidated stockade still visible, and a small settlement of Delaware, Shawnee, and Tuscarora peoples said to be living nearby, signs of the woods abounded. Its boundaries were still remarkably "fluid at the edges"; it had the haphazard quality of a new place.[29]

The town's first inhabitants were also a study in contrasts. The most privileged were a tight-knit clique of proprietors' men. They had political connections and economic ties to other, more elite town investors like Penn associate Edward Shippen, Receiver-General Lynford Lardner, merchant Samuel Neave, and trader George Croghan. But unlike these Philadelphians whose interest in Carlisle was distant and speculative, these townspeople were there to stay; Carlisle was to be their home. These men, most of whom were Scots-Irish, some of whom were related by marriage or other family ties, staked their and their families' futures on building this town in the interior. And their careers were on the rise at mid-century because of such willingness to take risks. In exchange for appointed posts in the county, and access to lucrative land and trade deals, they served the proprietors in the interior. Thus, a combination of service and opportunity drew them to Carlisle. Virtually all of them were original applicants for lots in town. They and their descendants formed the town's core leadership class for decades to come.[30]

Although their life experiences and occupations varied, their connections to the proprietors raised expectations that they would fill the void left by Croghan's hasty departure and help make Carlisle what Penn envisioned. Some, like Irish-born Robert Callender, Michael Teaffe, or Croghan's partner, William Trent, were experienced men of the woods. Callender, an integral figure in the town's first two decades, was already an established fur trader and associate of George Croghan. As an "Indian trader of Carlisle," he orchestrated much of Carlisle's trade with Native peoples of the Ohio Valley until his death in the 1770s.[31] Others, like the Irish-born John Armstrong and Francis West, who were also immigrants, brought different skills, connections, and loyalties to Carlisle. They arrived willing to serve the proprietors, but expected lucrative personal returns for their efforts. Armstrong, who quickly became one of Carlisle's foremost political and military leaders, immigrated to Pennsylvania after 1740, settled in York County, and was elected to the Assembly, where he distinguished himself as a friend of proprietary interests. "Against his own judgment" he was convinced "to remove to Carlisle" by Richard Peters, who recommended him as "the most proper person to manage the Proprietary Affairs in and about Carlisle," and appointed him deputy surveyor. Armstrong, like others among this group of proprietary stalwarts, arrived in Carlisle expecting "his removal" would be "made advantageous to him."[32] So, too, did merchant Francis West. A more recent arrival from Ireland, he quickly distinguished himself as loyal political servant to Penn. West also brought the added advantage of connections to the Philadelphia merchant community in his brother, William, who was also among the first applicants for town lots and a dry-goods merchant in Philadelphia with dealings in the fur and skin trade. The West brothers surely expected rewards for the trade connections they brought with them to Carlisle.[33] Then there was Hermanus Alricks, a Dutch merchant born in Delaware. He was new to the interior, but eager to make his way there. Alricks moved to Cumberland County shortly before its formation, obtained several appointed political posts, then won election as one of the first two assemblymen from the county in 1750. Although he was one of few non-Irish members of this clique, his marriage to Francis West's sister, Ann, won him an indispensable kin connection to other Carlisle leading men.[34]

Carlisle's more ordinary colonists shared qualities with the above group. As their surnames suggest, many were Scots-Irish and likely recent immigrants. They, too, brought a variety of occupational and craft specializations needed to make Carlisle a town. Indeed, among Carlisle's first lot applicants were two blacksmiths, a wheelwright, two saddlers, a tanner, a shoemaker, a cooper, a feltmaker, a brewer, two hatters, a tailor, a weaver, a carpenter, three bricklayers, and two silversmiths. There were three shopkeepers as well. Historian Merri Lou Schaumann has been able to identify others as gunsmiths, joiners, and tavern keepers. These colonists, including those like weaver Robert Killpatrick, who "has his family with him," shared one important quality that distinguished them from those with ties to the proprietors.[35] They risked their lives and those of their families on Carlisle's founding *without* the benefits of Penn's patronage to support them; they were not proprietors' men. That meant they had no safety net; the risk was all their own. Some of them—like the carpenter, bricklayers, and joiners, for example—were there to build the town's infrastructure. Others—like the brewer, tailor, weaver, shoemaker, shopkeepers, and tavern keepers—were there to offer needed services or consumer goods to locals and those passing through town. Still others—like the wheelwright, blacksmiths, saddlers, gunsmiths, hatters, tanner, feltmaker, and perhaps the silversmiths and weaver—probably supported the fur trade. Their work in facilitating the movement of men and goods, the processing of hides, or the manufacture or repair of metal or cloth goods probably served the town's traders. Although of a different rank, Carlisle's craftsmen, retailers, and small-scale merchants also had vested interests in seeing the town prosper.

Then there were still others, including five women, two of them widows, who settled the town. Less information exists about them. One of the women, Elizabeth Ross, kept a store or tavern; she may have fled an unhappy marriage to begin a new life in Carlisle. Ross prospered enough to appear regularly on the town's tax rolls and write a will conveying the proceeds from the sale of her house and lot to her grandchildren in 1773.[36] Others, by contrast, were of humbler origins, perhaps making their living working as laborers, haulers, or petty retailers. They were joined at the bottom of the town's social ranks by indentured servants and slaves, individuals who remain mostly anonymous because they did not apply for lots or build houses. Early Carlisle had small populations of both servants and slaves. In 1765, for example, townspeople owned twenty-six servants and twenty-one slaves, which likely represented between 3 and 4 percent of the town's total population. Still, they were there, and their presence shaped the town. Carlisle's leading men held some of them. Surveyor John Armstrong, for example, had two slaves, while merchant John Montgomery owned two slaves and a servant. Tanner Robert Miller, with four, held the greatest number. He clearly used his three servants and a slave to work his tanyard. Even Carlisle's two Presbyterian ministers held bound laborers. The New Light, George Duffield, held a servant, while the Old Light, John Steel, had two slaves. Other evidence, though sketchy, suggests that a disproportionate number of the town's bound laborers may have been women or girls who worked as domestics. Servant girl Margaret Bar, for instance, served Thomas Parke and his wife in the early 1760s, while Thomas Kinkead and his wife Elizabeth kept a servant girl and a "Negro girl name Rose," whom he permitted to learn to read after his death in 1772. Since they were both "girls," Kinkead had probably acquired them in the 1760s.[37] From its start then, colonial Carlisle was a town built by a variety of individuals, some of them identifiable, others anonymous.

As these colonists arrived and began to build their town, wood was the obvious choice for most early structures, either in the form of log, or in a few cases, frame buildings. News that townspeople have "built their Houses principally with your Timber in the manner as was done at Lancaster" came as no surprise to Penn and his officials. The Cumberland Valley had plenty of trees; Penn's surveyors had noted the "well Timber[e]d Land" nearby when deciding where to locate the town.[38] Yet building a log home, even a small one, was an arduous process. Trees had to be felled, trimmed, and hauled into town. The logs were then squared, notched, and the structures gradually assembled. Although carpenters likely served those who could afford it, many others probably labored to construct homes on their own with the help of only family and neighbors. When George Hook, one of Carlisle's earliest residents, died in 1762, for example, he left behind a lot "with a cellar walled" and forty-five logs, fifteen of which were "squared," thirty of which were still "round." He also had thirty-three more "squared" logs sitting in the woods nearby "ready for bringing home."[39] Who assisted him in this arduous process before he died is unknown. Yet he had at least obtained the logs for his house without incident. Other town residents were not as lucky. They found that gathering the needed logs for their homes was the first challenge awaiting them. It also sometimes put them at odds with Penn's agents, who believed town building should be orderly. As Peters explained, colonists were supposed to go to the surveyor's "Man," who first "mark[ed] the Trees wanted and then they are fell[e]d & cut up, so that no more waste is committed than [that] wh[i]ch I believe you [Penn] wou[l]d be pleased with." Waste was intolerable; the proprietors did not want too many of their trees "destroy'd." Conflicts arose, however, when some colonists simply cut down the trees they needed to the "Great Damage" of the proprietors. Poachers were hauled into court and fined.[40]

A considerable minority of privileged residents built more substantial and permanent structures right from the start. At least one settler, joiner William McCoskrey, even chose brick for his home.[41] But even with three bricklayers in town, brick houses were rare in colonial Carlisle, as they were elsewhere in the American interior. Most townspeople of means opted for stone structures instead because limestone was in such plentiful supply. Even in the early 1750s, as the town was just beginning, demand for stone construc-

tion materials was great enough to support a lime kiln and stone quarry on
the square, and there was at least one mason at work in town by late 1751.[42]
One of the town's first stone structures was built by Scots-Irishman John
McCallister, a tavern keeper, and the first town resident to patent ownership
of his lot in 1753. McCallister's house, located along High Street on the east
side of town, was a two-story stone building, nearly 2,000 square feet in total
dimension. In addition to this structure, the property, which he described
as "very convenient for store or tavern keeping," and which he operated as a
tavern from 1751 to 1756, had "stable room for 80 horses," a detached kitchen,
and garden. Stone structures like McCallister's, or tavern keeper William
Buchanan's "large stone house," with "a good kitchen[,] stables and garden . . . suitable for a publick house," constituted the central core of Carlisle's
housing stock for many decades to come.[43] These impressive stone structures
surely lent an air of prosperity and permanence to the town during its first
years of existence.

Such structures also exemplified the class diversity that marked Pennsylvania's urban interior settlements at mid-century. Carlisle, like other towns of
the interior, was not an open-country neighborhood like its rural hinterlands,
but a soon-to-be densely packed urban place. Its townspeople were economically diverse. A minority of them called upon substantial resources when
constructing their new lives in Carlisle. William Buchanan and his family,
for instance, were experienced colonists of the interior who had moved west
from Lancaster County. When they arrived, they opted to build a grander
stone dwelling; their choice was not unusual. Some colonists wanted to make
their mark in Carlisle; many of them had come with the intent to stay. In this
way, population persistence was as much a part of the story of the American
interior as was migration and movement.[44]

A new town needed a core group of committed residents to transform
it from plan to place. In Carlisle, even though population persistence rates
ranged between only 41 and 44 percent during the colonial period—figures
comparable to other interior places of the time—some colonists came, bought
or rented town lots, built dwellings and businesses, and made their lives there
for the long term.[45] In fact, the lot patents issued in colonial Carlisle read like
a "who's who" of prominent families whose descendants persisted in Cumberland County into the nineteenth and twentieth centuries.[46] For these colonists, their choice of building materials signaled a willingness to put down
roots and assert their self-appointed status as community leaders.

Regardless of their construction material or size, Carlisle's first houses stood as testaments to an emerging townscape. This pleased Penn. Despite setbacks, he had progress to celebrate; a group of "proprietors' men" had taken up residence there and they and their neighbors were building a town. Even Richard Peters, a perennial pessimist, was pleasantly surprised by "the New Town of Carlisle" he visited in 1753. "Upon the whole," he reported, Carlisle "made a much better appearance than I expected." By his calculations, there were "Six very good Stone Houses, several good frame Houses[,] and a large Number of Log Houses" standing in the town, "in all making the Number of Sixty Five Houses." Although "the far greatest Number" were "small" and "triffling," residents, he observed patronizingly, had "done as well as their Abilities would permit."[47] The town had substance. And others agreed with his assessment. Two years later, Carlisle was "the first town of note" British Gen. Edward Braddock encountered in interior Pennsylvania. As a place "which from a wilderness about eight years ago is now become a flourishing town," Braddock noted that Carlisle included "some very good [homes] . . . built in a genteel taste."[48] Credit for such infrastructure went to townspeople; their labors gave meaning to Penn's grid.

Townspeople were also building other parts of Carlisle's townscape during the 1750s and 1760s, including the central square. Construction of these spaces also reflected the interplay between the town's plan and the choices made by its first inhabitants. For Penn, the square was to be the town's focal point, its real and metaphorical center. Designed to sit at the intersection of the two main streets, it was intended to reinforce the geometric order of the grid. All town lots adjacent would front it; the inhabitants of structures on these lots would look out their windows and into the bustle of court and market days and gatherings at the church[49] (see figure 4). Despite such careful plans, however, its construction did not happen as intended. Miscommunications during its survey and the mistaken actions of several colonists who dug cellars for their homes on parts of it meant that the square was not laid out as he devised. House lots did not front it; there was no street encircling it. Rather, it was just a big open, and mostly empty, space. Sometime after the town's resurvey in 1762, and definitely by 1765, the two main streets formally bisected it, dividing the square into four separate and equal quarters (figure 5; see also figures 1 and 4).[50]

In this way, the square was not a focal point for the expression of provincial authority, but a literal embodiment of Carlisle's evolving function as a crossroads. It was the place where the two main roads intersected. Penn had mixed reactions to these developments. At first he chastised the governor

Figure 5. *Public Square of Carlisle, Circa 1860.* This photo, attributed to Charles L. Lochman, who came to Carlisle in 1859, looks northwest across the square. It shows a mostly open space bisected by the town's two main streets, Hanover and High, which stood in stark contrast to the more grand central square of public buildings Thomas Penn had originally conceived. Left to right in the photo are the courthouse, the three-story Washington Hotel, the spire of the First Reformed Church, and the First Presbyterian Church. The roof of the market house built in the early nineteenth century occupies the right foreground. Lochman's apprentice, A. A. Line, reproduced and copyrighted this view in 1909. (Courtesy of Cumberland County Historical Society, Carlisle, Pennsylvania.)

for not following his instructions, and sent new ones. But after officials attempted unsuccessfully to implement his "beautiful and commodious" plan, Penn acquiesced. In the summer of 1752, after several exchanges with his officials across the Atlantic, he "very readily consent[ed]" to leave things as they were, taking account of the townspeople's "desire" and "think[ing] it most for our private Interest to do so."[51] Although the square did not look exactly as he intended, he still hoped its evolving form would help make Carlisle the kind of town in-between he envisioned. Residents, he conceded, might not want a market, prison, or Anglican church on the square, but if they consented to build a courthouse at its center, he would rest contented. Compromise, he surely recognized, was part of the town building process. Central squares, like their towns, did not always evolve according to plan. Philadelphia's squares, for example, did not become the focal points of his father's city either; Philadelphia prospered for over a century without a center.[52]

Still, Penn did not give up hope that residents would implement some other features of his plan. Although it did not look as he intended, he took comfort that "in that great Square there is ground enough Left for all Publick Buildings and a Market Place."[53] But progress on those structures stalled as well. Town residents had no plans for a market house; they did not erect one until the nineteenth century. And the courthouse and prison were going nowhere fast. Penn and his agents were frustrated. Colonists did not share their goals; they were more eager to erect houses than public buildings. County courts could always meet for a time in someone's dwelling or a tavern.

Old World experiences might also have influenced colonists' actions. Courthouses and prisons, as any colonist knew, were built symbols of cosmopolitan legal and political authority. In America and Ulster, the place from which so many Carlisle townspeople hailed, the British had used town planning and the erection of central squares and public buildings as tools to assert their dominion over the wilderness and its native inhabitants. In seventeenth-century Ireland, government buildings were, according to one historian, "the visual representation of fundamental political change." As evidence of the plantation scheme, they embodied the authority of newly arrived British and Scottish immigrants over the native Irish and their "Old" English brethren.[54] Many Carlisle townspeople, whose ancestors were the Scottish beneficiaries of this urban system, surely understood how such markers of authority could affect their lives; their memories likely informed their reactions to Penn's plans. Proprietors' men like John Armstrong, for example, who emigrated from Enniskillen, the first borough in Ulster to be incorporated during the plantation period, certainly must have recalled how English structures of authority could work to one's benefit—as they had likely done for his ancestors in Ireland.[55] Or, as Britain's eighteenth-century treatment of these same Protestant dissenters proved, they could also work to one's detriment. British authority often cut two ways. Carlisle's colonists, many of them immigrants and not all from the same privileged background as Armstrong, would have been keenly aware of this fact. Moreover, in Pennsylvania, these structures were also the hallmarks of a distant proprietary establishment that some deeply mistrusted. Set within these contexts, even though it was said that a prison was "much wanted" by those like Armstrong who had aligned themselves with the proprietors, it had not been built because too many others did not want it. The construction of a courthouse or prison, Penn's opponents knew, would formally acknowledge the town as county seat, thereby marking a victory for the proprietor and English colonial authority.[56]

This situation presented another challenge to proprietary officials. But this one could be finessed. Getting the people of the county to "determine at Last, to build the Court House and Prison there," according to Penn, simply required "prudent management" by the governor.[57] Hamilton followed Penn's advice. He first ordered the county courts relocated from Shippensburg to a temporary log structure that stood on one corner of Carlisle's largely vacant square.[58] Then he went to work behind the scenes, and his actions paid off. Although some in the county reacted angrily, he finally won the struggle over Carlisle as the county seat by 1753. To Penn's "great satisfaction" a newly elected group of county commissioners "put an end to the controversy" and accepted Penn's offer of funds to help construct the public buildings.[59] By the summer of 1753, townspeople were "building a good Prison of Stone" one block off the square. Although they were agreeable to erecting it on the square, as Penn called for, Hamilton gave them a lot on High Street instead.[60] Town officials also erected a stocks and pillory in 1754. The county courts continued to meet in the log structure on the square until a new brick courthouse was built on the southwest corner in 1765. Their actions gave Penn "room to hope" that "they will gain the Reputation of a more orderly People."[61]

As Carlisle grew and more people took up lots and built houses, Protestant meetinghouses began to dot Carlisle's townscape. These elements of the townscape also represented compromises between the proprietor's and colonists' interests. Indeed, in an age when ethnicity and religion were the foundations of cultural identity and community, Carlisle's first meetinghouses and churches were hallmarks of townspeople's ethno-religious diversity. But the predominance of Presbyterians among the town's first inhabitants also distinguished Carlisle as a center of what some scholars characterize as a Scots-Irish and British borderlands ethno-cultural hearth. Throughout the eighteenth century, the Cumberland Valley was noted for its predominantly Scots-Irish, Irish, and Scots Presbyterian populations.[62] One scholar calculated the county's population to be mostly Scots-Irish (with some English) in 1760; another observed that by the 1780s "Cumberland was almost universally recognized as the most Scots-Irish Presbyterian county in the state."[63] Carlisle reflected the patterns of its county. A conservative estimate suggests that more than half of town's first inhabitants had Scots-Irish, Scottish, or Irish surnames, a pattern that held through the century, despite the growing number of German colonists after 1770.[64] Most were also practicing or converted Presbyterians. This is significant because Presbyterianism became a defining facet of Scots-Irish identity in America. Over the long term, it united colonists from Scots and Irish backgrounds, minimized the class distinctions among them, and, as one historian notes, became "a rallying point for self-understanding and group consciousness."[65]

Yet this unity was not immediately visible in Carlisle during the 1750s. Several active Presbyterian congregations already existed in the Valley, one of them dating back to the 1730s. Like other Presbyterian congregations across the middle colonies by the 1740s, they were fractured by changes prompted by waning economic isolation and the convulsive arrival of New Light piety during the Great Awakening.[66] Thus, as Carlisle's Scots-Irish colonists arrived in the 1750s, they brought with them powerful but divided spiritual priorities as Presbyterians, coupled with a sense of urgency inspired by competition from Anglicans, the denomination whose church Penn hoped would occupy the square. The first group of Presbyterians staked their claim to space soon after the town's survey when several townspeople—including John Armstrong—joined by New Lights from the Meeting House Springs congregation just north of town, began a new urban congregation. In 1757, they erected a wooden meetinghouse on the corner of Hanover and Pomfret, one block south of the square. In 1759, they installed the Rev. George Duffield as their minister. Duffield, born in Lancaster County to Ulster immigrant parents, was a New Light Presbyterian educated at the College of New Jersey. He served in Carlisle until 1772.[67]

This New Light congregation was joined almost simultaneously by a rival. Old Lights from the Meeting House Springs congregation also moved to town joining like-minded town residents to erect their own frame meetinghouse one block north of the square. Among this new congregation's leaders was another Irish immigrant, John Montgomery. Montgomery, born in 1727, had arrived in the Cumberland Valley while still in his teens. He settled in Carlisle sometime between 1751 and 1753. Once there, he rose through the town's economic ranks as a merchant. By the 1760s, he was among the top 10 percent of the town's taxable wealth holders; by the late 1770s, he was the wealthiest man in town. More significant to Carlisle's history, Montgomery translated his wealth into political authority. He was a respected Presbyterian elder, soldier, and political officeholder on the local, state, and eventually national levels. He later helped found Dickinson College and was one of its first trustees.[68] In 1759, with Montgomery's help, Carlisle's Old Light congregation installed its own minister, the middle-aged Rev. John Steel, yet another Irish immigrant who came to America in 1742 and was ordained in 1744. His appointment, unlike Duffield's, had the weight of authority behind it because it came at the behest of the Presbytery, and not just the local congregation. The Presbytery wanted the congregations to reunite.[69]

Ulster Presbyterians thus made their mark on Carlisle's townscape. Yet, although numerous, they were not united. With two competing Presbyterian congregations, each with its own minister and meetinghouse on opposite sides of the square, Presbyterianism was initially a divisive, rather than unifying, force in early Carlisle. The New Lights, especially, were enraged by their rivals. To them, Steel's installation represented the Presbytery's betrayal of their interests. As Rev. Duffield wrote in 1759: "Our affairs here look with an aspect as gloomy both in Church & state as when our Indian Enemys infested our Borders." The installation of Steel, his rival, had "revived a party spirit . . . and very generally disgusted our People up this way."[70] The town's Presbyterians were fractured. Those divisions had a long-term influence on the town's history, for they established intracommunal patterns of contention that perpetuated themselves in the secular realms of town politics and society for decades to come.[71]

Presbyterianism had other effects. The prominence of Presbyterians undercut Penn's plans for an Anglican-dominated town. Although Penn likely was not pleased by such developments, he and his family were accustomed to working with Irishmen; he was thus willing to compromise, especially with the Old Lights. As evidence, in 1766, colony officials granted Steel's Old Light congregation building rights to the northwest corner of the square. After sponsoring a lottery to raise funds, Steel's congregation began construction of the large stone meetinghouse, completed by 1772, that stands today.[72] With the construction of this structure, the Presbyterians claimed a prominent place at the town's center. Although they had "avoided the place you once pitched for a church," and Anglicans ultimately beat them to the square, their meetinghouse, as Penn's nephew John later observed, was "the most conspicuous, and the best built" of any church in Carlisle.[73] Colonists thus made Carlisle a Scots-Irish Presbyterian town. Completion of this meetinghouse, especially when accompanied by Duffield's departure to a new post in Philadelphia and the founding of the Presbyterian grammar school that became Dickinson College, went a long way toward reuniting Old and New Lights. As the Revolution approached, the stone meetinghouse on the square symbolized a new, more unified Presbyterian community (see figure 6). But in a colony known for its pluralism, Presbyterians were not the only Protestants staking claim to Carlisle. Rather, they competed with others—particularly Anglicans and sometimes Lutheran and Reformed Germans, though not Quakers—for souls and space on the townscape. Anglicans, in particular, formed a sizable and powerful minority of the town's inhabitants. This development was no accident. "The interests of the Church of England and the proprietary," as one historian observes, were "closely allied" in eighteenth-century Pennsylvania.[74] This was especially true in interior settlements like Carlisle where Quakers had no discernible influence. In these towns, Anglo equaled Anglican. Carlisle's planners were all Anglican; they included Cookson, the surveyor; Peters, who was an Anglican cleric; Governor Hamilton; and Thomas and Richard Penn. So, too, were some townspeople. When an Anglican missionary passed through town in the spring of 1752, he noted that in this "place where they have no church and no missionary ever was before," he was "surprised to find so many disposed to our Ch[urc]h in a place where there never had been any but Dissenting Teachers."[75]

Even so, Carlisle's Anglicans were smaller in number and not as formally organized as their Presbyterian neighbors. With the only nearby church in York County, until the 1760s, the Valley's Anglicans were served only by itinerant missionaries like the Ulster-born Thomas Barton. At that point, Rev. William Thomson, the Anglican son of a local Presbyterian minister, took up residence in town.[76] Equally significant, many of Carlisle's Anglicans, like the ministers who served them, were not of English, but were of Irish, Scots, or Scots-Irish ancestry. In this way, their Anglo identities represented a compromise. Like their counterparts in other proprietary towns such as Easton, they were Anglicized, and likely identified as Britons. But they were not Anglos ethnically.[77] For them, religion was a channel to patronage and power in the colony, rather than a formative component of their ethnic identity. Carlisle's Anglicans made their presence felt through the work of ministers like Barton and Thomson and proprietors' men like traders George Croghan and Robert Callender. They formed a church—perhaps as early as 1752 says one history—and likely used the log courthouse on the square for their services. This gave them a claim to the square that they formalized in 1762 when they began to erect a new church, completed in the late 1760s. St. John's Church

Figure 6. *Public Square of Carlisle.* This nineteenth-century view depicts Carlisle's square as seen from the east. On the left are the courthouse and town hall. On the right in the foreground is St. John's Episcopal Church, and on the other square, near the center, is the First Presbyterian Church, completed in 1772. This engraving comes from Sherman Day's *Historical Collections of the State of Pennsylvania,* published in 1843. (Courtesy of the Cumberland County Historical Society, Carlisle, Pennsylvania.)

was a two-story stone structure that stood until the larger and grander building that stands today was erected in the 1820s (figure 6).[78]

Carlisle's Anglicans quickly claimed their own spot on the townscape, and once established, St. John's challenged Presbyterian predominance. Their church and its place on the square symbolized the extension of proprietary and British colonial authority into the interior much as Penn planned. Although the church's many Irish-born congregants did not fully fit the Anglo character of the wider colony and empire, St. John's nonetheless included many prominent families. Over time, these Anglican families, aided by the organizational power of the Church of England and their political connections to the proprietors, played pivotal roles in shaping the town's history.[79]

Finally, Carlisle's German colonists put their ethno-religious marks on the townscape. Cumberland County's German population was small during the colonial period, especially when compared to the nearby counties of York or Lancaster. German churches thus took longer to make their place on the landscape. Nonetheless, both a Lutheran and a Reformed congregation formed between 1763 and 1765. Unlike their Presbyterian and Anglican counterparts, who erected substantial stone meetinghouses during the 1760s, Carlisle's German congregations shared a single log structure located just south of the square until 1807.[80]

With the establishment of Carlisle's German congregations, colonial Carlisle's ethno-religious landscape was mostly complete. While St. John's Church most clearly symbolized the culture and interests of the proprietor and British empire, the Presbyterian churches especially—but the Lutheran and Reformed congregations too—demonstrated the extent to which Carlisle's townscape represented compromises between the proprietor's vision and the diverse ethnic and religious cultures of its inhabitants. In this way, Carlisle was a microcosm of the complex cultural dynamics at work in the mid-Atlantic interior. Thomas Penn and his agents had planned the townscape, but only the town's colonists—those Scots-Irish, Irish, Scots, English, German, or in a few cases Dutch or French peoples who built, lived, worked, and worshiped in Carlisle's first structures—determined what it looked like or how it functioned.

Other landscapes also took shape as townspeople gave meaning to the spaces they inhabited in their daily lives. Log, stone, and frame houses imprinted class interests onto Carlisle's townscape. New public buildings like the courthouse and prison, meanwhile, heralded the arrival of provincial authority, while the formation of various Protestant congregations and the construction of meetinghouses and churches marked the townscape with residents' diverse ethno-religious and cultural identities. The construction of these visible structures was critical. They signaled the town's birth while simultaneously illustrating the myriad ways that Carlisle's evolution represented a series of compromises between proprietary aspirations and townspeople's class, ethnic, and religious identities.

But there was more. Carlisle's townscape was also shaped by broader forces of economic growth affecting the colony, mid-Atlantic, and British Atlantic world at mid-century. Carlisle was founded during a period of phenomenal growth in Pennsylvania, one that coincided with a massive movement of immigrants to America and the explosive growth of the consumer economy. That meant that if it was to survive and thrive as a town it could not exist in isolation; its townscape had to be connected to others via networks of transport, exchange, and communication.[81] Thomas Penn recognized this when he planned it; Carlisle's reason for existence was to serve as a place in-between in his colony. Colonists recognized it as well. As they arrived with their families—sometimes with servants and slaves in tow—and took up their lots and built houses, they worked not only to establish themselves, but to carve out Carlisle's economic identity as a town in the interior. Their challenge was to build an urban economy capable of providing their livelihoods and the consumer goods and services they desired. This meant making Carlisle into the kind of crossroads place that would meet these needs. They had to found businesses to provide goods and services. They also had to forge communication and transport links within and beyond the Valley. Perhaps most important, they had to form exchange networks that would connect them to Atlantic markets and consumer economies. Defining Carlisle's economic identity as a crossroads place was thus a complicated process, depending in large measure on the choices made by the town's first inhabitants.

Yet Carlisle's first residents were not of one mind. They came to town with multiple objectives. Some craftsmen, like the carpenters, bricklayers, and joiners who applied for lots in 1751, were there to build the town. Others played more pivotal roles in defining Carlisle's economic identity. They did so in ways more explicitly reflective of their class and occupational interests than their ethno-religious identities. They included the many traders, merchants, storekeepers, and haulers associated with the fur trade whose enterprises were supported by a host of craftsmen and laborers in town; their activities will be discussed in Chapter 3. There were also many innkeepers and shopkeepers. Their taverns and stores served local patrons. Yet these businesses were also geared to take advantage of Carlisle's pivotal location at the convergence of pathways heading west and south. Their owners aimed to serve migrants, travelers, and traders moving through town, thus their businesses integrally shaped Carlisle's identity as a crossroads place.

One traveler described Carlisle as "mostly compos'd of People who keep Shops and Public Houses."[82] Five taverns were likely operating there by 1753. By 1764, with 182 taxable inhabitants and a total population numbering perhaps close to 1100, nineteen individuals had petitioned the court for licenses, several of them returning repeatedly to renew their applications; another fourteen people were charged with keeping unlicensed "tip[p]ling houses" before 1764.[83] During its first thirteen years of existence, conservative estimates suggest that Carlisle had at least twenty different drinking establishments. That meant there was approximately one tavern for every fifty townspeople, a ratio that exceeded even Philadelphia, whose provisioning one scholar termed "extraordinary."[84] And these patterns persisted through time. Historian Merri Lou Schaumann has identified fifty-five separate sites where taverns existed between 1750 and 1840. Twenty-four taverns operated in 1798 alone, a time when Carlisle's population stood at just under 2,000 people. Even by the close of the century, Carlisle contained approximately one tavern for every eighty-three men, women, and children living there.[85]

Carlisle's taverns served myriad purposes. As social spaces, they brought people of diverse ranks, ethnicities, and religions together. Although the ethnic identity of their keepers, like the "fat Irishman" who served one traveler passing through town in the 1780s, likely influenced the clientele they attracted, taverns nonetheless assisted in integrating the community and assimilating Carlisle's immigrant colonists to colonial America. In the American interior, says one historian, taverns were "nodes around which neighborhoods developed," and Carlisle was no exception. But tavern keeping also served other local functions by offering Carlisle's disadvantaged poor relief.[86]

Because not everyone prospered, some townspeople took up tavern keeping as a potential escape from economic hardship. Oliver Wallace, who occupied one of first lots built upon in Carlisle, requested a "Licence to Retail Beer" in 1751. Being "very Aged and past Labour," with a "Known bodily Infirmity," he looked to tavern keeping in his North Street house for the income he needed to survive in this new town. That he persisted on town tax lists until 1764 hints that selling beer was a workable plan.[87] Eleven years later, Thomas Patton, "Not Being Eable to Work at farming as Formerly by Reason of Wanting my Helth [health]," wanted a tavern license "in order of Making A Livelyhood for my Familey."[88] For these men and others, old age, physical disability, and economic necessity drove them to tavern keeping; it was a survival strategy in the urban interior. Local associations were equally important in sustaining these businesses. As Wallace explained, he had "for some time . . . Sold Beer" in Carlisle, and in consequence had come "to trust Several person[s] in this County with the greatest part of his Substance."[89]

Yet in a town at a crossroads, Wallace's and Patton's businesses relied on more than just local patrons. Rather, with so many migrants, traders, travelers, and, during wartime, soldiers and refugees passing through, tavern keeping was an especially public pursuit. Retailers positioned themselves to participate in an Atlantic-based commerce conducted by people on the move across the region, and they knew it. For example, Alexander McCain, an original applicant for a town lot, had "no Trade but intends [to be a] Merchant." He saw the town's commercial potential.[90] Tavern keepers were likewise aspiring; they desired to keep taverns in hopes of financial gain from this commercial growth. Walter Denny, who migrated from Chester County to Carlisle, prefaced his request for a license in 1758 by explaining how he had "been O[p] pressed this Severall Years With Travelers which passes" his "House." "Having allways kep[t] a privet [private] house," he wanted to make his business "publick."[91] Carlisle's selection as the staging ground for Gen. John Forbes's 1758 expedition against Fort Duquesne also likely inspired Denny's request. Evidence suggests that his application was a wise move. While assembling his troops in Carlisle, Forbes's second in command complained bitterly that "all these new recruits are getting debauched in the taverns." By 1759, even soldiers standing guard at the barracks on the town's border were "found drunk" on liquor they probably purchased from the town's tavern keepers.[92] In this way, Carlisle became a crossroads of commerce and empire.

Trade and migration also generated considerable business for Carlisle's innkeepers. Andrew McIntyre, John Kennedy, and Robert Hammersly all spoke of the "Accommodation of Travellers" in their petitions for licenses in the 1750s and 1760s.[93] McIntyre, a carpenter-joiner by trade, kept the Sign of the Indian Queen in the two-story stone structure he owned near LeTort Spring on the corner of High and East Streets; he operated this tavern with help from his wife Martha and four children from 1754 until his death in 1761. His estate inventory shows that he did well. Aside from his eight-room stone tavern house with a parlor, bar room, dining room, and several bedrooms for guests, he owned a slave, two other lots in Carlisle, another in York, and a plot of land near Shippensburg.[94] Tavern keeping was a route to prosperity for him.

More important, tavern keeping helped define Carlisle as a crossroads place. Roads brought potential customers through town. But taverns and other retail establishments—especially when coupled with a growing craft economy of blacksmiths, saddlers, wheelwrights, and gunsmiths offering the services to keep people and goods moving—made it a place where they wanted to stop. Without a doubt, by erecting a "Suitable" house and providing "all Necessarys" for business, Carlisle's tavern keepers drew people to town; they made it a "convenient" place to stay.[95] Furthermore, as locals and many travelers, migrants, traders, refugees, and soldiers from all over the Atlantic world converged in these spaces for refreshment, lodging, conversation, and news, taverns became microcosmic places in-between that exemplified Carlisle's role in the mid-Atlantic.

Yet townspeople did more than construct buildings and retail establishments like McIntyre's Sign of the Indian Queen. In defining their town's economic landscape, they also reshaped the region's geography by building

roads. These physical links were the foundation of a communications infrastructure necessary for interior economies to expand. In this way, they were
essential to defining what Carlisle would be and how it would function.[96]
Much like the Native pathways that preceded them, roads brought people
and goods to and through Carlisle; they embodied continuities between the
region's past and present. Yet roads also marked unique Euro-American connections forged among places, cultures, and markets. Particularly in the interior, roads also helped colonists overcome isolation. Beginning in the 1740s
and continuing long after Carlisle's founding, roads in Pennsylvania, as historian Patrick Griffin explains, "connected enclaves to frontier entrepôts tied
into the growing city of Philadelphia, and from thence to a larger Atlantic
World of trade."[97] There was much at stake in building them, and people had
different interests in the outcome.

For these reasons, roads took different forms in interior Pennsylvania.
Road building was influenced in part by the proprietors. Provincial roads,
typically major arteries, were inspired by colony leaders. Most of them were
ordered to be laid out by the governor and council, sometimes upon the advice of the proprietors. These roads, typically called Great Roads or King's
Highways, were tools of imperialism. Much like maps and town plans, they
imposed a socially constructed reality on the land and colonists.[98] They functioned as routes for speculation, trade, and the extension of political authority
by Penn's officials. Because they were most often roads connected to the port
of Philadelphia, they funneled colonists into the interior while at the same
time encouraging them to send their products back to the city's markets. In
this way, provincial roads benefited the proprietor and his officials.[99]

In and near Carlisle, the most important provincial road was the "Great
Road" from Philadelphia, the path that brought most Euro-American travelers, migrants, and traders to Carlisle. The "Great Road," which was ordered
in 1735 and surveyed in 1744, generally followed the ancient Allegheny Path
near the Susquehanna (see map 1). Travelers coming northwest out of Philadelphia picked up this road west of Reading. From there, the road continued
west, crossing the Susquehanna at Paxtang, or Harris's Ferry, then headed
southwestward to Carlisle. Once at Carlisle, it intersected with other trails
to become the Virginia Road, which then headed southwestward down the
Cumberland Valley, through Shippensburg and Chambersburg, and finally
into Maryland and Virginia. The Great Road was an immensely important
route for Carlisle's and the colony's development. It functioned effectively as
a northern branch of the Great Wagon Road, to which it was connected by

the Conoy or Conewago Path, which crossed the Susquehanna at Conewago and then came into Carlisle from the southeast. As such, the Great Road was the primary artery conveying migrants, traders, and troops to town. It was also the road that colonists used to carry their produce to markets, especially Philadelphia.[100] And Penn's officials planned it this way: the LeTort Spring site's proximity to the road had been a key factor in determining Carlisle's location. This road, provincial officials believed, would ensure that Carlisle grew to be the place in-between that Penn envisioned. Many Carlisle towns-people shared this vision; their taverns and shops were geared to meet the needs of the people traveling along it.

Most roads were not provincial roads, however. County courts were the primary creators of roadways in Pennsylvania, which gave colonists considerable influence over road construction in the Cumberland Valley. Because county court decisions were difficult to oversee from afar, road building sometimes highlighted disjunctures between provincial and local visions of development. Colonists in and near Carlisle had their own notions of how roads could be used to connect their seat to places within and beyond the Valley. They put their own stamp on the region's emerging transportation and communication networks by building the roads that they wanted. Their actions made clear that roads were critical to their lives. They knit together the local community and established connections to other regions. In an area where water transport was unworkable, roads took on heightened importance; they were the only way in or out of Carlisle.[101]

Although local residents requested the construction of roads for different purposes, they agreed on the vital need to build connections within the Valley and to Carlisle. Regardless of their ethnic identity or religious affiliation, the farm families who settled the town's hinterlands knew that accessing Carlisle was critical to their survival. The town was fast becoming an important population center in the Valley; by 1760, for example, it already contained 15 percent of the county's population.[102] More important, as the seat of government, headquarters of the provincial surveyor, an emerging market center, and home to meetinghouses, churches, taverns, and shops, it was the place rural residents needed access to in order to process their land claims, protect their property, sell their produce, attend worship services, and socialize. As a measure of these needs, the county courts heard twelve separate requests for roads to or from Carlisle in the three years following the town's survey. One group of colonists living near North Mountain put forward a typical petition in 1753. They wanted a "straight road" from their "places of Abode" to Carlisle to aid them in traveling to town and meeting.[103] Others settled east of town also wanted a road laid out that would permit them "to travel to and from the s[ai]d town of Carlisle."[104] Later, in 1774, these same petitioners requested another road to Carlisle, "for want of a road to Carry there [their] Produce to Market."[105] For these rural dwellers, following the patterns of others across Pennsylvania, road building was a way to forge a new social and economic order within Penn's woods. Roads to Carlisle were thus "much wanted and . . . of great Use to the Publick" because, as these rural colonists said, they were for "the Convaniency of Your Petitinors Comeing to Market with their products (see map 3)."[106]

Building physical links to Carlisle signaled another phase in the process of regional definition that had been under way since the first Euro-American colonists entered the Valley in the 1730s. Roads connected farmers to the markets and meetinghouses of the county seat, and laid the foundation for the expansion of trade and communication networks across the region. Yet in a region where grain production was a critical component of the agricultural economy, roads also linked producers to rural processors and urban merchants. In this regard, Carlisle was only one destination to which residents sought access. Millers, for instance, had a stake in seeing the local grain economy prosper; mills were expensive investments. Because they needed customers with grain to grind and access to merchants who purchased flour for resale, millers were eager to erect roads to their mills and Carlisle.[107] But local grain farmers had equally important stakes in getting their produce to miller and merchant. The 1753 request for a road northward from Carlisle to James Chambers's mill and then through one of the passes over North Mountain was another early statement of locals' need to access both "Mill and Market."[108] Roads thus linked producers, processors, and retailers together, fostering symbiotic economic relationships within the county, and between county and town. Yet because much of this produce was ultimately sold off to other merchants supplying the Atlantic world, these roads also overcame isolation by allowing colonists to participate in commercial worlds beyond the Valley.

This pattern of knitting Carlisle into webs of economic association across the Valley and beyond continued throughout the colonial period as the local population and grain economy grew. In 1769, for example, some county residents argued that a road from Carlisle to William Thompson's mills was "much wanted" because it would be of "great use" to the public "to carry the Produce of their Plantations to Market."[109] Roads between mill and market had other benefits as well. As another group of county residents explained, because "a Fulling Mill[,] Grist[,] and Merchant Mill have been lately Built near the mouth of Letart [LeTort] Spring," they wanted a road "to Places of this Nature." Such a road would bring traffic to the mills that would benefit those who resided nearby, as well as the millers.[110] Rural residents, this petition implies, wanted connections to sites of economic production and exchange in the Valley. They also wanted roads to bring people—and business—to their farmsteads. In this way, roads expressed the kind of economic exchanges residents wished to sustain among themselves. They were two-way links that reached outward toward other places and people and inward toward home.

Inside or closer to Carlisle, where the accelerating "publick" demands of this new town affected the lives of colonists, road building focused more explicitly on broadening access to customers and markets. Colonists in and near the seat often used roads to forge inter-regional connections. This made sense. If Carlisle's markets were to have economic weight within the mid-Atlantic, they had to be connected to others; the colonists livelihoods' depended on it. Yet how and what connections would be built varied over time and according to residents' economic interests. In the 1750s, one of the top priorities for many was establishing more connections to points east, ultimately aiming at Philadelphia. Surely Penn and his officials were pleased when locals turned their attention toward building better routes to John Harris's Ferry on the Susquehanna at Paxtang; in most cases these routes heightened the significance of his own Great Road in the Valley's development. In 1752, for example, some residents requested a road from Harris's Ferry to connect to the "New" road to Carlisle.[111] In 1758, another group requested another road from John Harris's Ferry to Carlisle. This road, they argued, was "very much wanted & would be very beneficial to such persons as Travel from [the] said Ferry & other parts of this province."[112] The ferry, which Harris's father, John, a Yorkshire immigrant, had established some years before, was their primary link to the eastern regions of the colony. Easier crossings of the Susquehanna enhanced Carlisle's trade connections to Philadelphia. Such roads also supported John Harris, Jr.'s interests, as they encouraged colonists to make the crossing at Paxtang rather than farther south, from which Harris profited by collecting tolls. Finally, these roads also facilitated Harris's access to Carlisle, where he had numerous economic interests.[113] Roads thus symbolized how residents looked outward for opportunity, while also encouraging outsiders to look to the county in pursuit of gain.

Yet those living close to Carlisle did not always build roads that coincided with the proprietor's goals for his colony. Just as they constructed a townscape representative of their own class, ethnic, and religious identities, they also built roads reflective of their economic interests and personal connections. They had their own visions of their region's potential. Some of their aspirations, like their eagerness for connections to the south—particularly to Baltimore, the emerging market center on the Chesapeake—clashed outright with Penn's vision by challenging Philadelphia's primacy. But looking south for Atlantic-world market connections made sense in the Valley. Native Americans had oriented their transport needs on a north-south as well as east-west axis. The river valley, as the Susquehannock experience showed, was a natural migration corridor. More important in the eighteenth century, Baltimore Town was a growing port with accessible markets. For colonists living west of the river, it held several distinct advantages over Philadelphia. Because northern Chesapeake markets were more decentralized than Philadelphia's, sellers could sometimes bypass large wholesalers, thus engaging in a more direct trade, less muddled by middlemen. Then, too, getting there did not require an expensive ferry crossing over the Susquehanna. Better still, there was a growing network of roads to this new city that were already being built by York County residents.[114]

To take best advantage of these opportunities, Carlisle-area residents reached south almost immediately upon the town's founding. York Town, a stop on Great Wagon Road, was their first destination, even though it meant having to cross over South Mountain. In 1751, for example, residents said that the construction of a road leading from Carlisle to one of the gaps in South Mountain was "much wanted by the Inhabitants" because it would link to the recently opened York County road stretching from that mountain pass to York Town.[115] York Town was an important access point. Personal connections drew some to it. Surveyor John Armstrong, for example, had lived there before moving to Carlisle. Others owned property there. But York was important in another way because, like Lancaster and Carlisle, it was a hub of colonial transportation routes; getting there offered access to other places south (figure 7).[116] In this way, Cumberland's colonists tapped into existing or budding transportation infrastructures to benefit themselves and their new seat.

While York was a destination in and of itself, colonists were most interested in it because of the connections it offered to the new and growing markets of the upper Chesapeake, including Joppa, Patapsco, and especially Baltimore.[117] These were the markets they really wanted to reach, despite Penn's wishes. Surely Penn and others groaned when Robert Hammilton

View of a pass over the South Mountain from York Town to Carlisle

Figure 7. *Road from York to Carlisle.* This illustration, from the *Columbian Magazine*, May 1788, depicts a bucolic scene on the road between these two interior Pennsylvania towns. Road petitions, by contrast, suggest that this was a heavily traveled route in the eighteenth century, as it offered access to the growing port of Baltimore and other ports on the northern Chesapeake. (Courtesy of the American Antiquarian Society, Worcester, Massachusetts.)

expressed the views of many in and near Carlisle when he complained in 1752 that the road from Carlisle to the York County line had not been completed "to the great Obstruction and Hindrance of Trade to York Town and Pattapsco in Maryland."[118] To the Penn family, trade between Carlisle's and Maryland's port towns represented a threat to their interests. Although Philadelphia merchants supplied some of the imported goods sold by their Baltimore counterparts, Baltimore was not Philadelphia. Just as important, the Penn family had fought a long-term border dispute with Maryland because they feared their rival's influence on the interior. The possibility of losing trade to Maryland had been one of the factors weighed in choosing Carlisle's site. Officials did not want colonists to have a choice of markets. For those actually living west of the river, however, Patapsco, the area in and around Baltimore, was an advantageous market destination. Over time, the push to connect with these Chesapeake markets gained momentum. In 1771, a group of county residents petitioned for a road from several of the mills on LeTort Spring just outside Carlisle "to fall into the Baltimore Road," because, as they explained, they "at present have no direct Road from [the] said mills to the Baltimore Markett."[119]

The rise of Baltimore and other market towns on the Chesapeake had a significant impact on the Cumberland Valley even during the 1750s and 1760s. In Cumberland County, as in York to the south, colonists in search of additional or more cost-effective markets oriented their commercial connections along not only an east-west but also a north-south axis.[120] Colony boundaries and proprietary interests were of little consequence to them. Instead, following the lead of the Susquehannocks who used the north-south Susquehanna Valley to their best advantage, colonists built roads to York and Baltimore as building blocks of communications networks facing south. These roads, from the perspective of Thomas Penn and his officials, symbolized the unpredictable nature of developing the interior. The autonomy locals had over road building, much like the autonomy they had in constructing their town, gave them authority to craft a town whose identity as a place was partly independent of Penn and his agents (see map 1).

Roads ultimately defined Carlisle and shaped its history. Penn could plan the town and its first inhabitants could construct it, but in an interior area where water transport was lacking, their efforts were for naught without roads. Roads were the physical routes that linked Carlisle to the rest of the Atlantic world. Crucial to the survival of the town and its inhabitants, roads gauged Carlisle's role as the hub of its county. They also embodied how colonists simultaneously embraced and resisted the will of proprietary authority. Perhaps most important, roads—whether headed east, west, north, or south—made Carlisle a crossroads place. They gave Carlisle a chance to "flourish" as a town in-between because they made the town a "publick" destination to travel to and through. Roads, in short, literally put Carlisle on the map. As one colonist hinted when he advertised his plantation "on the great road to Carlisle" for sale in 1753, "Carlisle Town" was fast becoming a conspicuous geographical marker for peoples—Native American as well as Euro-American—moving into and through the mid-Atlantic interior. Yet in the 1750s and 1760s, who controlled the new map being drawn was in dispute.[121]

CHAPTER THREE

New Lines Drawn

IN MAY 1768, Joseph Rigby, an agent of the Philadelphia trading firm of Baynton, Wharton, and Morgan, noted in a letter to his employers that he hoped to forward the lead he was holding at the company's warehouse in Carlisle with the troops who would soon be "going up" to Fort Pitt.[1] Although at first glance this seems a routine correspondence, it was not. Rigby's presence in Carlisle and the description he offered of his activities in town confirmed how much Carlisle had changed in the seventeen years since its founding. It was no longer a remote village, or even a developing crossroads of migration and retail commerce. Instead, the town functioned as an essential way station in a long-distance fur and skin trade that stretched from Native American communities of the early American West to major Atlantic world markets in Great Britain. Carlisle, in short, had become—in one important respect at least—exactly the kind of place in-between Penn envisioned. Long-established Native paths led the town's many traders and haulers west to the Native peoples of the Ohio Valley who hunted, trapped, and processed the pelts that supplied this trade. Roads built by provincial officials and local colonists led to Baltimore, but they also connected town merchants to the export markets of Philadelphia. Equally significant was the presence of outsiders. With their warehouses and agents like Rigby positioned in Carlisle, firms like Philadelphia's Baynton, Wharton, and Morgan had staked their own space on the townscape. Their arrival heralded Carlisle's role as what Governor Hamilton had once described as a depository of the fur and skin trade for the colony.

But Carlisle was also much more. Roads and fur trading brought not just Philadelphians but fear to town. And during the late 1760s, in the wake of the Native violence unleashed during the Seven Years' War and then Pontiac's Uprising, these fears assumed the forefront of townspeople's consciousness. These fears cast Carlisle as a central stage for expressions of hostility toward Native peoples and the traders—sometimes outsiders, sometimes their neighbors—who served their interests. Carlisle thus grew contentious; it divided upon itself. Within this climate of hatred and suspicion, pelts and trade goods took on new, more ominous meaning as reminders of potentially predatory Native peoples and the destruction they might wage on the town and its Scots-Irish inhabitants. For many townspeople, the trade thus became something to be resisted because it heralded danger: those men who trafficked with Indians were soon the targets of intense suspicion and antagonism.

Joseph Rigby knew this well. He worked nervously that May in consequence. Earlier that spring townspeople had begun to confront trade agents whom they suspected of supplying Native peoples with the tools of their destruction. Rigby was one of those whom they suspected. As he reported anxiously to his employers in the same letter: "We are Surrounded by Ja-b-t-s- [Jacobites?] who are continually prying into every Waggon and package that comes to the Gate to know the Contents, and often ask whether, there is any powder or Lead going back to kill the Sc-th [Scotch] Irishmen."[2] The climate in Carlisle, he made clear, was tense. His neighbors, he knew, were furious. Believing there were traitors in their midst, they feared for their lives. But he was scared as well. Rigby wanted to serve his employers, but he and other agents were unsure what townspeople would do next. In response, they found themselves employed in increasingly clandestine work; to keep the trade moving they had to hide goods from their neighbors and conceal shipments as they went out. Rigby's note confirmed these tactics as well as his desperation. He sent the firm's lead west with the troops that May as a cover. Local Scots-Irish colonists, he knew, might well sabotage a shipment hauled by packhorsemen, but troops were another matter; colonists would leave them alone.[3] To get the trade goods west and serve the interests of his employers, therefore, he went against the will of neighbors. Such extraordinary times, his note implied, required extraordinary measures; this was anything but routine practice.

Rigby's note and the mood of contention it relates raises intriguing questions about Carlisle's early history, the functions the town served in the mid-Atlantic interior at mid-century, and the relationships among its inhabitants.

Carlisle had become a town in-between in the trade by the late 1760s. Situated at the convergence point of roads from the east and Indian pathways from the west, Carlisle's location made it an attractive way station for colonists who were traders and trade agents of Philadelphia merchant firms (see maps 1 and 2). But being a town in-between also had unanticipated consequences. Roads brought outsiders and their diverse interests to town. Some of these outsiders, like Rigby, worked for merchants eager to harness the town's resources to serve their needs for profits. Others were Native peoples whose presence, though mostly distant, had a powerful affect on the psyches of local inhabitants. Together, the real and symbolic influence of these outsiders pit neighbor against neighbor, and divided the community in ways that heightened a particularly intense brand of Scots-Irish localism born of fear and hatred. In these ways, Carlisle became not just a town in-between for trade by the 1760s, but a kind of ground zero for the expression of contention and hatred in the mid-Atlantic interior.

Native Americans were familiar to Carlisle's inhabitants. Although most Native peoples had relocated west before the town's founding, they nonetheless continued to assert their presence in and near town from the 1750s until the 1770s. One of the earliest reminders of Carlisle's heritage as a Native place came in 1753, when several Ohio Valley chiefs "Sent very Boldly" to the governor "to Come and Meet them at Carlisle."[4] As they explained, the "unsettled Affairs to their Country . . . would not allow them time to wait on your Honour at Philadelphia," as was customary. Instead, "return[ing] homeward" following a conference with the Virginians at Winchester, they wished to follow one of their ancient routes leading up the Valley to Carlisle, a meeting place more convenient for them (see maps 1 and 2).[5] The conference that followed that October was a low point of intercultural diplomacy. The long peace that characterized Native-Euro-American relations between 1720 and 1750 was breaking down rapidly amid growing imperial rivalries between the French, English, and their Native allies; this meant that little could be accomplished at Carlisle. Over four days, these Ohio Valley peoples sought to reduce tensions in the Ohio Valley, drive the French from their lands, and promote their friendship with the English while preserving their independence.[6] Specifically, they wanted Pennsylvania to better regulate its traders and speculators. In their view, the arrival of "more Traders than are necessary" and land-hungry Virginians eager to build a "strong House" on the Ohio had prompted French incursions into the region. Pennsylvania, they argued, should "call back the great number" of its traders. Traders should carry less rum and more of the powder, lead and "other valuable Goods" that would aid Native peoples in their struggles against the French.[7]

The commissioners who represented Pennsylvania at Carlisle—Benjamin Franklin, Isaac Norris, and Richard Peters—offered little in response. The colony was concerned about French and Virginia moves into the Ohio Valley. They were also sympathetic to "the *miserable* Condition of these Indians" and desperately wanted "the Continuance of our Friendship."[8] But they were also at a disadvantage because they had no real power to act. With their "hands . . . tied up by the Principles of the Assembly," whose Quaker representatives would not allow the trading of ammunition for defense, they "cou[l]d do no more," Peters explained, "than make general Professions of Friendship and distribute some Presents." Therefore, nothing changed; distrust between Natives and colonists persisted, speculators and colonists continued to push west, and traders' traffic in liquor continued. The fate of the Ohio Valley remained uncertain. The Carlisle conference was a failure.[9]

Yet the conference set precedents for Carlisle's future. By summoning Pennsylvania officials to Carlisle, these Ohio Valley Native peoples destabilized diplomatic authority and subtly reminded Pennsylvanians of their heritage as claimants to the Cumberland Valley. Governor Hamilton was "perplexed" by their request and suspicious of their motives. Knowing that not all Ohio Natives opposed the French, he questioned their loyalties to Pennsylvania. Furthermore, knowing that they were returning from conference with the Virginians, he feared they were trying to pit colony against colony. He also worried about how the Six Nations might respond to Pennsylvania negotiating directly with peoples they considered their dependents. Would this negatively affect the colony's diplomacy with the Iroquois?[10] There was also the thorny issue of location. Although one of Carlisle's planners, Hamilton "did not like that the Indians should alter the Place of treating with them" and at first "saw no Necessity for the Governor's indulging" them "at a Place so distant from Philadelphia." Carlisle was a seat of local government and trade, while Philadelphia, "which used and ought to be" the location for "treating" with Natives, remained the place for diplomacy.[11] In this way, treating with Indians at Carlisle represented another unanticipated shift in the town's function. In response, although Hamilton noted his "Unwillingness to gratify the Indians in their desire of treating at so great a distance," he accepted their invitation. There was a catch, however. He would not attend—his representatives would meet them. That is how Franklin, Norris, and Peters found themselves venturing westward on the Great Road, charged with acting in the "Publick Good." [12] The Ohio Natives had succeeded in shifting diplomacy westward. "All Persons at Ohio," said one observer, "would have their Eyes on the Reception of those *Indians*, now at *Carlisle*." [13]

These Natives demonstrated their authority in more direct ways as well. Upon their arrival in Carlisle, this group of nearly one hundred men, women, and children—including Mingo (Iroquois), Delaware, Shawnee, Miamis, and Wyandot peoples—staked out a prominent place on the townscape. As Franklin recalled, they "lodg'd" themselves "in temporary Cabins" of their own construction "built in the Form of a Square just without the Town." [14] Surely Carlisle's first colonists, many of whom were constructing their own homes and businesses along the town's streets, noted the Indians' proximity and the striking similarities between their town, which contained many log cabins organized around a square, and the temporary Native camp that had been erected just beyond their town's border. Here was a powerful reminder of the Native place LeTort Spring had been not long before.

These Ohio peoples sent an even bolder reminder of their presence at the conference's conclusion. Although fears of "quarrelsome & disorderly" drunken Natives had prompted Franklin, Norris, and Peters to forbid liquor sales to them during the conference, once "Business was over" they were given "Plenty of Rum." That night a large group of drunken Indians, male and female, took over Carlisle and "made a great Bonfire in the Middle of the Square," the town feature Penn most associated with order. They were, as Benjamin Franklin described with a note of horror, "quarrelling and fighting" with one another: "Their dark colour'd Bodies, half naked, [and] seen only by the gloomy Light of the Bonfire, [were] running after and beating one another with Firebrands, accompanied by their horrid Yellings." Together, he recalled, they "form'd a Scene the most resembling our Ideas of Hell that could well be imagin'd"; there was "no appeasing the Tumult." [15] Many townspeople no doubt felt the same way. With drunken, disorderly, semi-nude Indians dancing madly around a fire at the center of their new and only partially built town, some inhabitants must have wondered what might come next. In dramatic fashion, these Indians had temporarily reclaimed Carlisle as a Native space.

Not all townspeople were repulsed by these drunken revelries, however; some were curious rather than threatened. Carlisle was a town of traders, as well as haulers, packhorsemen, and craftsmen associated with the trade. For these men, Indians meant economic opportunity. Among the town's first inhabitants was trader and proprietors' man Robert Callender; he was a business partner of George Croghan in the 1750s. By the 1768, however, the forty-two-year-old Callender was a leading trader in his own right, with extensive contacts in Philadelphia and the Ohio Country. He made his family's home in Carlisle while also maintaining a country house and sizable mill complex along the Great Road from Harris's Ferry. There was also Stephen Duncan, another Scots-Irishman, town pioneer, and Presbyterian. Duncan, nearing forty years of age in 1768, was an attorney and dry goods merchant who dealt in deerskins on the side (see figure 14). Then, too, there was Christopher Vanlear. The Dutchman Vanlear was a tavern keeper who left his wife Elizabeth in charge of his business while he hauled goods for the trade.[16] Finally, there were the many—mostly anonymous—craftsmen, retailers, and laborers, even a few slaves, who participated in the trade in ways large and small.[17] Together, these men made fur trading a communal enterprise.

Their work also acquainted these men with Native American ways of exchange, treaty making, and celebration. Because they saw Indians, particularly the Ohio Valley peoples, as trade partners rather than threats, they likely welcomed to them to Carlisle for treaty making that fall. They wanted to make deals, not stage confrontations. As proof, some Carlisle traders, it was said, had even supplied the Indians with much of the rum that they were drunk on that night as they danced madly around the bonfire on the square, which was no surprise. Carlisle residents had a history of selling liquor illegally to Natives. In the two years before the conference, thirteen townsmen, including tavern keeper John McCallister, owner of one of Carlisle's first stone houses, were indicted by the county court for "Furnich[ing] divers Quantitys of Rum[,] Brandy & other strong . . . Liquors" to Native peoples. Cumberland County's fur traders were also notorious for their irregularities in trading.[18] Indian drunkenness, therefore, did not revile these townspeople the way it did Franklin or their neighbors. Earning their livelihoods by encouraging Native indulgence, these traders saw business in this conference.

In hindsight, traders and liquor loomed large in official explanations of the Carlisle conference. One "Man of Credit at Carlisle" said that the "whole" conference had been nothing more than "a vile Scheme of the Indian Traders," many of whom were probably his neighbors. The Indians, he said, "were not sober when in Council, but received their Directions from the Traders present."[19] Consequently, Pennsylvania's commissioners had been "told a great many lies" at Carlisle.[20] Traders and liquor were thus to blame for the failure of the Carlisle meeting. Because "the Traders of this Province," as

Richard Peters observed the year before, "are in general worthless, expensive, dishonest men, a Prey to the Indian Women, and regardless of publick or private Faith," their involvement boded ill for the conference. No wonder nothing good came from it.[21]

Native Americans returned to the Cumberland Valley when Pennsylvania's interior erupted in violence in 1754. Although the Carlisle conference had happened only the year before, new events transformed tensions into violence. George Washington had surrendered to the French at Fort Necessity after pushing against them and their Native allies to assert Virginia's Ohio Company claims; the Albany Congress had failed to secure an intercolonial union; the controversial land purchase at that conference had infuriated Native people. Then, British forces under General Edward Braddock were soundly defeated along the Monongahela. Arrogant and ill-informed British military leaders, meanwhile, alienated many of their Native and colonial allies. In Pennsylvania, efforts to negotiate peace with the Delawares, longstanding allies of the colony, were hampered by the Indians' lingering anger over the unjust 1754 land purchase. Peace was also hampered by the struggles between proprietary and Quaker parties in the colony. In response, western Delawares aligned themselves with the French. Suddenly, as historian Francis Jennings explains, the "brawling" in the Ohio country, which the Carlisle conference had failed to discourage, "served as an excuse for powerful Englishmen who wanted to fight France" to make their move, and the Seven Years' War—or the French and Indian War, as it was often called in its North American context—was on.[22]

In Carlisle, the coming of war signaled the first of several turning points in the town's history. Authority over the region shifted as a British imperial apparatus bent on conquest, spearheaded by the British Army and supported by a host of colonial troops and Natives loyal to the English cause, supplanted proprietary influence in the region. Simultaneously, Native attacks on colonists, sometimes stretching as far east as the Susquehanna Valley, undermined townspeople's sense of security and intensified negative reactions to Native peoples. Hell, as townspeople discovered, was a relative thing. It could be observed at a distance, as Franklin suggested that night in Carlisle, or experienced more intimately. Indeed, when "a Powerful Army of Cruel Merciless and Unhuman Enemies" of mostly Shawnees and Delawares descended on parts of the county in a series of targeted raids intended to retake lands claimed by the Iroquois and Pennsylvania, colonists in and near

Carlisle were powerfully reminded that Indians could do worse things than dancing drunkenly around a bonfire. Rather, they could turn on their colonial neighbors in violent ways by destroying those with whom they had only recently shared economic and even personal ties.[23]

As attacks persisted, colonists' fears of Native Americans reached new heights. Rural residents feared for their lives and property; townspeople feared Carlisle would be attacked; and Philadelphians like Governor Robert Hunter Morris feared for the colony's well being. Many believed that unless these attacks were checked quickly by British and colonial military forces, the "counties of York and Cumberland"—spatial buffers between Native America and the Delaware Valley—"w[ould] be entirely Evacuated, and the River Sasquehannah" would "become the frontier on that side."[24] Such concerns intensified as Native-French raids drew closer to Carlisle. By 1758, British General John Forbes, in Carlisle to command the expedition against Fort Duquesne that was intended to squash these raids, confirmed that Native warriors were "scalping every day and have broke up all the settlements in [the] neighborhood."[25] The same year, another officer noted that Native raids outside nearby Shippensburg had "allarm'd the Inhabitants very much." With two killed and two others taken prisoner, locals were so upset that they were "incapable of giving advise [advice] how to Act upon the offencive, as their views are only turn'd [on] how to defend themselves.[26] By all accounts, Indians bent on remaking their former territories into Native spaces had turned Pennsylvania topsy turvy.

Especially alarming were reports of refugees flooding into interior towns. In Carlisle and York there could be "seen Men[,] Women[,] and Children who had Lately Lived in great affluence and plenty reduced to the most extreme poverty and distress."[27] Most of them fled interior settlements to the north and west in "the greatest Distress and Confusion imaginable"; they were left with nothing. With "the whole Country to the West of this place [Carlisle] . . . abandoned," Carlisle was fast becoming an important refugee town.[28] More striking was that these refugees had not come far; they were townspeople's rural neighbors—and friends. Before the war, these colonists had traveled recently constructed roads to Carlisle to attend meeting or market. By contrast, during this time of great "Uneasiness," with "several skulking Indians daily seen" as close as four or five miles from Carlisle, these farmers and their families traveled these same roads hurriedly to seek refuge in town after abandoning their farms.[29] By all accounts, chaos reigned. One trader confirmed, "all the People have left their Houses betwixt this [Carlisle] and the Mountain, some come to Town and others gathering into little forts."[30] Carlisle had thus become yet another kind of town in-between; only this time, it was not a crossroads of commerce or way station of trade, but a refuge where interior colonists took stock, desperately trying to answer the "single Question" of "whether they shall go West, and take a Chance of saving their Estates, or East, and lose all?"[31]

While violence raged in the mid-1750s, Pennsylvanians bickered about how to respond. Outraged colonists, some of them displaced persons, others supporters of the proprietary party, wanted an armed defense. They were afraid of Indian violence, angry about what they had lost, and frustrated by the pacifism of the colony's Quaker-dominated assembly. Colonists at the southern end of Cumberland County petitioned the Assembly to put aside factional politics and pacifism and offer colonists "Relief" from their "very Mallencolly [melancholy] Circumstances." They were willing "to Defend our selves"; they did not expect eastern colonists to fight for them. But they needed arms and ammunition "to help in a Ruining Country."[32] Their calls for defensive action were echoed by the colony's governor, who also wanted "a Just and Equal Militia Law." This happened in 1756 when the proprietors and Assembly compromised in their long-standing struggle over the taxation of proprietary lands, and the Assembly appropriated a substantial sum for " 'the King's use.' "[33] The colony could finally organize its defense.

Though never attacked, Carlisle was a center of interior defense. It was one of the first interior places fortified in 1755. That summer, the governor noted that "the People," although "much disheartened and inclining to quit their plantations," had "laid the Ground for a wooden Fort in the Town of Carlisle."[34] Although whether this fort was completed remains uncertain, some kind of stockade stood on either the west side of the public square or inside it by 1756. Its presence, and the fifty men who staffed it, offered security to townspeople and refugees flooding into town.[35] Carlisle also had British and provincial troops for added protection. Because of its strategic location on the "new Road" over the mountains "along which any forces that shall be raised for the Ohio Service must go," Carlisle was the place, the Governor argued, where troops—including the remnants of Braddock's Army—"should be posted" to secure the "plentiful Country" of the province's west.[36] They were, although with some delay. British troops began arriving in 1757. They were housed at the "barracks for the Soldiers," a large encampment the size of two football fields enclosed in earthen ramparts, which began construction just north of town in 1756 (figure 8).[37] In 1758, many others joined them when

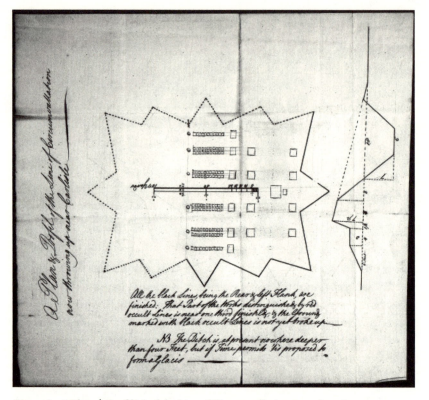

Figure 8. *A Plan & Profil[e] of the Line of Circumvallation now throwing up near Carlisle.* British military engineer Thomas Bassett drew this sketch of the Carlisle encampment in 1757 while it was under construction. The "works," as it came to be called, was more than two football fields in size. It served the British during the Seven Years' War and the Americans during the Revolution. Later, during the 1780s, some of the buildings were home to Dickinson College. (Courtesy of the Huntington Library, San Marino, California.)

Carlisle became the staging ground for the Forbes expedition against Fort Duquesne. In addition, after local militia companies formed in 1756, "great Numbers" of provincial volunteers "from Lancaster and York Counties" were also "coming in every Day" to Carlisle "to our Assistance."[38] Carlisle housed many fighting men. For some townspeople, the military presence was sufficient to lull them into a sense of security.

For others, however, that was not enough, especially during the first two years of the war. Forts took time to build and British troops took time to arrive. Equally significant, Major General Edward Braddock's ambush and defeat along the Monongahela demonstrated the vulnerability of European forces against Native enemies. His defeat also unleashed a new series of raids across the interior that sorely tested the defensive line of fortifications Pennsylvanians were hastily erecting. With the interior in "the utmost Confusion, [and] not knowing what Hand to turn to," many in Carlisle felt they did not have time to wait. Provincial forces were organizing and some townsmen, "being more afraid of the Indians . . . than of the French," took it upon themselves to wage their own offensive against Pennsylvania's Native enemies. They did so with the governor's sanction.[39]

Their target was the western Delawares' village of Kittanning, a settlement along the Allegheny, about forty miles northeast of Fort Duquesne and almost two hundred miles northwest of Carlisle (see map 1). This "Town of our Indian Enemies" had special meaning to many interior colonists. It was the home to the reviled Delaware chief, Captain Jacobs, who led several brutal raids, including one destroying Fort Granville (figure 9). It was also the holding ground for many Euro-American captives.[40] John Armstrong, Carlisle surveyor and proprietors' man, led the attack that September 1756. He had just assumed the rank of captain of the militia and commander of provincial forces west of the Susquehanna; he had also distinguished himself as a vocal critic of Pennsylvania's fort-based defense. Kittanning, the raid he staged with nearly 300 militiamen, many of them locals—including his second-in-command, his neighbor Robert Callender—was the most memorable and brutal expression of his military vision.[41]

Armstrong and his men targeted Kittanning for a surprise attack to ensure their success. They first marched west along the Frankstown Path, the more direct but challenging trader's path from Carlisle to the Allegheny River (see maps 1 and 2). Then, hearing the "whooping of Indian Warriors at a Dance," they stopped just outside, organized themselves, and attacked at daybreak, killing as many Natives as they could and burning the town. During their attack, Captain Jacobs "gave the War Whoop" and "defended his House bravely through Loopholes in the Logs." He would not surrender, however, but instead shouted out in English that "he and his men were warriors" who "would fight while life remained."[42] In response, Armstrong's men set his house afire and shot and scalped him, his wife, son, and at least nine others. When it was over, thirty to forty Delawares lay dead, some of them shot, others burned to death in their homes. The town lay in ashes.

For dealing this "greatest Blow the Indians have received since the War

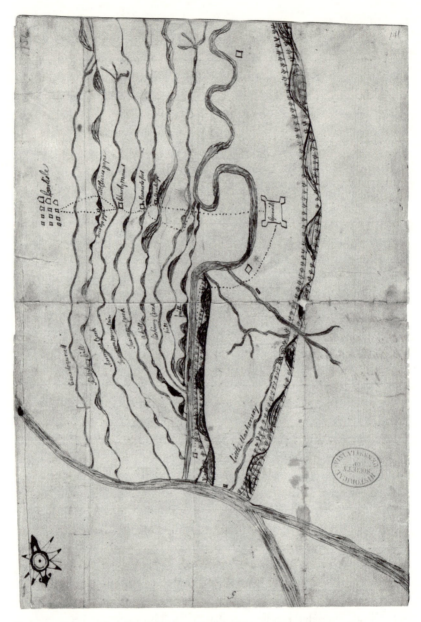

Figure 9. *Route to Fort Granville from Carlisle.* This crude map, drawn by an unknown mapmaker, probably dates to 1756. It offers a conceptual depiction of how interior settlers perceived the terrain they moved through as they traveled from Carlisle, depicted as a grid on this map, to Fort Granville, probably along Native American paths. (From the Lamberton Scotch-Irish Collection. Courtesy of Historical Society of Pennsylvania, Philadelphia.)

began," Pennsylvanians celebrated Armstrong and his men as heroes.[43] He and his officers were rewarded with money in exchange for the scalps, prisoners, and plunder they acquired. Admiration for them swelled when they "generously" donated this blood money to their fellow militiamen to encourage future expeditions. This gesture showed them to be "Gentlemen" who had not gone "against the Enemy from a mercenary Motive, but from a Regard for the Service of their King and bleeding Country."[44] They were not greedy or savage, but noble. Philadelphians, in particular, feted the wounded Armstrong (he had received a ball in his shoulder during the raid) and his officers with silver medals and money as expressions of their thanks for their "Courage and personal Bravery." The Penn family granted him land at the townsite he destroyed.[45]

Despite such celebrations, however, there was another, more troubling reality at work here. At Kittanning, Armstrong and other Carlisle men, including Callender, a "friend" to many Ohio Valley Native peoples before the war, engaged in the same kind of intimate violence as their enemies. They had not simply murdered, but scalped men, women, and children. This raid was thus a clear example of the bloody and brutal "counter-terror" colonists waged on Ohio Valley Native peoples during the war. It also demonstrated how, in this struggle to reassert Euro-American authority over the interior, some townsmen were willing to take violent action to protect their communities. They would not sit idly by on the sidelines as war raged around them.[46]

Kittanning also raised issues about the war's effect on Carlisle. The praise heaped on Armstrong illustrates that there were benefits as well as costs to this war. Townspeople suffered along with their rural neighbors in the 1750s—the persistent fear that "we in these Parts lie much exposed" and "expect daily to be attacked here," suggests the debilitating hold fear had on townspeople's psyches.[47] But while townspeople were "Sufferers in the late Calamities," their sufferings were mostly secondhand. More significant, Carlisle reaped considerable benefit from the war. Armstrong's expedition, for example, brought the town fame as home to fierce Indian fighters. The war was also a catalyst of growth when Carlisle became a refugee town and military staging ground. These functions brought people and war-related service activities to town, thereby demonstrating the ironic way that chaos generated positive outcomes in some communities of the interior.[48]

Growth happened in a number of sectors during the war; population was one of them. In contrast to most of the colony's interior, which experienced "widespread settlement retreat" during the war as rural colonists reversed migration patterns toward the interior, Carlisle expanded demographically. Between 1753 and 1764, its taxable population increased from 105 to 182 individuals, a gain of 73 percent (which translated into a population of perhaps 500 or 600 expanding to more than 1,000 individuals, and perhaps as many as 1,100, in eleven years). This was the highest rate of growth during the town's first sixty years; it was driven by several factors.[49] Colonists stayed put because wartime dislocations held migration in check. Carlisle's population swelled with refugees, some of whom likely stayed and became tax-paying residents. Furthermore, as a military staging ground, Carlisle was also temporary home to a large contingent of British soldiers, colonial militiamen, and, for a brief time, two parties of Cherokee and Catawba warriors who came north to join the British. British troops started arriving in 1757, once Britain made reconquering the Ohio Valley one of its highest priorities. Their numbers increased dramatically after Brig. Gen. John Forbes, the fifty-one-year-old Scotsman charged with leading the British assault on the French Fort Duquesne, chose Carlisle as the depot and assembly area for his expedition. Soon thereafter, when Forbes's force numbered nearly 7,000, one officer counted 6,400 men at Carlisle.[50] The town was no longer a small settlement of the interior, but a pivot point of British military maneuvers (see figure 8).

Although a mass influx of British regulars could create tensions within a town, their arrival in Carlisle also had positive effects. Troops passively deterred attacks on the town, thus calming colonists' fears. Soldiers also patrolled the county's hinterlands and safeguarded farm families working their fields. As one officer recalled, he did not know exactly how many "enemy Indians" remained in the area, but he was doing "everything in my power to make their situation uneasy to 'em."[51] An interior population wearied by attacks and fear welcomed his approach. The troops' arrival also spurred growth in Carlisle's economy because soldiers brought business. Just as Carlisle's tavern keepers were eager to see business from Native peoples and provincial officials during the Carlisle conference in 1753, so did they welcome soldiers who spent money in their establishments. British officers knew this as well. As one officer observed, "unless Carlisle & Shippensburg are of late miraculously altered in point of Morals, the old game at either of those seats of Virtue & good manners would undoubtedly be play'd over; especially as it is intended the men should receive their Pay there, to enable them, more & more, besides having their pockets pick'd by Tavern keepers."[52] Troops brought opportunities for profit to retailers; as Chapter 2 discussed, their presence inspired some townspeople to become tavern or storekeepers.

More significant to the local economy was Carlisle's function as a supply and provisioning center, first for the Forbes expedition, and later for troops stationed in the West. Indeed, once the crown committed to fighting this imperial contest against the French in North America, it needed a transportation and supply infrastructure to support military operations in the interior. That required building roads to transport men and materials west and establishing supply depots and staging grounds at strategic locations like Carlisle to collect and house men and materials. Fulfilling these demands promised jobs and money for colonists. Job opportunities took various forms. The construction of the Forbes Road, the major wagon road that took Forbes's troops from Carlisle and over the Alleghenies toward Fort Duquesne, was a massive undertaking requiring surveyors and countless laborers to complete. When work commenced, there were 150 men on the project. More joined them, however, when they encountered obstacles in cutting this road over the mountains (see map 1).[53] There were also plenty of other jobs to be had. Unskilled laborers became drivers of wagons and haulers of goods. The Army also hired craftsmen to manufacture and repair supplies. Forbes's second in command, Col. Henry Bouquet, for example, noted hiring a "good" local gunsmith, "a skillful farrier," and their apprentices at Carlisle.[54]

Carlisle's leading men also found employment with the army. In fact, those who won coveted supply agent positions for Forbes's army reads like a who's who of town elites. Trader Robert Callender, Armstrong's lieutenant at Kittanning, became wagon master general. Bouquet characterized him as a "very useful man because of his knowledge of the country." Callender, with a captain's commission, had evidently traded fighting Indians for profiting from the fights others waged against them.[55] Adam Hoops, a "very energetic" trader who had been indicted for selling liquor to Indians in 1753, became subcontractor for provisions. After fighting Natives while defending McDowell's Mill in 1755, he also switched to supplying the army.[56] Andrew Colhoun became forage master, and William Lyon, John Armstrong's nephew, oversaw contractor's agents and provisions at the magazine. John Byers managed wagons in Cumberland County. Francis West, another pioneer and proprietors' man, and Carlisle tavern keeper William Buchanan, victualed provincial troops at Forts Littleton, Loudoun, Morris, and Carlisle.[57]

That these Carlisle men occupied such prominent positions in supplying Forbes's army was no accident; they lobbied for these jobs. The lure of business sparked their interest. Bouquet remarked with surprise on how many merchants had asked to follow the army; some, he thought, might even come "of their own accord" and "without wages."[58] These men knew first-hand that fighting Indians was dangerous work. But supplying troops might bring profit while allowing them to conduct illicit trade with some of their former Native trade partners, establish future trade contacts, or scout lands for purchase. Initially, Bouquet was "very glad" for men like Callender "to have some profit." Over time, however, he grew suspicious. "No one in this country can be relied on," he said. "At all times, private interests outweigh the general welfare."[59] Self-interest, rather than concern for the common good, inspired their involvement in the war.

The army did more than employ people, it also demanded supplies from them. Staging a major interior campaign was a monumental undertaking that the British could not carry out on their own. Forbes and his troops were dependent on the local population for virtually all of their provisioning and transport needs. To that end, the British established a "Grand Magazine" and the "Kings Stores" at Carlisle; these structures added to the warehouses, domestic and retail structures, and public buildings dotting the townscape.[60] Those employed by the army then tried to fill these structures by acquiring the resources held by local colonists, but often met with frustration. British officers complained that "the Country" was "Deficient" in its contracts and its colonists reluctant to part with their horses and wagons.[61] Even so, they gathered a remarkable quantity of materials in the area. Meadows "near or about Carlisle," for instance, were taken "for the use of the army," their owners paid for their use. All kinds of forage, such as hay and oats, and provisions, such as flour, rum, whiskey, hogs, cattle, and sheep, were gathered from colonists in and near town.[62] One official, for example, talked of collecting "all" the hay within ten miles of Carlisle in autumn 1759. The same year, another reported that there were one thousand horses in or near town, and the army "contracted" hundreds of wagons. For the better part of two years, Carlisle and its residents were a major center of military service and supply activity in the colonies. Said one observer: a "spirit of Activity prevails here that does at Philadelphia."[63]

Still, townspeople's reactions to the hustle and bustle around them were mixed. Many innkeepers, traders, and merchants welcomed the army's business, while others were more cautious. Remarkable changes had taken place in the short time since the town's founding. Native raids first brought fear and refugees to town. Then, a huge group of British military men descended. Although they were there to protect and serve British imperial interests, their presence transformed Carlisle and placed huge demands on colonists' resources. Not all townspeople were happy about this British presence or their conduct of the war. John Armstrong, for one, was fearful for interior colonists' safety, and he spoke out. Men, he said, should be learning "the essential parts of Service" rather than doing things like building roads. He also worried that once the expedition moved west, the remaining "Troops, and colonists about Carlisle will Suffer hardship at this Season of the Year, for want of convenient Cover."[64] To Armstrong, leader of the province's western forces, local needs outweighed imperial concerns; the army's first duty was to colonists. Yet for his cautiousness, Armstrong found himself "in a very unfavourable light" with British officers who dismissed him as a "timorous & Confused" man.[65]

Other colonists, especially the "country people," were "obstinate" and "unfriendly" toward the military men in the midst.[66] Their hostility especially perplexed the often haughty Bouquet, a European who expected colonists to spring to action. Instead, they feared being "ill treated," a "Jealousy," as one county official explained, that arises "from some Unfair Usage, which they alledge, some of 'em have formerly rec'd from Officers in the Army."[67] In a county populated by Ulster immigrants, one wonders how many of these alleged abuses happened in Ireland? Did they resist the army as a familiar institution of British imperial authority that they or their ancestors had experienced in the Old World? Regardless, colonists refused press warrants by sending "their Wagons & horses out of the Country." When they supplied goods or livestock, Bouquet believed they "kept the Best at home," even though it was "Not agreeable to Contract." Good will alone, Bouquet knew, would not bring the provisions he wanted.[68] Colonists wanted money for their property or produce. But because many "Country People" also "have but little Faith in Military Payments," they began "to grumble" anytime they did not get a fair deal.[69]

The army was caught in a bind. Authority, not just cash, was in dispute. Rural colonists, and some townspeople too, contested army officials' right to compel them to do anything. They were outsiders, after all. Were not colonists' services voluntary? And why, colonists wondered, should they do others' bidding, especially if it impinged on their personal interests? Such questions came to the fore after Native raids subsided. "The Country People," noted one official, "Appear prejudiced Against, & Backward to Enter into the Service of the Crown." In Carlisle, drivers were hard to find because "The People here are all a sleep."[70] County justices, meanwhile, fearing challenges to their own tenuous authority, were loathe to compel their neighbors' obedience. To British officers it thus seemed that "civil authority" was "completely nonexistent in this county."[71] Bouquet asked the governor to pressure local officials to do their duty. Army officials, meanwhile, advertised and paid high prices for needed supplies and services. They continued to remind colonists that "The King has a right to Their Service on paying."[72]

The eventual success of the Forbes expedition eased the threat of Native attacks on Pennsylvania's interior by late 1758. Despite challenges, British forces under Bouquet finally took Fort Duquesne after the French, abandoned by their Native allies, deserted it.[73] This and other British victories elsewhere in the colonies and Canada, however, did little to foster a uniform sense of security among colonists in the Cumberland Valley. Unease, fear, suspicion, and sometimes hostility remained the watchwords as Carlisle moved into the 1760s. Having experienced a violent clash of cultures and empires, and with memories—or at least stories—of destructive raids still vivid, some townspeople and rural colonists remained leery and sometimes hostile to Natives and the British military. To them, Indians especially, but the British, too, were outsiders whose interests potentially threatened their own. People's fears were confirmed particularly after Native peoples, led by the Ottawa leader Pontiac and inspired by the nativist message of the Delaware prophet Neolin, launched another series of devastating raids on Pennsylvania's interior in 1763. Indians were savages.

Intercultural relations in the mid-Atlantic were especially volatile in the early 1760s. During Pontiac's Uprising, Native peoples asserted their right to self-determination in violent ways, and colonists responded in kind. Most notorious was the Paxton Boys' brutal murder of a group of Conestogas at Lancaster in late 1763; this was an especially bloody gesture intended to intimidate Native peoples across the interior. Such spiraling patterns of violence, say scholars, had long-term effects. These incidents hardened the divide between Indians and interior colonists by intensifying animosities between them. Among some colonists, fear and anger morphed into hate.[74] Such heated emotions, and the desires for revenge they inspired, as historian Richard White notes, were not "without cause."[75] Two brutal wars and a decade of terror waged by both sides had "poisoned intercultural relations in the Pennsylvania backcountry," says another scholar.[76] The upshot was the rise of "the 'bad Indian' as a prevalent negative representation in the 1760s." In fact, with the rise of a powerful "anti-Indian sublime," a rhetoric promulgated through lurid tales of Native violence, Indians were no longer noble, but savage. They were enemy others whose barbarity set them apart as outsiders;

they made "white people" suffer.[77] Such negative attitudes, most scholars conclude, paved the way for a "proto-racism" that unified colonists by classifying
Indians as a distinct and inferior race.[78] But as historian Peter Silver notes and
Carlisle's experience confirms, this picture is more complicated. The effects
of this hate were more insidious. Anti-Indian sentiments set up an opposition
between Natives and Euro-Americans. But because not all Euro-Americans
hated Indians uniformly, hate also became a political weapon to use against
each other. It established a "standard of loyalty" on which the actions of
others within the community could be judged.[79]

Some Carlisle residents shared the anti-Indian sentiments of their rural
neighbors. They, too, believed that Native peoples were "resolved to kill all
the white Folks, except a few."[80] But Carlisle's response is also instructive
because some townspeople rejected these sentiments. Attitudes to Native
peoples varied considerably; not all interior colonists were Indian-haters by
the 1760s. Native Americans no doubt loomed large in the town's collective
consciousness. Nearly ten years of intermittent war with Indians generated
huge stresses. Uncertainty about the future was high. But townspeople reacted differently to it. Some blamed Native peoples for their predicament.
Others, however, in contrast to most historians' portrayals of Pennsylvania's
interior colonists, did not. They distinguished between Native friends and
enemies. This was so even during the Seven Years' War when at least sixty
Cherokees, who came north to support their British allies, walked Carlisle's
streets unmolested. Acknowledging one's friends, townspeople knew, was important. While there, the Cherokees, for instance, helped secure the interior
by conducting raids against other enemy Indians.[81]

These sentiments grew stronger once warfare ceased and postwar economic conditions offered additional incentives to cultivate Indian friends.
Because many townspeople were dependent on the fur and skin trade for
income before the war, many of them held that renewed trade relations were
central to Carlisle's future. Farmers and others unconnected to the trade
could reject Indians as brutal savages, but the town's many traders, trade
agents, merchants, retailers and artisans who serviced the trade, and the
packhorsemen and wagon drivers who hauled goods for it, could not afford
to indulge in such anti-Indian sentiment. Rather, reestablishing Carlisle's exchange economy demanded tolerance of Native trade partners. In the wake
of two wars, these men, their families, and servants were probably fearful of
Indians; they certainly did not consider them their equals. Yet that did not
make them racists or proto-racists, but pragmatic businessmen. Thus, once

violence ceased, they wanted to trade with Indians, not kill them. They put animosities aside in the interests of commerce.

But just because all townspeople did not hate Indians did not mean that hate was absent in Carlisle. As Peter Silver argues, anti-Indian sentiment was also a tool Euro-Americans used to beat up on each other. It "made possible a politics of opposition to everything and anyone who could be suspected—credibly or not—of threatening the people."[82] This was certainly true in Carlisle, where, as agent Joseph Rigby's comments at the opening of this chapter suggest, Carlisle became a community divided upon itself. Hate made townspeople hyperconscious of their own interests and identities; it brought tensions to the forefront. It also bred a particularly virulent form of ethnic localism that held sway among some members of the town's Scots-Irish. Townspeople coalesced; they grew bold. Driven by fear, armed with hatred and suspicion, and united by a shared ethno-religious heritage, they challenged others' loyalties. By directing hostility toward any individual or group they perceived as acting in ways destructive to their interests, they fostered this tension. They confronted outsiders like provincial authorities, Quaker merchants, and the agents of Philadelphia trading firms like Rigby's. They also challenged those of their Scots-Irish neighbors whose economic interests in the fur trade and friendliness toward Indians called their allegiances to the community in question. Their actions deeply divided Carlisle, remaking the town into a central stage in the interior where hate drove neighbor to confront neighbor.

Wartime experience was one genesis of Indian hating. But the antagonism townspeople directed toward other Euro-Americans also had more complicated roots that reached back to the 1750s. Some stemmed from tensions with proprietary officials over the town's founding; others derived from internal status and religious disputes among townspeople about the effects of proprietary patronage and the Great Awakening in their community. By the 1760s, however, the fur and skin trade was the most divisive, becoming a lighting rod for the expression of tensions about Indians' and outsiders' role in Carlisle. To understand why the trade was so important, one must grasp how the postwar trade worked. Products had changed; deerskins, rather than beaver pelts, were the preferred item. Markets had changed as well: Britain's growing empire expanded credit and improved transport, and at least in theory, the trade was more heavily regulated than in the past. British authorities administered it, casting it as an imperial enterprise. To curtail abuses, they sought with mixed success to license traders, fix prices, forbid liquor sales, and hold trade to military garrisons. Simultaneously, roads constructed during the war expanded its scope and reach. These factors together created a larger, more competitive, and riskier trade controlled by bigger firms with greater access to capital and credit.[83]

Carlisle was part of this context. This meant, though, that those towns-people eager to resume the trade, first in the late 1750s and then following Pontiac's Uprising, found that things were different. Their neighbors hated Indians, while outsiders like Pennsylvania's Commissioners for Indian Affairs and Philadelphia firms like Baynton, Wharton, and Morgan had new influence in this more complex trade. Locals thus had less independence than before. By the 1760s, the town's traders found themselves mostly employed as agents of others. Carlisle was no longer a place where an enterprising colonist might venture a short distance to a Native village to barter for pelts.

The trade still held allure, however, and those partaking of it had choices regarding how to participate. Even before the war's end, a few Carlisle men like Francis West allied themselves with the provincially sanctioned trade establishment led by Pennsylvania's Commissioners for Indian Affairs. These nine commissioners, appointed by the province in 1758, were granted what was supposedly a monopoly on the trade. They controlled the colony's trade posts—including one at Fort Pitt—fixed prices for goods, and sold pelts in Philadelphia. The commissioners' existence reflected Pennsylvania's efforts to better regulate trading. For town pioneer West—an Irishman, Anglican, and proprietors' man who had spent time as a trader in the 1750s—joining these provincial traders made sense. At a time of heightened regulation, working for the commissioners offered him access to the trade. The commissioners also included other proprietors' men, most notably his brother William, a Philadelphia merchant, trader, diplomat, and assemblyman; he thus worked among friends. Yet West's choice was also a bold one. The commissioners' powers were limited; their monopoly was more theoretical than actual. More significant, their enterprises were funded mostly through the Quaker-dominated Friendly Association, an organization founded to promote peace with the Iroquois and eastern Delawares through trade and diplomacy. For West, therefore, joining the commissioners also meant aligning himself with a group of powerful Philadelphia Quakers, men who opposed his loyalties to the proprietor and that many of his Scots-Irish neighbors reviled for their pacifism.[84]

Although West risked the ire of his neighbors, he never earned it. Stationed in Carlisle, West acted as a middleman for the commissioners, working mostly with Quaker trader James Kenny. Kenny operated the Pittsburgh trade house where he acquired pelts, in one case "three Hundred & Eight fall Deer skins, Weight fifteen Hundred & Six Pounds." He then relayed them to his "Friend West" via the Forbes Road. West in turn "forward'd" them on to "ye Commiss[ione]r for Ind[ia]n affairs in Phila[delphia]."[85] West oversaw a sizable operation at Carlisle, one his neighbors would have noticed. Among his duties, he maintained the commissioners' warehouse, where he sorted and stored pelts. As he explained: "as the Deerskins[,] Furrs[,] and Sundry Goods . . . brought here from Bedford in the Beginning of the Snow [were] very wet and without any Invoice, I was obliged to spread out the skins and Furrs in the Store House."[86] He also presided over an extensive array of English trade goods. "In Store" at Carlisle in 1763 were "two half Faggots of Steel," an assortment of "Matchcoats" [a woolen mantle], and "Seventeen Barrs of Iron," in addition to an assortment of fabric, thread, sealing wax, bed lace, wrist bands, arm bands, "ear Bobbs," "Hair plates," gunlocks, wampum, ink powder, and quills—all "Sundry Goods . . . design'd for [the] Pittsburgh Trading House."[87] West's work positioned Carlisle to resume its function as a way station. His neighbors were evidently pleased enough by the commerce that brought to refrain from acting on their suspicions of outsiders, particularly Quakers, in their midst.

But that restraint did not hold. As the trade resumed fully in the mid-1760s and new outsiders arrived to administer it, tensions over Indians and outsiders came to the fore. This situation grew from the choices made by those insiders who followed different avenues to the trade than Francis West. As proprietors' men, they mostly shunned employment with the antiproprietary Friendly Association and instead aligned themselves with the crown's administration of the trade, which was spearheaded in Pennsylvania by William Johnson's deputy, George Croghan.[88] This choice made sense. Johnson and Croghan were fellow Irishmen and woodsmen; Croghan had long-standing ties to Carlisle and some of its traders. Working for them, therefore, meant joining a mostly Irish, or Scots-Irish enterprise. But not quite. Croghan brought his friend Samuel Wharton and the Quaker merchant firm of Baynton, Wharton, and Morgan into the trade. Thus, aligning oneself with the crown also meant working for a group of Philadelphia Quakers—a compromise. Still, Carlisle traders were undeterred. Quakers may have been enemies to their neighbors, but Carlisle's fur traders were more flexible. They were accustomed to a trade that had been long populated by colonists of diverse ethno-religious backgrounds. Their ambitions drove them to work for

Baynton, Wharton, and Morgan and positioned the firm to be the primary and most controversial outside player in renewing Carlisle's role as a town in-between in the fur and skin trade.

Baynton, Wharton, and Morgan were not typical Philadelphia merchants. Unlike their competitors, they saw opportunity, rather than discouragement, in the fur trade of the 1760s. Encouraged by Croghan, who estimated the value of the Illinois beaver trade at £100,000, Baynton, Wharton, and Morgan plunged forward and sponsored a series of ambitious, costly (pledging upward of £75,000 in 1766 alone), and distant ventures into the formerly French-held Illinois country. Although their goal was to capture the trade, land, and military supply contracts of these territories, their ventures were colossally unprofitable and the firm went bankrupt in the 1770s.[89]

Despite their ultimate failure, executing these elaborate ventures brought the firm to Carlisle. To keep goods and pelts moving over such distances, they needed way stations to rest horses, store goods and pelts, and house trustworthy agents who would facilitate the trade for them. Carlisle was one of these places, Pittsburgh the other. Haulers carried wagon loads of English goods from Philadelphia to Carlisle along the Great Road. Once there, agents sorted, repacked, and transferred these goods to pack horses (but sometimes back into wagons) and sent them out with new carriers along the Forbes Road up to Fort Pitt. Other agents then reloaded the goods onto riverboats heading down the Ohio and up the Mississippi where still others offloaded them in the Illinois country. On the return, the whole process was carried out in reverse, at least until 1770 when they began sending goods downriver to New Orleans.[90]

Managing these extensive and distant operations took manpower. The firm's partners certainly played their roles. George Morgan supervised the trade at Kaskaskia; John Baynton and Samuel Wharton oversaw business in Philadelphia and England. But they also needed lots of help from hired agents. In fact, at least five men—Ephraim Blaine, Joseph Dobson, John Irwin, Joseph Rigby, and Joseph Spear—oversaw the firm's operations in Carlisle from the mid-1760s until the early 1770s. All of them were Scots-Irish (or perhaps Scottish), Anglicans or Presbyterians, and literate; all of them were also experienced in the trade. These were economically ambitious men. Ephraim Blaine, for instance, entered military service during the 1750s. He served as a commissary sergeant in the British army, earned the rank of lieutenant, and eventually commanded Fort Ligonier. After the war, he was a prominent Carlisle merchant and miller. When the American Revolution began, he used his military service and experience with Baynton, Wharton, and Morgan to win appointment as Commissary General of Purchases. Men like Blaine were also politically connected; most had personal ties to Croghan and his associate, Robert Callender. These men thus operated within the privileged political orbit of the proprietor.[91]

Once employed, these agents, like West, served as vital middlemen in the trade. This job included running the company's warehouse. In 1766, Ephraim Blaine described his duty's there:

> Thomas Day is come Down and has Deliver'd me Twenty one loads of
> Deer Skins, which came from the Beaver[.][92] There is one of the Girtys
> [perhaps Simon?] with five Loads that is not come Yet[,] but I Daily
> Expect him, Day has been a Good Deal Careless in not Worming the
> Skins he Brought Down—there is forty Skins which I think Quite
> Damag'd, & Several Other a little Touch'd with the Worms[.] . . .
> I have this Day Rec[eive]d Ten Loads of Dress'd Leather and
> Parchment, which I have Examin'd and find them all Verry Safe[.]
> I have about four wagons to load off which I hope will be Done the
> first of next Week.[93]

Blaine, an experienced fur trader and merchant with strong ties to Carlisle's Scots-Irish Presbyterian community, described his duties nonchalantly. But his was no easy task, for he managed thousands of pounds of valuable pelts in any given year.[94] Traders and haulers came "down" to Carlisle with pelts; Blaine sorted through them, assessed their quality, then loaded the best of them "off" to Philadelphia. His primary responsibility was to keep the company's goods "Verry Safe" and the trade moving. He did other things as well. Acting as a broker, he traveled west to Fort Pitt to buy and sell as the firm's representative.[95] Finally, he managed the firm's extensive land holdings, which included surveying new lands and overseeing the 2,000-plus acres the firm owned in Cumberland County.[96] His job was a big one.

Keeping the trade in motion was the most challenging task. Agents had an enormous quantity of stuff to move. At one point in 1766, there were 140 horseloads of goods in Carlisle awaiting transport west. During one eighteen-month span three years later, another agent noted that he sent out 445 horse-loads and 100 wagons of goods.[97] More significant, to keep trade moving, agents depended on the services of other townspeople. They needed wagon haulers, wagons, packhorses and drivers to move goods, and the services of artisans to build barrels, service transport vehicles, shoe horses, repair guns, and manufacture goods. They also required laborers, including servants and slaves, to do grunt work around the warehouse. In 1765, for example, William Trent, Croghan's former partner, owned a servant and slave, and Baynton, Wharton, and Morgan agent, Joseph Spear, had two slaves. Robert Callender even employed his neighbors, most likely women, to manufacture Indian shirts.[98] Trading thus cut across status, occupational, ethnic, and class lines in Carlisle; it was a communal enterprise.

Even so, the trade did not function without challenge. In a town where many were hostile to Indians and sensitive to outsiders, agents found that obtaining the horses, wagons, and men needed to move goods was especially difficult. Haulers and drivers no doubt recalled lurid stories of wartime Indian raids on Pennsylvania's roads and trails. These memories made travel to the Ohio Country an unappealing prospect; why risk losing their lives or livestock on the trail? Agents had to offer economic incentives to convince colonists to work as drivers and haulers, or hire out their horses and wagons. To do so, they followed the model of British army officials during the war by paying locals for services rendered. Agents, especially those with strong ties to Carlisle, also coaxed the participation of friends and family by offering personal reassurances that work for the company did not threaten their interests or the community's.

But there were gaps. Wagons, for instance, were sometimes difficult to obtain. While a partner in the company in 1762, Robert Callender sent the firm some 1,928 pounds of "dressed leather," 900 raccoons, and 346 pounds of fall skins. He also wanted to send an additional "Six or Seven Waggon load[s] more" but could not do so until "Wagons Can be got to take them."[99] Packhorses were also difficult to hire. Packhorsemen were particular about the quantity, size, and weight of goods they transported. The large and weighty "Half Barrels" of sugar and coffee the company sent, for instance, were challenging to find men to transport. As agent Joseph Rigby explained, it was "vast trouble to engage the Packhorsemen to meddle with them," because most carriers "say they will cut the Horses Hips and through their Sides." He was in an awkward position; he wanted to serve his employers, but his neighbors were reluctant. His dilemma was resolved only "after one or two had taken them" (perhaps by persuasion or offers of higher pay) and "the rest came into it with Less Reluctance, though they complain[ed] of the extraordinary size of the Casks."[100] As this incident demonstrates, townspeople's cooperation was crucial to keep the trade operating.

Economic considerations certainly influenced townspeople's reaction to the company and its agents, just as they shaped reactions to the British military during the war. Townspeople had multiple interests—in a region where there was a "Great Scarcity of Money," one might suspend one's fear of Indians and suspicion of outsiders if cash wages were being offered for one's goods or services. But this arrangement worked only when the company was flush. When Baynton, Wharton, and Morgan's finances declined, agents faced a predicament.[101] People expected their pay. As agent John Irwin explained, the men who wintered the company's horses "is now Demanding pay, and Says they Cannot want it any longer." So were the drivers who had hauled goods to Sandusky months earlier; they "have been this long time Warmly applying for their pay." Irwin was tired of "put[ting] them of[f] with Storys."[102] But the situation worsened. By 1768, with the company's Illinois ventures failing, the firm was going broke. Agents had no cash and little credit. Townspeople reacted angrily. By summer, agent Joseph Dobson anticipated "a Severe Check." The signs were there. One person had already refused his bill of credit saying he "would take no more of ye Company bills" because he already held too many of their unpaid notes. Dobson knew that "if this Should once Gett wind hear we will Gett no more People to Carry for us," and operations would halt.[103]

Dobson's reactions to the mounting pressure from his neighbors made things worse. He had a volatile temper, haughty attitude, and few friends. He was particularly obstinate in negotiating with craftsmen, which locked him into disputes with several Carlisle coopers. He claimed the coopers were dishonest; they produced leaky kegs and then demanded high payment. The coopers, however, had a different story. They saw the agent of a failing company trying to swindle them. They were correct. As a stall tactic, Dobson disputed charges and refused to pay them. After he claimed one cooper overcharged him, for instance, Dobson demanded that he "Get a fresh bill Drawn to my Likeing." When the cooper demanded payment, Dobson made up excuses, telling him that he needed the partners' permission before paying him. Then, he intensified the situation by chiding the cooper for his greed, saying that he "was in to[o] Great haste for his mon[e]y." The cooper, irate, declared that "he would have" his money. But Dobson, determined to "Keep him out of it," then "bid" the cooper to "Get it in the best manner he was able."[104] The cooper set off for Philadelphia to take up the matter with the firm's partners.[105]

This heated exchange illustrates the tenuous relationship agents, and by extension the company, had with townspeople. Craftsmen like the cooper were willing to work for the firm, but only if they received compensation for their services; their tempers rose when they did not. When agents responded to hostility with more of their own, tensions spiraled. As the company's situation in Carlisle deteriorated, Dobson harbored grudges. As he said about the cooper: "I mortally hate the Rascale," because "he has affronted me Several times" with his "saucy" attitude.[106] He made no secret of his loathing for his neighbors and did everything in his power "Never [to] Speak to any of them, but when I Can[']t help it or Go into one of their house[s]." In short, he did everything possible to distance himself from the community. But this only made things worse because his "method of Living alone and Not Asscoating [Associating] with them" made them "thing [think] me an odd Kind of person."[107] Indeed, although his surname suggests that he shared a common Scots or Scots-Irish ancestry with his neighbors, his behavior, economic alliances, and perhaps his religion (some of Carlisle's most prominent traders were Anglicans) cast him as an outsider. His status raised suspicions about him and reinforced townspeople's wariness to the company.

Yet townspeople also made choices about whom to confront. Not all traders were outcasts. Dobson was incredulous, for instance, when Robert Callender—who had left his partnership with the company to become one of its chief rivals—trumped him by employing craftsmen whose services he typically commanded. In 1768, he reported that Callender, who "never Speaks to me Now Nor I to him," was working in "secret" with other former company agents to stage their own ambitious venture to Fort Chartres in the Illinois country. To prepare, he engaged the town's coopers to prepare 150 kegs to carry 1,500 gallons of rum.[108] Not long afterwards, Dobson watched again in agitation as Callender employed "a Great many hands," probably women, servants, and perhaps a few slaves, to make a large quantity of Indian shirts for his trade.[109] Callender had set Carlisle abuzz with manufacturing activity at a time when Dobson was struggling to get anything accomplished. He could do this because he was an insider, and that status that won him the cooperation of his neighbors. A shrewd businessman, Callender knew his neighbors expected economic rewards for their work. And as a town pioneer, Callender had legitimacy among his neighbors. Callender knew people and understood the interests they weighed. With this information, he could persuade them that his western enterprises were their own. But there were ironies. By all accounts, his ventures depended mostly on peddling large quantities of rum to the Indians. This was an illegal trade that many colonists opposed in the wake of the Native violence of the war years; alcohol, they believed, fueled savagery. Still, many townspeople put aside their concerns to work for their neighbor. In this case, neighborly ties and compensation for one's labors trumped fears of drunk and unruly Indians.[110]

While Callender enlisted his neighbors, Baynton, Wharton, and Morgan's agents faced growing animosity. These feelings spilled out into the public sphere in the fall of 1768 when a Carlisle wagon driver sued Dobson for wages he had been denied. In fact, the man brought suit "in Less than half an hour" after Dobson said he "would not pay him." The court's judgement went against Dobson and he was fined. For Dobson, this judgement was a highly personalized attack, one symptomatic of the broader insider-outsider dynamics and ethno-religious tensions at work in Carlisle by the 1760s. Before the hearing, Dobson, writing with a note of cynicism, was "pretty Sure" of the outcome, for the plaintiff was one of the justice's "own Dear Breath[r]en." The driver was a Scots-Irish Presbyterian, an elder in the meeting, and, as Dobson noted sarcastically, "a man of Note hear." Dobson knew that the justices "would order me to pay the fellow for the[y] are his friends and Dont Love me much . . . Nor indeed Do the[y] [love] any Body but one of their own Creatures." Even his witness, Stephen Duncan, a Carlisle merchant with ties to the company, "Did not Say much in my favour." According to Dobson, this was "because the[y] all three [the plaintiff, justice, and witness] belongs to the Same Meeting."[111]

Justice had not prevailed by Dobson's reckoning. Instead, a cabal, united by their common Presbyterian—and by extension Scots-Irish—heritage, set the county's legal establishment against him and the company. The implications of their actions, he knew, were far reaching. His public sanctioning signaled the rise of a potent localist mindset among some of the town's Scots-Irish Presbyterians that would thereafter seek to police all of the company's activities in Carlisle. Hate was a potent force; it fueled the "Hidden Villainy" that Dobson saw everywhere about him each day in Carlisle.[112] More significant, hate had mobilized a sizable segment of the town's population along ethno-religious lines. It brought ethno-religious factors to the fore, creating an "us," united in its shared Scots-Irish and Presbyterian identity, to oppose a "them," whose Quakerism, hostile agents, and shady business practices violated communal interests or standards. For Dobson, an outsider whose company could no longer offer him the financial means to buy townspeople's goodwill, this was an ominous development. His future in Carlisle looked grim, and he knew it. "God help me," he wrote his employers, "if Ever the[y] Gett any Claw against me in the Law," because they "hate you and me."[113]

This virulent Scots-Irish Presbyterian localism was made more potent by townspeople's fears of Native peoples. More was at stake here than disputes over lost wages for goods or services; townspeople perceived that their lives were in danger. Hidden villainy existed on both sides. Baynton, Wharton, and Morgan's agents were not just uncooperative and unneighborly, they were engaged in a secret trade in powder, lead, and knives to the Indians sponsored by their firm.[114] In the context of 1768, a year when intercultural tensions were rising and another Indian war seemed possible, this was unacceptable. The firm had crossed a line. In peddling arms and ammunition to Native peoples, its trade threatened colonists' lives. In response, angry townspeople and other local colonists did everything possible to sabotage the firm. Packhorses were suddenly mostly unavailable.[115] Dobson and fellow agent Joseph Rigby relied instead on troops to relay goods to Fort Pitt as they marched west. John Armstrong, who was no fan of traders and their Quaker employers, failed to deliver Dobson's letters to company partners in Philadelphia. Dobson interpreted Armstrong's action as another attempt to undermine the company.[116] Haulers carrying goods from Philadelphia, meanwhile, broke trunks "all to Pieces" to steal goods from them, while another man delivered his goods "Very badly" with "14 Gallons of wine Drank and Sugar wanting."[117]

A seasoned agent, Dobson took some of these actions in stride. He knew, for instance, that "some Rascales . . . would Destroy ye Licquor and Goods" and could thus dismiss some incidents as the hazards of a trans-Atlantic trade.[118] But he also recognized that what was happening in Carlisle was different. These were not random acts, but sabotage. A critical mass of townspeople was furious at the company because they resented its trade practices. To drive out the firm and their agents, they were using the courts, disrupting the flow of goods, pelts, and information, and most significant, staging pointed acts of personal intimidation against the firm's agents.

The most notable of these confrontations happened one May morning in 1768 while Dobson loaded horses bound for Fort Pitt. "Several of the towns people Came about me," he said. He was "Greatly Mortified" as they surrounded him ominously and asked pointedly "whether I had Got Powder and Lead in those Bundles to Kill the Scotch Irish."[119] Was Dobson, they wondered, helping to arm Indians against them? This was an astonishingly bold question posed by townspeople who perceived their lives at risk. And in singling out Dobson they labeled him a traitor. Indeed, when read literally, their question asked if he, not the Indians, planned to murder them. Dobson was not one of them, but a murderer, they charged. But there was more. This personalized act of intimidation also targeted the firm. Townspeople wanted Baynton, Wharton, and Morgan to know that the gig was up on the company's games.

This pointed message spoke to townspeople's memories of Indian violence and the tensions pitting various Euro-American ethno-religious groups against each other at mid-century. Their question also expressed a strong sense of their group identity as "Scotch Irish." They portrayed themselves as a distinct and potentially victimized people, definitely not a "people with no name." But equally important, their identity remained fluid and was not determined solely by their Old World ancestry. Rather, in Carlisle, townspeople earned their position in the community's ranks by their Presbyterianism and loyalty to their neighbors. They also worked together for the common interest, which during the 1760s focused particularly on resisting incursions from Indians and outsiders. Yet having to earn one's place had ramifications, for it meant that not all Scots-Irishmen belonged. Some, like Dobson for example, did not fit the mold. Despite his Scots or Scots-Irish ancestry, his actions and alliances precluded his inclusion. He was not one of them.

Townspeople's potential victimhood also shaped their Scots-Irish identity. Their question to Dobson hinted at their broader belief in a conspiracy between Philadelphia Quakers and Native peoples of the Ohio country to "Kill the Scotch Irish." They held that Dobson and the firm's Quaker partners were fueling a war of extermination against them with their trade. These were powerful charges, but they knew the firm's partners would understand their message. Their confrontation with Dobson took place only four years after the Paxton Boys' uprising. This event had generated an enormous pamphlet and cartoon literature lampooning Quaker hypocrisy on defense and vilifying them for trading arms to Indians, which Pennsylvanians were acutely aware of. To them, the "Quakers' special closeness with Indians was the other side of an undue distance from other Europeans, whom they despised."[120] Quakers and Indians were not simply outsiders and thus suspect; they were united enemies. That left the Scots-Irish as the victims of these conspiratorial foes. Such an intense sense of victimhood, or the potential for it, prompted townspeople to accost Dobson as he worked that May day. The firm's trade, their actions suggested, must not threaten their lives.

Recognizing the highly charged nature of this confrontation, Dobson tried to diffuse it quickly. Contrary to "my Temper," he "answer[e]d them Very mildly" and denied their charges, although he was lying. He had "not Sent any Lead yett," he told them, but he planned to do so soon. Dobson was not foolish. He knew he was "Environed with Enemys" and thus had "to Smother my Resentment" to them because they held the reigns of local power.[121] He may also have been scared, although he did not admit it. Colonists near Carlisle, he knew, had a history of violence toward Baynton, Wharton, and Morgan and their agents. Three years earlier, in a confrontation that became famous in its retelling, a group of colonists, mostly Scots-Irishmen, their faces blackened, and calling themselves the "Black Boys," attacked the firm's wagon train as it headed to Fort Pitt carrying goods for the Indian trade. As James Smith, the most famous of them later explained, "country" people like him were "alarmed" when they heard news in 1765 that "a number of wagons loaded with Indian goods, and warlike stores," including arms, knives, and liquor, were being sent to Fort Pitt.[122] The trade, they knew, was not yet officially reopened and arms and ammunition sales were still banned as trade items. The company thus acted illegally. More significant, armed Indians had the potential to act violently against already fearful colonists like Smith. As he concluded, this trade was "a kind of murder," conducted "at the expence of the blood and treasure of the frontiers."[123]

In response, Smith and approximately fifty colonists from near the Maryland border, confronted the traders and demanded that they immediately "store up their goods."[124] Robert Callender, then one of the firm's partners and leader of the pack train, responded. He refused their request and even chided them. Still, to preserve peace, he let them inspect several barrels that were free of contraband goods in hopes of putting them off. Some woodsmen who were satisfied departed. But twenty men, including Smith, stayed; they were suspicious. Callender had sway among his town neighbors, but his persuasive powers were limited among country people like Smith. The next day, "blacked and painted," Smith and his compatriots attacked the pack train again as it moved up Sideling Hill, not far from Bedford, and shot several horses (see map 1). They allowed traders and drivers to flee to safety. Then Smith and his men burnt sixty of the eighty loads they carried, including all the lead, tomahawks, and scalping knives they found; the casks of rum they spared for themselves.[125]

Although soldiers at nearby Fort Loudon were sent to apprehend them as "robbers," Smith staunchly defended the Black Boys' actions.[126] A drinking song of the time perhaps best exemplified his views. It condemned Baynton, Wharton, and Morgan as a firm that tried "To profit itself by public blood." The Black Boys, by contrast, were "patriots" who, in destroying the property of the traders, acted "for their king and country's good." Their actions showed that interior colonists would not tolerate the illegal trading of arms to Indians, especially when directed by outsiders motivated solely by "party interest" rather than the common good.[127] Dobson and other agents certainly remembered this attack. They recalled the destruction of the firm's property and knew of other attacks that followed. Smith and the Black Boys had thus shown that they were deadly serious about policing the company's trade practices; the exchange of trade items that threatened colonists' lives or interests would not be tolerated. In fact, for a time, "it was common knowledge" on the Pennsylvania interior "that persons concerned with the Indian trade would be stopped and their possessions inspected."[128]

Still, the Black Boys' actions were mild compared to the brutal violence that took place elsewhere in Cumberland County. Agents knew about these incidents as well. During the 1760s, colonists, they realized, policed Indians as well as traders, generating an escalating pattern of violence. In 1760, for instance, colonists murdered the Indian, Doctor John, his wife, and two children in their cabin on Conodoguinet Creek, only a few miles north of Carlisle. Governor Hamilton, condemning such "horrid practices," issued a reward for the capture of their killers.[129] More significant were the strikingly brutal murders of Indians by colonist Frederick Stump that took place in the winter of 1768, just as sentiment against Baynton, Wharton, and Morgan heated up in Carlisle.

Although Stump lived in the remote Middle Creek settlement near the forks of the Susquehanna, some sixty miles north of Carlisle, his actions had bearing on the town's history. Stump was a thirty-three-year-old, Lancaster County–born German. In an appallingly brutal and unprovoked act, he and his German-born, nineteen-year-old servant, John Ironcutter, murdered and scalped ten Native American men, women, and children "in the most cruel and inhuman manner" possible.[130] Stump, a part-time rum dealer, had sold this multiethnic group of Indians liquor and gotten them drunk. When they got a bit unruly and threatened to kill him, however, he beat them to it. He murdered them all and then threw their bodies into a frozen creek. He and Ironcutter then went to their nearby settlement, killed the four who remained, and burned their cabins to the ground.[131] Despite their strong anti-

Indian sentiment, local colonists met the news of these events with horror; such brutality was unwarranted. A posse of county colonists responded by capturing Stump and Ironcutter and taking them to the county jail in Carlisle. But then provincial officials got involved and events took an unexpected twist. Fearing that Stump's violent actions would be read as a declaration of war by Native peoples, Pennsylvania officials acted. This "wicked, rash Man," as Governor John Penn described him, would be made an example along with his servant. They were to be transferred to Philadelphia where they would stand trial.[132]

Stump's brutal actions were a powerful example of colonists' violence against Indians in the 1760s. But once he arrived in Carlisle as a prisoner, he also took on symbolic meaning as a victim of outside interests, particularly a provincial establishment intent on punishing him to placate the Delawares. Furthermore, even though he was German, not Scots-Irish, and many were horrified by his actions, locals identified with his plight. They were infuriated that he was to be tried in another county. Justice and political authority were at stake here. Governor Penn's decision deprived county residents of legal authority over their own. Consequently, two days after his arrival in Carlisle, a mob of seventy or eighty armed men, most of them said to be "p[e]ople from the Frontiers" rather than the town, surrounded the jail, confronted the three local magistrates, including John Armstrong, and gained entrance to the building after holding a pistol to the jailer. Although the magistrates used "Force & Argument" to dissuade them, "in less than then ten Minutes" they rescued him and his servant "in open triumph and violation of the Law." Stump and Ironcutter were never seen again.[133]

From provincial officials' perspective, this act of defiance was a "most daring Insult upon the Laws of the Country." County officials agreed with such assessments; they were in "real distress" about this incident. As Armstrong observed, "*we* are deceiv'd and disgrac'd at once." Stump's cold-blooded murder of these "friendly" local Indians, and locals' dramatic rescue of him from jail, showed just how high tempers were in 1768. Indeed, while their rural neighbors targeted Indians, inside town, "rioters," as Armstrong termed them, directed their anger at any Euro-American individual, institution, or authority acting counter to the community's interest.[134] In this way, the antagonism directed against provincial officials during the Stump affair must be read as another facet of the same loathing townspeople expressed toward other Euro-American outsiders like trade agents in the 1760s and

British military officials in the 1750s. Colonists in and near Carlisle did not want to be told what to do. They claimed authority over themselves and their community, and were willing to defend it.

Agents like Dobson and his partner Joseph Rigby knew the score. They felt the hate of the town's Scots-Irish; heard about the destruction caused by the Black Boys; and witnessed Stump and Ironcutter's break from jail.[135] Authority, they knew, was in dispute in colonial Carlisle. But not just any authority was in question; rather, residents sought control over their economic and political lives. And they claimed this right as Scots-Irish colonists. This was a highly focused dispute, but it was also one with broad-reaching cultural and ethno-religious implications. Dobson and Rigby acknowledged these tense circumstances in their reports. As Rigby's letter at the opening of this chapter argued, for example, he and Dobson were "Surrounded by Ja-b-t-s" who pried into the firm's wagons and asked whether arms and ammunition were being sent to kill "Sc-th Irishmen."[136] Jacobites? Interesting. In the context of the British Atlantic this was an incendiary term, one Rigby hesitated to spell it out fully lest his letter be read by others. It implied that the enemies he and Dobson faced were of a surprisingly familiar kind. He associated them with the long-standing Stuart opposition to the British crown, an opposition that stood for Catholic rights, as well as broader political freedoms and agrarian rights in Scotland and Ireland into the mid 1760s. In labeling them as such, Rigby acknowledged their significance by stigmatizing them as troublemakers of a particular Old World vintage.[137]

The year 1768 was thus pivotal in Carlisle. With a power struggle underway, more townspeople turned against the firm and its agents. More demanded payment for services, while rumors of a new Indian war heightened fears of traders who were supplying them with arms. Emotions and tempers ran high. In response, Dobson, growing more fearful of his neighbors' wrath and conscious of his status as an outsider, carried out more of his duties covertly; he knew that revealing the true contents of the shipments he sent out would infuriate his neighbors. When six boxes of knives arrived from another agent in Baltimore, for example, three of them "wet through," Dobson shut himself in his house, "Lett no body in," and working "all my Self," he unpacked ninety dozen knives, wiped them down, and repacked them in clean, dry paper. His activities had to be kept secret, for he knew that "if the[y]," meaning his Scots-Irish neighbors, ever "saw Such a Quantity of Knives the[y] would think the[y] were for Scalping people." He was undoubtedly correct. Many townspeople would have been greatly troubled by the sight of these knives, for there was an immense quantity of them, over 2,300, that Dobson judged were "the Handsomest and best made for [the] Indian markett or french men that Ever I Saw." To Dobson, the sight of these knives was intriguing and even exciting. Their beauty and the memories they evoked triggered positive associations in his mind. He remarked with a note of nostalgia that "the[y] [the knives] are Just the Same make that I used to See with ye french and Indians 20 years a Go[,] all Sloaping and Sharp to the point."[138]

Although the "Indian Trade brought great wealth into this part of the Country" during the 1750s and 60s, it also provoked tension and disruption.[139] The fur and skin trade built Carlisle into a way station between regions by the 1760s. The town was a setting for treaty making; it was a refuge where interior colonists fled during times of unrest; it was a strategic launching pad from which the British staged and supplied one of their most important military offensives of the Seven Years' War; finally, it was a conveniently located trans-shipment point where a Philadelphia trade firm with interests in the Illinois country placed agents to oversee the movements of goods and peltry between east and west.

At the same time, the trade paradoxically tore Carlisle asunder. It intensified political and cultural rivalries and worsened the ethnic, religious, and cultural tensions that fostered hate. Equally important, the trade created winners and losers. Trader Robert Callender was the most notable winner. He reinvented himself during these two decades. First, as a fur trader, later as an Indian fighter at Kittanning, as wagonmaster general for the Forbes campaign, partner of Baynton, Wharton, and Morgan, and finally as one of their chief rivals in the Illinois trade, Callender successfully rode the often treacherous waves of change sweeping the mid-Atlantic interior at mid-century. Although he never obtained great wealth, he gained social capital. Many, though not all, of his neighbors also benefited from the opportunities the trade offered. Tavern keepers and shopkeepers found that the movement of people and goods through town was good for business. Others earned income by hiring out their horses and wagons. Haulers and drivers, as well as many of the town's craftsmen, found work, which offered important sources of income during tough times.

Others were less fortunate. By the 1760s, Indians were mostly alienated as threatening outsiders. For them, Carlisle was no longer the kind of contested terrain they might claim for treaty making, even temporarily. Some Carlisle

residents were willing and even eager to trade with them, but few were willing to host them as visitors or tolerate them as neighbors as they had in the
early 1750s. Cultural lines between peoples, though by no means imperme-
able, were drawn and Indians stood on the outside. Then, too, inside Carlisle,
imperial conflict, interior warfare, and the changing context of the fur and
skin trade fostered ethno-religious alignments that fractured the town's Euro-American community. A Scots-Irish, Presbyterian "us" mobilized against
a "them" of various outsiders whenever the town's safety or political authority
was threatened. Yet it was the stark divisions among Carlisle's Euro-American
colonists, marked by townspeople turning on their neighbors as enemies like
never before, that most affected the town and its inhabitants.

There was a tragic side to Carlisle's development during the 1750s and
1760s, one that went beyond the bloodshed of the frontier wars of the time.
For those of the town's Scots-Irish Presbyterian community who opposed
agents like Dobson, hatred—motivated by fear and likely intensified by
Old World divisions—left them defensive and reactionary. Such opposition
pulled them together by encouraging their assertion of a distinctive local
identity. But there were also costs, because it divided them. Men like Dobson
who were the objects of their wrath were shunned. He was trapped in a town
where he did not belong or want to be. As he admitted to his employers, "if it
was not for the business that you are Pleas[e]d to favour me with . . . I believe
I would not Live Long in this County." Carlisle, he noted disdainfully, "is
a Dead Place."[140] But Dobson was also dead in a metaphorical way. He had
gambled and lost. By 1769, the company he worked for so diligently was falling rapidly into bankruptcy and his neighbors hated him. He was trapped.
Because "my mon[e]y is at interest here," he explained, he was "obliged . . . to
Reside hear a few years Longer."[141] Perhaps then Dobson, although a prickly
and sometimes unsympathetic character, should be seen, like Native peoples,
as a victim of the sometimes cruel workings of the Atlantic world economy
and cultural politics at mid-century. Despite its potential for riches, the fur
and skin trade brought him few tangible rewards. As time progressed, he sank
into obscurity, falling in status on local records from gentleman to yeoman,
and finally disappearing from Carlisle's public records entirely by 1779.

Thus, as the 1760s closed, Carlisle and its inhabitants were important
players on a real and metaphorical road of imperial politics, trade, and cultural relations stretching from Europe, across Pennsylvania, and into America's westward and southern interiors. Yet while the road and Carlisle's place
on it were firmly established, how this road was to develop through time, and

who, exactly, was going to control it, remained unclear. Indians were mostly, though not entirely, eliminated from the picture near Carlisle. So were the French with Great Britain's victory in the Seven Years' War. Yet Great Britain, Pennsylvania's proprietors, profit-hungry Philadelphia merchants, and a host of competing ethno-religious groups inside and outside the town remained, each with its own interests in controlling the region and its real and metaphorical access ways.

CHAPTER FOUR

War and Revolution

SOON AFTER THE signing of the Declaration of Independence in July 1776, John Montgomery—one of Carlisle's wealthiest men by the 1770s and chair of the county's Committee of Inspection and Observation, the political body then governing the town—wrote "With pleasure" to John Hancock, president of the Continental Congress, to "assure you that a noble Spirit appears amongst the Inhabitants here." According to a proud Montgomery, who was a successful storekeeper, soldier, and local politician, "the spirit of marching to the Defence of our Country is so prevalent in this Town, that We shall not have Men left sufficient to mount Guard."[1]

Carlisle residents, Montgomery argued, were excited by the challenge before them. Like many other Americans, they had imbibed in the "Spirit" of revolution sweeping the colonies in 1776 and were eager to fight. But unlike others swept up in the excitement of the American cause, their enthusiasm was not new. Rather, these townspeople and their rural neighbors had already established a pattern of service. The year before the county had raised one of America's first rifle battalions, commanded by another Carlisle leading man, the forty-year-old Scots-Irishman Colonel William Thompson, an experienced soldier who had fought alongside John Armstrong against the Delawares at Kittanning. Thompson's battalion, as it was called, marched north to defend Boston in 1775 and then fought gallantly in Canada; Thompson, a newly appointed brigadier general, was taken prisoner there. His men, however, fought on without him at New York, many re-enlisting in 1776.

Montgomery, like other local Whigs, was immensely proud of this battalion's fortitude. But he assured Hancock that the county was willing to do more; they had five additional army and three militia companies prepared to send to George Washington's aid.[2] Just let them join the fight. "The good men of Cumberland County," said another local Whig, stood in "readiness . . . to March on the shortest Notice."[3]

Montgomery's letter said much about Carlisle residents' enthusiastic mood in 1776. Townspeople, like their county neighbors, did not wish to remain on the sidelines. Rather, by seeking to position themselves between British enemy outsiders and American communities like Boston and New York that needed defending, they expressed their desire to be central players in this war for independence. And they were well prepared for this challenging task. Having negotiated their town's function as a place in-between and their role as its mediators during the 1750s and 1760s, Carlisle men were accustomed to weathering risk, uncertainty, and conflict between regions and peoples. This was part of their town's history and their personal experiences as its inhabitants. Thus, taking the bold move to join the Revolution did not frighten them. They were ready to insert themselves into the middle of this British-American conflict. But still, while assuming such risk when negotiating the spaces between others was familiar, Carlisle's residents approached the Revolution with an unprecedented collective spirit of unity and eagerness. This was something new. During the 1760s, being a people in-between had fostered a climate of suspicion, distrust, and hostility among Carlisle residents, often dividing neighbor from neighbor and pitting insiders against outsiders. By contrast, in 1776, not even ten years later, with a new group of outsiders, the British, having invaded "our Country," as Montgomery termed it, residents put aside the quarrels that separated them, reigned in their ethnic localism, and united behind an American cause that transcended their town. This struggle, unlike others in the recent past, was not just about them or the mid-Atlantic region; it focused instead on the uncertain fate of a new United States of America. In response, a powerful revolutionary élan gripped the town; it captured townspeople's imaginations and spurred them to action.

War and revolution set significant changes in motion that simultaneously built on and shattered precedents in Carlisle's twenty-five year history. Some of these changes, like the spirit of voluntarism Montgomery detailed, were readily visible in town—officials could literally count the number of men willing to serve. So, too, were changes in the townscape as the Revolution altered Carlisle's meaning and function as a place. War dramatically reconfigured America's Atlantic trade by shutting off British markets. Meanwhile, wartime diplomacy held Native American neutrality, not trade, as its primary goal. In consequence, the fur and skin trade, a mainstay of Carlisle's colonial economy, declined dramatically.[4] And thus, with Carlisle no longer functioning as the town in-between West and East that it had been since its founding, townspeople found themselves scrambling for new senses of purpose and communal identity. But they did not scramble for long. The war offered new opportunities to serve, while Congress quickly assigned Carlisle new wartime functions as a holding site for prisoners and as a critical supply and arms manufacturing depot for the Continental Army. These functions confirmed the town's continuing role as a place in-between, but they simultaneously reconfigured how that betweenness was expressed and experienced.

There were other significant changes. Although these shifts were less visible, they were equally momentous in how they affected townspeople's lives. War and revolution posed a dizzying array of choices to all Americans, and Carlisle townspeople were accustomed to negotiating their options. But because more was at stake in this conflict than any before, townspeople—both those who served and those who remained on the homefront—had much to weigh when deciding how to respond. The American Revolution thus posed new and dramatic risks and opportunities for all Carlisle residents that had to be negotiated with particular care and caution.

As the American Revolution began, the town's mood was optimistic, even buoyant. Carlisle residents like John Montgomery had good reason to brag of their contributions. The town's early and warm response to America's cause was exceptional compared to other communities in Pennsylvania; Montgomery did not exaggerate. The town's middling and lower sorts, joined by their county neighbors, flocked to join the ranks of several army and militia regiments raised locally. Many leading men, meanwhile, jumped even faster to volunteer for leadership positions in politics and the military; a surprising number became key figures in the Revolution's vanguard. Indeed, Carlisle was home to three signers of the Declaration of Independence—James Smith, George Ross, and, best known of all, James Wilson, a Scottish born, American-trained attorney who became one of the nation's leading conservative politicians. Equally significant, besides William Thompson, Carlisle also produced several other high-ranking military officers early in the war; they included John Armstrong, Major-General in command of the Pennsylvania militia, and another Scots-Irishman, William Irvine, who, like Thompson, rose to the rank of brigadier general in the Continental Army. Ephraim Blaine, the fur trader who was an agent of Baynton, Wharton, and Morgan in the 1760s, became the army's Commissary General of Purchases by 1780. Carlisle even claimed one of the war's legendary female figures, Mary Ludwig Hays McCauley. She was the servant who accompanied her husband to the battlefield at Monmouth in 1778 and whose heroic actions in hauling water to the troops earned her the nickname "Molly Pitcher."[5]

But Carlisle residents were also exceptional because they were enthusiastic about the *idea* of revolution even before the war began. Beginning in 1774, and perhaps earlier, they were fired up about British measures imposed on the colonies and identified strongly with the plight of Massachusetts. Their supportive, even radical, stance stood in stark contrast to the slow and lukewarm responses from many others in Pennsylvania, particularly in the Delaware Valley.[6] At a town meeting held at the Presbyterian church on the square during the summer of 1774, almost nine months before the first shots were fired at Lexington and Concord, Carlisle residents made their position public. This meeting, the town's best-known prewar expression of anti-British sentiment, was convened at the behest of town leaders, particularly many of its Scots-Irish or Scots leading men like Montgomery, Armstrong, Wilson, Robert Callender, and soon-to-be military leaders like William Thompson and William Irvine. It was intended not as a rowdy protest but as a peaceful attempt to voice political opposition to Britain's Intolerable Acts, Boston's punishment for the Tea Party. More specifically, the meeting was a response to a circular letter from Pennsylvania's political leaders, including Wilson's mentor, the moderate John Dickinson, which called on Pennsylvania's Whigs "to rally the friends of colonial liberty in every town of the Province."[7]

John Montgomery presided over this "very respectable Meeting" of these "friends" of liberty. From it came seven resolves that expressed local sympathy for Boston's suffering, called for united actions to redress the colonies' grievances—including nonimportation of British goods—and pledged locals' willingness to "contribute to the relief of their suffering brethren in Boston."[8] The last resolve initiated the formation of a county committee of correspondence; its members were to be drawn from among the town's proprietors' men, many of them organizers of the meeting. The new committee included Montgomery, Armstrong, Wilson, and Callender, as well as Blaine, Thompson, and Irvine. Those in attendance then selected Wilson, Irvine, and attorney Robert Magaw—later a Continental Army colonel—as their deputies to the first Continental Congress. Not long afterwards, county voters further committed themselves to America's cause by selecting a new thirteen-member committee of observation to oversee public affairs and enforce the boycott. As one historian notes, the appointment of nearly one hundred people to act as enforcers of the boycott was "an indication" of the county's "fervor."[9]

Carlisle was a town prepared to resist; town residents wanted others to know that. As another local leader asserted proudly, for example, "ever since the Tyrannical Measures taken by the King and Parliament of Great Britain to enslave these (now) Free and Independent American States," he had "Join'd heartily in the Opposition for the Support of Freedom." British tyranny would not be tolerated by him or others. By his reckoning, it was the "uniform attachment to the Independence of the United States" that distinguished his fellow townsmen and him from others in the state.[10] That six hundred local men came forward to take the oath of allegiance to the United States confirmed his observations. Locals could put aside their differences and gather behind a cause. "No people," historians note, "held representative government more dear than did the Scotch-Irish settlers of Carlisle."[11]

But what brought them to this position? Why were so many local men supportive of revolution? And how did Pennsylvania's interior, of which Carlisle was an integral part, earn its reputation as the state's strongest pro-American, anti-British region?[12] Without doubt, the large number of Scots-Irish immigrants in Carlisle and the county influenced the intensity of local commitment. These immigrants came to Pennsylvania seeking opportunity because Britain's colonialism had constrained them or their families in Ulster; they had already felt the pinch of British regulation and did not wish to do so again. Equally important was their Presbyterianism. In Ireland, British authority had defined them as dissenters and subordinated them to Anglicans. In Pennsylvania, their religion excluded the most privileged among them from the colony's Quaker aristocracy. Several scholars say these unjust and exclusionary experiences encouraged them to view the world as "a struggle between freedom and tyranny, between Dissenters and Anglicans, and between a virtuous people and a selfish, dissolute aristocracy."[13] Shared anger and frustration thus fueled their fervor. But that was not all—there was another issue at stake. Presbyterians feared that Britain's attempts to regulate the colonies would also bring the imposition of an established church to America. For this reason, it was no accident that Carlisle's revolutionary leaders counted several Presbyterian church elders among their numbers, or that they chose to hold their first public meeting in the Presbyterian meetinghouse on the square. Not just politics, but fundamental ethno-religious issues tied to their personal and group identities were in dispute. Presbyterianism defined their opposition to Britain, much as it had prompted them to oppose the Quaker party's preference for royal government in the colony the decade before. The coming revolution thus morphed the ethnic localism that divided the town in the 1760s into a potent component of a new American identity set in opposition to Great Britain. In response, Carlisle's Scots-Irish Presbyterians found themselves central players on the state and national stage.[14]

Townspeople also had significant personal motives for joining this revolution. Status considerations, in particular, loomed large in fueling men's zeal. Sensing personal opportunities in the dramatic changes sweeping America, local men seized on them. War and revolution had prompted various upheavals across the colonies; in Pennsylvania, where the Revolution became a dual rebellion against British and provincial authority, the turbulence was especially profound. The proprietors were gone. Thomas Penn died in 1775. The Revolution then formally ended proprietary control, marking a monumental political turning point in the colony's history.[15] In Carlisle, such change had dramatic ramifications, for the proprietary town was suddenly without its proprietor and the lines of authority governing the town were unclear. Some town and county residents rejoiced; long suspicious of the proprietor's goals, they now were free of his officials' meddling. But for a core group of the town's leading men who had long supported Penn in return for patronage, the demise of the proprietorship left a significant void. They rushed to fill it by joining the revolutionary cause; tapping into the evolving lines of American authority was a strategy to re-anchor their status.

The war also drove pacifist Quakers from positions of provincial political leadership, particularly in the colony's assembly. Their withdrawal left an even bigger political power vacuum in its wake. This paved the way for a dramatic internal revolution in Pennsylvania politics when a group of radical politicians, led by a coalition of lower and middling sorts that included many Scots-Irishmen of the interior, seized power in 1776. These new leaders, which included a number of prominent Cumberland County men, expressed their vision for a more representative government in the new state constitution they drafted—a plan of government one scholar calls "the most radical . . . of the Revolutionary era."[16] Suddenly Carlisle residents, like other Pennsylvanians, scrambled to claim their place in the new political landscape rapidly taking shape around them. They sensed correctly that men of the interior had new opportunities to lead the state in ways they had been mostly shut off from before. Thus, seeking eagerly to prove that they were more than just "a parcel of upstart[s]" from the interior, they seized what they justifiably perceived as a new political day.[17]

The dramatic political shifts prompted by war and revolution offered townspeople unprecedented chances for advancement. Carlisle's leading men, the group who spearheaded their county's political opposition, pursued them with vigor; seeing opportunities for leadership, economic advancement, and even assimilation in the Revolution, they adapted quickly to the shifting political landscape of the 1770s. Proprietary patronage was gone, but with political representation broadening, the Revolution offered them new access to significant positions of authority in state and national politics. And unlike other Scots-Irish proprietors' men in towns like Easton or Allentown who withdrew from the conflict or became loyalists, Carlisle's leading men, although mostly politically moderate or conservative, remained firmly committed to the cause. They hoped that the American Revolution would advance their careers by earning them favorable reputations beyond the interior. Equally important, because so many of them were immigrants, service to the new state and nation promised firmer status as Americans.[18]

James Wilson, probably the best known of Carlisle's leading men, exemplifies this pattern. The Scots-born Wilson came to Philadelphia in 1765, just as anti-British sentiment was building. After reading law with John Dickinson (about the time he was writing his *Letters from a Farmer in Pennsylvania*), Wilson began practicing law, working first in Reading, and then Carlisle by 1770. Ambition brought Wilson to Carlisle; its bar, which was more open than others, offered him greater prospects of advancement. Once in town, he ingratiated himself to court officials and cultivated friendships with the town's Scots-Irish leaders, including Armstrong, Montgomery, and newcomers like physician William Irvine. He found success quickly as an attorney. When the Revolution began, however, his sights shifted; he saw a chance to leave Carlisle behind and advance to a political life in the metropolis. Wilson thus positioned himself carefully. He participated actively in Carlisle's public political protests and wrote his own critique of parliamentary authority. By 1778, with his political fortunes tied firmly to the state and nation in Philadelphia, Wilson sold his Carlisle house and moved his wife and three children to the city. He left the interior behind by riding the tide of Revolution. Yet his opposition to Pennsylvania's radical constitution, legal defense of the Penn family's estates, and later support for the U.S. Constitution earned him a well-deserved reputation as a conservative. Like many of his privileged Carlisle neighbors, Wilson, though an opportunist, was no political radical.[19]

Wilson took the political route to advancement. Many of his neighbors, by contrast, leaned instead toward military service as Continental Army officers. William Irvine is perhaps the best example. Irvine was an Ulster immigrant, born in Enniskillen in 1741. Coming from a well-to-do family, he trained as a physician at Trinity College, Dublin, before serving as a surgeon in the British Navy during the Seven Years' War. He came to Carlisle upon emigrating to America in 1765, likely drawn there by John Armstrong, another Enniskillen immigrant and friend. Once in Carlisle, as only one of two physicians practicing in or near town, he achieved modest economic success, falling into the top 20 percent of taxpayers, and, like Wilson, developed friendships among the town's leading men. But he remained restless and dissatisfied. Unlike his neighbors, he played no apparent public role in the town's political workings and was unmarried.[20] His friend Armstrong even remarked in 1772 that Irvine had a strong desire to "go to Sea and afterward settle in Ireland" again.[21] Soon after, however, his circumstances changed. He married fur trader Robert Callender's eldest daughter, Ann, and she brought him economic resources and kin connections to the proprietors' men who controlled the town. Then came the Revolution, which offered Irvine an opportunity to serve the nation. Irvine leaped at the chance, having had British naval experience—here was a possibility to put his experience to use in America as a way to establish himself and advance his career. Between 1776 and his death in 1804, he served as a colonel and a brigadier general in the Continental Army, including a stint as commander at Fort Pitt from 1781 to 1783. Once established as an officer, he parlayed his experience into other forms of national service. He was elected as a delegate to Congress in 1786 and 1793, helped to settle the Whiskey Rebellion in 1794, and in 1800 was made Superintendent of Military Stores for the army.[22] For Irvine, the Revolution offered myriad opportunities for advancement. Military service put him on the national stage and won him status and authority.

Carlisle's leading men were not the only locals to jump on the revolutionary bandwagon for personal reasons. The area's middling and lower sorts had their own reasons for supporting the Revolution that were rooted in their experiences as artisans, retailers, laborers, and farmers. A number of scholars argue that Pennsylvania's lower and middling sorts found their real and metaphorical voice during the Revolution. The collective political voice they found, particularly in rural Cumberland County, was a radical one willing to challenge the existing order in the interest of promoting greater social equality and political democracy. Much like their privileged urban neighbors, they used the disruptions of war and revolution, and the power vacuum created with the end of proprietary and Quaker leadership in Pennsylvania, to carve out new authority for themselves as radical state politicians and military leaders. New opportunities abounded and they seized them as well. Cumberland County, for example, was home to farmer Robert Whitehill, a leader of the state's radical faction, and one of James Wilson's chief political opponents.[23] It was also home to James Smith, leader of the Black Boys, the frontiersmen who forcibly policed the fur trade in the 1760s. When the Revolution began, as Smith explained, he did not attend meetings in Carlisle or draft resolves—he acted by redirecting his experience fighting outsiders toward fighting the British. Smith served as a western representative and then fought for the Continental Army in New Jersey. Later, as a colonel, he turned to the militia and took up fighting Native peoples in the West. For this former Indian captive and frontier vigilante, the Revolution offered the chance to legitimize his authority and express his identity as an independent man of the interior by fighting for the American cause. By risking his life to fight the British, a man some considered a bandit won acclaim as a revolutionary and a patriot. Much like his more privileged neighbors Wilson and Irvine, the Revolution gave Smith's life story new meaning.[24]

Personal motives among the county's middling and lower sorts also took more ideological forms. Many local men volunteered for service to advance the broader political principles of liberty and democracy that they held dear. In doing so, they made the American cause their own; no matter what their economic status, the men of Cumberland County were "desireous to Assist in the Present Struggle in Defence of American Liberty."[25] Their enthusiasm distinguished them from many others in Pennsylvania, especially during the war's first years; "central Pennsylvania," as two scholars note, "provided the core of the state's support for the cause."[26] More significant, they served despite having had firsthand experiences with especially brutal forms of intercultural warfare during the 1750s and 1760s, a fact that earned them notoriety. As one army officer writing from Carlisle noted: "The Pennsylvanians think themselves inferior to none in Zeal, Bravery, or Conduct."[27]

Though such claims contained hyperbole, they also had basis in fact. Responding to calls for volunteers following the battles of Lexington and Concord in the spring of 1775, for instance, some 3,000 local men enlisted in the militia; they accounted for nearly three-quarters of Pennsylvania's entire quota. Two of these regiments were among the first sent to aid Washington in the battles for Long Island.[28] Even before Americans declared their independence, militiamen were willing to risk their lives to fight British tyranny in locations far distant from their homes; they sought to place themselves at the center of the action. Their actions confirm that their motives went beyond localized concerns for defense of family, home, and community; rather, they fought because larger ideals that they held dear were at stake. Some of those ideals, particularly of a democratic political sort, came into stark relief in the governance of the county's militia, which gained a reputation as being particularly radical. As historian Steven Rosswurm notes, the Cumberland County Committee of Privates, the elected body representing the county's militia, was known for its egalitarianism; it made bold, but ultimately unfulfilled, calls for annual elections of officers, equal votes between officers and privates in courts martial, and the replacement of whipping with fines.[29]

Then, too, there was the service local men gave to Thompson's Rifle Battalion, the only regiment of the Pennsylvania Line to march in defense of Boston in spring 1775.[30] Thompson's battalion was drawn mostly from Cumberland County. Two of the companies came exclusively from Carlisle; one was captained by the grandson of Tobias Hendricks, one of the first Euro-American colonists in the Valley.[31] In hindsight, their intense commitment to fighting this war of independence helped secure American liberty. It also solidified their identity as Americans and men. In the war's aftermath, they sought recognition for the dangers they faced while fighting the British, especially so early in war. For example, after being taken prisoner at the Battle of Trois Rivières, William Thompson, to his great frustration, sat out the rest of the war as a paroled but unexchanged prisoner unable, he said, "to share in the honour and danger of defending his country." Still, he took pride that "even his enemies acknowledged he had done his duty and behaved gallantly." He had not surrendered, but was "taken in the field with his sword in his hand."[32] For Thompson, demonstrating bravery and honor on the battlefield legitimized his personal claims to authority as an American. His service also helped to move Carlisle from the periphery to the center of this conflict.

His men showed similar desires to "shar[e] in the dangers of [t]his country."[33] After the war, their service was a cornerstone of their identities. Henry McEwen, for instance, a private in William Hendricks's company, was among the first locals to volunteer for Thompson's battalion in 1775. During his year of service, the company marched to Massachusetts. McEwen, like his fellow soldier, New Jersey–born Philip Hornbaker, who also enlisted at Carlisle, fought first at Bunker Hill and then trekked "through the wilderness to Quebec," where they suffered serious defeat by the British in January 1776.

Many were killed, including Hendricks, who was shot through the chest. Others were wounded, including McEwen, who was stabbed through the hand with a bayonet. Still others, like McEwen and Hornbaker, were taken prisoner along with Thompson. McEwen was paroled and finally exchanged in 1778. He did not serve again. Hornbaker, however, reenlisted, returning to the battlefield at Monmouth and later joining the New Jersey militia.[34] To these men, as to Thompson, their early and voluntary service demonstrated their ardor for America and their worthiness as men.

Cumberland County men also offered service in the Sixth, and later Seventh, Pennsylvania Battalions, authorized in 1776, commanded by William Irvine. Irvine's battalions, like Thompson's, were tight-knit with a strong local feel to them; they illustrated how town and county residents could overcome their differences and unite to serve the American cause. Comprised mostly of Scots-Irishmen, the Seventh Pennsylvania was also knit together by its members' mostly shared ethnic identity.[35] Irvine, the commanding officer, thought well of his men, many of whom were his neighbors and fellow countrymen from Ireland. As he noted: "My Battalion is more than full & many of the men are fine fellows indeed."[36] His men felt equally strong attachments to him. Even Francis O'Hara, one of the sizable minority of Irish Catholics who served alongside their Protestant brethren in the Seventh Pennsylvania, stayed with Irvine for the duration of the war. Loyal to the cause and the officers they served under—sometimes even "declar[ing] they will enlist with no other"—men like O'Hara followed Irvine to various fronts in eastern America, including Bunker Hill, Quebec, Long Island, New York, Trenton, Monmouth, Brandywine, and Germantown.[37] They had an intense commitment to the cause and their commander.

By the end of the war, with the county having raised thirteen infantry companies for the Continental Army, locals took enormous pride in their community's contributions to the cause; in volunteering they had placed themselves and by extension Carlisle at the war's center. Their eager service demonstrated, as one young volunteer said proudly, an indisputable "patriotic Spirit & a readiness to Serve his country in all cases."[38] As militiamen and soldiers they risked their lives to serve the war's many theaters, from Boston and New York to Canada, and from Philadelphia to Yorktown. In retrospect, because they remembered defending America as their primary motive for fighting, they portrayed themselves as men who transcended the local and embraced the national. Militiaman James Irwin, for example, was proud that he had "voluntarily marched for the Defence of American Liberty at the beginning of the war." He served "Voluntarily" and even without pay to defend residents of Northumberland County when they were under attack.[39] Brice Smith was another militiaman "of Fidelity & Patriotism."[40] The Irish-born John Tate, a resident of nearby Shippensburg, first volunteered for militia service at the age of eighteen. Although a newcomer to America, he went "against the Tories" at Philadelphia and Monmouth. Soon after being discharged, he was "hired . . . to fill out a draft" and fought at Brandywine. Tate served a third term of enlistment when he volunteered again in 1781.[41]

For Irwin, Smith, and Tate, men of humble means who were accustomed to operating on the margins of British society in Europe and America, military service was a potent force shaping their identities; it imbued them with pride and status. For the Irish-born Tate, as for some commanding officers like Thompson or Irvine who were also immigrants, soldiering was a vehicle of assimilation into a new culture. Fighting for the defense of their new country won soldiers the right to claim an identity as Americans. Military service also accorded them new respect as men. Officers got the added bonus of military titles, which along with their service established their status as gentlemen in America. But there was more—military service was also a democratizing force. Choosing to serve fostered a collective sense of purpose and belonging that gave even ordinary soldiers standing in the nation's public sphere. By war's end, having distinguished themselves as brave men and superior American patriots, they expected public recognition and the right to participate on a more equal basis in society.[42] Theirs was a highly personal commitment to American liberty. It was also one expressive of a proto-nationalism. As Isaac Thompson, a private from Thompson's Rifle Battalion explained, he enlisted because troops were "being raised to defend the rights of the then colonies against the encroachments of the British Parliament."[43] He, like others, identified these "rights of the then colonies" as their own; they were citizens, not subjects. In these ways, serving either the political revolution or the military war offered Carlisle men new opportunities for advancement. The risks were enormous, but there was much to be gained. Carlisle men knew this well, but were willing to risk all by positioning themselves as central players in this revolutionary war.

Carlisle men and their neighbors in the county reached out in large numbers to volunteer for political and military service; they were enthusiastic and dedicated patriots who were eager to pull themselves from the periphery of the conflict to its centers. Yet the town's revolutionary élan during the war's early years was built on more than some men's fervent ideological commitment to change or their ambitious pursuit of self-interest. With the fate of the nation up for grabs, more was at stake in the Revolution than individual destinies and personal identities. That fact came into focus sharply as war and revolution arrived quickly and visibly in town, reorienting Carlisle's geographic situation in the mid-Atlantic, altering the townscape, redefining its functions as a place in-between, and affecting all townspeople—male and female, privileged and poor, free and unfree.

Changes in the townscape were among the first and most significant signs of the Revolution's arrival in Carlisle; they signaled shifts in the relevance of the mid-Atlantic's geography and direction of the town's history. With the fighting war distant from the town and the political revolution headquartered mostly in Philadelphia, Carlisle was no longer the same kind of town in-between it was in the 1750s or 1760s. Most Americans, including Carlisle residents, had redirected their attention away from the Native peoples and trade of the West and toward repelling the British invasion of America's coastal communities. For townspeople, this marked a major change in their geographical orientation as they suddenly found themselves more often facing east, north, and even south, rather than west—the direction of so much of their energies and animosities during the colonial period. This also meant that although Carlisle remained a town in-between, its betweenness was no longer shaped along an east-west, but instead along a north-south, trajectory; the town's situation in the mid-Atlantic, in short, had changed. Furthermore, the demands of fighting this war gave new meaning to the town itself by reconfiguring the townscape and the accompanying senses of place, purpose, and function that defined it. Still though, not everything was different; fundamental continuities remained from the colonial past. The very real changes wrought by this war and revolution still built on Carlisle's betweenness in the mid-Atlantic. Meetinghouses, churches, and the courthouse, for example, were the structures that framed the daily workings of colonial Carlisle, while stores, taverns, and warehouses had signaled its role as a way station in the fur trade. War and revolution, by contrast, thrust new town spaces and structures, like the jail and the public works, into the foreground of people's consciousness; their prominence was grounded in the central functions they and the town served during the war. In this way, even though Carlisle was no longer a proprietary town nor a way station in the trade, as a holding place for prisoners of war and a critical supply and arms manufacturing center for the Continental Army, it continued to function as a place in-between others in the mid-Atlantic.

Congress recognized Carlisle's potential to serve the war from the start. They instigated the first noticeable shift in the town's function in the mid-Atlantic when they designated Carlisle—along with Reading, Lancaster, and York—as places for the "disposition" of prisoners taken in the battles for Canada in late 1775. As centrally situated interior towns distant from the fighting but still easily accessible by road, Congress saw these Pennsylvania towns as ideal safe havens for those they wanted removed from the action.[44] For Carlisle, this new role as home to high-profile prisoners of war heralded the first of many wartime changes that were not of residents' own making; it signaled how the war came to them, whether they wanted it or not. The gravity of this charge became clear as the first prisoners arrived. Among them was a group of ten English officers and their servants, which included Major John André and Lieutenant Edward Despard. André, the infamous British Adjutant General tried and executed some years later as a spy for his role in Benedict's Arnold's defection to the British, was one of a group of young British military officers who were defeated by a force led by Richard Montgomery and captured at St. John's. They were held first in Lancaster County until fears of loyalist uprisings prompted their removal to Carlisle.[45] Arriving at a time when anti-British sentiments were running especially high in town, their presence posed a dilemma for Carlisle's Whig leaders. Where would they be housed? How would they be protected? Even more worrisome, what influence would they have on the community? Would they sway those who remained uncommitted? To resolve the question of lodgings, town leaders designated several ordinary town buildings for their confinement. In doing so, however, they inadvertently elevated these buildings from their humble status as dwellings to central focal points in Carlisle's townscape and structures of considerable importance to the nation's security.

Local histories confirm these shifts. According to these works, Irishman Samuel Stewart's modest stone tavern house along one of the town's two main streets gained considerable notoriety when it became the temporary home of André, Despard, and their servants in 1776.[46] The arrival of these well-known British officers inspired much curiosity, and perhaps even some commotion. Because anti-British sentiment was so intense in Carlisle early in the war, they were not welcome arrivals. Town residents—many of them overtly hostile, a few others perhaps sympathetic—watched intently as these two British prisoners were granted the courtesies extended to gentlemen, to roam freely inside town and beyond into the Valley, coming and going from their quarters on a daily basis. Their presence further galvanized local anti-British sentiment; although the war was distant, their presence reminded residents of the Revolution's proximity.[47]

Many townspeople were repulsed by these enemy gentlemen living in their midst. They witnessed the freedom of movement granted these officers; the humble sorts among them also likely observed the genteel care and accommodations accorded to these prisoners as men of status and rank. Resentment grew, and in a town in which residents had never been shy about expressing their displeasure with governing authorities or outsiders, its civilians made their objections known. As André reported, he and Despard were "every day pelted and reviled in the streets"; they were "fired at" and even "waylaid by men determined to assassinate us." Furthermore, townspeople, whom André described disdainfully as a "greasy committee of worsted-stocking knaves," knew exactly where to find them. With two notorious British prisoners in residence, Stewart's tavern was a structure locals knew well; it stood out on the townscape. Yet this tavern and its prisoners also drew much attention to Carlisle from outsiders, casting the town once again as a central stage for the collective expressions of local tension and uncertainty. As proof, at one point in 1776 when tempers against Britain were especially high, a militia company from the countryside marched into town, assembled outside the tavern, and began calling for the two men's lives. Local lore holds that it was only the intercession of Stewart's neighbor, Mrs. Ramsey, that turned back the crowd, thus sparing their lives.[48]

These prisoners had more insidious effects on town dynamics; their presence made Carlisle's Whig leaders tremendously nervous. The war had just begun and many local revolutionaries, despite all evidence to the contrary, were uncertain of their neighbors' loyalties. They especially feared the apathetic and perhaps hostile who remained hidden among them and wanted desperately to stifle internal dissent in order to preserve the pro-American unity that distinguished Carlisle from other, more divided Pennsylvania communities. For these reasons, they were concerned about the effect of these prisoners' "Conversation[s]" on their neighbors. Such men, they noted, had already "influenced many weak & ignorant Persons . . . in Town, as within the six Miles around it." Even worse, with the servants of these British officers moving about town dressed in the "hunting Shirts & Trousers, the Uniform of our People," local Whigs worried that some of their more humble, less educated, and less committed neighbors might closely identify with them and facilitate their escape; these prisoners were a potentially problematic influence.[49]

Their fears were genuine. Although most residents, caught up in the heady enthusiasm for America during the war's early years, remained resolutely set against these two famous prisoners and the nation they represented, some former British soldiers as well as loyalists, though limited in number, posed threats to Carlisle and its expanding number of military installations. The most dramatic scare came ironically enough in 1776, the same year that so many town inhabitants were caught up in the fevered pitch of the new war. Carlisle merchant John Holmes revealed a plot by a British deserter, a Scot, to raise one hundred loyalists to attack the town's public works and burn its stores. By Holmes's account, this plot was part of a widespread conspiracy in the county that stemmed from the subversive influence of these prisoners of war in Carlisle. Although this plot was never carried out because Congress sent two companies of soldiers to guard the public works, it heightened fears of how the influence of high-profile British prisoners might sway local people. These concerns persisted until André and Despard were marched off to new quarters in New Jersey in late 1776, where they were exchanged and returned to service.[50] With their departure, local tumult subsided for a time and Stewart's tavern receded into the background of Carlisle's townscape; it was no longer a structure of central public import.

Although Congress relocated André and Despard, it continued to use Carlisle as a safe and centrally located interior site to house prisoners. After the British occupied Philadelphia in 1777, the prisoners housed at Carlisle were prominent American loyalists, not British prisoners of war, and they were lodged in the humble public spaces of Carlisle's jail rather than private structures like Stewart's tavern. The war refocused Carlisle's townscape yet again by elevating another structure, the jail—the simple and coarsely built stone building on the corner of High and Bedford Streets—to a new position of public prominence. It was another symbol of the Revolution's arrival in Carlisle.[51]

Conditions at the jail also attracted negative attention from Congress. This happened when two of the men held there, Major Richard Stockton of New Jersey and Dr. John Kearsley of Philadelphia, both privileged American gentlemen, began a letter-writing campaign to protest the deplorable conditions of the jail. Kearsley, an ardent loyalist who had taken a public stand against the Revolution and been beaten, arrested, and jailed for his actions, began by drafting a letter to the county committee. Having been held previously in the jail in nearby York, where he was housed as a gentleman might expect, Kearsley was shocked by the extreme and often hostile conditions he experienced in Carlisle. His accommodations were unfitting a gentleman and perilous to his health, he said. Describing himself in a "Critical" condition after nearly a year of imprisonment, Kearsley, fearing for his life, explained that "the room in which I have my Lodging is so open and Cold that it has brought on me a . . . fever which has ended in a Dangerous Obstruction of the Liver." He requested either that the room be "altered" or that he be transferred to a more acceptable apartment, noting that he "hardly [thought] the Committee of Cumberland mean to take away my Life." Although Kearsley's fears were well founded (he died shortly after writing this letter), he hoped at this point in 1777 that county officials "will do what is Humane and necessary for their own Honor."[52]

Eight of his fellow captives, including the other gentleman Stockton, echoed Kearsley's complaints when they wrote Congress. Suggesting that they had a comparative perspective on Pennsylvania's jails from being held first at Philadelphia and then York, they argued "that this Prison [in Carlisle] is perhaps the worst on the continent[,] being rather a ruin then a Gaol." Due to its shabby construction, they complained that "every part" of the building "distributed Air as thro the holes of a Cullender [colander]." Such a horrible draft was "destroying" their health. Furthermore, because there was no glass in the windows, they were "Obliged to sleep in one room without any thing but . . . one Blanket." Asking to be "relieved in the Premises" based on the laws of nations, rules of war, and gentlemanly codes that typically softened the treatment of high-status men like themselves, they noted that "Humanity is the Characteristic of a civilized People." They asserted that their accommodations were not just an insult, they were inhumane, and expected their former fellow British subjects in Congress to do something to address their concerns.[53] Carlisle committeemen were ultimately sympathetic. They agreed that prisoners' complaints were "Truth"—these accommodations were "unfit for a Gentleman."[54] Congress seconded this conclusion and called on them "to have the gaol made as comfortable as circumstances will admit."[55] Given Kearsley's untimely death, Carlisle's jail embodied how Whig-Tory clashes played out in the most physical ways during the war. As loyalist gentlemen found themselves shivering from the cold in a crude stone structure with open windows, they were willing to make their plight a national issue by bringing it to the attention of Congress.

But there was more. The sudden prominence of the jail was minor compared to the dramatic shifts in the townscape taking place on the town's northern border. Congress needed a safe location for prisoners, but the army's need for arms and supplies was even greater. This brought renewed attention to the armory and barracks built on Carlisle's northern outskirts during the Seven Years' War. After being mostly abandoned during the 1760s, the public works, as it was called by the 1770s, was again abuzz with activity in 1776 (see figure 8). Congress called for the construction of a magazine for the storage of arms and gunpowder as well as an adjacent laboratory for the manufacture of munitions on the site.[56] This move was meant to encourage the domestic manufacture of arms and artillery in order to wean the American army from its dependence on imported or captured British weapons. More important to Carlisle's history, Congress chose this site for these functions for the same reasons that Native peoples, the Penn family, colonists, fur traders, and the British army were drawn to the location in the past: it was situated conveniently between others in the mid-Atlantic. Its location west of the Susquehanna was advantageous since it was likely safe from British takeover, but not inaccessible. Roads connected it to other regions, which meant that supplies could be moved easily from there to points east, west, north, and south. These paths also linked it to raw materials, including grain, livestock, and iron produced in the Cumberland Valley. Sitting between the different theaters of war, Carlisle was a most suitable location for the army's manufacturing and supply efforts.[57]

In response to Congress's call, the works revitalized and expanded into a more extensive complex of structures. During the war's first years, the army established a brickyard on site, and in addition to the magazine, constructed new buildings to house shops for the manufacture of cannon, shot, harnesses, barrels, nails, and gun carriages. They also erected new barracks. By all accounts, this expansion was a major undertaking that took several years to complete. Some of these structures were reportedly built by a group of Hessian prisoners confined at Carlisle. Others were built by local men who had enlisted in the war effort. Irish immigrant Adam Logue, for example, recalled that after enlisting in a company formed in Cumberland County he spent the first five months of service working in "the Continental Brick yards" at Carlisle where "he assisted to manufacture Brick" and "to erect Barracks and a magazine at said place." After volunteering for the Battle of Long Island, he returned to Carlisle where he "was again put to work in the . . . Brick yards." He finished out his two-year term of service there.[58] The complex that Logue helped to construct eventually included a military hospital and training school for artillerists. It was eventually renamed Washingtonburg to honor the army's commander.[59] Although some later complained that no

"Proper foresight" was used in constructing this complex—leaving some structures, for example, without roofs—no one disputed the way it altered the townscape or Carlisle's functions in the mid-Atlantic.[60] Described by one observer as "an immense pile of buildings, far exceeding anything in this part of the country," the works was an imposing complex of structures that assumed the foreground of the local landscape.[61] It heralded the Revolution's arrival in Carlisle in a most physical way. Yet it also exemplified the central role the town played in the war effort and embodied how Carlisle remained a town in-between.

The works was important in other ways. It was the larger of two ordnance depots and manufacturing centers—the other was in Springfield, Massachusetts—that supported army operations in the north for the duration of the war. Carlisle's public works thus embodied in microcosm some of the key economic shifts taking place as America struggled to move from a colonial to a national economy that could supply more of its own needs. Its significance as a center of domestic weapons production, repair, and storage only increased after Philadelphia fell to the British in 1777 and Carlisle became, according to one historian, "the center of the artificers business in Pennsylvania."[62] Falling under the authority of Lieutenant Colonel Benjamin Flower, Commissary General of Military Stores, the works was staffed primarily by two depot companies of ordnance technicians. The first company, consisting of some eighty men, manufactured arms, especially cannon. The second company, with just over seventy men, repaired and maintained arms, and fabricated ammunition.[63]

The artificers were a diverse group of artisans and laborers whose activities as arms manufacturers and repairers—and status as soldiers—was never clearly defined by Congress or the army.[64] In some locales, artificers served in artillery companies that spent most of their time in the field, repairing guns as needed for combat units. Carlisle's artificers, by contrast, were a mostly stationary labor force that made only rare excursions outside the works. Private William Ferguson, for example, recalled going on only two tours during his three years of service at the works. The first was a month-long trek up the Juniata to "the Lead mines" to gather up the stores that had been left there. As he explained, "we bro[ugh]t cannon, shovels, [and] picks . . . down the river in boats." The second was a journey up the north branch of the Susquehanna following the devastating loyalist-Indian attacks on the Wyoming settlements in northeast Pennsylvania. On this trip, Ferguson gathered coal for use at Carlisle's foundry.[65] As Ferguson's experiences suggest, because the artificers at Carlisle engaged in only limited scavenging expeditions outside the works, these approximately 150 men, most of them lower or middling sorts, were a near-constant wartime presence in the town. They temporarily swelled the ranks of the town's inhabitants, whose migration west was checked by the war. Their presence was another significant reminder of the war's arrival in the Cumberland Valley and Carlisle's central role in it.[66]

The artificers were also a predominantly skilled labor force drawn mostly from Pennsylvania and the mid-Atlantic. In Capt. Isaac Coren's company, the more fully documented of the two, most men came from Cumberland, Philadelphia, or Northampton counties, while others were drawn from Lancaster, Bucks, and York counties; one each came from Maryland and New York.[67] Although there were laborers among them, most were experienced craftsmen like William Denning, a blacksmith from Philadelphia who served four years at Carlisle as foreman of the cannon foundry.[68] Other smiths and forgemen manufactured cartridges, and repaired muskets and bayonets. Still others, like Isaac Wall, a carpenter, worked in what he called the "Factory" and "was employed at the Carpenter business for the use of the army." There were wheelwrights, harnessmakers, tinners, and turners stationed there as well.[69] The presence of such concentrated numbers of army artisans, especially when coupled with the town's resident craftsmen, ensured that Carlisle was one of the more important hubs of skilled manufacturing activity during the war.

The artificers made significant contributions to an often desperate American effort to defeat Great Britain. These men recognized and took pride in this fact. Still, like other soldiers, they perceived their contributions in highly personal terms; their wartime experiences became defining ones in shaping their identities. If the accounts of William Ferguson are any indication, Carlisle's artificers took considerable pride in fulfilling the orders of Congress and the army, and in practicing a craft that enabled them to create works of power and beauty. As Ferguson explained some years after the war, while stationed at "Washingtonburg" in 1778, he was "employed in making the carriages of cannon, ammunition wagons and traveling Forges for the United States army." As he recalled, a reciprocal relationship existed among Congress, the army, and the artificers, in which the manufacturing enterprises at Carlisle stood at its center. As he explained:

> Orders were sent on to us from the army for what was wanted and we made [it] agreeably to calls forwarded to us[.] At one time we made fifteen cannon carriages for eighteen pound cannon which were sent

on to Stony Point after that place was taken by Genl[.] Wayne[']s army[.] [D]uring the time we were at Washingtonburg there were two cannon made by William Denning made of wrought iron, the one a three pounder and the other a six pounder, we mounted them on very handsomely finished carriages[.] [T]hey were painted red at the muzzle, the remainder with alternate black & white rings—the one had "The Queen of France," the other "Genl Wayne" painted on them in large letters[.] After they were finished we tried them at target and found they shot extremely correct—If I remember correctly, I think they were taken towards Fort Pitt—I have since heard that the British took one or both of them and have them now mounted in Dover castle.[70]

Ferguson remembered a seamless operation at Carlisle in which artisans like him worked hard and "agreeably" to fulfill army requests. The products of their labors were then relayed by wagon to the front lines. Their work was also a model of quality and efficiency. They did not simply fill these orders; instead, he and his fellow artisans took great care in building cannon and carriages that were "handsomely finished," colorfully and patriotically deco-rated, and—most important—fired "extremely correct." Even the British, he implied, recognized their worth, for why else would they mount them in one of their own castles some years later?

The American Revolution began and made its presence felt in Carlisle in the mid-1770s, setting the stage for political and social change, and reconfiguring the townscape. These changes posed many tough choices for townspeople. During the first years of the war, when enthusiasm for the cause was great and the high-profile prisoners housed in town helped solidify the opposition to Britain, many local men chose to actively support the war and the political revolution it represented. As they flocked to participate in local committees or the new state government and volunteered in large numbers for army and militia service, it would appear by their actions that their decision to become revolutionaries seemed easy. It was not. Service, whether in politics or the military, often meant leaving wives, children, farms, and businesses behind. Soldiering, in particular, meant risking injury or death, potentially leaving families destitute. Still, it is imperative to remember that the men who served were not the only townspeople who faced choices; nor was the only choice regarding whether or not to serve. Rather, Carlisle's civilian population, in-cluding those men who could not or would not serve—as well as the town's many women, children, and even servants and slaves—faced equally important questions regarding how they would respond to the momentous events reshaping their nation, town, and lives. As they quickly discovered, battle zones need not be nearby for war and revolution to affect a community. How they would cope with those effects was up to them.

Wartime activities at the public works probably posed the greatest array of choices for Carlisle's civilians, especially as the war progressed. While the manufacturing and repair of arms performed by artificers like William Ferguson were the primary activities at the works, the facility also served other critical, nonordinance-related supply functions that relied heavily on the local population. As a quartermaster depot and commissary magazine by 1777, for instance, Carlisle was the headquarters of Deputy Quartermaster John Davis and, more important, of Ephraim Blaine, the fur trader, farmer, miller, and revolutionary who rose through the ranks of the Commissary Department to become Commissary General of Purchases for the army by 1779.[71] The army's needs in this region were tremendous. At one point in the war, the commissary staff at the works provided food and forage for the nearly 5,000 men and 1,000 animals associated with the army. Meanwhile, the Carlisle magazine supplied both the French forces at Newport and the Sullivan expedition into Iroquois country. Carlisle was thus central to army supply efforts.[72]

But the army did not accomplish such feats alone; the Quartermaster and Commissary Departments depended heavily on town and county residents for the supplies and services they needed. This was not unusual—these departments simply followed the time-honored army practice of drawing their provisions from civilian populations. Near Carlisle, there was a more immediate and specific model to emulate—the one pioneered by British officials provisioning the Forbes expedition in 1758. In the 1750s and 1770s, army officers or their agents relied heavily on local residents to obtain the supplies, foodstuffs, forage, and related services needed to support the war effort. But there was a catch, for such strategies placed the army in a dependent position. Supply agents had to convince civilians that it was in their best interests to supply the American war effort. To do so, it was said that officers like Davis had to develop a "general acquaintance & intimacy with the people"; his goal was to use powers of persuasion to convince locals to give up their goods.[73] Davis evidently met with some success. Unlike the Swiss-born Colonel Henry Bouquet, who found building this intimacy a challenging task because he was an outsider, Davis had the advantage of being an American; Blaine was even a long-time Carlisle resident. Moreover, Davis and Blaine had the additional advantage of supplying a war effort cast as a grand political struggle against tyranny, which many locals supported fervently. For these reasons, many locals cooperated in providing supplies.

Then there was the issue of money. The army offered to pay for the goods it needed, a powerful lure to local residents. Cash was in short supply in the region; even men of "considerable Property" felt its "great Scarcity" as the Revolution began in 1776.[74] Many civilians thus cooperated with army supply agents because they welcomed promises of pay or IOUs for their goods and services. John Glen was one of them. Although he never fought, he was "Employed" for several years "in the Service of the United States as [a] Contractor for Lumber & c. for the Use of the Publick workes Near Carlisle."[75] Others, particularly many of the town's skilled craftsmen—such as smiths, saddlers, and carpenters—joined him. They quickly discovered that wartime supply and manufacturing efforts placed a high premium on their skills, which expanded their clout in the local economy. Carlisle residents responded by reaching out to build closer ties between the works and town. A 1779 request for a new bridge over the LeTort, for example, captured the sentiments of many townspeople. It described the "very many Waggons and Teams, . . . , traveling between Carlisle and Washingtonburgh" and noted that a new bridge would serve the "greater Ease and Conveniency of Strangers, as of the Inhabitants."[76] Townspeople knew that it was in their economic interest to construct physical links between these two places. The works brought "Strangers" to town, and considering the hostility some townspeople directed at Native peoples and trade agents during the 1760s, this probably troubled some. But the works was also the single most important center of local commerce during the Revolution, thus locals were flexible. They sought "Ease and Conveniency" in accessing this site because it was so central to their town's wartime identity.

Many town and county residents welcomed the opportunity to serve the American cause and earn money by assisting the army's supply and manufacturing activities headquartered at Carlisle. But local supply and manufacturing efforts actually predated the organization of the army's staff departments and their extension into the interior. As early as 1775, for example, Cumberland County's volunteers "very generally offered their Service," but needed arms and supplies to outfit them. This demand continued into 1776 when eleven companies were ready to march and three more preparing "if they can get Arms."[77] These needs placed great pressure on civilian craftsmen, who worked hard to meet a large portion of the local demand. Yet outfitting the army was not the only charge, there was also the militia. Raising and supplying it placed additional demands on locals. With so much going to the army, some county officials feared that there would not be sufficient guns to supply over one-third of the militia. Nevertheless, with "the welfare of this country at heart," they contracted with "the best Gunsmiths in this County" to make a hundred rifles.[78] Finally, there was plenty of repair work to be done, which provided additional employment for gunsmiths like George McGunnegle, a middling Carlisle artisan who serviced arms for the militia.[79]

As officials scrambled to put a gun into the hands of every militiaman and army volunteer, they turned to local artisans—sometimes desperately—to provide needed arms, supplies, and services. Evidence suggests that many Carlisle gunsmiths responded favorably; so did other artisans. Carlisle saddler Charles Cooper, for instance, made scabbards for the army's French guns. He was also engaged to make "a Number of Cartouch[e] pouches, bayonet belts, and Scabbards, for the use of the Militia."[80] In providing these goods and services, civilian artisans like Cooper gained cash—or the promise of it. By laboring for the nation, they also assumed a new kind of public identity even though they did not fight the war.

Self-interest was one of the most significant factors influencing local craftsmen's choice to provide needed services or supplies for the war. In a town populated by retailers and artisans, many of whom had participated in supplying the British army during the Seven Years' War, townspeople knew the opportunities war presented. They offered their services as a strategy to preserve or better the material condition of their lives. This was true of both the town's better and middling sorts. As historian E. Wayne Carp notes, for instance, those joining the army staff departments, although inspired by patriotism, were also spurred by self-interest. Ephraim Blaine, the Carlisle merchant and trader who became Commissary General of the Army, certainly joined the department in the hope of profiting from his service. He and other officers knew that during various colonial wars, staff departments "were often the route by which men made fortunes and founded family dynasties."[81] They anticipated similar returns from the Revolution. Although few found the riches they hoped for, wartime service did bring connections and other tangible returns. Blaine, for instance, did not get rich from his service—he was mostly broke by war's end—but he earned a position of national prominence that helped position his family in politics for generations to come.[82]

The war also benefitted those of Carlisle's middling sorts who were willing to offer their services. Aside from earning pay or IOUs, artisans like the gunsmith McGunnegle and the saddler Cooper also got other, less obvious rewards for the skills they possessed. Those artisans with high-demand skills, in particular, found increased buying and bartering power in the local economy. Skilled work for the army or militia became a valuable kind of currency in Carlisle. Artisans gained credit for goods purchased from local retailers by supplying the war effort. McGunnegle, for example, was a regular patron of Assistant Quartermaster Samuel Postlethwaite's Carlisle store. There he purchased supplies of beer, whiskey, and other liquor in exchange for providing goods and services needed by the Assistant Quartermaster. Whereas before the war, he made fire irons, tongs, and toast forks to pay for his liquor, during the war, McGunnegle reconciled his debts by doing such things as supplying Postlethwaite with twenty-two muskets for the army on one occasion, eleven on another, and by "cleaning and Repairing 60 Muskets for Col[one]l Irvine[']s Battalion."[83] Another gunsmith, Abraham Morrow, also had many exchanges with the Assistant Quartermaster. For the "sundr[y] Repairs Done to Muskets for Col[one]l Irvine[']s Bat[talio]n" in 1776, Morrow received £35 and a steady supply of toddy, eggnog, beer, whiskey, and wine from Postlethwaite. This pattern continued through 1777, as Morrow continued to repair rifles in exchange for a mix of cash and credits at Postlethwaite's store.[84] Clearly, the work these civilians performed influenced the war's course and Carlisle's role in it. Without their services, men could not fight.

Locals' choice to participate had other effects. As the above examples suggest, artisans like McGunnegle and Morrow who possessed valuable skills like gunsmithing commanded increased clout in an economy geared to supplying America's and Pennsylvania's fighting forces. Personally, they gained significant quantities of cash or credit. Although this did not make them wealthy, it likely kept them out of debt while offering them access to the consumer goods, especially the liquor, they desired. This is significant. At a time when cash was in short supply, and boycotts, then shortages, put many consumer goods out of reach, the ability to acquire items without incurring significant debt put one at a distinct advantage. Equally important, artisans' high-demand skills earned them bargaining power over retailers like Samuel Postlethwaite. Assistant Quartermaster Postlethwaite, an Anglican probably of English descent born to a Lancaster County resident, was an experienced merchant. He was a former trader at Fort Frederick in Maryland in the 1760s who relocated to Carlisle sometime after 1768. At the time of the Revolution, Postlethwaite, a wealthy merchant and militia colonel, counted himself among the town's privileged.[85] But no matter what his experience or authority, as an assistant quartermaster, Postlethwaite depended on his more humble neighbor McGunnegle to provide the arms he needed to supply the troops and fulfill his duty to Congress. Such dependence likely meant that rates of payment were negotiated; artisans like McGunnegle were surely able to drive up compensation rates for their services. Equally important to understanding the Revolution, these examples suggest how entangled privately owned businesses and individual accounts became during the war. As the postings in Postlethwaite's store ledger illustrate, the war's demands penetrated the private workings of Carlisle's economy. Because wartime needs linked the livelihoods of civilian artisans, retailers, and laborers to the professional reputations of officials and institutions overseeing the Revolution, the lines between civilians and soldiers were not so distinct after all.

War and revolution posed other, less profound choices for Carlisle's civilians. Wartime activity at the works brought several hundred men to town to staff the Artificers' Regiment and the Commissary and Quartermaster Departments, most of them young and many single. This dramatic expansion of the town's population had a significant impact on the tenor of local society. Quite suddenly, Carlisle had a temporary surplus population, predominantly male, that desired entertainment and social interaction. Residents thus faced choices about how to respond to the social demands of war.

Evidence shows that Carlisle's many tavern keepers jumped at the opportunity to serve new patrons, much as they had during the Seven Years' War. And soldiers at the works were ready and willing to patronize their taverns, despite officers' efforts to curtail access to them, which they scorned as stages for rowdy behavior. One commanding officer who was concerned that "no disorder happen in camp," ordered that none of his men could "presume to leave the Camp to the distance of half a mile, without leave" from the officer in charge. To enforce his order, several men were sent "to Examine the streets of Carlisle" each evening. If any soldier "not having a written permission from a Command[ing] officer shall be found in the town, such soldier shall be made a prisoner & punished."[86] Despite such orders, soldiers still made their way to town, where they found tavern keepers ready to serve them. Carlisle thus remained a lively retail hub, even during the war.

Townspeople also opted to socialize with soldiers outdoors. Open spaces on the town's borders, for example, offered informal settings for rowdier forms of entertainment like horse racing that lured civilians and soldiers. Yet the two groups, one composed mostly of outsiders, did not always get along. On the first day of one race in 1778, with tempers fueled by the air of competition and plenty of liquor, "there was a great deal of fighting with Clubs." One officer, an observer noted, "was struck with a Club on some Difference" that arose between the officer and another man. Although this fight was finally stopped, it was "not without the Expence of some bloody Heads." The next day, guards were ordered to the race grounds to preserve the peace."[87] Whether inside the town's taverns or outside at the races, the war created circumstances in which civilians and soldiers, and officers and enlisted men, drank and socialized together in informal but sometimes rowdy and violent ways.

Carlisle's wartime social scene took more genteel forms inside the homes of the town's leading families. Social rituals such as calling and courting opened wartime socializing to women as well as men. Some women, like the wife of one of the officers commanding the artificers, arrived in town with their husbands hoping to establish new social networks in their temporary town of residence. For Mrs. Lukens, the wife of Major Charles Lukens of York, the challenge of relocating to Carlisle was not so much about wartime hardship or being an army wife as it was the task of adapting to a new social world that was dependent on the sociability of new neighbors. As one of her husband's companions observed, she came "to like Carlisle better and better," because it seemed like "the People are more social now [in 1777] than they ever were before."[88] The war and the new people it brought to town thus changed the social scene in ways that some outsiders interpreted as for the better.

Other women, like the daughters of Carlisle's leading families, found new social outlets with the women and many men, especially officers, who arrived with the army. Soldiers took full advantage of the courting opportunities available when local young women showed willingness to spend time with them. Recruiting officer John McDowell was happy to visit with the town's most charming and attractive young women. Writing to a friend, he noted that he and another officer, accompanied by "two of the first young Ladies of this Place," had gone on a day's outing to the nearby town of York. Taunting his friend with news of this trip, McDowell noted that "I have a great Mind, if you don't soon order me to Camp—to marry some of those Angels for *Spite*."[89] To McDowell, his fellow officer, and their female companions, socializing sometimes temporarily eclipsed the more strenuous demands of war. Wartime life in Carlisle was not just about hardship and risk. Rather, as a central place for wartime recruiting and supply activities, the Revolution lent a new social vibrancy to town.

Despite the town's enthusiasm for the war and the myriad opportunities it presented, not everyone in Carlisle supported the Revolution; there were cracks in the local consensus from the start. Not all men wanted to volunteer their service, not all civilians wanted to manufacture supplies and repair arms, and not all townspeople wanted to socialize with the large number of soldiers in their midst. Not everyone was pleased with how war and revolution redefined their town and its functions in the mid-Atlantic. Further complicating the situation were especially contentious state politics that polarized residents into opposing camps; rivalries between radicals, moderates, and conservatives influenced how townspeople responded to their neighbors, wartime developments, and newcomers. Even among those townspeople who did support the changes happening around them, their unity and elán were conditional; most expected tangible returns for the risks they bore for the American cause. Taken together, then, Carlisle's response to the Revolution was far more mixed than it appeared. Although the town was never beset by the kind of internal civil war between patriots and loyalists that marked other Pennsylvania communities, it had its groups of resistant and reluctant.[90] Their hostility, apathy, or, as the war wore on, widespread weariness and frustration, countered the intense enthusiasm of their neighbors, especially by the late 1770s and 1780s. Carlisle residents thus had a variety of responses to war and revolution. They opted into or out of the conflict for different reasons, and sometimes they even changed their minds as the war progressed. In keeping with their colonial past, they remained a remarkably independent lot.

The conditional nature of Carlisle's support for revolution was evident among the town's leading men, the ambitious group of Scots-Irish and Scots revolutionaries who spearheaded the town's anti-British stance early in the war. These Whigs, like many other privileged urban dwellers in the mid-Atlantic, were moderate, sometimes conservative, in their revolutionary politics. They strongly favored political independence from Britain, but in placing a high premium on order, they opposed social revolution at home. Even though they were strongly committed to the war against Great Britain, they thus raised serious challenges to the Revolution's radical direction in Pennsylvania. They made clear that their support for America's political revolution was not unthinking, unconditional, or without reservation; they had their own political principles, which they did not intend to compromise. In particular, they adamantly opposed the state's radical constitution and reviled the Test Oath radicals instituted to affirm it. They justifiably feared that if the Oath were used as a weapon of persecution and harassment across the state, it would divide residents against one another and undermine the social order and their position in it.[91] This was not the kind of revolution they wished to wage.

Such opposition posed a dilemma for them, however. They knew that acting on their beliefs meant going against their state's political grain; it risked alienating them from positions of political power and earning them the hatred of their economically humble but politically radical neighbors in town and county. Still, they made their choice to oppose their state's radical turn. Several, for example, refused the Oath and thereby forfeited their offices.[92] Others worked more collectively to oppose radical authority. Indeed, because "'the Sensible and vertious [virtuous] part of this County'," said William Thompson, wanted "'to set this Villainous Constitution aside;'" they joined with other moderates and conservatives across the state to forge their own, independent political course as anti-Constitutionalists, or Republicans.[93] With James Wilson leading the charge in 1776, they set out to prove their point when Wilson and others drafted thirty-one resolves critiquing the state's new constitution as "'Inconsistent with the principles of free government.'"[94] But these men could do only so much. With one estimate suggesting that two-thirds of the state supported the new constitution, their choice placed them in a distinct minority. That meant they had to accept what they could not immediately change. Instead, they suffered the consequences as elections went to radicals; Wilson, for instance, was tossed from office. They also swallowed their pride and accepted that the county would be "full and Stinking with yellow wiges" as the state's radical government appointed local justices more sympathetic to their agenda.[95] Yet they also persevered, waiting for the opportunity to retake control of the state, which finally happened as the war wound down in 1782.[96]

Town leaders were not the only ones making tough choices and suffering the consequences, however. Some, like the middling John Wilkins, an ambitious entrepreneur, initially embraced the Revolution as his own but then rethought his actions when faced with intense hardship. The Pennsylvania-born Wilkins, of Welsh and Scots-Irish parentage, moved to Carlisle in the 1760s and established himself as a tavern and storekeeper.[97] When the Revolution commenced he, like many of his neighbors, "immediately randevoused on the side of the Americans." In fact, he was "one of the first captains of Militia chosen in Carlisle." After being so commissioned in 1776, Wilkins raised a company of sixty-four men, paying their bounties, wages, and rations "out of my own money" for half a year. Although he was eventually compensated for his expenses, currency depreciation left him with nothing. When additional economic hardships that undermined his business interests on the homefront compounded this loss, he found himself facing financial ruin. "My property," which he had worked so hard to accumulate, "was dwindling to nothing." In response, Wilkins resigned his commission in 1778 to "go home to pay attention to my family and private property." There were limits to his commitment; with a wife and family, he could not risk all. Thus, when it looked like "the great faith and strong belief in conquering the British," might also be "the means of my Destruction," Wilkins left the war to return to a small homestead outside Carlisle where he "began to farm with spirit to keep my family together and wait with pations [patience] the will of the Almighty ruler and director of all things." For Wilkins, as for others, joining the war effort was a conditional action. In his case, economic self-preservation ultimately outweighed his ideological commitment.[98]

Other townspeople, by contrast, were either less dedicated or indifferent from the outset. As John Armstrong observed as early as 1775: "Our Volunteering Schemes have a generous appearance," but "they are freight [fraught] with confusion and lyable to the greatest uncertainty."[99] This pattern of behavior reappeared in late 1776, the year when excitement about the war was at its height.[100] Revolutionary enthusiasm was more fleeting than initial impressions suggested. Yet this made sense. Carlisle's ordinary sorts did not act with one mind, nor were they completely unified. Rather, from the start of the war, some resisted or opted out of service whenever possible, while others simply sought to minimize the potentially disruptive impact the war might have on their lives.

As the war continued on into the late 1770s, the tendency to opt out intensified. War weariness, compounded by economic hard times, turned fleeting spirits to apathy and sometimes outright disaffection. Fewer men stepped forward to serve; fighting was no longer in their best interest. This trend was already evident by 1777, when one army official noted that "recruiting comes on slowly" in Carlisle. "Men," he said, "are not to be had hardly at any Rate in this State."[101] And his was not an isolated observation. As one scholar confirms, finding men to fill the ranks of the militia and army became a major issue for recruiters in Pennsylvania's interior through time. With the initial excitement over the Revolution having died down after the first year or two of the war; with few loyalists around to generate internal strife; and with the theaters of war with the British and Native Americans located to the distant east, west, and south, fewer men felt pressure to join the war effort.[102]

Economic factors further discouraged service. This was particularly true for the militia—county officials had little money to support the men who served. There were signs of trouble early on—even in 1776, county leaders complained that "our Stock of Cash is run very low."[103] They desperately needed money "for the maintenance of the Familys of our Associators as are called into actual service." These were working men, many of them town laborers and county farmers; their families—particularly their wives— were "not of [the] Ability to maintain themselves in the Absence of such Associators."[104] Again, a year later, local officials wondered "how the Militia are to be paid their Subsistence?" This was "a Matter of Much Inquirey by the Militia who have far to march before they can draw rations."[105] Over time, with no money to support their families on the homefront, and no funds to support them while serving, militia service held decreasing appeal. Why serve when the economic costs were so high?

Army recruits faced their own dilemmas. For the most part, the army had the resources to pay its soldiers. But the war inflated wage rates on the home front, which discouraged men from enlisting. As one recruiter explained: "there is no such thing as getting Men whilst Wages in the Country are so high." With British markets closed during the war, domestic production of goods ramped up, especially in areas distant from the fighting, like the Cumberland Valley. Consequently, Cumberland County farmers who found themselves pushing production to meet the demand for grain to feed the army were "giving £5 p[e]r month for common plough men." To local laboring men assessing their self-interests, the choice was clear: why "be so foolish, . . . as to list for 50%" when one "can get double and stay at home."[106] Even servants were difficult to recruit. "The People," as one recruiter explained, "will not give up so useful a part of their Property without knowing for what."[107] Masters also had significant economic considerations to weigh during such uncertain times; they did not wish to lose their investments.

These patterns intensified in the early 1780s. Upon arriving in Carlisle in 1781, one officer remarked with frustration that "there is nothing doing in this County by the Classes for the recruiting Service."[108] He was not the only one to complain. Even William Irvine, who was so enthusiastic about the soldiers of his battalion at the start of the war, became increasingly annoyed at his neighbors' apathy as the war neared its end. Locals, he said, "are very slow, indeed." In fact, "they seem quite indifferent about the matter." By his reckoning, the central obstacle the army faced in convincing local men to fight was that "the people in general seem as easy and secure as if there was not War in the Country."[109] Much had changed. Whereas in the mid-1770s, Carlisle men had identified strongly with the plight of Massachusetts, casting its fate as a grand struggle for America as for themselves as its inhabitants, after nearly six years of fighting, war had grown tiresome, especially when the fields of battle were distant. By 1781, many locals no longer cared what happened in southern campaigns remote from their town. The war was simply not as pressing on their lives or interests. Still, such indifference bewildered town leaders. Why did so many of their neighbors behave as if "Every Thing Goes on here as Usual."[110] Had they forgotten war was still raging? No, they had not. Local apathy was not a new problem. As county lieutenant John Carothers put it in a conciliatory letter to Congress in 1778, the town's Whig leaders were "greatly disappointed" in their neighbors. Although he and other "Spirited friends to our American cause" had "done everything" in their "power to induce" local men to "turn out" to join the fight, few had done so, and recruitment quotas remained unmet. It was clear that not every local man joined the war as enthusiastically as some of his neighbors.[111]

Apathy persisted even after devastating Tory-Indian raids on Pennsylvania's northern interior—such as the Wyoming attacks of 1778—raised new alarms about how "Indians Continue their Savage cruelty upon our frontiers" in ways reminiscent of the Indian wars of the 1750s and 1760s.[112] Not even when fears of "Emenent Danger, from the Savages" prevailed in distant parts of the county, and the roads toward Carlisle were said to be "crowded" with what one witness estimated as "not less than four thousand Souls" fleeing the frontier, were local men motivated to serve.[113] Unlike other parts of the Pennsylvania interior, Carlisle townspeople appeared unafraid. Contrary to the claims of scholars, they displayed no great desire to fight Indians. Instead, with economic ties to the fur trade severed and agents of that trade no longer working in Carlisle, townspeople no longer had much stake in policing Native peoples. Indian problems had moved on, past them. Thus, with the British theater of war situated to the distant east or south and the Tory-Indian threat focused in areas far to the north and west, many men of the Cumberland Valley chose to stay home rather than fight.[114] To town leaders, such lack of response was appalling. County lieutenant John Carothers, for example, was "heartily Sorry that the State of Pennsylvania in general and this County in particular Should be found So extremely backward in marching out in defence of rights so invaluable as those for which the Americans are now contending." This was especially so, as he noted with some embarrassment, "when one manly effort would in all human probability work out our political salvation."[115] Townspeople, he suggested, were making the wrong choice in refusing to serve—they were turning their backs on Carlisle's heritage as a place and a people in-between.

To complicate matters further, able-bodied men were not the only townspeople opting out. Through time, Carlisle civilians got fussier about supplying services and materials for the war effort; some even refused to participate. Their refusal demonstrates how the existence of commercial ties between the army staff at the public works and townspeople, and between local Whig officials administering the war and the town's artisans, did not guarantee consistently cooperative or harmonious relationships among them. Residents had options, and like other civilian communities near Valley Forge or in New York City, townspeople chose whether and how to fill the army's call for supplies.[116] Their actions reveal that they had decidedly mixed responses to the war's economic demands. The war had come to them, after all, and while some welcomed it, others did not. Thus, as some townspeople rejected the army's calls for supplies, they made it clear that not everyone was equally enthusiastic, nor uniformly cooperative, about the demands placed on them by the wartime supply and manufacturing efforts on their town's northern border.

Economic relations between Congress, the army, the works, and local artisans and retailers thus remained conditional throughout the war. Their interactions were shaped by civilian expectations that contributors would receive just compensation for their goods and services and by army policies that discouraged impressment of goods. More important, exchanges depended on cash to keep them active. That expectation presented problems from the start of the war because local officials were cash poor and civilians did not work for free. For example, Carlisle's tavern keepers, many of whom supplied militiamen with food before the appointment of a commissary agent, made it clear that they expected payment for each meal they provided. Similarly, those Carlisle "Mechanicks" who repaired guns and made cartouch[e] boxes and pouches also expected compensation in a timely manner. When these same craftsmen "Stood in Need of some Money to enable them to Carry on the Work," as one local leader explained, lack of payment worked in reverse by slowing or halting their participation.[117] Like their neighbors who worked for the agents of Baynton, Wharton, and Morgan in the 1760s, no payment equaled no goods and services; and no goods and services temporarily halted wartime supply efforts.

For those administering the war, much like agents in the colonial fur trade, this posed a dilemma. To obtain needed goods and services, they had to have funds "Sufficient to answer the demands" of these workers.[118] But with "our Stock of Cash . . . run very low," as one official explained, and with runaway inflation and devalued currency looming as national issues as the war continued, local officials wondered how they would pay for the goods and services they contracted. In response, they begged state officials for more cash.[119] And they pushed local craftsmen "to Compleat the full Complement of Muskets," by "urg[ing] the Workmen to their duty and Interest."[120] In this way, local officials sometimes used pressure tactics, including calls upon patriotism and threats of shame, as weak substitutes for the cash they did not have on hand.

In a town where ideological commitment was strong in many quarters, calls to "duty and Interest" no doubt held some sway. But they held only limited compulsory power among the civilian population. Consequently, work sometimes slowed or stopped. "Several Innkeepers," state officials noted, had "greatly distressed the Militia on their March, by refusing to Supply them with necessary provisions." Others, by contrast, "imposed upon them by exacting [the] most extravagant prices."[121] Near Carlisle, "Tavernkeepers were unwilling to accommodate the Men, unless the Price of a Meal is increased, because every kind of victualing is become dearer."[122] Through these actions, civilians made clear that their economic self-interest, sometimes aimed at profit, other times at survival, was central in spurring their wartime supply efforts. When locals, like the "Mechanicks" who outfitted Associators with arms, demanded payment, they did so knowing that "all such People are paid in the other Counties in this State;" and they expected the same in their county because they did not work for free.[123]

Tensions mounted as the war continued and civilian expectations of gain collided with America's—and the army's—worsening economy. Compounding the problem were ineptness and inadequacies in the army's Commissary and Quartermaster Departments, which prompted a clash of interests.[124] In Carlisle, consequences were most visible at the public works, the place where the war effort most closely intersected with the local community. By 1779, with war continuing, revolutionary spirit fading, and little cash around to inspire production, townspeople had few incentives to maintain their economic ties to the works and its staff, thus the artificers there were mostly left to starve. As one of their officers explained, his men were so "starving for want of bread" that they requested that the Quartermaster Department "furnish" them with transportation so that they might "go about 20 Miles for a load of Wheat"; they were desperate enough to go find their own food.[125] Provisioning took on crisis proportions with national implications a year later when, with the addition of several more artificer companies from Philadelphia after its laboratory closed, the men at Carlisle's works fell into "absolute Famine." Things were so bad, it was said, that "No Work is done." They were "kept," as another officer described, "in a very odd kind of way."[126]

The artificers were caught in a double bind. On the one hand, because "the Artificers Regiment at this place has always kept the County bare," as William Irvine explained, there were relatively few provisions left to claim by 1780; a combination of their needs and wartime shortages had exhausted supplies.[127] But then, there was the worsening American economy, which also had its effects. Shortages of cash, inefficiencies within the Quartermaster and Commissary Departments, and runaway inflation compounded the artificers' dire circumstances. Local farmers who still had livestock were either unwilling to part with their property on questionable terms of credit or were demanding "a most scandalous price" for their possessions. With economic risk having increased dramatically, farmers were reluctant to sell what little they had to the army. When they did cooperate, they did so on their own terms.[128] This left the artificers at the works to subsist for months on flour and whiskey, while wanting for pay and clothing. Yet they still had choices. In this case, much like their civilian neighbors, with no support for them or their services, they "did not think themselves obliged to Work."[129] Their commitment was also conditional. Some officials administering the war acknowledged the reasonableness of their position. Soldiers had the right to expect food for their service; as one official put it, they could not be forced to work when the public "cannot enable them to eat."[130] But the Board of War disagreed. Winning the war was its first concern. To do so, the board needed Carlisle's artificers to work whether they had pay and provisions or not. Referring to what they saw as the "Ill temper of the Artificers at Carlisle," the board found it "lamentable that the Public should be in this Situation." But with little cash on hand, "it is not in our Power to remedy it."[131] They could do little to provide for the artificers, but wartime supply and manufacture had to go on.

Because so many of the army's armaments were manufactured or re-paired at Carlisle's works, the artificers' dire situation had ramifications for the final years of war: How could arms be manufactured or repaired for the army when starving men refused to work? Their situation also had signifi-cant effects on Carlisle. With little pay or provisions in the early 1780s, the artificers were pushed to make other decisions that went beyond production stoppages at the works. In a fight for survival, they were left "wand[e]ring about" town, pushed by circumstances into an every-man-for-himself men-tality that undermined their commitment and set them up to compete with townspeople for jobs. As one official described it, those of the artificers who were lucky got "private Employment" and "receive[d] a Support from what they earn[ed]," while those who were "not fortunate enough to get private Work are in a State of absolute Want." As a result, "No Discipline can be enforced."[132] Some especially desperate soldiers even used criminal means to obtain wages, food, and clothing. In 1781, the year when the artificers' situ-ation was especially desperate, soldiers Charles Jones and John Perry, prob-ably tired of starving at the works, were taken into custody for entering "Mr Callender's Still House" and taking "a quantity of Bacon Out of said House in a Felonious Manner."[133] Perry, a nailsmith at the works who characterized his two years of service as "faithful" and "honest," was found guilty and sen-tenced to death later that same year for yet another crime—he had stolen bed-clothes, bottles, and other household goods out of a Carlisle home. Although Perry protested his innocence, arguing that he had purchased these stolen goods from another soldier at the works, the fact that he needed a coverlet hints at the dreadfully poor condition of the artificers.[134] War and revolution had thus made their presence felt in Carlisle in more sinister way. By forcing soldiers to act against civilians in a desperate attempt to survive, the declin-ing state of affairs in Carlisle demonstrated how choices made during war could have especially divisive impacts on a community. These circumstances demonstrated that being a town in-between during wartime was not always a good thing. War and revolution brought opportunity to Carlisle, redefining its role and function in the mid-Atlantic in significant ways. But at the same time, serving as a holding site for prisoners and an arms manufacturing and supply depot for the army had significant drawbacks. Residents discovered this sometimes quite painfully as years passed, finding themselves coping with greater economic and personal challenges than they had anticipated.

Whether one was a politician, soldier or civilian, young or old, or male or female, Carlisle residents could not avoid the significant changes war and revolution brought to town. Fighting this war redefined the community and reconfigured how its betweenness was expressed and experienced. For some residents, such as the many men who served in its political and military ranks, the American Revolution demanded great sacrifice. Yet it also offered them new opportunities for leadership, service, and increased status or economic gain. For these reasons, they reached out, eagerly volunteering because they wanted to be central players in this armed conflict with Great Britain. Their actions illustrated that Carlisle would not remain a community on the sidelines. By contrast, for the town's civilian population—especially its artisans and retailers—the Revolution's arrival in town offered them chances to earn income while meeting some of the war's enormous supply and service demands. Because their work helped to keep the Continental Army supplied, their efforts also highlighted Carlisle's central importance to the future of the nation.

Then, too, there was the townscape. War and revolution gave new meaning and function to various town structures. The public works, for instance, suddenly loomed large on the town's borders as a center of wartime commerce and production, as well as home to many soldiers. Inside town, private buildings like Stewart's tavern, or public buildings like the county jail, suddenly merited new degrees of local and national attention. Such shifts in the town's form and function also altered townspeople's daily lives in fundamental ways. Even though Carlisle was distant from the fighting, was never occupied by the British, and was not beset by civil strife between Whigs and Tories, war and revolution nonetheless had a remarkably pervasive influence on the town and its inhabitants. Such developments as the steady flow of artificers and other soldiers through the works, the economic opportunities and frustrations that accompanied the army's arrival, the housing of British and loyalist prisoners within the town's borders, and the new social dynamics that accompanied each of these changes brought the war home to even the most uncommitted. As a kind of local ground zero in the mid-Atlantic interior, Carlisle remained a town in-between, and as such, no one in town could avoid the war or its myriad effects.

This meant that when the war approached its conclusion in the early

1780s, this was also a communal event accompanied by significant change and a host of mixed reactions and emotions. Many Carlisle residents, unsurprisingly, celebrated the war's end elaborately and joyfully. General William Irvine, then commander at Fort Pitt, honored Cornwallis's surrender at Yorktown in 1781 with the firing of nineteen pieces of artillery and a patriotic display of colors.[135] To him, as to others who had risked their lives to fight, the war's end made the prospect of returning to Carlisle and his loving wife and family a welcome reality.

Other residents rejoiced initially, but then grew circumspect. They were concerned about their futures, recognizing that the community and nation that stood before them was no longer the colonial world that had existed only a short time before. The state of the economy, especially, troubled many. It was "in too unsettled a state" for many townspeople's tastes, and trade "present[ed] a Dull aspect, on acco[un]t of the Scarcity of Money."[136] Such developments raised fears in the minds of some. John Montgomery, for example, was less sure of the state of the nation, his community, and his financial well-being at war's end. Finding himself no longer a revolutionary booster, but a citizen trying to make his way in the new nation, he feared the effects a general drop in prices would have on Carlisle and his finances. As one of the town's wealthiest men, he had much to lose.[137]

Still, he was not the only one to express such fears, or to voice genuine concern about the conduct of his neighbors in the postwar world he envisioned. Many town leaders were baffled by the changes they saw around them. One prominent attorney lamented how "lands in this County have fallen in price very much since the Peace."[138] John Armstrong was more direct. He feared that a general financial crisis was setting the stage for a speculative boom that would eventually undermine the social fabric of Carlisle and its county. Observing with amazement that "there are no less than ten new houses of Stone or Brick going on in this town" even though "money is almost invisible," and characterizing some of his storekeeper and attorney neighbors as "Nabobs" for their irresponsible speculative practices, Armstrong lamented the estimated £25,000 debt sitting on the books of local merchants. In frustration, he exclaimed, "is it not high time that all ranks should change their gates?"[139] What, he wondered with trepidation, had the American Revolution actually wrought in Carlisle? In 1787, when he wrote, the answer was still not fully clear.

CHAPTER FIVE

Still In-Between

IT WAS DECEMBER 26, 1787. Another year nearly over, but with little to celebrate. The 1780s were a tough decade in America. The Revolutionary War was won, but victory had costs. In Pennsylvania, these costs included a postwar economic depression that worsened cash scarcity, accelerated declining land prices, gave rise to property foreclosures, and encouraged speculation. Then there was the continuing struggle between radicals, moderates, and conservatives for control of state politics, which remained heated. Still, though, some Carlisle townspeople, particularly its politically cautious leading men, had cause for optimism that winter day. Just weeks before, the state convention had ratified America's new Constitution; it was only the second state to do so. That gave them hope. The Constitution, they believed, would restore prosperity and order to America. It would also help them claim power from the radicals who had controlled Pennsylvania's government since the Revolution.

And so, on that late December day, Carlisle's Federalists busied themselves preparing a parade and ceremony to honor the new Constitution, which was to be held on the public square. They planned to issue several public proclamations, fire a cannon, and light a bonfire.[1] These activities seemed innocuous enough. Philadelphia, Lancaster, York, Easton, and nearby Chambersburg had already staged their own peaceful "demonstrations of joy."[2] But Carlisle was unlike these towns. As a town in-between it had a history as a divided, contentious, and sometimes violent place; the Revolution had done nothing to alter that fact. A parade staged here, therefore, had potential to become disorderly. Moreover, the Constitution that Carlisle's Federalists wished to celebrate was adamantly opposed by most county residents and some of their Carlisle neighbors. Carlisle's Federalists knew this, but still persisted in their celebration. They would revel in their victory whether their neighbors liked it or not.

The stage was thus set; this would be no ordinary parade. Festivities began at five o'clock that evening when Federalists called their neighbors out of their homes with the ringing of a bell and the beating of a drum. Supporters of the Constitution assembled on the streets. But soon a group of Antifederalist protestors appeared, "armed with bludgeons." They had also prepared for the occasion. Angered, in particular, by Federalist threats to break the unilluminated windows of all who opposed the Constitution, Antifederalists confronted their neighbors on the square and demanded a halt to the celebrations. Major James Armstrong Wilson, a Continental Army veteran who had served under William Irvine, stepped forward from the cannon he manned to defend his Federalist compatriots. As he noted with irony, he knew a "people so pregnant with liberty . . . would not wish to hinder their neighbors to show marks of joy." Antifederalists were in no mood to listen, however. They pelted him with staves and then beat him to the ground (he died several months later, possibly from wounds sustained during this attack). A "general confusion," or riot, ensued. Federalists hurled insults. Antifederalists attacked several celebrants. Most people ran off, however, frightened by the melée. Afterward, with the public square to themselves, Antifederalists carried out their own ritual; they set the cannon afire and burned a copy of the Constitution while shouting "loud huzzas" and damning its supporters. They won the first round.[3]

Carlisle's Federalists did not give up, however. The next day they returned to the square armed with muskets and bayonets, determined to carry out their celebration. For two hours, they celebrated by lighting a bonfire, verbally affirming the Constitution and its ratification, and shooting off volleys of muskets and cannon. Then they retired to a tavern. Immediately afterward, Antifederalists appeared again, announcing themselves with a drumbeat, and quickly proceeded to the courthouse. From there, they staged another counterdemonstration. Only this time, they went further. They paraded the streets with a cart carrying effigies of two of Pennsylvania's most well-known Federalists, Chief Justice Thomas McKean, and—more important to Carlisle's history—their former neighbor, James Wilson, whose effigy they specifically labeled "the Caledonian." Next, "with shouts and most dreadful execrations," according to Federalist observers, they hanged then "committed" the effigies "to the flames" in symbolic acts condemning two of Pennsylvania's most vociferous advocates of the new government. With these dramatic actions, two days of "rioting" came to a close.[4]

The Carlisle riot, as it was called by its detractors, was a momentous event for the town and nation. Set in the context of Carlisle's thirty-six-year history, this event confirmed Carlisle's heritage as a contested town in-between in the mid-Atlantic. Once again, the town's streets were the setting for the kind of hostile and violent confrontations between competing groups that had marked Carlisle's colonial past. Townspeople remained as politically fractured and confrontational after the Revolution as before, it seemed. Antifederalists' labeling of Wilson's effigy as "the Caledonian" illustrated the persistence of ethnic tensions as well. Not much had changed.

But there were important differences. More was at stake. A war had been fought and won, and a new republic born. In the troubled times of the 1780s many Americans, including townspeople, were uneasy. They feared not just for themselves, but for the future of their new nation. Still, these fears did not unite but divide, because Americans diagnosed the threats to the new nation differently. Some, like Carlisle's Federalists, believed economic downturn and democratic excess threatened the republic's stability. Others, including Carlisle's Antifederalists, feared that an evolving American aristocracy was undermining republican liberty. In this climate, Carlisle's riot, "one of the most widely reported events during ratification," according to historian Saul Cornell, took on heightened national importance.[5] Occurring at a time when popular resistance was gaining momentum across Pennsylvania, and nearly coinciding with the conclusion of Shays's Rebellion—the uprising of western Massachusetts farmers that began the year before—the clash between Federalists and Antifederalists at Carlisle expressed in microcosm the tensions plaguing America overall. The riot either confirmed fears that the Revolution's achievements might be lost to anarchy, or gave one confidence that democracy from below might prevail.[6] In either case, this riot had a significant impact on Carlisle's identity as a place. As a ground zero for the expression of tensions between the Constitution's supporters and its opponents in the late 1780s, Carlisle's betweenness took on far more metaphorical meaning than in the past. Being a town in-between was no longer measured just by the number of trade goods and furs passing through, or the quantity of supplies gathered or manufactured there for the army. Rather, as the town's political fate took on import to the nation at large, Carlisle and its residents assumed a central place in the nation's political consciousness.

But why Carlisle? How had it become so central to the expression of these tensions? More than just the Constitution was at stake—the townspeople who confronted each other on Carlisle's streets during those two days in December fought over the nation's as well as their town's past and future. And there was much to argue about. Politically, revolutionary-era clashes between the state's radicals and conservatives perpetuated existing ethno-religious and class antagonisms in Carlisle, pitting the town's conservative political leaders against their more radical neighbors in town and especially the county. Then there was the problematic postwar economy. Economic distress was palpable in interior Pennsylvania. A "Gloomy aspect . . . Hangs over us," wrote one contact of William Irvine.[7] In Carlisle, taxable property values had declined since the war. Townspeople owned fewer livestock than they had in 1779, and slave holdings had dropped 25 percent, a reflection of economic hard times and the state's 1780 gradual emancipation law.[8] More problematic was the uneven impact of these dislocations. Some suffered intensely, while others saw improvement postwar. The result was a widening chasm between the economic haves and have-nots. Finally, the newly founded Dickinson College stirred local tensions. The college brought a host of new, outside influences to town while shifting expectations about the kind of community Carlisle might become. Taken together, these factors generated intense stresses within the community. All that was needed was a spark like Constitutional ratification to ignite them. With that, Carlisle exploded in violence.

That Carlisle would play a pivotal role in the politics of the early republic was not evident as the Revolution concluded in the early 1780s. The town had contributed more than its share to the American cause. But with the war won, soldiers and officers stationed at Carlisle went home and the public works closed; the town was no longer needed as an army supply and manufacturing center. New county formation, meanwhile, reduced Cumberland County by nearly two-thirds; this meant that Carlisle was no longer the de facto capital of Pennsylvania's west as it had been during the colonial period.[9] The town had thus lost crucial components of its wartime identity as a town in-between. Instead, Pennsylvania's and the nation's attention shifted east to Philadelphia and New York, each for a time America's capital, where American political leaders faced the daunting task of crafting a nation. Although the republic was established, big political questions loomed large in the nation's collective political consciousness. How would this republic function? In particular, would it rely, as many of the nation's prominent leaders hoped, on the quiet virtue of its citizens? Or would the new republic rest on individuals actively claiming their place in a more participatory political order, as many ordinary Americans schooled in the politics of revolution believed it should?[10]

The answers to these questions were especially complicated in Pennsylvania, the state where American politics had taken its most radical turn during the Revolution. The state's radical leadership was enthusiastic about the participatory politics of the Revolution. They saw a citizenry eager to claim its place in the republic and expanded the franchise and civil liberties in response. But there was a downside. Their wartime Test Oath and vociferous persecution of loyalists and neutrals earned them enemies. And they were unable to collect taxes or hold down prices. Thus by the 1780s their frustrated opponents, the state's Republicans, stood ready to assume the helm. With the state's and nation's future at stake, these conservative politicians were fearful of republican excesses. They opposed the state's radical constitution and decried the divisive politics of the radical majority. Pennsylvanians, they argued, needed to be taught restraint.[11]

But how to instill that restraint was the issue. Ratifying the U.S. Constitution seemed the best way by 1787, and later, in 1790, drafting a more conservative Pennsylvania constitution was another. But in the early 1780s—with the Revolution only just won and radicals still mostly in control—new, conservative plans for government were not the answer. The time was not right. Pennsylvania's Republicans had to advance their agendas through other means, like education. That they looked in that direction was no surprise; many Americans believed that an educated citizenry was critical to sustaining the republic. As testament, between 1776 and 1800, sixteen colleges opened in the United States.[12]

Philadelphia physician and Republican politician Benjamin Rush was among those Pennsylvanians who argued most passionately for education as a tool for building political virtue and stability among the state's citizenry. Founding colleges, he suggested, would ease political chaos. To rescue "the state from the hands of tyrants, fools, and traitors," Pennsylvania's conservatives had to target the hotbed of state radicalism, the west side of the Susquehanna, and found a college there that would serve as "a nursery of religion and learning" for its interior residents.[13] New generations of leaders, educated from "infancy" to be virtuous men, would act responsibly to safeguard "the liberties of the first state in the Union," a place, said Rush, that was "already a little nation" in and of itself.[14]

Establishing a college was no easy task, however. Higher education was highly politicized in the mid-Atlantic and had been for some time. Because universities were primarily training grounds for ministers, the Great Awakening and the bitter divisions it engendered among Protestants spilled into higher education. Such splits were particularly acute among Presbyterians, among whom Old and New Lights had competed in the 1760s to control institutions like the College of New Jersey at Princeton. Old Lights lost that battle. Then came the Revolution. Political divisions between radicals and conservatives in Pennsylvania intensified religious rivalries. In 1779, as a strike at one of the state's remaining vestiges of conservatism, radicals seized control of the College of Philadelphia, ousted its Anglican founders, and appointed a Presbyterian as provost. Although many Presbyterians hailed this as a victory, not all were happy. Some, including Rush and many of Carlisle's leading men, opposed this move. They read this takeover as another sign of their political alienation.[15]

Rush grew more determined to found a college in response. But where? His friend and fellow Republican, John Montgomery, offered the answer: Carlisle. It fit Rush's criteria perfectly; it was located west of the river at a convergence point of commerce and culture; furthermore, some of the state's leading radicals, such as Robert Whitehill, hailed from its county. Equally significant, some Carlisle gentlemen were willing to work with him on this project because they also opposed the state's Radicals. They were Presbyterians, some of them Old Lights, and they were eager to bring higher education to Carlisle.[16] Already on Congressman Montgomery's agenda was a plan to lobby the state to expand Carlisle's grammar school, chartered in 1773, into a larger academy. Rush and Montgomery soon transformed this idea into a more ambitious plan for a college. Together they would make Carlisle a center of higher education in the state's interior; if successful, Carlisle's postwar betweenness would have new cultural as well as political meaning.[17]

They began work in 1782, a good year for the state's Republicans. Republicans held a majority in the state house and had elected John Dickinson president of the Executive Council.[18] But still, founding a college was an uphill battle because radicals, many of whom were also Presbyterians, sensed an ambush; they saw Rush's plan for what it was—politically and religiously partisan. Nor were all Carlisle Presbyterians supportive. John Armstrong, a

New Light who sent his son to the College of New Jersey, initially opposed it; he was unconvinced of the need for a theologically conservative college.[19] Rush lobbied him in response. He reminded Armstrong that "the University of Philadelphia" would never be the "nursery" of the Calvinism they held dear. He also argued from a more pragmatic perspective. Education should be accessible to all Pennsylvanians, he reminded Armstrong. "The expense of an education in Philadelphia alone" was "sufficient to deter farmers from sending their sons to the University of Philadelphia," and the College of New Jersey was too distant "from the western counties of this state."[20] Most important, according to Rush, this new college would train the region's next generation of leaders. In a town where gentlemen like Armstrong were more politically conservative than their rural counterparts, this argument held sway. As Rush asserted, "the happiness and prosperity of every community, . . . depends much on the right education of the youth." A college at Carlisle would thus school "the minds of a rising generation" to "promote the real welfare of this State." Armstrong agreed and threw his support behind their plan.[21]

There were also important ethnic dimensions to the college's founding. Rush, a Philadelphian, critiqued most of the state's interior residents as rustics. As a Presbyterian, he was especially vexed by the Scots-Irish; too many of them were uncouth radicals in need of "virtuous principles and liberal knowledge."[22] Only education would "soften the tempers of our turbulent brethren," he said, by teaching them how to be Americans. Education would "inspire them with liberal sentiments in government and religion, . . . teach them moderation in their conduct to other sects, and . . . rescue them from the charges of bigotry and persecution that are so often brought against them." To boot, it would school them to value hard work, thrift, and clean living.[23] And the Irish were not the only target of Rush's plans; he felt that Pennsylvania's Germans would benefit as well. As the other major non-English ethnic group of the interior, Germans must also "be *enlightened*," said Rush. "Too many" of them "imagine the whole business of life to consist in *labor,* and all its happiness in *gold and silver* and fine *plantations*." To become Americans, this "uninformed body of people" needed education.[24]

Rush's plans surely sounded familiar to Carlisle residents. He was not the first outsider to attempt to reorder the town to suit his ends, nor was he the first to critique the Scots-Irish. His approach and attitude resembled those of Thomas Penn. Rush, like Penn, positioned himself as the cosmopolitan authority who knew what was best for the interior. Penn had planned the townscape to instill order and serve his economic interests. By contrast, Rush hoped that education would school locals in political moderation more in keeping with his own sensibilities—his goal was to end political radicalism in the state. But there was more. Of particular significance to the town's history, Rush and Montgomery resurrected older, colonial-era notions of Carlisle's identity as a place between east and west in arguing for its advantageousness as a site. In phrasing reminiscent of Penn's surveyors, for example, Montgomery explained that Carlisle was "pleasantly Situated in a rich and healthy part of this State." Because it was situated "nearly in the center of the same," it was "one of the most Suitable places that could have been thought off [*sic*] for the erection of a College."[25] With "an immense country" open to it "over the mountains," Rush believed that Carlisle was "the key to our western world."[26] In keeping with the town's colonial history, Rush chose Carlisle as the site for his college because of its central position between east and west in the state. If his plans succeeded, they would realign the north-south geographic orientation that had reshaped the town's functions during the Revolution.

Carlisle's college became reality in 1783. In the fall of that year, as Republicans gained momentum in state politics, the Pennsylvania Assembly issued the college's charter; its name attested to their growing strength. Dickinson College honored conservative politician John Dickinson and acknowledged his financial donation to the school.[27] Its seal, which was designed by Rush, symbolized the republican idealism on which it was founded. It contained a cap of liberty and a telescope placed above an open Bible accompanied by the motto written by Dickinson, *Pietate et Doctrina tuta libertas*, or "religion and learning, the bulwark of liberty," a phrase that embodied Rush's beliefs.[28] As chartered, Dickinson College served the commonwealth. It was a nonsectarian institution funded by state and private subscribers under the management of forty trustees from all regions and religions in Pennsylvania. In reality, however, Presbyterians, both Old and New Lights, and Carlisle gentlemen dominated its governing board. In fact, reading like a who's who of the town's leading men, trustees included John Montgomery, John Armstrong, James Wilson, William Irvine, attorney Robert Magaw, and merchant Stephen Duncan. Dickinson thus enjoyed the de facto status of being the first state-supported sectarian institution in Pennsylvania; Rush and Montgomery had mostly gotten their way.[29]

Their victory was short-lived, however. Much as Penn and his surveyors discovered in the 1750s, Dickinson's founders quickly realized that overseeing the operations of a college posed different challenges than planning it—especially at a distance. There were hurdles to surmount, including funding. During the economic hard times of the 1780s, money was hard to come by. John Dickinson's generous donation was not enough. The college not only began on shaky economic ground, financial matters would plague it for decades to come.[30] The school also needed a physical home; the small, dilapidated brick structure that housed the grammar school would not suffice. With the help of James Wilson, the trustees successfully petitioned Congress to lease them the shuttered buildings at the public works. Although crude structures, they were large enough to house a school. Equally important, the college needed equipment, a curriculum, faculty, and a principal. The trustees mostly borrowed Dickinson's curriculum from existing institutions.[31] Among the first faculty appointments was Rev. Robert Davidson, a graduate of the College of Philadelphia, assistant minister of the First Church of Philadelphia, and a favorite of Rush. Davidson was named professor of history, geography, and belles lettres; he was also called to minister to Carlisle's First Presbyterian Church on the square. James Ross, master of the grammar school, was named Professor of Languages. The college's first principal was to be the Scots Presbyterian minister, Rev. Charles Nisbet, a highly regarded Old Light, protégé of John Witherspoon, and friend of American independence.[32]

Nisbet was central to Rush's plans. Early on, Rush pinned his hopes on convincing Nisbet, whom he described as "a moving library," to vacate his post in Scotland and come to the American interior to head this "new-born infant" institution.[33] After much flattery and assurances, Nisbet agreed. He sailed for America with his wife and four children in 1785. After staying for a time in Philadelphia, the forty-nine-year-old Nisbet and his family traveled west to Carlisle, arriving in town on the auspicious day of July 4th. The mood that day was festive, perhaps even a bit rowdy. Locals had gathered to celebrate the anniversary of American independence, as many communities did in the 1780s. But this particular year was special—they were eager to welcome this outsider into their community. Upon hearing of his approach, townspeople, along with the Carlisle troop of horses, met Nisbet on the road and escorted him first to a picnic and then to town. Once there, with the courthouse bell ringing to announce his arrival, he was met with "joy and congratulation, and was received and treated with all the marks of respect and esteem which distinguished . . . long expected strangers." He was sworn in as Dickinson's first principal the next day.[34] Everything had started well. Townspeople may not have taken kindly in the past to strangers, but they welcomed Nisbet. To an elated Rush, "a new sun is risen upon Pennsylvania."[35]

Alas, this sunrise was brief. Nisbet was disappointed, even shocked, by what he found in Carlisle. The college, he discovered, existed mostly in name only. There were few students. The college building (a "'hogpen'" as he described it) and the house provided for him were in disrepair. Much to his dismay, with no position on the Board of Trustees, he had little authority. He did not even have a church to minister to, since Davidson presided over Carlisle's First Presbyterian. As a middle-aged immigrant accustomed to life in Scotland, Carlisle was a coarse, unappealing town to him. Finally, his cantankerous personality intensified when he and his family grew ill soon after their arrival.[36] After finding himself confined to his deplorable Carlisle house while ill, Nisbet hit a breaking point. In fall 1785, he resigned and said he was returning to Scotland. Despite boosters' claims, Nisbet disputed that Carlisle was centrally located or in any way advantageous; he considered it rather a sickly and depressing place located on the edge of civilization.[37] He preferred to go home rather than risk "falling a sacrifice to the climate."[38]

The Board was stunned. They initially refused to accept his resignation, but then capitulated, critiquing Nisbet as a deserter and weakling. An exasperated Rush proclaimed that he was nothing more than "a mere machine in the hands of his wife and children" who were homesick for Scotland. But just as the Board resigned itself to this setback, they were surprised again when Nisbet rescinded his request and asked to be reelected. Rush, completely flabbergasted and pitying Nisbet as "*insane*" and his wife as "*foolish,*" nonetheless agreed to his reelection. He had pinned the college's reputation on him, after all. Nisbet was thus reappointed; he remained Dickinson's principal until his death in 1804.[39]

Although Rush was willing "to forgive and forget all of Dr. Nisbet's failings," the cleric's actions were a major reversal for the college.[40] Nisbet's complaints revealed that larger issues were in dispute, which reflected not only the college's shaky foundation, but the transitional state of Carlisle's society, economy, and political culture in the 1780s. Dickinson College was a far more infant institution than Nisbet anticipated. Even more significant, Carlisle was not the peaceful, pastoral, and "handsome town, free from luxury, and other vices," that Nisbet had been led to expect.[41]

Nisbet had arrived at a pivotal time in the town's history. Although "inhabited by Indians and beasts of prey" only "30 years ago," Carlisle had become, in some respects at least, a "sample of the rapid progress of population and improvement in Pennsylvania."[42] Despite the postwar economic downturn, the town was doing well by some measures. Carlisle had several hundred houses and businesses. Many were crude log structures, but others were built of stone or brick. It had public buildings of law and government, as well as meetinghouses and churches. After 1783, it even had a college to call its own, which was exceptional; Dickinson was the thirteenth college chartered in America, and only the second in Pennsylvania. More significant, in 1785, the same year Nisbet arrived, the Pennsylvania-born German George Kline, only twenty-five years of age at the time and a recent arrival in town, started publication of the *Carlisle Gazette*, the first newspaper of Pennsylvania's interior. By 1810, he was one of seven book and print tradesmen at work in the town.[43] In addition, by the 1790s, Carlisle was a stop for the mail stage traveling across the state. Market days were held twice weekly on the center square, and the town's streets were lined with retail establishments and craft shops.[44] As one traveler reported in 1789, "business is good, and there are many stores" in Carlisle. "There is a good printing press, and almost all trades are carried on here, in particular the making of nails and good beer."[45] Through time, Carlisle had evolved from a town of tavern keepers, merchants, storekeepers, and traders into an economically diverse commercial and cultural crossroads serving its hinterlands and the mid-Atlantic. This also meant that its betweenness as a place was grounded on more than just metaphorical political or cultural attributes. Rather, with an increasingly diverse economy, as well as a printing press and a college, Carlisle's betweenness had tangible qualities that proved especially dynamic.

The expansive range of occupations residents held was one gauge of Carlisle's function as a new kind of commercial crossroads in the early republic. Pennsylvania began conducting an occupational census every seven years beginning in 1776. The limited records extant for Carlisle show that an average of sixty-seven different trades were practiced there between 1793 and 1807.[46] Advertisements in Kline's *Carlisle Gazette* reveal a greater range, naming over ninety different occupations being practiced in and near the town after 1785. Such occupational diversity undoubtedly reflected a maturing urban economy, one built on western trade and two wars. It also signaled the myriad economic shifts taking place during the early republic as townspeople continued to define and redefine themselves and their town in response to necessity and enterprise.

Retailers—including shopkeepers, merchants, and tavern keepers—still predominated, much as they had during Carlisle's colonial past.[47] But their niche in the local economy was changing. Whereas earlier, many retailers earned income by acting as middlemen between western Native peoples and Philadelphia merchants, or by serving traders and agents who did, circumstances were different by the 1780s. The fur trade was gone, and with the Revolutionary War won, supplying and servicing the military was a thing of the past. If these retailers were to survive the postwar economic downturn, they had to respond to new commercial opportunities offered by export merchants in Philadelphia, and especially Baltimore. That meant remaking themselves into different sorts of middlemen who served an expanding grain trade. The grain trade was mostly a good economic bet in the postwar mid-Atlantic. As historian Brooke Hunter notes, not all sectors of the American economy were equally depressed postwar. In particular, grain exports, spurred by increased demand for foodstuffs in the West Indies and Europe, expanded rapidly in the 1780s, increasing prices and spurring economic growth in the Delaware Valley, the center of American production. Growth spread outward to interior areas where retailers worked cooperatively with farmers and millers to tap into this lucrative trade.[48]

The grain trade anchored Carlisle's postwar recovery. It also shaped town-county relations by knitting together urban and rural sectors of the region's economy more tightly than before. Grain production was not new to the Cumberland Valley; it had been part of the region's economy since the 1730s. Nonetheless, its expansion in the 1780s, particularly when combined with the end of the fur trade and wartime supply functions, fostered new degrees of economic interdependence between town and county. This was especially evident in Carlisle where merchants, all of whom also participated in the depressed dry goods market, found they needed the grain trade more than ever to survive or thrive. The account books of one unidentified merchant from 1789 confirm this pattern: during a time of severe cash shortages, grain and flour were critically important mediums of exchange. One local customer, for example, earned £15 credit with the twelve barrels of flour he brought to the store in June. This merchant also received bushels of unprocessed wheat from farmers as payment for merchandise eleven different times during a seven-month period in 1789. On these occasions, an average of once per month, he then contracted with a local miller—most often Charles McClure—to grind this grain into flour that could be transported and sold. In September 1789 alone, McClure received store credit in four instances for grinding seventy-six barrels of "flower" at "diff[eren]t times."[49] Although this merchant never specialized to the extent of flour merchants in Philadelphia, he nonetheless cultivated an economic niche for himself as a middleman in this trade, replicating patterns of earlier merchants who had acted as agents of fur traders. Unlike his counterparts in the 1760s, though, he no longer dealt with Native peoples, but rather with other Americans. There was another major difference—he was not an employee, but rather an independent businessman.

In addition, Carlisle—as a traveler noted in 1794—had become "the market where the grain from the surrounding area is brought to be transported from here to Philadelphia by wagons."[50] Thus, by arranging for the transportation and sale of flour to export merchants in Philadelphia and Baltimore, this same Carlisle merchant also positioned himself as a middleman between interior producers and coastal markets. This cemented economic connections between regions in ways reminiscent of the fur trade. During the last seven months of 1789, for example, he engaged a local man to haul produce, likely including grain or flour, to Philadelphia or Baltimore on thirty-three instances. Seven percent of the credits issued in his daybook during this period were granted to men like David Williamson, whom he employed for "Halling 12 Barrels flower to B[alti]more" and for "Halling 12 Bushels Salt from Baltimore" back to Carlisle. Other evidence from his account book confirms his extensive dealings with Baltimore and Philadelphia merchants. To his Baltimore contact, merchant John Holmes—a former Carlisle resident—he sent 126 barrels of locally milled flour between June and December 1789. In return, he received over 200 barrels of salt, three barrels of herring, and one of mackerel. During the same period, he sent an additional forty-three barrels of flour and six kegs of butter to unnamed merchants in Philadelphia as payment for shipments of dry goods and other unspecified "sundries."[51] For this merchant, as for his colonial predecessors, economic isolation was not an option. To make a profit or achieve a competence, Carlisle merchants had to adapt to the market demands of their time. In the colonial period that meant serving the fur trade. In the 1780s, by contrast, it entailed selling flour to Philadelphia and Baltimore merchants engaged in supplying the sustenance demands of the Atlantic world. In either context, however, in functioning as an essential crossroads of commerce, Carlisle was also an important town in-between; it was still a way station that goods or products moved to and through on their way elsewhere in the mid-Atlantic.

Flexibility was therefore essential to economic survival in postwar Carlisle. Despite the opportunities trading in grain offered, with the dry goods markets depressed, debts high, and cash in short supply, these were still tough economic times. Merchant Joseph Givin's advertised willingness to sell his goods "at the most reduced prices, for Cash or Country produce" in 1788, for example, hints at the challenges retailers faced in the cash-poor economy of the interior. For Givin, it was better to collect country produce than not sell his goods at all.[52] He was not alone. Although payments in kind were not as liquid as cash, Carlisle's merchants used them to supplement stock and perhaps supply personal needs. For example, hatter John Isett earned store credit for the fur hat sold to Samuel Pickering and tobacconist John Morrison purchased goods by supplying "course" and "fine" tobacco for resale. While the merchant probably wore the two coats and jacket he received from tailors William Petrikin and William Levis in 1789.[53]

Trade in kind was, in fact, more common postwar than it had been in the past. For example, during the 1770s, customers at Samuel Postlethwaite's store settled 28 percent of their accounts with cash. By the 1780s, cash payments to another Carlisle merchant fell to 24 percent of his total. Although the total percentage of his accounts paid rose by the 1780s, locals were somewhat less likely to pay for their purchases at his store with cash and nearly twice as likely to pay with produce, goods, or services instead.[54] Equally significant, these patterns imply a two-way process of adjustment. While Carlisle merchants were more willing to accept payments in kind, local consumers likely felt more intense pressure to pay their accounts in a timely fashion. With a "great multiplicity of Law Suits brought against the poorer sort of People" in the county court "at a Time of so great scarcity of Cash," according to one justice in the early 1780s, the "very distressing" economic conditions of people in post-revolutionary Carlisle pushed retailers, producers, and consumers into new economic relationships whether they wanted them or not.[55] Economic innovation was inspired by necessity as well as choice.

Merchants and shopkeepers, while important, were not the sole economic actors in the local economy. A diverse and increasingly specialized array of artisans were also at the economic forefront by the 1790s, their activities also redefining Carlisle's function as a town in-between. Some of them, like the town's coopers (barrel makers), an occupational category on the rise, supported the grain, and by extension whiskey, trade.[56] Others did not. Those in the cloth production and apparel trades participated in parallel exchange networks that bridged economic gaps between town and countryside, much like the grain trade. Shoemakers, weavers, and tailors accounted for nearly 17 percent of the town's workforce after 1793.[57] Like grain merchants, these tradesmen depended in part on rural producers and processors, such as fullers and tanners, for their business. The weaver, Robert M'Bride, for example, noted in 1795 that he had purchased a new loom "for raised work . . . for

weaving double and single Coverlids [coverlets], Diaper and White Coun-
terpains [bedspreads]," implying his desire to produce finished goods made
of wool obtained from livestock raised by local farmers, and probably spun
into yarn by their wives and daughters.[58] Interdependence also worked in the
opposite direction. Fullers (artisans who finished cloth by processing it in a
mill) depended on cooperation from urban retailers to sustain their trades.
Vincent Gribble, fuller at a mill on the Yellow Breeches just south of town,
took cloth—woven by weavers like M'Bride—at John Hunter's tavern in
Carlisle. Peter M'Cann, another fuller just north of town, picked up cloth for
fulling every three weeks at Jacob Crever's store. When fulling was complete,
cloth sometimes returned to Carlisle, this time to craftsmen like Jacob Miller,
who "carrie[d] on the BLUE-DYING Business, in all its Branches," at his shop
on York Street.[59]

The cloth production trades paralleled the grain trade in another way—
they were changing rapidly postwar. Cloth production was expanding in
directions that linked these tradesmen and their products to more distant
raw materials and finished goods markets. There were hints of these changes
before the Revolution. In the early 1770s, the large quantities of wool and tow
cards (tools used for carding wool and flax) that four Carlisle merchants purchased in Philadelphia suggest that there were already extensive cloth production networks operating in the region.[60] Whether this production supplied
cloth for the final years of the fur trade or met local needs is unclear. After
the war, locals began producing cotton cloth. One store's accounts reveal
customers purchasing anywhere from twenty-one to slightly over one hundred pounds of raw cotton that they were presumably carding and perhaps
spinning in their households or businesses. Several merchants stocked cotton cards for sale in their stores. By 1795, weaver Robert M'Bride had even
opened what he called a "COTTON FACTORY," where he produced an assortment of "Striped Cottons" for his customers.[61] The rise of cotton cloth production demonstrates how postwar changes in American textile manufacture
affected Pennsylvania's interior urban communities. Specifically, cotton cloth
production, dependent as it was on non-local raw materials, linked Carlisle
to a distant market economy fueled largely by the labors of enslaved African
Americans. This simultaneously undercut the interdependent associations
that bound rural producers to town merchants and artisans.[62]

The cloth production trades not only sealed Carlisle's function as a central site of exchange between town and country, they also connected Carlisle

to economic and cultural worlds that transcended the interior. The functioning of this trade only further reinforced Carlisle's economic identity as a town in-between in the mid-Atlantic. Yet there were significant differences from the colonial era. In the town's postwar economy, European influences and metropolitan goods, rather than western ideas or products, loomed particularly large. This meant that goods and ideas tended to flow eastward through town more often than in the colonial past. The town's hatters, tailors, and seamstresses, for example, had few connections to the region's agricultural economy; the materials and styles they used were imported. Their work brought metropolitan, even European, products and cultural ideals into the Cumberland Valley, making Carlisle an important site of cultural diffusion in the interior. In fact, these tradesmen and women cultivated Carlisle customers by flaunting their experience in London, Philadelphia, or Dublin. Alexander Biggs was a "Taylor, from London" whose work was "performed as well as any master in Philadelphia." The English immigrant William Petrikin, tailor and "Ladies Habit-Maker from Britain"—a man who earned fame as one of Carlisle's leading Antifederalists and defenders of their riot—pleased many customers in Philadelphia before setting up shop in Carlisle. Andrew Murray promoted himself as a tailor from Dublin, suggesting that European experience was a sign of quality work and current tastes.[63] Cosmopolitan cultural connections were important selling points for these artisans. In promoting themselves in this way, however, they also situated Carlisle's identity in a broader commercial and cultural orbit that transcended the interior, as well as the mid-Atlantic.

Still, these were not the only strategies these craftsmen used to market themselves. In highlighting their connections to the genteel and "most fashionable" cultures of Europe and America, they implicitly promised to bring cultural sophistication to Carlisle.[64] Alexander Biggs, for instance, performed "every branch of the business in the most elegant taste and newest fashion." The hatter Jacob Shuler made only "LADIES and GENTLEMEN'S HATS in the newest fashion" and "of the best materials."[65] Biggs and Shuler tapped into the same kind of rising cultural and class consciousness that inspired town leaders like John Montgomery to seek a college for the town. Their advertisements demonstrate that not all outside influences need be threatening to community interests. Stylish goods were status markers that Carlisle's wealthier men and women might employ to differentiate themselves from their poorer neighbors. These goods divided the community, but unlike the knives and gunpowder traders sold to Indians in the 1760s, clothing did not imperil anyone's well-being. Instead, in a region sometimes criticized by outsiders for its lack of refinement, fashionable dress was a way townspeople signaled that they were not the coarse bumpkins that many perceived them to be.

Female artisans followed similar patterns, but were more likely to target other women. Milliner Miss Patty Stuart was from Philadelphia and "wishe[d] to inform the Ladies in Carlisle" that she was "acquainted with the Newest Fashions." Milliner Mary M'Cormick made "New Fashioned Bonnets; Wire Caps; Cloth and Silk Cloaks; . . . Ladies Caps, and Head Dresses," which "she can form in the newest and neatest modes."[66] Women were important shoppers and consumers in late eighteenth-century America. Aside from the 1760s and 1770s, when their boycotts helped spur the Revolution, women had more choices and economic power in the eighteenth-century marketplace because of the consumer revolution.[67] In Carlisle, female artisans made every effort to cultivate their business by offering wares they thought would appeal to customers. They even created retail spaces, like Susannah Thompson's store or Elizabeth Vanlear's tavern, where they might feel welcome.[68] Some male artisans followed their lead, appealing directly to locally privileged women. Tailor William Petrikin "solicit[ed] the patronage of the ladies of Carlisle and county adjacent, which he hop[ed] to acquire by his care and punctuality."[69]

Other artisans targeted the town's leading families by cultivating demand for luxury craft items that conformed to metropolitan styles. By the 1790s, Carlisle had five clockmakers, three watchmakers, and several silversmiths. Among the best known was Jacob Hendel, a highly skilled clock and watchmaker, jeweler, and silversmith, who relocated to Carlisle from Lancaster in 1796. In his shop in his two-story stone house on High Street, he noted that "CLOCKS of all kinds are executed by him, . . . Watches repaired, and all manner of JEWELLRY and SILVER WORK done." Not only did he make "Eight day and Thirty hour Clocks" to grace the parlors of local gentry, he also crafted more specialized pieces "shewing the rising and setting of the Sun, the increase and decrease of the Moon," while doing "All kinds of Gold and Silver work." Hendel is an especially important Carlisle artisan. He symbolized the German turn of the town's population in the late eighteenth century. As one of the region's finest clockmakers, his work embodied the town's move toward the production of more specialized and high-style goods.[70]

Hendel was not alone. A remarkable number of highly specialized itinerant artisans and tradesmen—from portrait painters and jewelers to dentists and music and dance teachers—passed through town during the early republic. Many of these artisan-professionals, like the dentist Mr. Dubuisson, who arrived from Philadelphia, or the portrait miniaturist, Mr. Peticoles from France, highlighted their connections to metropolitan places of the east or Europe. Like their counterparts in the apparel or clockmaking trades, they aimed to serve Carlisle's aspiring ladies and gentlemen. Music teacher S. Balentine, for example—who spent several months in town in 1792—taught violin, German flute, oboe, clarinet, bassoon, trumpet, French horn, and guitar. Those who patronized him while he resided at a local tavern were likely among the region's better sorts; they had the time and money for such leisured pursuits.[71]

Viewed as part of a larger economic picture, these changes—from the increased importance of the grain trade to the rise of specialized tradesmen who aggressively marketed their goods—illustrate the dynamism of Carlisle's early national economy and its centrality in the mid-Atlantic. Not all was gloom and doom. In fact, one New Yorker who "cast my Lott in this quarter," was "happy" to hear from his Carlisle friend "of the flourishing situation of Carlisle" in 1785.[72] Growth was uneven, however. Happening in fits and starts, it generated the kinds of booms and busts characteristic of the broader transition to capitalism taking place across America between 1790 and 1820. Much was in flux. By the 1790s, the Cumberland Valley was moving toward the industrial nineteenth century. In response, locals reinvented their businesses and themselves to suit the new economic climate, reasserting Carlisle's identity as a commercial and cultural crossroads, albeit one that stood between its hinterlands and various cosmopolitan markets in America and Europe. But ironically, just as townspeople more clearly demarcated class boundaries among themselves by purchasing consumer goods, like clothing, or pursuing an education at Dickinson College, occupational boundaries got more fluid. In the early republic, townspeople were more likely to switch occupations than in the past, and many pursued several occupations at once.[73] The German immigrant Adam Mattheis, for instance, was a blue dyer and coverlet weaver, cloth production trades that were related but required different skills and equipment. Wheelwright Moses Bullock, who arrived from Ireland in 1797 and opened a wheelwright and cane-making business, advertised a year later that he was also a "Windsor Chair Maker." Several years later, he started a brush-making business. Although Bullock always identified himself as a wheelwright first, he learned other trades. William Graham, who resided just outside town, was a wheelwright and chairmaker, who also did cane making, varnishing, and house painting.[74] Others took on tavern

or storekeeping as a second or third business. Several town physicians, unlike their colonial counterparts, ran apothecary shops. Hugh Holmes was a
tailor and grocer. Shoemaker John Webber sold dry and wet goods, did boot
and shoemaking and leather cutting. Nearly seven years later, he was also a
book and almanac seller. John Moser, another shoemaker, also kept a tavern,
the Sign of the Ship. Charles Bovard, a maker of weaver's reeds, ran a reed-
making shop, which he then expanded into a dry goods, hardware, and grocery store. A decade later, in 1802, he sold off his shop. Several years later he
was proprietor of a tavern, the Sign of General Washington.[75] It is impossible
to know the reasons for such patterns of employment. Was this an entrepreneurial spirit aimed at exploiting expanding markets and new supplies of
labor, or a strategy to overcome economic fluctuations, minimize risk, and
maintain year-round employment? Or was it some combination of all these
factors? Whatever the case, a powerful occupational dynamism took hold in
Carlisle. Many townsmen, supported by the labors of their wives and children, servants, and a dwindling number of slaves, took on multiple and sometimes unrelated occupations from practicing skilled crafts to retailing.

In another sign of industrialization, Carlisle workplaces grew more specialized as craftsmen geared their shops for the production of specific goods.
Beginning in the late 1780s, artisans used new terms to describe their workshops and products. By 1798, Samuel Criswell was no longer a gunsmith, but
the proprietor of a gun "factory"; Lewis Foulke ran a "Nail Factory"; and
tobacconist Andrew Crouse ran a "manufactory" rather than a shop.[76] Other
examples of this specialization exist. In 1798, Misters Hanna and Martin announced that they had "commenced and intend[ed] carrying on the Boot and
Shoe-making, in all its various branches." Five years later, after Hanna went
solo, he advertised himself as a boot and shoe "Manufacturer." Tallow chan-
dler John Gray followed a similar pattern. In 1802, he "commenced . . . the
Tallow-Chandling and Soap Boiling Business." By 1805, his business had
grown into a "Soap and Candle MANUFACTORY," where he "mould[ed] and
dipped" candles, sold soap, and had a "handsome assortment" of dry goods
and groceries for sale.[77]

Some of these artisans surely employed such terminology as a marketing
strategy to sell familiar goods in novel ways. But use of "factory" and "manufactory" also signaled broader structural changes in the town's economy
as industry localized. Scholars argue that these terms symbolized the rise
of larger, specialized, and mechanized workplaces in America's nineteenth-
century urban centers; their use in Carlisle suggests that interior towns were

not exempt from these shifts.[78] John Duncan illustrates how such change played out in Carlisle. In 1787, the Scots-Irish Duncan, proprietor of a dry goods store and nailery, embarked on an ambitious plan to enlarge his business. Advertising for additional nailers, he boastfully stated that: "He has it now in his power to supply the country at his NAIL FACTORY, with Shingle Nails, Flooring Brads, Double Tens[,] Lathing and Cask Nails, and Sprigs of any size."[79] For Duncan, as for other craftsmen in Carlisle in the early stages of targeting a broader customer base, the term "factory" illustrated his ambitious plans and the enlarged scope of his enterprise. The growth of his business exemplified the dramatic change in some sectors of Carlisle's postwar economy. Carlisle remained a town in-between, but the forces defining its betweenness as a commercial crossroads shifted dramatically during the early republic. Industry, not just trade, shaped its economic identity as a place.

As the nineteenth century approached, Carlisle was anything but the pastoral village that Dickinson College's first principal, Charles Nisbet, expected upon his arrival. Instead, multiple economic changes were pushing and pulling the town toward the Industrial Revolution. Some townspeople embraced these changes. Eager to pursue new opportunities, they saw them as progress. Others simply weathered them as best they could, adapting their lives and businesses as necessity demanded. Still others resisted. How one reacted reflected one's class as well as cultural and personal interests. Some leading men, such as newcomer Charles Nisbet, were caustically critical of what they saw before them. Nisbet despaired about his new hometown: "Every thing here is on a dead Level; there is no Distinction here except wealth which few People possess here, tho' many live in Luxury."[80] To Nisbet, culture and education were the hallmarks of genuine standing, not fancy consumer goods. Others of the middling and lower sorts were equally critical, but for a different reason: they felt excluded from postwar opportunity. But rather than writing of their displeasure, as Nisbet did, they took a more active approach. As historian Terry Bouton describes, county residents obstructed roads in the late 1780s as a desperate strategy to defend against attacks on their economic well-being from tax collectors and moneyed men. Still other town and county residents struck back by committing crimes, including violent ones. Burglary, armed robbery, and riots increased across Pennsylvania during the 1780s and 1790s, especially in rural counties like Cumberland.[81]

Migration was another response. While new townspeople arrived, including many Germans, many others migrated away in the wake of the

Revolution. Population persistence rates, which typically held at slightly over 40 percent in earlier decades, dropped to 33 percent in the thirteen years after the war. Thus, between 1782 and 1795, nearly 67 percent of the town's taxable inhabitants disappeared from the town's tax rolls. Only the arrival of newcomers saved Carlisle from population decline during this time.[82] Wartime deaths of men who served account for some of the decline, but such figures also reflect accelerated rates of out-migration. Pension applications confirm this trend. Many former revolutionary soldiers, men of humble economic means likely to be negatively affected by postwar economic fluctuations, left Carlisle for newer territories in the South or West in the 1780s and 1790s. The New Jersey–born Philip Hornbaker, who had enlisted in Thompson's rifle battalion, lived near Harrisburg for a few years after the war, but upon the death of his wife moved to North Carolina for eight years "to look after a brother." He remarried and returned to Pennsylvania for a number of years, but then moved to Ohio where he remained "to look after my children."[83] The Irish-born John Tate, a soldier from William Irvine's regiment, lived for nearly a year in Baltimore following his discharge from his third term of service. He moved on to Pittsburgh, and then to North Carolina. In 1796, he relocated again, this time to Georgia, where he resided at the time of his pension application in 1832.[84] Other former soldiers followed similar patterns. Robert Thompson went to Ohio in 1801; William Alexander moved to Indiana; and the Irish-born John Torrence moved first to Lexington, Kentucky, in 1780, where he fought Indians under George Rogers Clark, and later to Ohio.[85] For those unable to benefit from Carlisle's postwar dynamism, more recently settled areas of the Carolinas and Georgia, as well as newly opened regions of the Ohio River Valley and beyond, offered economic opportunities—especially for landholding—that central Pennsylvania did not as it industrialized.

Emigrants envisioned a new and better future for themselves. Observers remaining in Carlisle, by contrast, viewed their moves with critical eyes. They held that continual migration was a negative force because it signalled that Americans did not think communally, but individually. "Every Man here," said Charles Nisbet disdainfully, "minds only himself."[86] Emigration thus equaled social instability to these more conservative observers. They also worried that this trend imperiled the American republic just as much as radical politics. This was why Benjamin Rush hoped that Dickinson College would teach the Scots-Irish to settle down; he held that they had to be taught "to prefer civil, social, and religious advantages, with a small farm and old land," because their continual migration into the "woods" undercut their political authority.[87] Nisbet went further—he was unabashedly critical. He did not understand his neighbors' propensity to move. "This country," he wrote, "is in a torpid state with regard to public spirit, arts and industry, and far from being united in politics." In fact, "private interest seems every where to be pursued in preference to the public good." The cause was "the ruinous practice of moving to the westward continues." Americans "have no attachment to their estates, but are ready to sell them whenever a buyer offers, and retire into the wilderness." Projecting outward from Carlisle, Nisbet concluded pessimistically that Americans were a mostly hopeless lot. "This new world," he observed with disdain, "is unfortunately composed, like that of Epicurus, of discordant atoms, jumbled together by chance, and tossed by inconstancy in an immense vacuum, it greatly wants a principle of attraction and cohesion."[88]

To Nisbet, a cultured immigrant who found himself immersed in this world of "discordant atoms" in Pennsylvania's interior, it came as little surprise that crises erupted. That Constitutional ratification was the issue around which his neighbors clashed so bitterly in late 1787 confirmed all that was wrong with Carlisle and America. How could Antifederalists object to this most worthy plan of government, he and other town leaders wondered? To Nisbet, a staunch Federalist, their objections made no sense: the Constitution gave him hope for an orderly American future. With "great strength of reason," said fellow townsman John Armstrong, he was "clear for adopting it."[89] Other town leaders and college trustees who favored the Constitution included John Montgomery and William Irvine, who was a delegate to the state convention. Even former Commissary General Ephraim Blaine, who had broken with other town leaders and supported the state constitution, appeared "its Friend."[90] When these men considered America's "situation at home (on the confines of anarchy) and our need of reputation abroad," as Armstrong wrote, "immediate adoption is . . . our wisest course"; there was no question about it. He and other supporters were "more apprehensive . . . of a failure in the duty of the people" than of any untoward actions by Congress, as "stale or careless jealousy, or prejudice and private motives, have thrown too many men into a political phrenzy" already. Was it not high time to stop this madness?[91] Furthermore, Armstrong and others believed that their neighbors supported it as well. Earlier that autumn, a Carlisle merchant and college trustee reported with confidence that "the People" were "well disposed to the federal Constitution." Although a few of their leaders opposed it or were lukewarm, "a great Majority of the People," this merchant said, "cry out for its immediate Adoption." They would carry the day, he predicted.[92]

But Carlisle's Federalists were wrong; support for the Constitution was not as widespread as they predicted. They were the minority in solidly Antifederalist Cumberland County.[93] Thus, when word got round of the self-congratulatory parade they planned to stage in Carlisle to celebrate state ratification, it ignited a violent response. Claiming that this partisan parade was "contrary to the minds of three-fourths of the inhabitants," Carlisle Antifederalists mobilized to protect themselves and their town.[94] Armed with anger born of old ethno-religious and class resentments, suspicion of new institutions like Dickinson College whose principal hated them, and concerned about their place in a postwar economy that was redefining the economic functions of their community, they took to the streets to assert their position in their town and nation. With the eyes of their opponents and the nation upon them, they fought to destroy aristocratic conspiracies directed against them and burned effigies of the two men most associated with the Federalist cause, Wilson and McKean. They drew on long-standing "plebian rituals" to occupy the town's center stage, express their frustrations, intimidate their opponents, and claim public authority to present an alternate vision of a different, more egalitarian America. The Antifederalists thus simultaneously asserted their own definition of Carlisle's betweenness and their role as its arbiters.[95]

The riot that ensued demonstrated exactly how outside issues could intersect with local tensions in such a town in-between and push them to a breaking point. Carlisle was a contentious community, a place where "people seem to have a bad opinion of each other," and had been this way since its founding.[96] Yet in 1787, it was not so much the presence of outsiders, but the influence of broader class, status, and political concerns that sparked confrontation. Carlisle's Federalists drew most of their supporters from the town's privileged ranks: politicians, merchants, attorneys, physicians, printers, and military officials. The Revolution had brought them opportunities for leadership and the political and economic shifts of the early republic offered them further advantage—they reveled in the cosmopolitan influences visible in their town. In fact, on the night of the riot, these gentlemen—the "respectable inhabitants of Carlisle," as they called themselves—convened at one of the town's taverns for "an elegant supper." There, in "the most perfect harmony, good humor, and conviviality," they gave twelve confident toasts to the Constitution, its political champions, and to the agriculture, manufactures, and commerce of America. Together, they affirmed what they believed was an established popular consensus in favor of the new plan of government.[97]

Antifederalists drew more heavily, but not exclusively, from the lower and middling sorts. Despite the fact that one critic denigrated them as "among the poor of this county," not all were. Judge John Jordan and radical leader Robert Whitehill were privileged men.[98] Still, most Antifederalists were not wealthy. As such, they more likely experienced the negative effects of postwar economic dislocation. Some, like one of their most vocal leaders, the tailor William Petrikin, even practiced trades that rendered them highly dependent on the patronage of the town's leading families. As Petrikin's advertisements for his shop demonstrate, participating in Carlisle's competitive postwar consumer economy meant convincing the town's leading ladies and gentlemen to purchase his services over another's. This left him dependent on their goodwill while simultaneously pitting him against his peers in ways that flew in face of revolutionary calls for American unity. Thus, Petrikin did not always realize the advantages of Carlisle's betweenness or its new cosmopolitanism. His pursuit of a livelihood and respectability placed him squarely within a status hierarchy that was anything but egalitarian. Perhaps this was one reason why Petrikin and others took such care to dress McKean's effigy in "a good Coat, . . . a pretty good hat & wig & Ruffl[e]d Shirt."[99] In fashionably dressing and then burning this effigy, they symbolically destroyed these markers of class authority while simultaneously challenging McKean's political authority.

Furthermore, in rejecting concepts of natural aristocracy extolled by Federalists like Charles Nisbet, Antifederalists also challenged Dickinson College, an institution whose mission as a kind of cultural crossroads was to educate a virtuous leadership class from the state's western interior. That goal sounded noble, but to Antifederalists it wreaked of exclusivity. Not all men of the interior could afford to send their sons to Dickinson; the college really aimed at educating the next generation of privileged men. To Antifederalists, fostering the rise of one class over others ran counter to the egalitarianism of the Revolution. Education, knowledge, and virtue, they held, were qualities that should be open to all as part of a more representative "plebian public sphere." When avenues to such cultural advancement closed, the town's Antifederalists protested their loss. They recognized that Carlisle's new status as a cultural place in-between did not benefit them.[100]

While disputes over class and cultural privilege fueled rioters' politics and actions, older ethno-religious tensions and insider-outsider dynamics fanned the flames. As historian Owen S. Ireland argues, Antifederalists actually worked against their economic interests in opposing the Constitution, for this new government would solve some of the burdens of rising taxes and decreasing farm prices under which they suffered. They did so, however, because ratification also brought long-standing ethno-religious antagonisms into stark relief. At the state level, a mostly Scots-Irish Presbyterian coalition, supported by Reformed Germans, pitted themselves in another bitter battle against the state's Quakers and Anglicans.[101] In Carlisle, by contrast, with few Quakers around to oppose, these antagonisms played out differently. Cumberland County's Scots-Irish split along geographic and economic lines over the Constitution, much as they had since the Revolution. Rural Scots-Irishmen of the county, who were mostly farmers, tended toward radicalism in state politics and Antifederalism in national politics. Their urban counterparts in Carlisle—who were attorneys, physicians, merchants, and often former proprietors' men—included many moderates, conservatives, and Federalists.

As ethno-religious tensions over the Constitution flooded into Carlisle in late 1787, they were expressed by the familiar insider versus outsider dynamic. Only this time, instead of townspeople pitting themselves against trade agents with Philadelphia connections as they had in the 1760s, they focused instead on outside cultural influences and the role and status of immigrants in the community. Who was a member of the community? Who was an American? These were the questions that the ratification debates raised locally, and each side had its own answer. When Carlisle's Antifederalists labeled James Wilson's effigy "the Caledonian," for instance, they symbolically condemned him for his Scots immigrant heritage as much as for his political positions. This act lent a distinct ethnic tinge to their protests. A Scots immigrant, their acts implied, could never adequately represent their interests. But immigrant outsiders were equally central to Federalist interpretations. With a note of disdain, one observer noted that it was local Irishmen who opposed the new plan of government; "they appear," he said, to "more prefer the English system."[102] Federalists also distinguished old residents from newcomers. They charged that members of the Antifederalist "mob" who had ruined their December celebrations were immigrants who "have come to this country within these last two years." As "men perfectly unknown" to members of the community, they were outsiders. "They are not amongst the respectable inhabitants of

Carlisle," argued one Federalist, and are "equally void of credit, character, and understanding."[103] These newcomers could never fully understand the needs of the town or nation in their estimation. Their actions, which were "really alarming," bordered on anarchy; they should "receive the reprobation of every honest citizen."[104] Antifederalists, not surprisingly, disputed these assertions. Some of them were immigrants, but they were also established members of the community. Their "characters," wrote the English immigrant tailor William Petrikin, "are so obvious as to be noticed with an envious eye."[105] They, too, were Americans and thus, in opposing the Constitution, positioned themselves "as patriots defending the Revolution."[106]

The upshot of this riot was a bitterly divided town. Antifederalists worked quickly to recruit more supporters in Cumberland and other nearby counties. By January, Montgomery reported that there was "a great Majority in opposition to the new Constitution."[107] Meanwhile, Federalist authorities struck back by jailing some of the rioters, but local militiamen mobilized and threatened a jailbreak. Tensions ran high. "Our Situation," wrote John Montgomery in early 1788, "is Exsceeding [sic]—Disagreeable." In an echo of the 1760s, he explained how neighbors once again snubbed neighbors, walking past them with "not a word Spoken."[108] Such a confrontational climate highlighted the qualities that brought the attention of men like Benjamin Rush to Carlisle in the first place. Antifederalists, said one gentleman, operated on "vain and puffed-up ideas." They were a coarse, uneducated "rabble" who pretended to act on liberty, but were unwilling to recognize their own "foolishness."[109] Yet such behavior also raised questions about the viability of Dickinson College. Could the college civilize the interior and overcome "that ignorance . . . which favours the designs of bad men" like those who led the riot?[110] The answer was unclear in 1788. The college's situation remained precarious; could it become the kind of cultural key to Pennsylvania's west that Rush envisioned?

More important, the riot won Carlisle infamy. As one traveler noted as he passed through town not long after: "This town is famous just now by the dissentions [sic] of its inhabitants, a part of whom are for the new constitution and a part do not wish to have it."[111] But such notoriety had broader implications. Aside from drawing much attention to the town, Carlisle and its riot was a lesson to America, one that boded ill for its political future. As Charles Nisbet explained, events at Carlisle "convinced" him "that in a Republic the Demagogues and Rabble-drivers are the only Citizens that are represented, or who have any Share in the Government." In this case, therefore, Carlisle's metaphorical betweenness had set the stage for the kind of class and political conflict that urged future caution. Looking outward from Carlisle, Nisbet concluded pessimistically that "the fate of this country is uncertain."[112]

Yet all hope was not lost; there was still cause for optimism. As historian David Waldstreicher argues, Federalist celebrations of the 1780s, however confrontational, were also marked by the "promise of regeneration" they offered their opponents. Federalists and Antifederalists could reconcile because they shared a common secular identity as Americans.[113] Americans also had faith and determination. As the cautious Benjamin Rush noted, it "is the prerogative of man to bring evil out of good, . . . it is the prerogative of God to bring good out of evil."[114] Carlisle, like America, had just enough of a foundation to overcome such "evil" in its midst; the town would persist. So, too, would its college, for Rush would hear of no other option. Dickinson graduated its first class of nine students only months before the riot, the trustees were on the brink of purchasing lands for a new building, and funding seemed more available than in the past. Just as important, despite all of the controversy and conflict over ratification, the "new government *will be* established," wrote Rush, and without "a civil war anywhere." For him, as for other conservative politicians of the republic, this was encouraging news, for the new government would preserve American nationhood. And because "our college," he noted confidently, "will revive with the commerce, agriculture, and manufactures of our country with the establishment of the new government," it would continue. *"All will end well,"* he concluded.[115]

CHAPTER SIX

Adapting to the Next Century

"UPON THE WHOLE," said one visitor, Carlisle had "a respectable appearance" by the nineteenth century. No longer was it the woods that Euro-Americans such as the fur trader James LeTort encountered in the 1720s when he built his cabin along the creek that later bore his name. Nor was it the fledgling interior town said to be "much at a Stand" in the 1760s when a host of fur traders, refugees, and soldiers brought together by the Seven Years' War and Pontiac's Uprising made it their temporary home. Instead, Carlisle residents of the early republic took great "pleasure" in the "improving" and even "flourishing Situation" of their borough; it was "a handsome village and Shire town" (figure 10).[1]

Carlisle had indeed changed over the half century since its founding. Its population was larger than at any time in its history. With just over 2,000 inhabitants by 1800, Carlisle was the fifth largest town in Pennsylvania.[2] The townscape was expanding as well. New public buildings, including a "handsome" new structure for county court offices and a new market house that opened in 1802, joined the existing brick courthouse, the "large & elegant" stone Presbyterian meetinghouse, and the Anglican church on the "spacious" public square.[3] One block east, the jail that Loyalist prisoners had complained about so bitterly during the American Revolution had been repaired and enlarged in 1790. And on the west side of town, a graceful new brick school building for Dickinson College was under construction; it would open in 1802.[4] The town's domestic landscape was also growing rapidly as a building boom expanded the number and quality of Carlisle's domestic structures.[5] As evidence, records produced in 1798, the year the U.S. government administered a Direct Tax on property (including dwelling houses) to generate revenue for a possible war with France, indicate that the 312 lots originally laid out by Thomas Penn's officials were densely occupied by nearly 300 houses and more than 450 outbuildings of varying shapes, sizes, and materials.[6] More significant than their quantity, was the size and style of these structures. Visitors described the newest houses as "neatly built" or "tolerable good ones"; some were even "very large & elegant."[7]

By 1800, Carlisle thus had an impressive appearance of status, permanence, and gentility that belied its past. To read the words of town boosters and some visitors, it was no longer a coarse colonial village of the mid-Atlantic interior; rather, it had come into its own as a prosperous and pleasing place. By all outward indications, townspeople had redefined their community and themselves by building upon the cultural clout Carlisle merited as home to Dickinson College, as well as the economic gains brought by its profitable

Figure 10. *Carlisle 1797.* A sketch by C. V. Colbert, Comte de Maulevrier. This is the earliest known sketch of Carlisle, made about 1797. The steepled building is the first courthouse. The old military barracks, or public works, are on the right. This bucolic scene was in keeping with the idealized image town boosters promoted near the turn of the century. (Courtesy of Cumberland County Historical Society, Carlisle, Pennsylvania.)

postwar grain trade connected to Philadelphia and Baltimore and its increasingly diverse and industrializing economy. Townspeople, in short, had pushed aside their town's colonial past and Carlisle's long-standing connections to the American West. Instead, they and their town assumed what residents implied was their and its rightful position between Baltimore and Philadelphia. A new day had dawned; and Carlisle became, like these cities, a town of the cosmopolitan east. Its betweenness narrowed to purely intraregional functions, and it sat more on the edge of the east than in the middle of the mid-Atlantic.[8]

But there were cracks in this neat narrative of progress and change. It was a one-sided story told by the town's privileged and powerful, and by European observers eager to see signs of cosmopolitan urban culture in the small communities of the new United States. The reality was more complex. Carlisle's prosperity was remarkably uneven during the 1790s and 1800s, and despite the town's impressively stylish structures, townspeople's claims to respectability and gentility were a façade in some respects. Poverty and coarseness, and not just prosperity and stylishness, marked the structures lining the town's streets. Then there was the continued influence of the American West, which loomed large in the economic lives of many residents: during the early republic, in fact, townspeople and their children looked deeper into the interior for the opportunities needed to shape their futures. Carlisle thus retained a critical defining quality of its betweenness as a place between east and west; it remained, like its colonial predecessor, a crossroads between regions, a place in the middle. It also remained a highly contested place. During the 1790s, Carlisle continued to function as the real and metaphorical space where angry residents came to express their frustrations, sometimes violently. This was yet another aspect of the town's history that had not changed.

There were thus other, more complex narratives to be told about turn-of-the-century Carlisle and its place in the mid-Atlantic. These stories, although far less progressive and celebratory, were far more compelling. Early republic Carlisle was actually a town of stark contrasts. This meant that behind the town's well-built public structures and its increasing number of stylish homes stood another, more complicated townscape and the diverse and sometimes conflicted community it embodied. Carlisle's history, in short, was not simply the triumphant evolutionary tale town boosters wanted it to be, and no amount of fancy structures or self-conscious assertions of status could alter that fact.

Rising economic inequality was probably the clearest manifestation of the contrasts that marked Carlisle as the nineteenth century dawned. Inequality was certainly not new; it had existed since the town's founding when some colonists arrived with resources sufficient to support the construction of impressive stone dwelling houses, while others lived in crude log structures. Yet the situation during the early republic was striking—the wealth gap among residents was widening sizably. Tax lists, for example, demonstrate that although total wealth was expanding, taxable wealth was increasingly skewed. In 1779, the top 50 percent of the town's taxable heads of household held 84 percent of the wealth, while the bottom 50 percent held only 15 percent. By 1795, the top half had increased their holdings; they held 87 percent of the taxable wealth, while the bottom half had only 13 percent. By 1808, the gap was even more pronounced; the top 50 percent of the town's taxable households possessed 97 percent of the town's taxable wealth, while the bottom 50 percent held only 3 percent. Moreover, in 1808, 18 percent of the town's taxable inhabitants (68 of 383 taxable heads of household) had no taxable property whatsoever.[9]

Clearly, some residents had benefited from the town's growth disproportionate to their neighbors. Property assessments of the Direct Tax of 1798 confirm these patterns. Those appraisals show that the top 50 percent of town residents owned property worth 85 percent of the total ($153,000), while the bottom 50 percent held only 15 percent of the total ($28,000).[10] Without doubt, the economic distance between Carlisle's haves and have-nots was widening by 1800, which mirrored patterns found in larger towns like Lancaster and cities like Philadelphia. In Carlisle, as elsewhere in Pennsylvania, opportunities for social mobility were uneven. Despite many signs of prosperity, economic dislocation persisted and was worsening. There were two Carlisles, one prosperous and one poor.[11]

Carlisle's townscape reflected this dichotomy. Like other urban landscapes of the time, it was characterized by "contradictory juxtapositions."[12] The new buildings on the square and the many impressive homes that lined Carlisle's main streets were signs of Carlisle's growth and prosperity; they attracted accolades from town boosters and visitors. But poverty marked the town as well. It was especially visible along the town's alleys and back streets where the mass of townspeople, like most Americans of the time, resided in small and simple one-story wooden or log structures.[13]

The dwellings of the men and women who occupied the twenty-nine lowest-valued properties in 1798 (the bottom tenth of the scale) exemplified their inhabitants' limited means and humble status in the community. In keeping with the tenancy rates of the town as a whole, nearly half (45 percent) of these twenty-nine houses were rental properties. Yet unlike those leased properties at the top of the scale that housed gentlemen, these structures were occupied mostly by day laborers and a few craftsmen, such as coopers. Women headed an unusually large number of these households—slightly more than one-third—suggesting how often single or widowed females found themselves relegated to a marginalized economic existence, even in the interior.[14] Material evidence also suggests that these structures were coarsely constructed and spatially cramped. Similar to their counterparts in nearby Shippensburg, Carlisle's poor resided in what one observer described as, "wretched huts of wood and logs and clay."[15] Inside these simple, one-story wooden or log structures with few windows, space was tight. These dwellings averaged only 353 square feet in total dimension. And because most were situated on cramped half, third, or quarter-lot parcels, outside space was limited. These structures were exceedingly small, multi-functional living quarters with little privacy. An example can be found from impoverished, sixty-three-year-old James Hutton, who said that he lived "on an alley, with a small log house thereon" in his pension application. This was presumably the same single-story, wooden house of 320 square feet with three windows that was valued near the bottom of the scale in 1798 at only $110. Hutton did not have much. He was one of Carlisle's growing number of lower sorts who did not enjoy the benefits of the town's growth during the early republic (figure 11).[16]

Carlisle's leading citizens responded in various ways to the economic disparities surrounding them. They played psychological games on themselves by focusing only what they wanted to see in their town. Particularly in public conversations about their community, they ignored the poverty around them and instead celebrated Carlisle's prosperity. When discussing the real estate boom of early republic Carlisle, for instance, town leaders marveled at how "the scene is changed." Whereas town lots were a "drag" not long ago with "vast number of good houses . . . unoccupied," postwar economic dislocations had given way to growth in the 1790s; by 1806, "every house was occupied." This change was met "with extreme pleasure," wrote the editor of the *Carlisle Gazette*; he and other privileged residents celebrated such a boom because as property owners it brought them financial gain.[17]

They also cast themselves as the primary engineers of Carlisle's progress. Tavern keeper James Pollock, who lived "in a good brick house," boasted that he had "assisted in cutting down the trees that built the first log house in Carlisle, and that trees grew on the spot where his house now stood."[18] For the prosperous Irishman Pollock, the town's transformation from woods to log structures and then good brick houses measured his achievement; he was

Figure 11. *John Reed or Joseph Sabolle House, Carlisle, Pennsylvania.* This log structure, dating to before 1790 and probably before 1779, is an extant example of the humble dwellings many of Carlisle's lower sorts occupied at the close of the eighteenth century. (Photograph by the author.)

a Carlisle success story. As an immigrant from Ulster, he came to Carlisle in the early 1760s. Once there, Pollock, like many of his neighbors, worked hard, acquired property, held various local offices, and became the respected proprietor of "a large and excellent tavern" on High Street.[19] Yet Pollock's hard work and success had broader implications for the town's history; his personal accomplishments exemplified the town's progress. As his words implied, he and other town leaders had literally built the town. This belief was something in which Carlisle's most privileged men, especially the oldest ones, took enormous pride: although John Armstrong and James Wilson, two of Carlisle's key colonial and revolutionary leaders, were gone—they died in the 1790s—other leading men, like Brig. Gen. William Irvine, remained; he was over sixty years of age and lived mostly in Philadelphia, but retained strong ties to Carlisle. Dickinson College's chief local booster, John Montgomery, also remained there; he was in his eighties, but did not die until 1808.[20] To these men and the rising crop of new town leaders like attorney James Hamilton, Carlisle's growth, prosperity, and its increasing cosmopolitanism was their legacy. They—not outsiders like Thomas Penn, or Baynton, Wharton, and Morgan, the British or Continental armies, or Benjamin Rush—had built Carlisle from a small village into "a large and attractive town."[21] This was Carlisle's history as they told it.

The town's leading citizens also banded together. Considering their impoverished neighbors the opposition, they developed a strong class cohesion that defined them as the town's cultural leaders. They touted their collective identity quite openly; one resident, for example, described his friends as "very respectable people among us." Another recollected years later that there was "a way of viewing life, standards of taste, breeding, feeling and hearing" that "reigned" among some in Carlisle.[22] These families prided themselves on their accomplishments. The men were successful professionals, including attorneys and physicians, politicians, merchants, and retailers; their wives often came from established Pennsylvania families. They had impressive homes filled with many of the latest consumer goods. They sent their sons to Dickinson College. Most important, in banding together, they wanted others to recognize them as the gentlemen and ladies they believed themselves to be. For this reason, they were surely pleased when Benjamin Rush, a cultured man of the metropolis, boasted that the "plentiful—elegant" dinner he had enjoyed at John Montgomery's home was "as well attended as any dinner I ever was at in a Gentleman's house in Philadelphia."[23]

Just as important, they made every effort to demonstrate their adherence to the values of a wider, cosmopolitan cultural realm. Their large, stylishly built, permanent houses were the most obvious manifestations of these aspirations. These structures were symbolic representations of themselves and the community they wished Carlisle to be. They were also among the most visible manifestations of the disparities that marked the town.[24] The size of Carlisle's most highly valued homes in 1798 offers powerful evidence of the privileged lives some townspeople enjoyed. The inhabitants of Carlisle's twenty-nine most highly valued properties resided in spacious two-story homes that averaged 2,300 square feet. These structures were nearly seven times larger than the homes of their neighbors at the bottom of the economic scale.[25] They were also architecturally stylish. By the 1790s, says one architectural historian, Carlisle was the "architectural showplace" of its county; the number of two-story homes, their size, and exterior detail were "unrivaled."[26] In distinguishing Carlisle's leading families from the coarse, poverty-ridden homes of their neighbors, these spacious and stylish two-story homes gave substance to their claims to authority.

These dwellings stood on sizable, full- or half-size lots where outbuildings such as kitchens, dairies, wash houses, and smoke houses segregated space in ways that reinforced the privileges they enjoyed. Whereas their poorer neighbors crammed themselves into small log structures on tiny parcels of land, these residents presided over sprawling complexes of domestic structures. All but three of Carlisle's twenty-nine highest-valued properties, for instance, had detached kitchens. Although outbuildings were not an innovation of the early republic, those that Carlisle's leading families had built by the 1790s were especially impressive. Many of these kitchens, built of stone or brick, were two-story structures substantially larger than the houses occupied by Carlisle's poor.[27] The size of these structures thus reinforced the visual impact of the dwellings they accompanied. Outbuildings also signaled the important spatial, social, and sometimes racial hierarchies operating within these households, which were another measure of their occupants' economic privilege. Detached kitchens, for example, removed food preparation and other domestic chores from the dwelling house. They segregated female domestics and Carlisle's remaining slaves from the dwelling house as well. One or more of John Montgomery's female slaves, for example, probably staffed the two-story stone kitchen that stood on his Carlisle property. Such specialization of space was another gauge of his privilege.[28]

Even so, the dwelling house remained the focal point of these properties because it best exemplified the family's public identity. Houses were significant consumer objects in the early republic. Their worth, size, and appearance measured their occupants' embrace of a more cosmopolitan cultural sphere.[29] By late eighteenth-century standards, the houses of these Carlisle families were impressive. Rarely living in homes constructed of wood (only two of the twenty-nine highest-value homes were made of wood or logs), these leading families built instead with the more durable materials of stone (59 percent of these twenty-nine houses) or brick (35 percent). Their use of these materials immediately distinguished their residences from the coarser, impermanent log homes of their poorer neighbors, or many of their colonial predecessors. Without doubt, these homes were built to last; they symbolized their owners' achievements and commitment to the community.[30]

Brick construction, in particular, had multiple connotations. Use of brick for these structures aligned Carlisle with the cosmopolitan design trends of the metropolis; it pointed residents east, rather than west, for their style and cultural cues. As architectural historian Nancy Van Dolsen confirms, Carlisle residents' frequent use of brick for their houses and outbuildings connected them to broader American and British building trends that were characteristic of the so-called housing revolution, an extensive rebuilding that took place in many of America's most cosmopolitan cities and towns during the early republic.[31] Brick, an especially neat construction material capable of forming highly regular external appearances, was closely associated with the polite housing of coastal dwellers. It was ideally suited to the symmetrical, classically inspired styles being adopted across America during the 1790s. That many of Carlisle's most privileged residents chose to build or live in brick structures, attested to their embrace of America's consumer and housing revolutions. But brick structures were not just symbols of architectural style trends, they were also status indicators. As the most expensive and labor-intensive building material of the era, brick houses were "statement[s] of personal status" in Philadelphia at the time. As brick became the preferred construction material for the homes of prosperous tradesmen, shopkeepers, merchants, and landed gentry across America during the early republic, these structures took on significant political meaning as well. The Federal style, for example, self-consciously asserted a unique American identity by aligning American architectural design with the great republics and classical forms of ancient times. Brick homes were not only more durable, but also more prestigious and consciously American.[32]

Carlisle's leading families were engaged in a broader, American process of cultural and class identification; their brick homes measured their commitment to the new nation as well as their community. Building in brick represented a significant choice over cheaper construction materials like wood or stone. This was true even in a town like Carlisle where several brickmakers and two brick factories operated by 1794.[33] Brick construction thus illustrated how consciously some townspeople were using metropolitan style trends as tools to craft their identities and that of their town. Brick construction highlighted their triumph over Carlisle's origins as a colonial town of the interior, while signaling their embrace of a present and future characterized by the prosperity, gentility, and republicanism shared by the best families of the new nation. Moreover, because brick was also among the most artificial of construction materials, one that took multiple steps to manufacture, its use signaled Carlisle residents' desire to present a highly constructed face to the world. These structures thus declared their residents' independence from the meddling of outsiders that had marked Carlisle's past and rejected the town's coarser origins as a place of the interior while simultaneously reinforcing the stories told of Carlisle's progressive and accomplished present.[34]

It thus was no accident that when Carlisle resident Abraham Hare replaced his old wooden house of 324 square feet in 1798, he chose to build his more spacious, two-story house with brick. Nor was it coincidence that tavern keeper John Hunter occupied a spacious two-story brick house (valued among the top 10 percent in 1798 at $1,730) that served as his inn—symbolically known by the Sign of General Washington.[35] But early republic Carlisle's wealthiest resident, James Hamilton, provides the best example. Hamilton, an attorney and later state supreme court justice, was one of the most prominent new leading men of Carlisle. He was born in Ireland in 1752 and came to Carlisle sometime in the early 1780s, where he established a lucrative law practice and worked his way up the town's social ranks. In 1798, he lived in the only three-story house in town. His property, one of the four highest valued at $3500, included a fashionable home built of brick, which he described as "commodious and well finished," a two-story brick kitchen, two-story brick office, and a "large" stone stable. In emulating the three-story Federal-era townhomes of cities like Philadelphia, Hamilton both announced his status and initiated a trend. By 1815, another resident remarked that "lofty buildings" like Hamilton's were "all the rage at present."[36]

Although one scholar notes with regret how a "homogenous American form" eclipsed many ethnic vernacular building traditions by the early 1800s, the architectural choices made by men like James Hamilton suggest that Carlisle's leading citizens embraced this homogeneity. They wanted to shed vernacular building traditions like log construction that harkened back to the town's founding and its history as a contested place.[37] Building in brick did the trick. As the seller of a two-story brick house with detached kitchen suggested in 1794, a spacious and spatially segregated house built of brick set the stage for a polite lifestyle. "This house," as he advertised, "is in a good part of the town, and has many conveniences to render it suitable for a genteel family that lives private."[38] It was no accident that good location, conveniences, gentility, and privacy converged in this sturdy brick structure.

Carlisle's leading citizens also directed their attention outward. To mold their town to what they wanted it to be, they also focused much time and energy on Carlisle's public structures. Buildings on the square, for example, got a facelift at the turn of the century. So, too, did Dickinson College, the institution on which much of Carlisle's claim to cultural clout in the mid-Atlantic rested. Dickinson was not doing well in the 1790s. Enrollment at the college had faltered as continuing financial problems and student rebellions over the curriculum left it in crisis. In response, trustees decided that a new school building was a must in order to bolster the school's sagging reputation. They began constructing "New College," a "large, elegant, and commodious" brick school building on the western edge of town. It opened in 1802 with great fanfare, but burned down a year later.[39] Disappointment followed. But hopes rebounded when shortly afterwards, personal connections brought Benjamin Henry Latrobe, architect of the U.S. Capitol and Surveyor of Public Buildings, on board as the designer of yet another building to replace it.

Latrobe, a champion of neoclassical style, designed "a large[,] Commdouse [commodious][,] and Elegent [*sic*] house . . . Built of stone" to house the college. It was a building meant to be in harmony with nature and the republican sentiments of the day.[40] The U-shaped structure was classically proportioned with arched windows, fan lights, a water table, and other classical details. To complement its natural surroundings, and thereby ground it firmly in its local setting, Latrobe "recommend[ed] that you should build your external walls of the lime stone of your Valley, rather than of brick."[41]

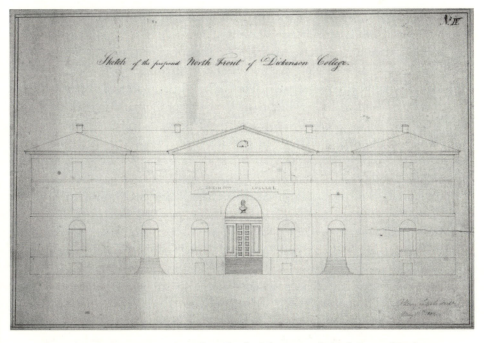

Figure 12. Benjamin Henry Latrobe, *Sketch of the Proposed North Front of Dickinson College,* Carlisle, Pennsylvania, May 18, 1803. In this original sketch by the British-born Latrobe, architect of the U.S. Capitol, he outlined a classically inspired structure for Dickinson College. (Courtesy of Dickinson College Archives and Special Collections, Carlisle, Pennsylvania.)

Said to have "an Eligent [*sic*] and Grand appearance" by the time faculty and students were admitted into it in 1805, this stylish building, its design a gift of Latrobe, was hailed as the most visible manifestation of townspeople's desires to follow the cultural styles of the early republic's cosmopolitan cities located to their east (figure 12).[42]

Yet Latrobe's choice to build in stone rather than brick, while a small and seemingly innocuous gesture, clouds this tidy scenario of cultural transmission from east to west. Instead, it suggests the important role choice played in adapting—and not simply adopting—metropolitan styles to the interior. Latrobe's preference for stone over brick represented his desire to incorporate locally available materials into his design: brick was for cities, not for a college intended to be the key to civilizing America's western inhabitants. But in using stone, he altered the pattern of cultural transmission to the interior and imbued "Old West," as it is called today standing at the center of Dickinson's campus, with local character. Dickinson's new stone school building reflected the town's past as a place of the interior; its use of local materials rooted the college in the complex history of a town and valley that had traditionally occupied a place between others in the mid-Atlantic (figure 13).

Latrobe's design highlighted the extent to which many Carlisle buildings were compromises between external cultural standards and local patterns of expression, need, and availability. With 59 percent of Carlisle's highest valued homes in 1798 constructed of stone, many townspeople agreed with Latrobe that quarried stone structures expressed refinement; brick was not the only option.[43] Yet such choices have important connotations for understanding Carlisle's evolving identity as a place. They demonstrate that Carlisle's leading citizens, like Latrobe, did not simply imitate the metropolis. Instead, they made choices by selecting styles and materials to suit their needs and tastes. William Irvine offers an example. He exhibited particular care in the construction of his "tolerably neat" and "large" stone house two miles outside town—a house one traveler described as "excellent."[44] But still, his use of stone construction allied his new home more closely to its interior surroundings or the monumental public architecture of the American colonial past than to the brick styles of the early republic. We do not know why Irvine—an educated, widely traveled professional man and leader—chose to build his new home in stone. But his choice illustrates how even Carlisle's leading men adapted metropolitan styles to suit their tastes and the availability of materials. Military and political service had brought him mostly to Philadelphia by the 1790s, but his choice of materials for his new house suggests how often he looked west to the Cumberland Valley and even further into the interior as the new century dawned.

Building fancy houses and school buildings accomplished only so much, however. Stylish structures lent an air of cosmopolitanism to Carlisle, but they did not eradicate poverty or coarseness. Carlisle's poor and the structures they inhabited were constant reminders of those in the community who had not prospered. When framed by Carlisle's origins as a town of the interior, local responses to poverty, while typical of reactions among privileged residents in towns across America, were also infused with a particular sense of urgency. Poverty and coarseness were potent reminders of Carlisle's beginnings as a small village in Thomas Penn's woods. Their continuation called

DICKENSON COLLEGE.

Figure 13. *West College, Dickenson [Dickinson] College, from a Sketch by A. Brackenridge.* This circa 1810 illustration depicts the constructed college building designed by Benjamin Henry Latrobe that still stands at the center of the college's campus today. Although West College, or Old West, stood on the western boundary of town, this engraving depicts it in a rural setting, one in keeping with the promotional literature put forward by the college's founders and boosters. Courtesy of Dickinson College Archives and Special Collections.

Carlisle's progress into question, for they undermined the triumphant history of the community that the town's leading men wanted to offer. Crude living conditions also reminded the town's privileged of their own, sometimes humble pasts. At the same time, as Carlisle's Antifederalist riot illustrated so powerfully, class differences generated contrasting worldviews. When these worldviews clashed, as they had in late 1787, they produced violence and disorder that threatened the community and besmirched its reputation in the mid-Atlantic.

In response, the town's leading citizens regulated their town. Some directed their energies at keeping Dickinson College afloat as a cultural institution. Higher education was something to which residents should aspire, and the college lent credence to citizens' claims to cultural respectability. Town officials acted—they attempted to reshape their neighbors' lives by legislating respectability, following patterns of urban policing begun in America's seaboard cities as early as 1700.[45] For example, when Carlisle was incorporated into a borough in 1782, officials placed great emphasis on "regulating the Buildings," and "preventing . . . nuisances." Provisions for the upkeep of roads, construction of public buildings, and regulation of water resources aimed at managing local infrastructure. Other regulations had strong overtones of class-based social control. Any "person" who dared to cast any "filth or annoyance" on any "street, lane or alley" in Carlisle would be fined. Distillers, soap boilers, tallow chandlers, and butchers—artisans of often humble economic means whose businesses were concentrated largely in Carlisle's northeast section—merited more attention. If any of them tried to collect "any stale, stinking or putrid fat, grease or other matter . . . so as to annoy any neighbor," they were fined for their actions. With survival no longer in question, town leaders wanted a community that was orderly and pleasing to the senses. As further evidence of their belief that the poor needed supervision, by 1804, they had obtained permission from the state to erect a poorhouse.[46]

Carlisle's streets and public spaces were difficult to control, however. Penn's town plan of long and narrow lots, many of which were subdivided into smaller parcels, encouraged dense, urban settlement patterns. Neighbors lived and worked remarkably close to one another. Furthermore, as the county seat and an important commercial crossroads for its hinterland, Carlisle was a bustling urban place. Its streets were filled with people who had come to do business in the local courts, trade with local merchants, or patronize the town's many taverns, stores, or craft shops. It was a noisy commercial town—not a quiet, pastoral village. Charles Nisbet confirmed this fact when he complained that he lived in a "noisy House" near the center of town, where he heard "nothing from Morning to Night, but Dogs fighting, People killing swine[,] Cows lowing, . . . The most quiet Neighbours we have are the Waggoners, tho' they rarely pass without Noise."[47] But noise was only part of the problem. Public disorder was the real threat, as it had been in the past, and many residents feared its onset. In 1793, for example, a *Carlisle Gazette* writer complained bitterly that it had been "long" practice for the town's "negroes" to collect on the public square in the evenings, go off to "disorderly houses" to get drunk, then "quarrel and fight and commit riots in the streets" on their way home "to the great disturbance of the inhabitants." Like those colonists who witnessed Native Americans dancing drunkenly around a bonfire in the center square in 1753, he and other "pious hearers" were tired of listening to their "horrid oaths and blasphemies." They were also probably afraid. Yet unlike 1753, when residents watched passively as Indians celebrated, this writer was bold and confident enough to demand action. As a citizen, this was his town, and he wanted borough officials to put an end to this behavior by establishing a curfew for African Americans.[48] To him, when Carlisle's "negroes" claimed the streets and dominated its public spaces, their noises signaled social transgression; they had to be stopped. More important, such incidents confirmed Carlisle's continued status as a contested place. The town's streets remained spaces in-between where African Americans, like Native peoples earlier, came to challenge the racial authority of their Euro-American neighbors.

Carlisle's streets also remained politically contentious spaces when they became a stage for boisterous political protest. This use of public space was especially difficult to regulate in a nation founded on traditions of popular resistance and celebration that took to the streets. Although wary of their consequences, borough officials could not ban spontaneous forms of political action from Carlisle's public spaces. Nor did they want to do so. It was local Federalists, including many of the town's leading men, who had staged the first public celebration of Constitutional ratification that provoked the riot of 1787. Still, in town leaders' minds, because parades did not contest authority but confirm it, they were different and preferable to riots. Local leaders were reminded of this distinction in 1794 when the Whiskey Rebellion provoked renewed public clashes with strong class-based overtones in Carlisle's public square.

In many respects, the setting for the events of 1794 were surprisingly familiar. As in 1787, disputes over national politics brought local tensions to a head in the form of public confrontation. Once again, Federalist politics, this time the economic threat posed to Pennsylvania farmers by a 1791 federal excise tax on distilled alcohol, occupied center stage in the controversy. Still, there was more in dispute. The mid-1790s were a particularly tense time. The French Revolution and the European war it sparked sharpened divisions between Federalists and Republicans, creating new political tensions. Carlisle's Federalist leaders, many of the same men who built fancy houses and tried to police the town's development, were simultaneously confident and wary. They were encouraged by their victory in 1787 and bolstered by the implementation of Pennsylvania's new, conservative constitution of 1790. Yet violent revolution in France had them worried: would this model inspire counter-revolution in America? Would it inspire another political showdown in Carlisle? Dickinson College's Federalist principal, Charles Nisbet, for one, took a very public anti-French stance. But the problem other town leaders faced was that not everyone shared Nisbet's sentiments; Carlisle was a town of economic, social, and political contrasts. Thus when France declared itself a republic in 1792, some townspeople were bold enough to challenge the political sentiments of their betters by ringing the town's bells to celebrate. They had their own views of France's revolution and were willing to express them.[49]

Then there were other state and local issues at stake. Ethno-religious politics had reared their head yet again in Pennsylvania. In the 1790s, however, it was not so much the Scots-Irish as the Germans who caused the commotion. Cumberland was one of four counties where its growing German population was demanding greater and thus more equitable political representation in the state. Although they still accounted for less than half the population in the county, they nonetheless wanted to shift the ethnic balance of local politics away from the long-dominant Scots-Irish Presbyterians, assuring more appointments for German-speakers who followed the Lutheran and Reformed faiths. Their calls for representation added an important an ethnic dimension to the buildup of local tensions.[50]

Then came the whiskey tax. Controversy over this tax pointed to broader economic and class disputes between ordinary Pennsylvanians and the privileged men who legislated for them. As historian Terry Bouton notes, protestors were frustrated over Congressional plans to finance war debt speculators, increase taxes, and create a national bank. Residents were also disgruntled over the state's disposal of the Erie Triangle, a nearly 500,000-acre tract in the state's northwest corner, to a group of speculators. This controversial land deal had particular resonance in Carlisle since James Wilson and William Irvine were members of the company that won control of these lands. Irvine even suggested their purchase, then surveyed these lands; his actions hint again at the westward direction of his gaze.[51] The whiskey tax protests expressed multiple tensions. Ordinary Pennsylvanians were frustrated by the link between economic power, or lack thereof, and political authority; their actions were intended to push the government to regulate itself to act on behalf of their interests. Although the most violent protests took place in agrarian western Pennsylvania, Carlisle was one of two sizable interior towns—along with Hagerstown, Maryland—where tensions grew intense enough to create small-scale riots. Much to the chagrin of town leaders who worked to achieve respectability and tell the town's history as a story of progress, Carlisle found itself back in national consciousness as a symbol of disorder. As a place in-between, it remained a kind of ground zero for the expression of myriad local tensions.[52]

But these tensions developed over time. Opposition to the whiskey tax brewed for several years. Formal protests against it did not begin in Cumberland County until the summer of 1794 when a group of farmers from Carlisle's hinterlands, inspired by the actions of other state residents, drafted a petition declaring it unjust. Others in the county resisted more physically. Some refused to pay the tax, while still others, in an echo of prerevolutionary protest activities, intimidated collectors to disrupt its implementation. Tensions came to a head in Carlisle in September when whiskey tax protestors took to the streets to demonstrate their frustration. Claiming the town's public square—the space its leading men had hailed as one of the most obvious measures of Carlisle's progress—they erected a liberty pole inscribed with the saying "'Liberty and no excise, O Whiskey'" on it. The next day, "a few of the friends to good government"—probably some of the town's Federalists who helped set off the riot of 1787—tore it down, causing "great agitation" among those who opposed the tax. Outrage spread quickly, which worked "to inflame the minds of the country people."[53] In response, nearly two hundred whiskey protestors appeared in town, some of them armed. Enraged at the tax, economic inequality, and destruction of their first liberty pole, they erected a new, larger pole inscribed with the bolder message of "Liberty and equality." The next day, following the lead of Antifederalists in 1787, they prepared another effigy of the hated Federalist Chief Justice Thomas McKean and "paraded along the streets with it . . . & burnt it." At night, while protestors drank excise-free whiskey around a bonfire on the square, a self-appointed guard patrolled the streets, firing guns to intimidate the opposition and making other kinds of noise to remind all of their grievances.[54]

Tensions among townspeople had again reached a high point. As with other conflicts in Carlisle's past, the community divided and neighbor turned against neighbor in response. Protestors "shun[ned] the conversations of any person they thought was opposed to their proceeding." The threat of violence lurked beneath the surface. Townspeople heard gunshots. Protestors were said to be carrying pistols beneath their coats; some even admitted their willingness to engage in violent confrontation, if needed. One protester, condemning these "damned Laws," said he would defend himself and his ideals. As he noted, "he had a good Gun & could shoot damned straight." Another declared that "he would be damned if some Lives should not be lost if attempts were made to prevent putting up the Liberty Pole."[55]

At its broadest, Pennsylvania's Whiskey Rebellion pitted "country people" against townspeople because farmers' interests were different than those of urban commercial men. Yet when these protests moved to towns like Carlisle, significant intra-urban class conflicts also emerged. This was especially evident during the second, more boisterous round of demonstrations in Carlisle. Inscriptions on the first liberty pole criticized the tax as a violation of distillers' liberty, thereby expressing the shared interests of farmers and distillers. The call for "Liberty and Equality" on the second pole—especially when coupled with the burning of McKean in effigy—pointed toward broader and more radical goals. They included achieving more democratic forms of political representation and economic justice that were applicable to all Pennsylvanians, farmers and townspeople alike. Furthermore, because the second protest was marked by the humble status of many participants, it confirmed Carlisle as a place of stark class contrasts. According to witnesses, for example, "very few men of property appeared among" these protesters; rather, these Pennsylvanians were among the many townspeople still searching for the opportunities the Revolution had promised. They were the residents who occupied the cramped log houses that lined the town's back streets and allies, and whose lives did not fit the progressive history their privileged neighbors wanted to tell of their town. Some also had direct connections to Carlisle's recent boisterous past. Some whiskey tax protesters were former Antifederalist rioters. Carlisle tailor William Petrikin, for instance, who gained the reputation as one of the town's most vocal Antifederalists when he spoke out forcefully against the dangers of aristocratic privilege in 1787, was implicated as a supporter of the whiskey rebels. His involvement confirms continuities with the town's past and certifies that urban as well as rural issues were at stake.[56]

Carlisle's whiskey protests were thus entwined in wider struggles over access to economic and cultural privilege in a town where the wealth and status gaps were growing. Carlisle was not exceptional in this regard; most whiskey protests happened in prosperous neighborhoods where the poor could see the growing prosperity of their betters.[57] Nonetheless, Carlisle's protests had their own dynamic. The town's history of confrontations, jailbreaks, and riots lent powerful credence to the actions of protestors in 1794; residents knew they meant business and were afraid of them. Most Carlisle gentlemen, for example, stayed away during the second demonstration. They had seen such protests turn violent before and they did not wish to take risks— they knew the authority that came with gentlemanly status was one of the things in question. One who did not stay away, Ephraim Blaine, the Army's former Commissary General, was chased out of town with his sister by "desperadoes" firing guns.[58] But still, town gentlemen also refused to concede. In holding their ground, even if only metaphorically, they too acknowledged Carlisle's status as a still-contested political space. Most were pleased when President George Washington and the federal troops sent to put down the rebellion converged on Carlisle as their staging ground to the west. It reminded them of the Revolution, especially as one of their own, William Irvine, commanded these forces. The presence of troops also bolstered their authority. But having others protect them was insufficient. As town leaders, they also wished to stand up for themselves. In response, Federalists claimed not only Carlisle's streets but also other public spaces such as its churches, where they waged a highly public war of words against the rebels. Charles Nisbet, for instance, condemned the rebellion in several sermons. But Robert Davidson, pastor at Carlisle's First Presbyterian church, expressed the views of his privileged compatriots most forcefully. As he noted in his sermon to the troops on the eve of their departure west: "That all men should be equal as to abilities, station, authority, and wealth, is absolutely, in the present state of things impossible." Rather, it was more important that "we . . . be obedient to lawful authority." Pennsylvanians must "respect the government" we "have made," he said. Order must be restored.[59]

Order was restored. The rebellion ended, mostly on its own. Yet Carlisle's whiskey rebellion resulted in two casualties, including the tragic shooting of a young boy by federal troops and the stabbing of a local man in a drunken scuffle with a soldier.[60] Protests over the whiskey tax thus powerfully demonstrated that laws and sermons would never contain the town's lower sorts. These residents had their own worldviews and were willing to act on them, even if it meant taking to the streets in opposition to the town's lead-

Figure 14. *Stephen Duncan House, Carlisle, Pennsylvania, built before 1794.* Although its exterior facade has been altered over time, this stone structure, assessed at $2,400 in 1798, was one of Carlisle's highest-valued dwellings. Duncan, a justice of the peace, county treasurer, member of the Pennsylvania Assembly, and trustee of Dickinson College, was a prominent merchant in town. This house was part of an extensive urban complex that included a stone kitchen house, storehouse, and stable. It is an example of how many Carlisle men continued to live in and build stone structures, even at the close of the century. (Photo by the author.)

ing men. This attitude marked yet another continuity with Carlisle's colonial past. Fiercely independent colonists, many of them immigrants, settled the town; their descendants and the newcomers who joined them over the years retained that quality as Carlisle moved toward the nineteenth century. Accustomed to lives lived between other places and peoples in the mid-Atlantic, they were willing to fight to protect their interests much as their colonial predecessors had done.

Carlisle's experience of the Whiskey Rebellion is especially interesting because there was more than just class conflict at work. This event made clear that other continuities marked the town's history. Compromise, in particular, was practically a Carlisle brand by the 1790s. Most notable was the tension that continued to exist between the ideals to which citizens aspired and the reality of their achievements. In an ironic twist, many of Carlisle's town leaders—the men most concerned about the public face of their town—most clearly embodied this tension. They were not exactly the genteel gentlemen they aimed to be, but hybrid men whose lives reflected the demands of their interior setting. The compromises they made were visible in everything from the houses they inhabited to the kinds of business interests they pursued.

First, consider their homes. The homes of Carlisle's leading citizens included important vernacular variations, despite their impressive size and style (figure 14). These variations had less to do with design ideals or individual desires than with the reality of their lives as working men of the interior and not cosmopolitan gentlemen of leisure. Carlisle was no longer a fledgling village by 1798, but a dynamic and economically diverse interior market town. As such, it was dominated by a decidedly "middling" group of leading citizens. In his study of wealth distribution in America, historian Lee Soltow found that in 1798 property values in America ranged from a low of $1 to a high of greater than $30,000. In Carlisle, by comparison, the span of enumerated values on the 1798 Direct Tax was much more limited, ranging from a low of $30 to a high of only $3500. By American standards of the time, Carlisle's leading citizens enjoyed only modest levels of wealth.[61]

Next, consider their business lives. These men—a collection of attorneys, tavern keepers, merchants, shopkeepers, and artisans—were not idly affluent patricians. Instead, as men of middling economic means, their lives, families, and ambitions demanded that they continue to work and sometimes even labor with their hands for a living, even though some carried titles of gentlemen, esquire, colonel, or general.[62] As William Irvine reminded his eldest son, for example, because "I can not give you a Capital," he would have to choose one of the "learned professions" that would allow him to earn "an independent living."[63] He, like his father, had to work. They were privileged men, but in Carlisle privilege was achieved by being industrious and entrepreneurial, much like the town's first colonists. Just as important, while men like Irvine, his son, and others looked east for their cultural and style cues, many also looked west for economic opportunity. These men and their sons continued to act as middlemen of sorts between the American West and the Delaware Valley—they had not left that aspect of Carlisle's betweenness behind. Some significant aspects of life in Carlisle thus had not changed much at all. Despite any outward appearances to the contrary, Carlisle remained an important commercial crossroads between regions. The business activities of its residents were still oriented on an east-west, and not just the north-south, axis that came into particular prominence during the American Revolution when Carlisle was a hub of wartime supply and manufacturing.

There were many examples of how this betweenness played out. Former Commissary General Ephraim Blaine and his son James, privileged Carlisle men, were among the many American traders who got involved in commercializing the deerskin trade of the lower Mississippi River Valley in the 1790s. James wrote to his father of purchasing skins and furs in Spanish-controlled New Orleans presumably for resale to markets in western Europe.[64] As partners in the firm of Blaine, Wilkey and Clark, the Blaines were also engaged in trading in the New Orleans flour markets. With an official passport allowing them to float goods down the Mississippi, the firm was evidently transporting flour from western Pennsylvania downriver at a time when prices were high because "the markett was nearly out of Flour."[65] These were the same kind of speculative, far-flung, western ventures that Ephraim and other Carlisle leading men had been involved in during the 1760s when Carlisle functioned as a critical way station in the fur and skin trade between the Ohio Country and Philadelphia.

William Irvine had his own western trading venture going as well. As a new immigrant and physician in Carlisle in the 1760s, he had mostly missed out on joining the speculative enterprises of his neighbors. By 1790, however, with national military and political leadership under his belt, his situation was different and he was ready to look west for economic opportunity. He partnered with the brothers Charles and John Wilkens of Pittsburgh in a scheme "to carry on a special trade and business in buying and selling" in western Pennsylvania. With the Wilkens brothers as agents in the field, and Irvine behind the scenes, the three intended to trade flour, whiskey, and salt to the Native peoples and settlers in Pittsburgh and Presque Isle in exchange for "considerabl[e] produce, money, and skins."[66] At the same time, Irvine was partnered with his brother and perhaps another relation to engage in speculative ventures in New Orleans. In 1789, while Spain still controlled the Mississippi River, he received a pass from the Spanish commander of Louisiana to "come down to settle in this Province with his family" and "to bring down his property" and "what produce so ever . . . such as Pelletry, Tobacco, Hemp, Flax, Flower, or any other production of the Country[,] free from duty." Although this permission was intended to promote long-term settlement in the region, Irvine and his brother—neither of whom had any intention of moving south—planned to use it for trade only, intentionally violating the spirit of the access they had been granted. While one of the partners went south to oversee business along the Mississippi, Irvine and his brother Mathew arranged for shipments of flour to be sent from Pittsburgh to Natchez and New Orleans. Their goal was to get the "uncommon price" of fifteen "hard" dollars per barrel of flour, and to earn additional money through the sales of butter, cheese, cider and mill or grind stones to needy settlers.[67] Clearly, for Blaine and Irvine, much as for Carlisle's fur traders in the 1750s and 1760s, the town functioned as a pivotal place in-between from which they could negotiate deals with partners or contacts in the east and suppliers, settlers, and even Native peoples in the west and southwest.

At least two other merchants used Carlisle even more directly as a transshipment point for imported dry goods going to retail stores in the newly settled lands of Kentucky. Merchant Samuel Postlethwaite set up his son, John, in the storekeeping business near Lexington in the 1790s. Two of his other sons left Carlisle for Natchez, where they became successful merchants. Another anonymous Carlisle merchant became involved in shipping goods from his Carlisle business to his "Kentucky Store" in the 1790s.[68] During several months in 1792, this merchant sent three large shipments of dry goods, groceries, and hardware totaling over £700 to Kentucky. Most of these wares he obtained from importers in Philadelphia. He then hauled them to his store in Carlisle, and sent them by wagon on to Pittsburgh. Last, he floated them by flatboat to his establishment in Kentucky. While the far-flung nature of this merchant's western ventures replicated the earlier, failed attempts of Baynton, Wharton, and Morgan to capture the Illinois trade, his actions were different because he worked independently; there was no evidence that he was an agent of his Philadelphia suppliers. By all indications, the risk he bore was his own as he maintained close, but autonomous, connections to his suppliers in the east and his customers in the west. Equally important, because he included locally produced goods in his Kentucky shipments—for example, one Carlisle blacksmith sent over three hundred pounds of bar iron in one of his shipments—his venture tied other Carlisle townspeople to the economic fortunes of the American West. For this merchant, as for others in Carlisle, although risk and transportation costs were high—hauling goods to Kentucky, for example, accounted for about 13 percent of his total expenditures—the expanding American West continued to offer the lure of potentially high profits from the sales of goods such as fabric, clothing, weapons, china dishes, books, and glassware.[69] Carlisle's identity as a place thus continued to take its cues in significant ways from its residents' western ventures. In another continuity with the past, it was its Scots-Irish and English residents who forged and perpetuated those connections.

Houses and properties of the town's leading men reflected not just their lofty ideals but the practical realities of their daily lives as men with fortunes closely tied to the American West rather than the eastern metropolis. While they were undoubtedly proud when others described them as "exceeding[ly] kind" and possessing "great politeness," their relatively limited economic means, working lifestyles, and distance from America's coastal cultural centers demanded a selective embrace of America's consumer and housing revolutions.[70] That meant that their dwellings had to suit their experiences as members of a working, western-oriented elite. Many could afford to use brick as the construction material of choice for their homes and outbuildings, thus expressing outward conformity with the increasingly important ideals of permanence, respectability, and gentility in America. But not all were willing or economically able to do so, especially when it came to the way space was organized inside and outside their homes. Urban dwellings, notes architectural historian Bernard Herman, embodied negotiation between cosmopolitan values and traditional practices.[71]

That was certainly true in the way these houses structured their occupants' lived experience. Business and family life, in particular, remained inextricably intertwined in virtually all Carlisle households, regardless of their occupants' wealth or social standing. Evidence from 1798 illustrates that the properties of Carlisle's most privileged families included few separate offices, workshops, or designated places of business. Only forty-six (15 percent) of all of Carlisle's almost three hundred properties had structures designated as "shops." Among the select group of most highly valued properties, there were no shops, and only two structures denoted specifically as offices. This meant that among this collection of attorneys, doctors, merchants, innkeepers, and artisans who worked for their living, the conduct of business occupied the first, if not the second, floor of their dwellings. Even though these leading citizens took on many outward trappings of gentility and cosmopolitanism, the organization of their dwellings and lots suggests that their transformation to polite patricians was incomplete. Social space was segregated on these properties; domestic laborers and slaves carried out many domestic chores in structures separated from the primary dwelling. But business and personal life continued to intermingle on a fundamental level.

Scholars emphasize that genteel houses of the late eighteenth century had become stages for the artificial and ritualistic. They were settings in which the walled partitions between front and back rooms, or top and bottom floors, preserved the increasing division between public and private space, as well as work and family life.[72] In Carlisle, by contrast, the public world of business—particularly retail trades like storekeeping and tavern keeping—regularly entered the homes of the town's affluent. Much like their neighbors of the middling and lower sorts, the town's leading families resided in multifunctional dwellings. Their houses could be "well calculated either for public *or* private purposes" as Sarah M'Donald noted in her 1789 advertisement for her tavern house—for most Carlisle people, wealthy as well as poor, a household's public and private functions overlapped in the family's primary dwelling.[73]

Tavern keeper William Rainey's 1801 advertisement for the sale of his property offers vivid testimony to such blending. Rainey's property, valued at $1400, was among Carlisle's higher-valued lots in 1798. His "old Stand," as he called it, was a wooden, two-story house with a "large Stone Kitchen and Piazza" and three rooms to a floor. "Long occupied as a Tavern as well as a store," he noted that one "convenient apartment," probably the addition, had been "adapted for a store room." Rainey's mention of his house's three rooms to a floor suggests that the interior of his home was not organized according to the four-room Georgian plan, but more likely according to the "Penn" or "Quaker" plan commonly used for taverns, or a common German form. His advertisement—specifically his description of how the house functioned as both a tavern and a store—suggests more important details about how often work and family life intersected in towns of the Pennsylvania interior.[74] Similar to their less-advantaged neighbors, the lifestyles of Carlisle's wealthier entrepreneurs, including tavern keepers like Rainey, continued to bear tan-

gible signs of the town's colonial past, a time when survival, competition, or
the quest for competency or prosperity dictated the interweaving of work and
home life.

Carlisle's lower sorts, many of whom were tavern keepers as well, pointed
to many of the same attributes as their privileged neighbors when advertising
their properties for sale or rent. For example, when tavern keeper and distiller
Charles McManus advertised his property for sale in 1801, he described it as
"the Tavern in which he now lives, with the whole of the premises, consisting
of, the Tavern and a Log Dwelling house, in front, and in the rear a Stable
well finished."[75] McManus's description of his property sounds much like
the one offered by William Rainey: on both properties business and family
life coexisted in a single dwelling. Yet in contrast to Rainey, McManus's log
house was valued at only $150 in 1798. Charles McManus and his family evi-
dently lodged their guests and themselves in a one-story dwelling measuring
a meager 720 square feet.[76]

Whether "large and commodious" or small and "convenient," both privileged and poor Carlisle residents built, rented, and purchased their homes according to the dwelling's perceived commercial potential. As David Lindsey
noted in his 1789 advertisement, his "convenient house, with good stabling,
with a good well of water in the yard," was "well suited for Store or Tavern."[77]
In an economically dynamic market town like Carlisle—an urban community that continued to function as a place in-between east and west as well as
north and south in the mid-Atlantic—commerce was an interest common to
all residents, regardless of their wealth or social standing. Large and stylish
houses built of brick and stone differentiated rich from poor, signaled long-
term commitment to the community, and confirmed Carlisle's embrace of
metropolitan cultural standards. Yet how these structures were utilized and
organized also gauged local economic conditions and social values. In a region
that witnessed considerable growth as it matured since its colonial-era founding, dwelling houses continued to reflect the working needs of their residents.
Privileged easterners may have basked in the genteel luxury of removing business from the home, but Carlisle's leading citizens—a mostly middling group
of professionals, merchants, retailers, and tradesmen—continued to involve
their homes and families in the daily conduct of their commercial affairs. As
the eighteenth century drew to a close, Carlisle's households and the town's
economy thus remained as intimately intertwined as they had been since the
town's founding in 1751. Much had changed and townspeople had proved remarkably adaptable, but important continuities in form and function linked

Carlisle to its colonial past. The town planned by Thomas Penn and his officials persisted. As such, its residents continued to sit in-between, rather than at the edge, of the mid-Atlantic.

The town and people of Carlisle, like other communities of the early republic, were enmeshed in a complex transformation at the close of the eighteenth century. As the new American nation matured, Americans faced the myriad opportunities and challenges posed by the practice of republican politics, the dynamism of an economy moving quickly toward industrialization, and the cultural quest of a young nation trying to define its identity. Yet how these complex processes of change played out, what effects they had, and how they paved the way for the future varied tremendously from community to community, and among individuals.

In Carlisle, this American maturation process took multiple forms and had diverse effects on the town and its inhabitants. By all outward measures, the town's leading citizens embraced these changes. They took enormous pride in their past, but they looked forward to the next century and their town's future. They had fought in the Revolution politically and militarily, and although they were frustrated by their state's radical politics, they welcomed the republic and its return to moderation after 1790. These leading citizens, most of them Scots-Irish Presbyterians, also wanted Dickinson College in their midst. As an institution of higher learning, and only the second college in Pennsylvania, it rewarded them with cultural authority as its trustees and patrons. Furthermore, as entrepreneurs, these same residents eagerly pursued opportunities offered them by America's lucrative postwar grain trade and its increasingly diverse consumer goods economy. They likewise profited from Carlisle's building boom during the 1790s. To these men and their families, the interconnected political, cultural, and economic changes transforming America during the early republic benefited them and their town immensely. And the progressive history they told of Carlisle and themselves as its founders confirmed their self-perceptions; they mostly wished to put their colonial past—a time characterized by the workings of the proprietors, Native Americans, fur traders, and sometimes cantankerous colonists—behind them and move on.

But in Carlisle, things were not so simple—they never were. The town's leading citizens offered only one part of the story. There were also plenty of middling and lower sorts whose experiences and perspectives differed; they offered an alternate narrative that was more critical. The contrasts between these groups came into stark relief in the many contexts where townspeople could not simply embrace the new politics, culture, and economies of the early republic, but rather had to adapt them to suit their lives, experiences, and the real, less uniformly triumphal history of their town. Adaptation involved making choices, sometimes balanced against serious constraints, about what one could do, and about how one would live one's life. Because Carlisle was not Philadelphia or Baltimore, but a prosperous interior town, its residents faced a different range of opportunities or challenges than the inhabitants of those cities. Consequently, townspeople discovered there were limits: not all aspects of life in the early American republic could be easily accommodated to Carlisle's unique conditions. Choice thus meant compromise. Carlisle would never be the fully cultured, cosmopolitan place its leading citizens wanted: its interior setting lent a roughness to its edges. Still, residents had options. While Carlisle's leading citizens had the advantage of more options, the town's middling and lower sorts were not without choice—nor were they shy about expressing the choices they made.

Yet there was a catch because choices had consequences, and not all of the outcomes were positive. Townspeople had to choose how to align themselves within the intensely partisan politics of the nation and state. As Carlisle's violent ratification riot and whiskey tax protests suggest, the choices they made polarized the town, pitting neighbor against neighbor on the streets in ways reminiscent of the ethno-religious confrontations and jailbreaks of the town's colonial past. Then there was the founding of Dickinson College. The town's leading Scots-Irish Presbyterians supported it as their cultural home. Their less-privileged neighbors resented its exclusivity; it was not there to educate them. Of considerable significance as well, was the postwar economic crisis and subsequent boom. As America recovered from the war and moved toward the industrial nineteenth century, townspeople had to choose economic activities and which markets to target. With the fur trade gone and dry goods markets depressed, those who best weathered the vagaries of the early national economy turned toward the grain trade and Baltimore. At the same time, and in an echo of past practice, many of the town's most privileged Scots-Irish and English residents looked west, rather than east, for investment opportunities and personal gain. For those with access, the furthest reaches of the American interior continued to have a powerful allure; it offered unprecedented opportunities for speculation.

So, what is the lesson to be learned from Carlisle's experience? At its most fundamental, Carlisle's history tells a story of adaptation and change parallel to the histories of other interior towns in America. Townspeople's choices, though individual and seemingly innocuous, were part of a broader trend, for they followed patterns of vernacular adaptation happening in other interior towns. What happened in Carlisle was not just unique, but representative. Functioning as a way station for ideals, standards, and practices to be gathered and adapted by townspeople to suit local needs, Carlisle's experience suggests how critical towns and their populations were to the adaptation of republican politics, metropolitan cultural standards, and proto-capitalist economic practices across the early American interior. Carlisle, like other towns, thus functioned not so much as a spearhead but as a translation point, or hub.

The adaptations residents made during the early republic confirmed their town's identity as a place in-between. Beyond the town's divisive politics, the impressive exterior facades of its stylish townhomes and public buildings, its growing market economy, or the wishes of town boosters to make their town face east, Carlisle retained a core component of its founding identity as interior town situated between regions and peoples in the mid-Atlantic. This betweenness continued to have real and metaphorical qualities. From a geographic standpoint, Carlisle's location had not changed. Although settlement had moved well beyond it by 1800 as Pennsylvanians made new claims to the interior, Carlisle still sat just near the state's center in the Cumberland Valley. Residents recognized it as an important town of *central* Pennsylvania. Furthermore, townspeople's economic and personal interests still positioned the town physically between the markets of the Delaware Valley, Baltimore, and the American West, much as they had during the colonial period. The only new speculative connections were to Kentucky and the Mississippi River Valley, which had replaced those directed at the unprofitable Illinois Country. Carlisle's betweenness was further defined by its tangible urban functions. Cumberland County had gotten noticeably smaller by the 1780s, but Carlisle remained the county seat and was an important local market center for its rural hinterlands (see map 1). New public buildings, including a market house bustling with activity, attested to that fact.

The town also retained key aspects of its metaphorical betweenness. Culturally, it remained a contested space where the privileged competed with the poor. Signs of this class struggle were readily visible in the townscape in 1800. Carlisle was, by all accounts, an attractive town, as evidenced by the praise of its many visitors. Yet a coarseness pervaded the townscape. The streets were "wide and well laid out" as one visitor said, for example, but they were also unpaved and unlit. The houses were large and "well built," but they were also

"heavy" and sometimes in "bad taste."[78] Within local society, the town's leading citizens, although diverse, ambitious, and entrepreneurial, were not patricians. Most dressed like gentlemen and ladies, had polite manners, and with a
college in their midst to "set a standard of fine intelligence," valued education
and civic responsibility. One resident later recollected that the "great ladies
of the town, looked, thought and talked as though they had come out of an
English novel."[79] Despite such lofty and probably distorted memories, however, these ladies and their husbands worked hard—very hard—much like
their poorer neighbors. To get ahead in Carlisle one had to be flexible, entrepreneurial, competitive—and sometimes lucky. This was another important
lesson parallel to the experience of other interior towns. Residents in urban
places like Carlisle earned their living through a combination of ingenuity,
skills, and hard work; in other words, they hustled. America's interior towns
were definitely not places where settlers went to rest on their laurels; they
were places very much in motion.

At the same time, as a town where the array of choices made so much
seem possible, Carlisle was a place where people came to pursue their aspirations and dreams; this was also a fundamental expression of its betweenness.
Native peoples were the first: they placed their villages there because of its
advantageous location between other Indians and Euro-American colonists.
Thomas Penn and his officials were next. They chose Carlisle's townsite because of the access it offered to Philadelphia and the Native communities
of the early American West. They hoped that the town would be a center
of orderly development and trade in their colony. Then there were Carlisle's
many industrious Scots-Irish colonists. These people in-between were willing
to risk hardship in the Pennsylvania interior in hopes of achieving material or
personal success by brokering trade with Native peoples while simultaneously
crafting deals with their Anglican and Quaker contacts in the Delaware Valley. Finally, even Congress and the Continental Army—and later Benjamin
Rush—were drawn to the site because of the town's potential to fulfill their
hopes and needs. Whether as a safe place for the manufacture of supplies for
the Army or as the home of a college that would civilize the interior, almost
anything, it seemed, was possible in Carlisle.

Because such potential did not always generate success, harmony, or happiness, however, Carlisle was also an especially contentious and contested
place in-between. There were thus winners, losers, and plenty of people who
fell somewhere in between in Carlisle. There was also a great deal of conflict.
These characteristics made Carlisle especially representative of urban experi-

ence in America's eighteenth-century interior. Some townspeople succeeded: a good number of colonists, for example, many of them Scots-Irish immigrants, built homes, established businesses, and raised families there, sometimes for generations. They assumed important positions of state, and even national, leadership. As immigrants who became established citizens, they were in many respects quintessential American success stories. But the experiences of some in Carlisle were not the experiences of all; not everyone succeeded or prospered there or in any other American town. Carlisle's history, like early America's history, was not just about winners. Those contrasts, not surprisingly. generated tensions and social strife. Outside planners like Penn and Rush were often frustrated—their ideals did not always translate neatly into realities in Carlisle. Entrepreneurs like Baynton, Wharton, and Morgan found their operations challenged by town dwellers who were threatened by their trade relationships with Native Americans. During the Revolution, Congress and the Army sometimes found their operations crippled by locals who would not work if they were not paid. More significant, however, were the experiences of the town's residents. Despite their hard work, not all of them found wealth or even competency. Instead, some found themselves shut out of prosperity as the wealth gap expanded at century's end. This meant that divisions between groups and ranks persisted, fueling a variety of class, ethnic, religious, political, and social tensions that sometimes spilled into the streets in violent protests against standing authority.

That these patterns persisted as 1800 approached demonstrates how challenging town life could be in the early republic. As urban places, market centers, and hubs of government and law, interior county towns like Carlisle were often stages for people's expressions of frustration and anger. As such, they reveal the multiple rifts cutting through American society as it entered the nineteenth century. Carlisle's ratification riot and the whiskey tax protests, for example, illustrated the considerable economic and political gaps that existed between townspeople, as did the gubernatorial election of 1799. In an election pitting two Presbyterians against each other, Carlisle's vote divided almost evenly, just barely tipping toward the Federalist candidate James Ross and away from the Republican convert Thomas McKean, the man Carlisle townspeople had burned in effigy twice during the 1780s and 1790s. This election contest, which McKean won to become governor, put Carlisle at odds with its county, many other towns, and the state.[80] It also demonstrated how politically divided the town remained. As such a contentious place, Carlisle thwarted many people's ambitions. To the great frustra-

ABBREVIATIONS

AHR	*American Historical Review*
Bouquet Papers	Henry Bouquet, *The Papers of Henry Bouquet*, ed. S. K. Stevens, Donald H. Kent, Autumn Leonard (Harrisburg: Pennsylvania Historical and Museum Commission, 1972).
BWM	John Baynton, Samuel Wharton, and George Morgan, partners in the Philadelphia merchant firm of Baynton, Wharton, and Morgan.
BWM Papers	Baynton, Wharton, and Morgan Papers, microfilm, David Library of the American Revolution, Washington Crossing, Pa., originals at Pennsylvania Historical and Museum Commission.
CCHS	Cumberland County Historical Society, Carlisle, Pa.
CG	*Carlisle Gazette*
Colonial Records	Samuel Hazard, ed., *Minutes of the Provincial Council of Pennsylvania, From the Organization to the Termination of the Proprietary Government,* 10 vols. (Philadelphia: Joseph Severns, 1851–1852).
Continental Congress Papers	U.S. Continental Congress, Papers of

	the Continental Congress, 1774–1789, microfilm, David Library of the American Revolution, Washington Crossing, Pa., originals at National Archives, Washington D.C.
DCA	Dickinson College Archives and Special Collections, Carlisle, Pa.
Deed Abstracts	John C. Fralish, ed. and compiler, *Cumberland County Archives, Series One, Records of the Office of the Recorder of Deeds*, 3 vols. (Carlisle, Pa.: John C. Fralish, 1988).
DHRC	Merrill Jensen, ed., *The Documentary History of the Ratification of the Constitution, volume II: Ratification of the Constitution by the States, Pennsylvania* (Madison: State Historical Society of Wisconsin, 1976).
DLAR	David Library of the American Revolution, Washington Crossing, Pa.
Forbes Headquarters Papers	Headquarters Papers of Brig. Gen. John Forbes, microfilm, David Library of the American Revolution, Washington Crossing, Pa., originals at University of Virginia.
GR	*Geographical Review*
Gratz Papers	Simon P. Gratz Autograph Collection, Historical Society of Pennsylvania, Philadelphia.
Hamilton Papers, CCHS	James Hamilton Papers, Cumberland County Historical Society, Carlisle, Pa.
Hamilton Papers, HSP	James Hamilton Papers, Historical Society of Pennsylvania, Philadelphia.
HEQ	*History of Education Quarterly*

HNAI	*Handbook of North American Indians*, gen. ed., William C. Sturtevant, 20 vols. (Washington D.C.: Smithsonian Institution, 1978).
HSP	Historical Society of Pennsylvania, Philadelphia.
Indictments	Clerk of the Court, Cumberland County, Pa., Criminal Court, Indictments, Cumberland County Historical Society, Carlisle, Pa.
IHS	*Irish Historical Studies*
Irvine Papers	William Irvine Papers, Historical Society of Pennsylvania, Philadelphia.
JAH	*Journal of American History*
JER	*Journal of the Early Republic*
JLHS	*Journal of the Lancaster Historical Society*
NYH	*New York History*
PA	*Pennsylvania Archaeologist*
PAPS	*Proceedings of the American Philosophical Society*
PA Rev. Gov't	Records of Pennsylvania's Revolutionary Governments, 1775–1790, Record Group 27, microfilm, 54 reels, David Library of the American Revolution, Washington Crossing, Pa., originals at Pennsylvania Historical and Museum Commission.
Penn Letterbooks	Thomas Penn Papers, Letterbooks, Historical Society of Pennsylvania, Philadelphia.
Penn OC	Thomas Penn Papers, Official Correspondence, Historical Society of Pennsylvania, Philadelphia.
Pennsylvania Archives 1	Samuel Hazard, ed., *Pennsylvania Archives*, 1st ser., 12 vols. (Philadelphia: Joseph Severns and Company, 1852).

Pennsylvania Archives 2	John Linn and William Egle, eds., *Pennsylvania Archives*, 2nd ser., 19 vols. (Harrisburg: Lane S. Hart, 1879).
Pennsylvania Archives 4	George Edward Reed, ed., *Pennsylvania Archives,* 4th ser., 19 vols. (Harrisburg: State Printer, 1900).
Pennsylvania Archives 5	Thomas Lynch Montgomery, ed., *Pennsylvania Archives*, 5th ser., 8 vols. (Harrisburg: Harrisburg Pub. Co., State Printer, 1906).
Pension Applications	United States National Archives, Revolutionary War Pension and Bounty-Land-Warrant Application Files, microfilm, David Library of the American Revolution, Washington Crossing, Pa., originals at National Archives.
PG	*Pennsylvania Gazette*
PH	*Pennsylvania History*
PHMC	Pennsylvania Historical and Museum Commission
PMHB	*Pennsylvania Magazine of History and Biography*
Road Petitions	Cumberland County, Pa., Road Petitions, Cumberland County Historical Society, Carlisle, Pa.
Statutes at Large	James T. Mitchell and Henry Flanders, eds., *Statutes at Large of Pennsylvania from 1682 to 1801,* 32 vols. (Harrisburg, Pa.: C. M. Busch, 1896–1919).
Tavern Licenses	Clerk of the Court, Criminal Court. Cumberland County, Pa., Hotel and Tavern License Applications, Cumberland County Historical Society, Carlisle, Pa., box 28.
Tax Rates	Cumberland County, Pennsylvania,

	Tax Rates, Cumberland County Historical Society, Carlisle, Pa. (microfilm).
Thompson, *Two Hundred Years*	D. W. Thompson, ed., *Two Hundred Years in Cumberland County: A Collection of Documents and Pictures Illustrating Two Centuries of Life in Pennsylvania* (Carlisle, Pa.: Hamilton Library and Historical Association, 1951).
Thos. Cadwalader Papers	Thomas Cadwalader Papers, Cadwalader Family Papers, Historical Society of Pennsylvania, Philadelphia.
Weiser Papers	Conrad Weiser Papers, Historical Society of Pennsylvania, Philadelphia.
West Papers	William West Account Books and Papers, Historical Society of Pennsylvania, Philadelphia.
Will Books	Cumberland County, Pa., Wills, Books A–F, Cumberland County Historical Society, Carlisle, Pa.
WMQ	*William and Mary Quarterly*
WPHM	*Western Pennsylvania Historical Magazine*
WPHS	Western Pennsylvania Historical Society, Pittsburgh

NOTES

INTRODUCTION

1. United States, Bureau of the Census, *Pennsylvania—County—CGT-T1-R. Population Estimates*, http://factfinder.census.gov/servlet/GCTTable?_bm=y&-geo_id=04000US42&-_box_head_nbr=GCT-T1-R&-ds_name=PEP_2006_EST&-_lang=en&-redoLog=false&-format=ST-2S&-_sse=on (2 January 2008).

2. Ibid. According to 2000 census figures, Allentown and Erie had 106,000 and 103,000 people, respectively; Harrisburg had 49,000. These towns are the third, fourth, and seventeenth largest places in the state, respectively, while Carlisle is ninety-sixth.

3. Borough leaders advertise Carlisle as a place where one finds "unique architecture, quaint shops, and overall serenity." Borough of Carlisle, *Welcome to the Borough of Carlisle*, http://www.carlislepa.org/index.asp?Type=B_BASIC&SEC={6590809D-F4BD-4-A02-81A6-520A7893997C} (8 October 2007).

4. For microhistory, see Richard D. Brown, "Microhistory and the Post-Modern Challenge," *JER* 23.1 (2003): 1–20; Jill Lepore, "Historians Who Love Too Much: Reflections on Microhistory and Biography," *JAH* 88.1 (2001): 129–44.

5. James T. Lemon, *The Best Poor Man's Country: A Geographical Study of Early Southeastern Pennsylvania* (Baltimore: Johns Hopkins University Press, 1972), 120–21.

6. For Carlisle's size in 1753, see Tax Rates, Carlisle, 1753. For its rank in Pennsylvania in 1800, see David J. Cuff and others, eds., *The Atlas of Pennsylvania* (Philadelphia: Temple University Press, 1989), 108; Lemon, *Best Poor Man's Country*, 125–26. For figures outside Pennsylvania, see United States Bureau of the Census, *Table 1. Rank by Population of the 100 Largest Urban Places, Listed Alphabetically by State, 1790–1990*, http://www.census.gov/population/documentation/twps0027/tab01.txt (12 October 2007); Christopher E. Hendricks, *The Backcountry Towns of Colonial Virginia* (Knoxville: University of Tennessee Press, 2006), 140.

7. Richard C. Wade, *The Urban Frontier: The Rise of Western Cities, 1790–1830* (Cambridge, Mass.: Harvard University Press, 1959; reprint, Champaign-Urbana: University of Illinois Press, 1996), 1 (quote), 27–34.

8. For the north, see John Frederick Martin, *Profits in the Wilderness: Entrepreneurship and the Founding of New England Towns in the Seventeenth-Century* (Chapel Hill: University of North Carolina Press, 1991); William Wyckoff, *The Developer's Frontier: The Making of the Western New York Landscape* (New Haven, Conn.: Yale University Press, 1988). For the south and west, see Hendricks, *Backcountry Towns*; John Reps, *Town Planning in Frontier America* (Columbia: University of Missouri Press, 1980); Lisa Tolbert, *Constructing Townscapes: Space and Society in Antebellum Tennessee* (Chapel Hill: University of North Carolina Press, 1999).

9. Sally Schwartz, *"A Mixed Multitude": The Struggle for Toleration in Colonial Pennsylvania* (New York: New York University Press, 1989), chap. 4. See also Henry Glassie, *Pattern in the Material Folk Culture of the Eastern United States* (Philadelphia: University of Pennsylvania Press, 1968), 1–33; Patrick Griffin, *The People with No Name: Ireland's Ulster Scots, America's Scots Irish, and the Creation of a British Atlantic World, 1689–1764* (Princeton, N.J.: Princeton University Press, 2001), 1–5; Liam Riordan, *Many Identities, One Nation: The Revolution and Its Legacy in the Mid-Atlantic* (Philadelphia: University of Pennsylvania Press, 2007), 1–13; Peter Silver, *Our Savage Neighbors: How Indian War Transformed Early America* (New York: W. W. Norton, 2008), chap. 1.

10. Lemon, *Best Poor Man's Country*, 13–23, 43–49. See also Richard R. Beeman, *The Varieties of Political Experience in Eighteenth-Century America* (Philadelphia: University of Pennsylvania Press, 2004), 204–6; Aaron Spencer Fogleman, *Hopeful Journeys: German Immigration, Settlement, and Political Culture in Colonial America, 1717–1775* (Philadelphia: University of Pennsylvania Press, 1996), 80–86; David Hackett Fischer, *Albion's Seed: Four British Folkways in America* (New York: Oxford University Press, 1989), 451–603, 633–42; Glassie, *Pattern in Material Folk Culture*, 36–64, 158–63; Gabrielle M. Lanier, *The Delaware Valley in the Early Republic: Architecture, Landscape, and Regional Identity* (Baltimore: Johns Hopkins University Press, 2005).

11. Michael N. McConnell, *A Country Between: The Upper Ohio Valley and Its Peoples, 1724–1774* (Lincoln: University of Nebraska Press, 1992), introduction–chap. 2. See also Colin G. Calloway, *The Shawnees and the War for America* (New York: Penguin, 2007), chap. 1; Daniel K. Richter, *Facing East from Indian Country: A Native History of Early America* (Cambridge, Mass.: Harvard University Press, 2001), 168–171; Amy C. Schutt, *Peoples of the River Valleys: The Odyssey of the Delaware Indians* (Philadelphia: University of Pennsylvania Press, 2007), 103–14.

12. For Anglican politics, see Beeman, *Varieties of Political Experience*, 208–16; James H. Hutson, *Pennsylvania Politics, 1746–1770* (Princeton, N.J.: Princeton University Press, 1972), 148–177; Alan Tully, *Forming American Politics: Ideals, Interests, and Institutions in Colonial New York and Pennsylvania* (Baltimore: Johns Hopkins University Press, 1994), 155–56. For Anglican identity, see Linda Colley, *Britons: Forging the Nation, 1707–1837* (New Haven, Conn.: Yale University Press, 1992), chap. 1; Lemon, *Best Poor Man's Country*, 43–49; Riordan, *Many Identities*, 22–27.

13. Riordan, *Many Identities*, 2 (quote), 25–27; Beeman, *Varieties of Political Experience*, chap. 8; Fischer, *Albion's Seed*, 451–603; Tully, *Forming American Politics*, chap. 7.

14. Fogleman, *Hopeful Journeys*, chaps. 3–5; Paul Douglas Newman, *Fries's Rebellion:*

The Enduring Struggle for the American Revolution (Philadelphia: University of Pennsylvania Press, 2004), prologue; Riordan, *Many Identities*, 6, 28–34; Marianne S. Wokeck, *Trade in Strangers: The Beginnings of Mass Migration to North America* (University Park: Pennsylvania State University Press, 1999), chaps. 1–3.

15. Griffin, *People with No Name*, 1 (quote), 4–8, chap 3. See also Wayland F. Dunaway, *The Scotch-Irish of Colonial Pennsylvania* (Chapel Hill: University of North Carolina Press, 1944; reprint, Baltimore: Genealogical Publishing, 1997), introduction–chap. 3; Riordan, *Many Identities*, 21–22; Wokeck, *Trade in Strangers*, chap. 5.

16. Dunaway, *Scotch-Irish*, chaps. 4–5; Griffin, *People with No Name*, chap. 4, esp. 104–8; Lemon, *Best Poor Man's Country*, 13–18, 43–49, 61–69.

17. Anonymous, "A Garrison Town in Pennsylvania Fifty Years Ago," n.d., HSP.

CHAPTER 1. CREATING A TOWN IN-BETWEEN

1. James Hamilton to Thomas Penn, November 29, 1751, Penn OC, 5:193 (first quote); Hamilton to Penn, April 17, 1753, ibid., 6:37 (second quote).

2. Hamilton to Penn, April 17, 1753, Penn OC, 6:37 (first quote); Hamilton to Penn, November 29, 1751, ibid., 5:193 (second quote). For the Scots-Irish surnames of the town's first residents, see Tax Rates, Carlisle, 1753.

3. Hamilton had inherited the proprietorship of Lancaster Town in 1734. See Craig W. Horle, Joseph S. Foster, and Jeffrey L. Scheib, eds., *Lawmaking and Legislators in Pennsylvania, volume 2, 1710–1756* (Philadelphia: University of Pennsylvania Press, 1997), 420, 449–54; Jerome H. Wood Jr., *Conestoga Crossroads: Lancaster, Pennsylvania, 1730–1790* (Harrisburg, Pa.: Pennsylvania Historical and Museum Commission, 1979), 2–6.

4. For principles of town founding, see Christopher E. Hendricks, *The Backcountry Towns of Colonial Virginia* (Knoxville: University of Tennessee Press, 2006), xiv, xviii; Emrys Jones, *Towns and Cities* (New York: Oxford University Press, 1966), 25–26, 39–40. For town founding as expressions of British colonization, see Gilbert Camblin, *The Town in Ulster: An Account of the Origin and Building of the Towns of the Province and the Development of their Rural Setting* (Belfast: William Mullan and Son, 1951), chap. 3; Raymond Gillespie, *Colonial Ulster: The Settlement of East Ulster, 1600–1641* (Cork: Cork University Press for the Irish Committee of Historical Sciences, 1985), chap. 7; Gillespie, "The Origins and Development of an Ulster Urban Network, 1600–41," *IHS* 24.93 (1984): 15–20. For towns as regulators of behavior, see Gregory Nobles, "Straight Lines and Stability: Mapping the Political Order of the Anglo-American Frontier," *JAH* 80.1 (1993): 29.

5. James T. Lemon, *The Best Poor Man's Country: A Geographical Study of Early Southeastern Pennsylvania* (Baltimore: Johns Hopkins University Press, 1972), 132–34.

6. George Craig, "Letters of Rev. Richard Locke and Rev. George Craig, Missionaries in Pennsylvania of the 'Society for Propagating the Gospel in Foreign Parts'," ed. Benjamin Owen, *PMHB* 34.4 (1900), 477 (first quote); Michel-Guillaume St. Jean de Crèvecoeur, *Journey into Northern Pennsylvania and the State of New York*, ed. and trans.

Clarissa Spencer Bostleman, 2 vols. (Ann Arbor: University of Michigan Press, 1964), 1:24 (second quote).

7. Hamilton to Penn, April 17, 1753, Penn OC, 6:37.

8. John R. Stilgoe, *Common Landscape of America, 1580 to 1845* (New Haven: Yale University Press, 1982), 3.

9. My discussion here draws on several key works in American landscape history. They include: Barbara Bender, "Introduction, Landscape—Meaning and Action," in *Landscape: Politics and Perspectives*, ed. Barbara Bender (Providence, R.I.: Berg, 1993), 1–3, 9; William Cronon, *Nature's Metropolis: Chicago and the Great West* (New York: W. W. Norton, 1991), 51–55; Matthew Dennis, *Cultivating a Landscape of Peace: Iroquois-European Encounters in Seventeenth-Century America* (Ithaca: Cornell University Press, 1993), 20; Simon Schama, *Landscape and Memory* (New York: Alfred A. Knopf, 1995), 9–10.

10. As quoted in Susan Q. Stranahan, *Susquehanna: River of Dreams* (Baltimore: Johns Hopkins University Press, 1993), note 7, 28. For Native American settlement patterns near the river, see Francis Jennings, "'Pennsylvania Indians' and the Iroquois," in *Beyond the Covenant Chain: The Iroquois and Their Neighbors in Indian North America, 1600–1800*, ed. James Merrill and Daniel Richter (Syracuse, N.Y.: Syracuse University Press, 1987), 75–91; Peter Mancall, *Valley of Opportunity: Economic Culture Along the Upper Susquehanna, 1700–1800* (Ithaca: Cornell University Press, 1991), 11–21.

11. John Smith, *The General Historie of Virginia, New-England, and the Summer Isles*, in *The Complete Works of Captain John Smith*, ed. Philip L. Barbour, 3 vols. (Chapel Hill: University of North Carolina Press, 1986), 2:106.

12. Francis Jennings, "Susquehannock," *HNAI*, 15:363.

13. George P. Donehoo, *A History of the Indian Villages and Place Names in Pennsylvania* (Harrisburg, Pa.: Telegraph Press, 1928), 215–16.

14. Ibid., 216–17. Donehoo argues that there were six Susquehannock villages in the lower Valley and at least another three located in the upper Valley in the early seventeenth century. For population estimates, see Mancall, *Valley of Opportunity*, 30–31; Stranahan, *Susquehanna*, 40–41. For descriptions of these settlements, see Smith, *General Historie*, 2:106. See also Jennings, "Susquehannock," *HNAI*, 15:362–67; Barry Kent, Janet Rice, and Kakuko Ota, "A Map of 18th Century Indian Towns in Pennsylvania," *PA* 51.4 (1981): 3–4.

15. Donehoo, *Indian Villages and Place Names*, 36–37, 215–19; Jennings, "'Pennsylvania Indians'," 75–76; Jennings, "Susquehannock," *HNAI*, 15:362–67.

16. Barry C. Kent, *Susquehanna's Indians* (Harrisburg, Pa.: Pennsylvania Historical and Museum Commission, 1989), 11 (quote); see also Donehoo, *Indian Villages and Place Names*, 212.

17. Jennings, "Susquehannock," *HNAI*, 15:363–67. See also Donehoo, *Indian Villages and Place Names*, 215–19; Charles A. Hanna, *The Wilderness Trail; or, The Ventures and Adventures of Pennsylvania Traders on the Allegheny Path*, 2 vols. (New York: G. P. Putnam's Sons, 1911), 1:26–28, 34–35, 45–56; Jennings, "'Pennsylvania Indians,'" 76–79; Amy C. Schutt, *Peoples of the River Valleys: The Odyssey of the Delaware Indians* (Phila-

delphia: University of Pennsylvania Press, 2007), 62–74. For Iroquois relationships with their Native neighbors in the seventeenth century, see Francis Jennings, *The Ambiguous Iroquois Empire* (New York: W. W. Norton, 1984), chaps. 6–8; Daniel K. Richter, *The Ordeal of the Longhouse: The Peoples of the Iroquois League in the Era of European Colonization* (Chapel Hill: University of North Carolina Press, 1992), chaps. 3 and 7.

18. For Conestoga, see James H. Merrell, *Into the American Woods: Negotiators on the Pennsylvania Frontier* (New York: W. W. Norton, 1999), 36, 107, 109.

19. Francis Jennings, "Iroquois Alliances in American History," in *The History and Culture of Iroquois Diplomacy*, ed. Francis Jennings et al. (Syracuse, N.Y.: Syracuse University Press, 1985), 41 (quote). For the Shawnees and Delawares, see Callender, "Shawnee," *HNAI*, 15:622–35; Colin G. Calloway, *The Shawnees and the War for America* (New York: Viking, 2007), chap. 1; Goddard, "Delaware," *HNAI*, 15:213–39; Hanna, *Wilderness Trail*, 1:88–160; Michael N. McConnell, *A Country Between: The Upper Ohio Valley and Its Peoples, 1724–1774* (Lincoln: University of Nebraska Press, 1992), 9–15; Mancall, *Valley of Opportunity*, 29–30; Schutt, *Peoples of the River Valleys*, chap. 3. For their lives on the lower Susquehanna, see George P. Donehoo, *A History of the Cumberland Valley in Pennsylvania*, 2 vols. (Harrisburg, Pa.: Susquehanna History Association, 1930), 1:26–28; Jennings, " 'Pennsylvania Indians,' " 76–80.

20. Schutt, *Peoples of the Valleys*, 64–65.

21. For Indian names, see Donehoo, *Indian Villages and Place Names*, 16–17, 42–44. For their villages, see Kent, Rice, and Ota, "Map of 18th Century Indian Towns," 8–11; Mancall, *Valley of Opportunity*, 31–39; Jane T. Merritt, *At the Crossroads: Indians and Empires on a Mid-Atlantic Frontier, 1700–1763* (Chapel Hill: University of North Carolina Press, 2003), 35.

22. Calloway, *Shawnees*, 11–21; Jennings, "Iroquois Alliances," 40–42; Calloway, "Susquehannock," *HNAI*, 15:366; Kent, Rice, and Ota, "Map of 18th Century Indian Towns," 3–6; McConnell, *A Country Between*, chap. 1; Schutt, *Peoples of the Valleys*, 64–74.

23. Patrick Griffin, *The People with No Name: Ireland's Ulster Scots, America's Scots Irish, and the Creation of a British Atlantic World, 1689–1764* (Princeton, N.J.: Princeton University Press, 2001), 104–6; Joseph E. Illick, *Colonial Pennsylvania: A History* (New York: Scribner, 1979), 109–10; Francis Jennings, "The Indian Trade of the Susquehanna Valley," *PAPS* 110 (1966): 406–24; Gary B. Nash, "The Quest for the Susquehanna Valley: New York, Pennsylvania, and the Seventeenth-Century Fur Trade," *NYH* 48.1 (1967): 3–40.

24. For LeTort, see Jennings, "Indian Trade of Susquehanna Valley," 406–24. See also Evelyn A. Benson, "The LeTort Family: First Christian Family on the Conestoga," *JLHS* (1961): 92–105; Robert G. Crist, *The Land in Cumberland Called Lowther* (Lemoyne, Pa.: Lemoyne Trust Company, 1957), 7; Donehoo, *History of Cumberland Valley*, 1:33; Frederic A. Godcharles, *Chronicles of Central Pennsylvania*, 4 vols. (New York: Lewis Historical Publishing Company, 1944), 1:61; Hanna, *Wilderness Trail*, 1:167–68. In 1734, LeTort was one of six traders that Shawnee leaders "desire[d] may have a License to come and trade with us." See *Pennsylvania Archives 1*, 1:425.

25. Eric Hinderaker, *Elusive Empires: Constructing Colonialism in the Ohio Valley, 1673–1800* (New York: Cambridge University Press, 1997), 22 (quote), see also 27; Jennings, "Indian Trade of Susquehanna Valley," 411–13; Merrell, *Into the American Woods*, chap. 1; McConnell, *A Country Between*, 37–38.

26. For the human dynamics of the region, see Wayland F. Dunaway, *The Scotch-Irish of Colonial Pennsylvania* (Chapel Hill: University of North Carolina Press, 1944), 59–61; John Florin, *The Advance of Frontier Settlement in Pennsylvania, 1638–1850: A Geographical Interpretation* (University Park: Pennsylvania State University, Department of Geography, 1977), 24–27, 55–58; David L. Preston, "The Texture of Contact: European and Indian Settler Communities on the Iroquoian Borderlands, 1720–1780" (Ph.D. diss., William and Mary, 2002), 97–98.

27. John Heckewelder, "Notes of the Travel of William Henry, John Heckewelder, John Rothrock, and Christian Clewell, to Gnadenhuetten on the Muskingum, in the early Summer of 1797," ed. John W. Jordan, *PMHB* 10.2 (1886): 128 (first quote); Anne Newport Royall, *The Black Book; or, A Continuation of Travels in the United States . . . ,* 3 vols. (Washington, D.C.: Printed for the Author, 1828–1829), 1:297 (second quote); Gottlieb Mittelberger, *Journey to Pennsylvania*, ed. and trans. Oscar Handlin and John Clive (Cambridge, Mass.: Belknap Press of Harvard University, 1960), 43 (third quote).

28. For the Cumberland Valley as migration gateway, see David Hackett Fischer, *Albion's Seed: Four British Folkways in America* (New York: Oxford University Press, 1989), 605–782.

29. For information on these colonists, see Dunaway, *Scotch-Irish of Colonial Pennsylvania*, 60–61. For Hendricks, see Merri Lou Schaumann, *Taverns of Cumberland County, Pennsylvania, 1750–1840* (Carlisle, Pa.: Cumberland County Historical Society, 1994), 121. For a map of the area, see John Armstrong's "Draught of a Tract of land known by the name of the Manor of Lowther," March 1765 (Lowther Manor Survey Maps), Thos. Cadwalader Papers, ser. 3, Box 186.13. For Newtown, see William T. Swaim, *Newtown: Precursor of Carlisle* (Harrisburg, Pa.: published by the author, 1904), 5–9.

30. Dunaway, *Scotch-Irish of Colonial Pennsylvania*, 60–61; Griffin, *People with No Name*, chap. 4.

31. Preston, "Texture of Contact," 99.

32. Theophile Cazenove, *Cazenove Journal 1794: A Record of the Journey of Theophile Cazenove Through New Jersey and Pennsylvania*, ed. Rayner W. Kelsey (Harrisburg, Pa.: Aurand Press, 1922), 61–62.

33. Preston, "Texture of Contact," chap. 2; Griffin, *People with No Name*, 100.

34. For Pennsylvania's eighteenth-century immigrants, many of whom moved into the interior, see Florin, *Advance of Frontier Settlement*, 11–22; Griffin, *People with No Name*, chaps. 3–4; Lemon, *Best Poor Man's Country*, chaps. 1 and 3.

35. For the shifting cultural dynamics of this region, see Calloway, *Shawnees*, 11–14; Callender, "Shawnee," *HNAI*, 15:622–35; Preston, "Texture of Contact," 100–3; Schutt, *Peoples of the River Valleys*, 65–74. For the balance among Iroquois, Shawnee, and Delaware authority in the region, see Hinderaker, *Elusive Empires*, 25–32; Jennings, "Iroquois Alliances," 38–44; Jennings, "'Pennsylvania Indians,'" 75–91; McConnell, *A Country*

Between, 5–16, 57–58; McConnell, "Peoples 'In Between': The Iroquois and the Ohio Indians, 1720–1768," in *Beyond the Covenant Chain*, 93–98. For the Shawnees and Delawares after their relocation to the Ohio Country, see Gregory Evans Dowd, *A Spirited Resistance: The North American Indian Struggle for Unity, 1745–1815* (Baltimore: Johns Hopkins University Press, 1992), especially chap. 2.

36. Donehoo, *Indian Villages and Place Names*, 16–17, explains that Pennsylvania officials were initially distressed when the Shawnees and others began to relocate westward. To entice them to stay, Pennsylvania provincial officials offered to reserve a tract of land between the Conodoguinet and Yellow Breeches for the Shawnee to settle. Most of the Indians, and traders like Chartier and LeTort, chose to relocate west instead; many ended up at Chartier's Town on the Allegheny River. For a description of the manor, see Copy of Warrant to Resurvey the Manor of Lowther, Thos. Cadwalader Papers, box 186.11 According to Kent, Rice, and Ota, "Map of 18th Century Indian Towns," 17, most Susquehanna Valley Indian towns were empty by 1755.

37. Margaret Van Horn Dwight, *A Journey to Ohio in 1810*, ed. Max Ferrand (New Haven: Yale University Press, 1912), 26.

38. Samuel Blunston to Thomas Penn, July 25, 1733, Penn Papers, Unbound Letters, HSP (quote). For the Penn family, see Lorette Treese, *The Storm Gathering: The Penn Family and the American Revolution* (University Park: Pennsylvania State University Pres, 1992; reprint, Mechanicsburg, Pa.: Stackpole Books, 2002), chaps. 1–2; Alan Tully, *Forming American Politics: Ideals, Interests, and Institutions in Colonial New York and Pennsylvania* (Baltimore: Johns Hopkins University Press, 1994), 262–64; Tully, *William Penn's Legacy: Politics and Social Structure in Provincial Pennsylvania, 1726–1755* (Baltimore: Johns Hopkins University Press, 1977), 3–22, 131–33.

39. James H. Hutson, *Pennsylvania Politics, 1746–1770: The Movement for Royal Government and its Consequences* (Princeton, N.J.: Princeton University Press, 1972), chap. 1.

40. Richard R. Beeman, *The Varieties of Political Experience in Eighteenth-Century America* (Philadelphia: University of Pennsylvania Press, 2004), 208–216; Tully, *Forming American Politics*, 260–303; Tully, *William Penn's Legacy*, 11–22, 41–43.

41. Preston, "Texture of Contact," 89.

42. For Penn's authorization of these licenses, see Thomas Penn to Samuel Blunston, January 10, 1734, Penn Papers, Unbound Letters, HSP. For quote, see *Lawmaking and Legislators 2*, 224. For more on Blunston, Cressap's War, and the Penn family's plans for settling the interior, see ibid., 2:220–31; Griffin, *People with No Name*, 101–7; Treese, *Storm Gathering*, chaps. 1–2; Tully, *William Penn's Legacy*, 8, 11–12. Tully explains (8) that the Blunston Licenses required no monetary payment and were offered to colonists with an implicit guarantee that they would be converted into regular titles when Penn obtained legal title. For the licensees, see "Blunston Licenses," Genealogical Society of Pennsylvania, *Publications of the Genealogical Society of Pennsylvania* (Philadelphia: The Society, 1895), 11:180–85, 269–75; 12:62–70.

43. Blunston to Penn, July 25, 1733, Penn Papers, Unbound Letters, HSP (quote); Lemon, *Best Poor Man's Country*, 60; Merritt, *At the Crossroads*, 24–28; Tully, *William Penn's Legacy*, 8–15.

44. *Pennsylvania Archives 1*, 1:495 (quote), see also 1:494–97; *Colonial Records*, 4:91–92. For one scholar's interpretation of this treaty, see Jennings, " 'Pennsylvania Indians'," 89; Jennings, "Iroquois Alliances," 45.

45. For the 1736 purchase as a bargaining chip in trade and diplomacy with Maryland, see Illick, *Colonial Pennsylvania*, chap. 7; Tully, *William Penn's Legacy*, chap. 1. For the creation of Cumberland County, see James T. Mitchell and Henry Flanders, eds., *Statutes at Large of Pennsylvania from 1682 to 1801*, 32 vols. (Harrisburg, Pa.: C. M. Busch, 1896–1919), 5:87–93. As Pennsylvania's sixth county, Cumberland fell behind Philadelphia, Bucks, and Chester, which were founded with the colony in 1682; Lancaster in 1729; and York in 1749 (the only other county west of the Susquehanna).

46. *Colonial Records*, 4:91.

47. Treese, *Storm Gathering*, 12 (first quote); Tully, *Forming American Politics*, 266 (second quote).

48. Illick, *Colonial Pennsylvania*, 174; Lemon, *Best Poor Man's Country*, 131–40; Donna Bingham Munger, *Pennsylvania Land Records: A History and Guide to Research* (Wilmington, Del.: Scholarly Resources for Pennsylvania Historical and Museum Commission, 1991), 88–99.

49. For Penn's town planning activities, see Illick, *Colonial Pennsylvania*, 174–82, 203–6; Lemon, *Best Poor Man's Country*, chap. 5; Munger, *Pennsylvania Land Records*, 57–60, 88–89; Treese, *Storm Gathering*, chaps. 1–2; Tully, *William Penn's Legacy*, chap. 2.

50. Thomas Cookson to James Hamilton, March 1, 1750, *Pennsylvania Archives 1*, 2:42–44.

51. James Hamilton to Thomas Penn, September, 24, 1750, Penn OC, 5:55.

52. Cookson to Hamilton, March 1, 1750, *Pennsylvania Archives 1*, 2:42–43. For the seven colonists on this site, see Land Releases, 1750–1751, Thos. Cadwalader Papers, box 186.2.

53. Richard Peters to Thomas Penn, July 10, 1750, Penn Papers OC, 5:31.

54. Peters to Penn, July 20, 1750, ibid., 5:39.

55. Cookson to Hamilton, March 1, 1750, *Pennsylvania Archives 1*, 2:42–44 (quote). See also Peters to Penn, July 20, 1750, Penn OC, 5:39.

56. James Hamilton, "Instructions to Nicholas Scull, Esq., Surveyor General," April 1, 1751, Carlisle Town Map Folder, PHMC, 48.3.

57. Cookson to Hamilton, March 1, 1750, *Pennsylvania Archives 1*, 2:42–44.

58. Thomas Cookson to James Hamilton, March 1, 1750, Thos. Cadwalader Papers, box 186.1.

59. Paul A. W. Wallace, *Indian Paths of Pennsylvania* (Harrisburg, Pa.: Pennsylvania Historical and Museum Commission, 1965; reprint, 1993), 19–21, 38. See also Swaim, *Newtown*, 10.

60. Hamilton to Penn, September 24, 1750, Penn OC, 5:55 (quote). For the New Path, see Wallace, *Indian Paths*, 115.

61. Wallace, ibid., 49.

62. Ibid., 49–54, 57, 115–16, 142–47. See also Donehoo, *Indian Villages and Place Names*, 42–43, 75–76, 82–85, 156–57, 167–70; Hanna, *Wilderness Trail*, 1:249, 274–89. Ac-

cording to Hanna (249), the Frankstown Path was the most important westward path before the 1750s, serving as "a main artery of communication between the East and the West" until the construction of the Forbes Road along the more southerly Raystown Path.

63. James Hamilton to Thomas Penn, April 30, 1751, Penn OC, 5:135 (first quote); Hamilton, "Instructions to Scull," Carlisle Town Map Folder, PHMC, 48.3 (second quote); Thomas Penn to Richard Peters, May 30, 1750, Penn Letterbooks, 2:309 (third quote). For the increased competitiveness of the fur trade at mid-century, see Hinderaker, *Elusive Empires*, 31.

64. Richard Peters to Thomas Penn, July 10, 1750, Penn OC, 5:33.

65. Locating county seats was serious business in eighteenth-century Pennsylvania. A seat was supposed to be a central and convenient location to its county. Interior seats were also to be located outside the orbit of Philadelphia, at least fifty-five miles away, so as to foster a profitable trade relationship with the city. See Illick, *Colonial Pennsylvania*, 174–75; Lemon, *Best Poor Man's Country*, 132–34; Munger, *Pennsylvania Land Records*, 88–89; Lisa Tolbert, *Constructing Townscapes: Space and Society in Antebellum Tennessee* (Chapel Hill: University of North Carolina Press, 1999), 20–23.

66. Cookson to Hamilton, March 1, 1750, *Pennsylvania Archives 1*, 2:42–44 (quote). Struggles over the location of county seats were not unusual in Pennsylvania; see R. Eugene Harper, "The Class Structure of Western Pennsylvania in the late Eighteenth Century" (Ph.D. diss., University of Pittsburgh, 1969), 169–70; Harper, "Town Development in Early Western Pennsylvania," *WPHM* 71.1 (1988), 15.

67. Richard Peters to Thomas Penn, September 5, 1750, Penn OC, 5:47.

68. The Inhabitants of the West Part of Cumberland County, Petition to Governor Hamilton, March 24, 1750, Penn Papers, Receipts for Beaver Skins for Tenure, etc., HSP, 12:40.

69. Ibid. Such petitions raised anxieties on the provincial level. Richard Peters spoke of how county residents had "warn[ed]" that towns being built in Maryland and Virginia "will entice away our Inhabitants." He worried about that prospect. See Richard Peters to Thomas Penn, April 5, 1750, Penn OC, 5:47.

70. David Magaw to Richard Peters, February 1, 1750, *Pennsylvania Archives 1*, 2:43 (quote). Shippen, it was reported, was willing to "exchange or sell you three hundred Acres of Land in that place" for a town; see Richard Peters to Thomas Penn, March 12, 1750, Penn OC, 4:197. See also *History of Cumberland and Adams Counties, Pennsylvania* (Chicago: Warner, Beers, and Company, 1886), 257–62; Conway P. Wing, *History of Cumberland County with Illustrations* (Philadelphia: James D. Scott, 1879), 243–47.

71. Cookson to Hamilton, March 1, 1750, *Pennsylvania Archives 1*, 2:43 (quote). See also Thomas Penn to Richard Peters, May 30, 1750, Penn Letterbooks, 2:310.

72. Penn to Peters, May 30, 1750, ibid., 2:309. See also Wing, *History of Cumberland County*, 23.

73. Cookson to Hamilton, March 1, 1750, *Pennsylvania Archives 1*, 2:43–44.

74. Hamilton to Scull, "Instructions," Carlisle Town Map Folder, PHMC, 48.3 (quotes). See also Penn to Peters, May 30, 1750, Penn Letterbooks, 2:309.

75. Penn had "determined to place the Town somewhere on the Waters issuing from

LeTort's Spring into the River Conedoguinet." As quoted in Thompson, *Two Hundred Years*, 18. For the name Carlisle, see Penn to Peters, May 30, 1750, Penn Letterbooks, 2:309. For instructions to purchase lands, see Hamilton to Scull, "Instructions," Carlisle Town Map Folder, PHMC, 48.3. In a lengthy letter to Penn, Cookson described how he purchased the town site from four colonists: Patrick Davison, William Davison, James Gilcore, and Peter Wilkie. His dilemma was that these colonists, aware of their advantageous bargaining position, demanded "very high" prices for their lands. Cookson "imagined you [Penn] wou'd think them [the prices] very extravagant in that Part of the Country," unfortunately "cheaper I cou'd not get them." These lands, he assured Penn, "were purchased as speedily and as cheap as was in my Power," and done so because both he and the Governor "thought it would be for your Interest to have those Lands even at the rates they insisted on rather than leave them in their Possessions." See Thomas Cookson to Thomas Penn, June 8, 1752, *Pennsylvania Archives 2*, 7:256–58. For additional details about these purchases, see Land Releases, 1750–51, Thos. Cadwalader Papers, box 186.2. According to these records, Cookson paid a total of £1655 for these seven tracts.

76. Lemon, *Best Poor Man's Country*, 124; Munger, *Pennsylvania Land Records*, 88–89.

77. For the purposes and goals of town planners, see David Hamer, *New Towns in the New World: Images and Perceptions of the Nineteenth-Century Urban Frontier* (New York: Columbia University Press, 1990), 85–86, 204–23; Lemon, *Best Poor Man's Country*, chap. 5; Stilgoe, *Common Landscape*, 3–4, 43–57, 77–83; Tolbert, *Constructing Townscapes*, 4–9, 21–23; Dell Upton, "City as Material Culture," in *The Art and Mystery of Historical Archaeology*, ed. Anne Yentsch and Mary Beaudry (Boca Raton, Fla.: CRC Press, 1992), 51–74; Upton, "European Landscape Transformation: The Rural Residue," in *Understanding Ordinary Landscapes,* ed. Paul E. Groth and Todd W. Bressi (New Haven: Yale University Press, 1997), 174–79; William Wycoff, *The Developer's Frontier: The Making of the Western New York Landscape* (New Haven: Yale University Press, 1988), 13–16, 42–52.

78. For the grid plan, see Sylvia D. Fries, *The Urban Idea in Colonial America* (Philadelphia: Temple University Press, 1977), 25–28; Hendricks, *Backcountry Towns*, 16–19, 145; Hildegard B. Johnson, *Order Upon the Land: The U.S. Rectangular Land Survey and the Upper Mississippi Country* (New York: Oxford University Press, 1976), 25–42; John W. Reps, *Town Planning in Frontier America* (Princeton, N.J.: Princeton University Press, 1969), 210–22; Dan Stanislawski, "The Origin and Spread of the Grid-Pattern Town," *GR* (1946): 105–20; Tolbert, *Constructing Townscapes*, 23–32. For the British perspective, see Gilbert Camblin, *The Town in Ulster* (Belfast: William Mullan, 1951), chap. 4; Raymond Gillespie, "The Origins and Development of an Ulster Urban Network, 1600–41," *IHS* 24.93 (1984): 15–29.

79. For "wide streets," see *Cazenove Journal 1794*, 56 (first quote). For Carlisle's plan, see Penn to Peters, May 30, 1750, Penn Letterbooks, 2:309; and Penn to James Hamilton, July 29, 1751, ibid, 3:78 (second quote). For more information about Carlisle's plan, see Milton E. Flower and Lenore E. Flower, *This Is Carlisle: A History of a Pennsylvania Town* (Harrisburg, Pa.: J. Horace McFarland, 1944), 3; Illick, *Colonial Pennsylvania*, 174;

Lemon, *Best Poor Man's Country*, 134. According to Harper, "Class Structure of Western Pennsylvania," 155, outlots were a typical feature of most Pennsylvania towns. They provided pasture land for livestock, offered space for future town expansion, and offered an investment opportunity for speculators. The British used them in Ulster as well. They also offered Penn additional opportunities for profit. Indeed, planning Reading had taught him that surveyors must acquire plenty of land near his towns, or "else we shall always sell cheap & buy at a dearer Rate which will not do in Large quantities." See Thomas Penn to Richard Peters, August 27, 1750, Penn Letterbooks, 3:49. For the payments made to surveyors to lay out Carlisle, see Peters Papers, October 12, 1750, December 26, 1751, August 24, 1752, Small Account Book, 4:3.

80. For Lancaster, see Bernard L. Herman, *Town House: Architecture and Material Life in the Early American City, 1780–1830* (Chapel Hill: University of North Carolina, 2005), 80–82; Wood, *Conestoga Crossroads*, chap. 1. For other towns, see Paul E. Doutrich, "The Evolution of an Early American Town: Yorktown, Pennsylvania, 1740–1790" (Ph.D. diss., University of Kentucky, 1985), 16–18; Liam Riordan, *Many Identities, One Nation: The Revolution and Its Legacy in the Mid-Atlantic* (Philadelphia: University of Pennsylvania Press, 2007), 28–34. See also Hendricks, *Backcountry Towns*, 18; Warren R. Hofstra, *The Planting of New Virginia: Settlement and Landscape in the Shenandoah Valley* (Baltimore: Johns Hopkins University Press, 2004), chap. 7; Alan Taylor, *William Cooper's Town: Power and Persuasion on the Frontier of the Early American Republic* (New York: Alfred A. Knopf, 1995), 200–205; Tolbert, *Constructing Townscapes*, 23–43. For the "Pennsylvania" or "Philadelphia" plan, see Wilbur Zelinsky, "The Pennsylvania Town: An Overdue Geographical Account," *GR* 67.2 (1977): 127–47. See also Thomas Winpenny, "The Nefarious Philadelphia Plan and Urban America: A Reconsideration," *PMHB*, 101 (1977): 103–13.

81. Anthony N. B. Garvan, "Proprietary Philadelphia as Artifact," in *The Historian and the City*, ed. Oscar Handlin and John Burchard (Cambirgde, Mass.: MIT Press, 1963), 177–201; Jean Soderlund, *William Penn and the Founding of Pennsylvania, 1680–1684: A Documentary History* (Philadelphia: University of Pennsylvania Press, 1983), 82–85; Beth Twiss-Garrity, "Double Vision: The Philadelphia Cityscape and the Perceptions of It," in *Shaping a National Culture: The Philadelphia Experience*, ed. Catherine E. Hutchins (Winterthur, Del.: Winterthur Museum, 1994), 3–4.

82. For the connections between father and son, see Lemon, *Best Poor Man's Country*, 98–109; Pierce F. Lewis, "The Northeast and the Making of American Geographical Habits," in *The Making of the American Landscape*, ed. Michael P. Conzen (Boston: Unwin Hyman, 1990), 97; Edward T. Price, "The Central Courthouse Square in the American County Seat," *GR* 58.1 (1968): 39–40; John Reps, *Town Planning in Frontier America* (Columbia: University of Missouri Press, 1980), 210–13, 221–23, 426–27; Stilgoe, *Common Landscape*, 77–83, 88–96; Dell Upton, "Another City: The Urban Cultural Landscape in the Early Republic," in *Everyday Life in the Early Republic*, ed. Catherine E. Hutchens (Winterthur, Del.: Winterthur Museum, 1994): 67; Winpenny, "Nefarious Philadelphia Plan," 107–8.

83. Penn to Hamilton, July 29, 1751, Penn Letterbooks, 3:78.

84. Thomas Penn to Richard Peters, September 28, 1751, ibid., 3:97. See also Stilgoe, *Common Landscape*, 94.

85. T. C. Barnard, "New Opportunities for British Settlement: Ireland 1650–1700," in *The Oxford History of the British Empire: Vol. 1, The Origins of Empire*, ed. Nicholas Canny (New York: Oxford University Press, 1998), 318.

86. Ibid., 318; Gillespie, "Ulster Urban Network," 15–20. See also Camblin, *Town in Ulster*, chap. 3.

87. Camblin, *Town in Ulster*, 33, see also plate 5; Anthony N. B. Garvan, *Architecture and Town Planning in Colonial Connecticut* (New Haven: Yale University Press, 1951), 35, 40; Twiss-Garrity, "Double Vision," 3.

88. Garvan, *Architecture and Town Planning*, 40 (quote); Camblin, *Town in Ulster*, 31.

89. Nicholas Canny, "The Irish Background to Penn's Experiment," in *The World of William Penn*, ed. Richard S. Dunn and Mary Maples Dunn (Philadelphia: University of Pennsylvania Press, 1986), 139–56; Mary K. Geiter, *William Penn* (Harlow, UK: Longman, 2000), 22–27.

90. Twiss-Garrity, "Double Vision," 3.

91. Richard Peters to Thomas Penn, June 12, 1752, Penn OC, 5:208, 211.

92. Peters to Thomas Penn, March 16, 1752, ibid., 5:217.

93. James Hamilton to Thomas Penn, November 29, 1751, ibid., 5:193

94. Thomas Penn to James Hamilton, July 29, 1751, Penn Letterbooks, 3:78.

95. Penn to Peters, May 30, 1750, ibid., 2:309 (quote). See also Charles Gilber Beetem, *Colonial Carlisle: Plans and Maps for the Design of Its Public Square* (Carlisle: Printed by the Carlisle Tire and Rubber Company, 1959); Flower and Flower, *This Is Carlisle*, 4; Merkel Landis, *The "English Church" in Colonial Carlisle* (Carlisle: Hamilton Library Association, 1949), 4–8.

96. Peters to Penn, March 16, 1752; June 12, 1752, Penn OC, 5:217–20; 5:208, 211.

97. Thomas Penn to Richard Peters, May 30, 1750, Penn Letterbooks, 2:310 (quote). For renaming as colonial practice, see Stephen Greenblatt, *Marvelous Possessions: The Wonder of the New World* (Chicago: University of Chicago Press, 1991), 82–85.

98. Treese, *Storm Gathering*, 17; Richard Pillsbury, "The Street Name System of Pennsylvania Before 1820," *Names* 17 (1969): 214–22.

99. Thomas Penn to James Hamilton, 1751, Penn Letterbooks, 3:87 (quote). For Thomas Penn's 1751 marriage to Lady Juliana Fermor, daughter of the first Earl of Pomfret, see Treese, *Storm Gathering*, 17. For Easton's plan and street names, see A. D. Chidsey, Jr., *A Frontier Village: Pre-Revolutionary Easton* (Easton, Pa.: Northampton County Historical Society, 1940), 19.

100. For the Jacobite Uprising of 1745, see Geoffrey Plank, *Rebellion and Savagery: The Jacobite Rising of 1745 and the British Empire* (Philadelphia: University of Pennsylvania Press, 2006), 40–52. For Carlisle, England and its connection to the uprising, see John Nichols, *The Gentleman's Magazine* (London: E. Cave, 1745), 15:675; 16:233.

CHAPTER 2. NEGOTIATING THE BOUNDARIES

1. Robert G. Crist, "John Armstrong: Proprietor's Man" (Ph.D. diss., Pennsylvania State University, 1981), 26.

2. Richard Peters to Thomas Penn, March 16, 1752, Penn OC, 5:217–20.

3. James Hamilton to Thomas Penn, April 30, 1751, Penn OC, 5:135 (quote). On the delay, see Thomas Penn to James Hamilton, February 25, 1750, Penn Letterbooks, 3:58; Thomas Cookson to Thomas Penn, June 8, 1752, *Pennsylvania Archives 2*, 7:256–58. On the price paid for these lands, Penn noted: "Mr. Cookson should sooner have purchased the Lands, which he might have had eighteen months since, perhaps for two thirds of the money." See Thomas Penn to Richard Peters, September 28, 1751, Penn Letterbooks, 3:97. For Carlisle's survey date of May 1751, see "Warrant to Resurvey Carlisle," May 5, 1762, Thos. Cadwalader Papers, box 186.7.

4. For the simultaneously cooperative and competitive nature of Indian-European relationships, see Jane T. Merritt, *At the Crossroads: Indians and Empires on a Mid-Atlantic Frontier, 1700–1763* (Chapel Hill: University of North Carolina Press, 2003), chaps. 1–2; David L. Preston, "Squatters, Indians, Proprietary Government, and Land in the Susquehanna Valley" in *Friends and Enemies in Penn's Woods: Indians, Colonists, and the Racial Construction of Pennsylvania*, ed. William A. Pencak and Daniel K. Richter (University Park: Pennsylvania State University Press, 2004), 180–200; Preston, "The Texture of Contact: European and Indian Settler Communities on the Iroquoian Borderlands, 1720–1780" (Ph.D. diss., College of William & Mary, 2002), chap. 2.

5. For the context of interior Pennsylvania in the late 1740s and early 1750s, in addition to the sources in note 4, see James H. Merrell, *Into the American Woods: Negotiators on the Pennsylvania Frontier* (New York: W. W. Norton, 1999), chaps. 4–5; Daniel K. Richter, *Facing East from Indian Country: A Native History of Early America* (Cambridge, Mass.: Harvard University Press, 2001), chap. 5.

6. Anonymous [likely Richard Peters] to Thomas Penn, May 5, 1750, Penn OC, 5:2 (first quote); Richard Peters to Thomas Penn, May 16, 1749, as quoted in Preston, "Texture of Contact," 117 (second quote).

7. *Colonial Records*, 4:570 (quote), 5:389. For the context of Native complaints and the treaty of 1749, see Preston, "Squatters, Indians, and Proprietary Government," 189–95.

8. *Colonial Records*, 5:394–95 (quote); Hamilton feared that squatters' continued presence might "occasion dangerous Quarrels" with the Six Nations and "be the Cause of much Bloodshed." For additional information, see *Pennsylvania Archives 4*, 2:107; James Merrell, "'The Cast of His Countenance': Reading Andrew Montour," in *Through the Glass Darkly: Reflections on Personal Identity in Early America*, ed. Ronald Hoffman et al. (Chapel Hill: University of North Carolina Press, 1997), 30–33.

9. Anonymous to Thomas Penn, May 5, 1750, Penn OC, 5:2.

10. Richard Peters to Thomas Penn, July 10, 1750, Penn OC, 5:31 (quotes). See also *Colonial Records*, 5:440–49; Silas Wright, *History of Perry County in Pennsylvania From the Earliest Settlement to the Present Time* (Lancaster, Pa.: Wylie & Griest, 1873), 9–10.

11. *Colonial Records*, 5:443 (quotes). See also Preston, "Squatters, Indians, and Proprietary Government," 196–97; Preston, "Texture of Contact," 120–22.

12. Richard Peters to Thomas Penn, October 23, 1750, Penn OC, 5:75 (quotes); see also 5:99. For another account, see *Colonial Records*, 5:445, where Peters asserts he carried out these actions "with a View to prevent an Indian War," and "to serve the neighboring colonies." For George Croghan's perspective, see Nicholas B. Wainwright, *George Croghan: Wilderness Diplomat* (Chapel Hill: University of North Carolina Press, 1959), 32–34. For a contrasting interpretation of these proceedings, one more inclined to take Peters at his word, see Preston, "Squatters, Indians, and Proprietary Government," 195–97.

13. *Colonial Records*, 5:449.

14. Richard Peters to Thomas Penn, June 22, 1750, Penn OC, 5:261 (first quote); second quote as quoted in Hubertis Cummings, *Richard Peters: Provincial Secretary and Cleric, 1704–1776* (Philadelphia: University of Pennsylvania Press, 1944), 155.

15. Peters to Penn, October 23, 1750, Penn OC, 5:75 (quotes). For Penn's pleased reactions, see Penn to Hamilton, March 9, 1752, Penn Letterbooks, 3:116. For historians' interpretations of these proceedings, see Cummings, *Richard Peters*, 150–56; Preston, "Squatters, Indians, and Proprietary Government," 195–99. See also Merrell, "'Cast of His Countenance,'" 31–32 and note 43; *Colonial Records*, 4:572.

16. *Colonial Records*, 5:438.

17. Richard Peters to Thomas Penn, October 23, 1750, Penn OC, 5:99 (first quotes), January 30, 1751, ibid., 5:121 (quote "disorderly & low"). For squatters' persistence, see James Hamilton to Thomas Penn, November 18, 1750, ibid., 5:89; see also Preston, "Squatters, Indians, and Proprietary Government," 197. Local protests took on new seriousness in 1752 when Peters got news that Penn's Maryland rivals had "spirited up a Number of poor infatuated People to sign a Petition to the King against me for burning their houses." See Peters to Penn, January 20, 1752, ibid., 5:213.

18. Richard Peters to Thomas Penn, January 30, 1751, Penn OC, 5:121 (quote). For Hamilton's response, see "A Message from the Governor to the Assembly," *PG*, August 30, 1750.

19. Wright, *History of Perry County*, 11–13. For the deceitful circumstances of the 1754 purchase, which Ohio Country Native peoples vehemently opposed and which was a driving force inspiring their raids on these lands during the Seven Years' War, see Merritt, *At the Crossroads*, 173–97; Preston, "Squatters, Indians, and Proprietary Government," 198.

20. Conrad Weiser to Richard Peters, April 1755, Weiser Papers, 1:53.

21. For Croghan's and Trent's application for Carlisle lots, see "Applyers for Lots in Carlisle," May 14–17, 1751, Thos. Cadwalader Papers, box 186.4. For George Croghan, see Andrew R. L. Cayton, *Frontier Indiana* (Bloomington: Indiana University Press, 1996), chap. 2; Charles A. Hanna, *The Wilderness Trail; or, The Ventures and Adventures of Pennsylvania Traders on the Allegheny Path*, 2 vols. (New York: G. P. Putnam's Sons, 1911), 1: chaps. 1–2; James H. Merrell, *Into the American Woods: Negotiators on the Pennsylvania Frontier* (New York: W. W. Norton, 1999), 81–83; Albert T. Volwiler, *George Croghan*

and the Westward Movement (Cleveland: Arthur H. Clark, 1926), chaps. 1–2; Wainwright, *George Croghan*, chap. 2; Richard White, *The Middle Ground: Indians, Empires, and Republics in the Great Lakes Region, 1650–1815* (New York: Cambridge University Press, 1991), chaps. 5–8. For the treaty held at Croghan's house near Carlisle, see *Colonial Records*, 5:431–36.

22. James Hamilton to Thomas Penn, June 19, 1752, Penn OC, 5:245.

23. Ibid. (quotes). For Croghan's role in the bankruptcy of Hockley, Trent, and Croghan, see Wainwright, *George Croghan*, chap. 2; Hanna, *Wilderness Trail*, 2:3; Volwiler, *George Croghan*, 32–49.

24. Hamilton to Penn, June 19, 1752, Penn OC, 5:245.

25. For the centrality of patronage in colonial politics, see Gordon S. Wood, *The Radicalism of the American Revolution* (New York: Alfred A. Knopf, 1991; Vintage Books, 1993), chap. 4.

26. Charles G. Beetem, *Colonial Carlisle: Plans and Maps for the Design of its Public Square* (Carlisle, Pa.: Carlisle Corporation, 1959), 23–25; Milton E. Flower and Lenore E. Flower, *This Is Carlisle: A History of a Pennsylvania Town* (Harrisburg, Pa.: J. Horace McFarland, 1944), 4; Donna B. Munger, *Pennsylvania Land Records: A History and Guide for Research* (Wilmington, Del.: Scholarly Resources, 1991), 88–89.

27. James Hamilton to Thomas Penn, April 30, 1751, Penn OC, 5:135.

28. "Applyers for Lots in Carlisle"; Tax Rates, Carlisle, 1753. For development on Carlisle's east side, see Martha C. Slotten, *From St. James Square to Tannery Row: Carlisle's Old Northeast Side* (Carlisle, Pa.: Friends of the Bosler Free Library, 1982), 4–8.

29. Lisa Tolbert, *Constructing Townscapes: Space and Society in Antebellum Tennessee* (Chapel Hill: University of North Carolina Press, 1999), 6 (quote). For the state of Carlisle in 1751, see I. Daniel Rupp, *The History and Topography of Dauphin, Cumberland, Franklin, Bedford, Adams, and Perry Counties* (Lancaster, Pa.: Gilbert Hills, 1846), 389–90; Civic Club of Carlisle, *Carlisle Old and New* (Harrisburg, Pa.: J. Horace McFarland, 1907), 10–11.

30. For information about these men, see "Applyers for Lots in Carlisle;" Crist, "John Armstrong," intro–chap. 1; G. B. Warden, "The Proprietary Group in Pennsylvania, 1754–1764," *WMQ* 3rd ser., 21.3 (1964): 367–89. For Lardner, see University of Pennsylvania, "Penn in the 18th Century, Penn Trustees, 1749–1800," http://www.archives.upenn.edu/histy/features/1700s/people/lardner_lynford.html (13 September 2008). For Neave, see Thomas M. Doerflinger, *A Vigorous Spirit of Enterprise: Merchants and Economic Development in Revolutionary Philadelphia* (Chapel Hill: University of North Carolina Press, 1986), 125.

31. *Deed Abstracts*, 1:29 (quote). Although Robert Callender played a pivotal role in Carlisle's early history, information on him is difficult to find because he left behind no comprehensive collection of personal papers. His taxable property is documented on Cumberland County tax lists from 1750 to the 1770s. Letters and reports written by him or about him are scattered throughout Pennsylvania's *Colonial Records*. For more about him, see Volwiler, *George Croghan*, 261–77; Judith Ridner, "Relying on the 'Saucy' Men of the Backcountry: Middlemen and the Fur Trade in Pennsylvania," *PMHB* 129.2

(2005): 133–62; James P. Myers, Jr., "Pennsylvania's Awakening: The Kittanning Raid of 1756," *PH* 66 (1999): 399–420.

32. As quoted in Crist, "John Armstrong," 12; see also 4–11; Alfred Nevin, *Centennial Biography: Men of Mark of the Cumberland Valley, P.A., 1776–1876* (Philadelphia: Fulton Publishing, 1876), 75–79.

33. Craig W. Horle, Joseph S. Foster, and Jeffrey L. Scheib, eds., *Lawmaking and Legislators in Pennsylvania, volume 2, 1710–1756*, (Philadelphia: University of Pennsylvania Press, 1997), 1055.

34. Ibid., 195–98.

35. "Applyers for Lots in Carlisle" (quote). See also "Categories of Applyers for Lots in Carlisle, 1751," the personal notes of historian Merri Lou Schaumann, who has been attempting to identify all of Carlisle's first appliers. I thank her for sharing these notes with me.

36. For Ross, see Will Book B, 183–84; personal conversation with Merri Lou Schaumann, April 2008.

37. For Carlisle's servant and slave population in 1765, see Tax Rates, Carlisle, 1765. There were 204 taxpayers and 28 freemen in 1765, which probably put the town's total population at somewhere between 1,200 and 1,300. Thus, Carlisle's forty-seven servants and slaves represented approximately 3.6 percent of the total population (with servants [twenty-seven of them] equaling 2 percent and slaves [twenty-one of them] equaling 1.6 percent of the total). See this tax list also for details about the holdings of individual Carlisle residents. For more about the servant and slave populations, see Tax Rates, Carlisle, 1753–1770. For Bar, see Will Book A, 136–37. For "Negro Rose," see Will Book B, 124–27.

38. Richard Peters to Thomas Penn, July 5, 1753, Penn OC, 6:73 (first quote); James Hamilton to Thomas Penn, September 24, 1750, Penn Papers OC, 5:55 (second quote).

39. As quoted in Merri Lou Schaumann, *Taverns of Cumberland County, Pennsylvania, 1750–1840* (Carlisle, Pa.: Cumberland County Historical Society, 1994), 56; see also *PG*, June 7, 1764.

40. Peters to Penn, July 5, 1753, Penn Papers OC, 6:73 (quotes); three individuals, William Houston, Benjamin Kid, and William Caldwell, were charged with trespassing and stealing trees in 1763—see Indictments, box 6.

41. *Deed Abstracts*, 1:17.

42. Rupp, *History and Topography*, 389; *PG*, November 7, 1751, where Samuel Lamb advertised himself as a "Mason at Carlisle Town."

43. For McCallister, see *PG*, March 20, 1753 (quotes). For more on McCallister, see ibid., January 29, 1756; "Returns of Survey for Patent, Carlisle, Pennsylvania," Land Records, PHMC, reel 5.117; Merri Lou Schaumann, *A History and Genealogy of Carlisle, Cumberland County, Pennsylvania, 1751–1835* (Dover, Pa.: M. L. Schaumann, 1987), 81, 210; Schaumann, *Taverns of Cumberland County*, 56. For Buchanan, see *PG*, January 8, 1756.

44. For Buchanan, see Schaumann, *History and Genealogy*, 196. For comparative perspectives on the urban interior, see Bernard L. Herman, *Town House: Architecture and Material Life in the Early American City, 1780–1830* (Chapel Hill: University of North

Carolina Press, 2005), chaps. 1 and 3; Tolbert, *Constructing Townscapes*, chap. 1. For persistence, see John Mack Faragher, *Sugar Creek: Life on the Illinois Prairie* (New Haven: Yale University Press, 1986), chaps. 14–16.

45. Persistence rates calculated from Tax Rates. Between 1753–1764, 44 percent of taxpayers persisted on local tax lists; between 1768–1779, the persistence rate fell slightly to 41 percent; between 1782–1795, it fell again to 33 percent; then from 1795–1808, it rose back to 43 percent. For more details, see Judith A. Ridner, "'A Handsomely Improved Place': Economic, Social, and Gender-Role Development in a Backcountry Town, Carlisle, Pennsylvania, 1750–1810" (Ph.D. diss., College of William & Mary, 1994), chap. 3, esp. 80. For comparative perspectives, see Richard R. Beeman, *The Evolution of the Southern Backcountry: A Case Study of Lunenburg County, Virginia, 1746–1832* (Philadelphia: University of Pennsylvania Press, 1984), 67; George W. Franz, *Paxton: A Study of Community Structure and Mobility in the Colonial Pennsylvania Backcountry* (New York: Garland, 1989), 161–65.

46. Returns of Survey for Patent, Carlisle, Land Records, PHMC, reel 5.117.

47. Peters to Penn, July 5, 1753, Penn OC, 6:73.

48. General Edward Braddock, September 23, 1755, "General Braddock's Campaign," ed. William Johnston, *PMHB* 11.1 (1887): 96.

49. For Penn's original instructions regarding the square, see Thomas Penn to Richard Peters, May 30, 1750, Penn Letterbooks, 2:309. For his later, updated instructions, see Penn to James Hamilton, July 29, 1751, Penn OC, 3:78; see also William Parsons, "Map of Carlisle" from an original sent by the Proprietors, May 23, 1752, Thos. Cadwalader Papers, box 186.5. For other maps, see "Carlisle Town Maps," Land Records, PHMC, folder 48.3. For more about the context of these plans, see Beetem, *Colonial Carlisle*, 6–8; Edward T. Price, "The Central Courthouse Square in the American County Seat," *GR* 58.1 (1968): 29–60.

50. Beetem, *Colonial Carlisle*, 6–8, 21; Merkel Landis, *The "English Church" in Carlisle* (Carlisle, Pa.: Hamilton Library Association, 1949), 4. Penn's plans were not followed exactly in Easton either, see A. D. Chidsey, Jr., *A Frontier Village: Pre-Revolutionary Easton* (Easton, Pa.: Northampton County Historical and Genealogical Society, 1940), 20. For Carlisle's resurvey, see James Hamilton, "Warrant to Resurvey Carlisle," May 5, 1762, Thos. Cadwalader Papers, box 186.7. For a reference to the streets bisecting the square by 1765, see Thomas Penn to Richard Peters, March 8, 1765, Penn Letterbooks, 8:231. For visual evidence, see John Armstrong, "Map of Carlisle," July 1768, Land Records, PHMC, 73/1:10.

51. Peters to Penn, March 16, 1752, Penn OC, 5:217–20 (quote "beautiful"). For Penn's original plan, see Thomas Penn to James Hamilton, July 29, 1751, Penn Letterbooks, 3:78. For his willingness to modify, see Penn to Hamilton, July 13, 1752, ibid., 3:142 (quote "consented").

52. "Copy of the Public Square in Carlisle, Cumberland County" from note of Thomas Penn, May 23, 1752, Thos. Cadwalader Papers, box 186.5. For other squares, see John Stilgoe, *Common Landscape of America, 1580–1845* (New Haven: Yale University Press, 1982), 96; Price, "Central Courthouse Square," 39–40.

53. Thomas Penn to James Hamilton, July 13, 1752, Penn Letterbooks, 3:142.

54. R. J. Hunter, "Ulster Plantation Towns, 1609–41," in *The Town in Ireland: Papers Read Before the Irish Conference of Historians*, ed. David Harkness and Mary O'Dowd (Belfast: Appletree Press, 1981), 65 (quote). For English town planning as colonialism in Ulster and America, see Leslie Clarkson, "Armagh 1770: Portrait of an Urban Community," in *The Town in Ireland*, 81–102; Anthony N. B. Garvan, "Proprietary Philadelphia as Artifact," in *The Historian and the City*, ed. Oscar Handlin and John Burchard (Boston: MIT and Harvard University Presses, 1963), 190–93; Price, "Central Courthouse Square," 31–36; John W. Reps, *Town Planning in Frontier America* (Princeton: Princeton University Press, 1969), 8–13.

55. Crist, "John Armstrong," 4–6.

56. Peters to Penn, July 5, 1753, Penn OC, 6:73.

57. Thomas Penn to James Hamilton, October 26, 1752, Penn Letterbooks, 3:168.

58. Flower and Flower, *This is Carlisle*, 4; Rupp, *History and Topography*, 385–88; Mary Ann and Barbara Jean Shugart, *History of the Courts of Cumberland County* (Carlisle, Pa.: Cumberland County Bar Association and Cumberland County Historical Society, 1971), 4.

59. Thomas Penn to James Hamilton, January 9, 1753, Penn Letterbooks, 3:180 (quote). For his offer of monies for the public buildings, see Thomas Penn to Richard Peters, July 17, 1752, Penn Letterbooks, 3:152. Until 1752, some locals continued to advocate for Shippensburg as the county seat; see Richard Peters to Thomas Penn, March 16, 1752, Penn OC, 5:217–20. Elections in November 1752 finally put an end to their calls; see Peters to Penn, November 18, 1752, Penn OC, 5:299.

60. Peters to Penn, July 5, 1753, Penn OC, 6:73 (quote). For Hamilton's offer of a forfeited lot, see James Hamilton to Thomas Penn, April 17, 1753, Penn OC, 6:37.

61. Thomas Penn to Richard Peters, January 9, 1753, Penn Letterbooks, 3:198. See also Flower and Flower, *This is Carlisle*, 4. Easton followed the same pattern: a permanent courthouse was not erected there until after 1765; see Chidsey, *A Frontier Village*, 206.

62. For Pennsylvania as cultural hearth, see David Hackett Fischer, *Albion's Seed: Four British Folkways in America* (New York: Oxford University Press, 1989), 451–603, 633–42. For the Cumberland Valley as a Scots-Irish region, see Donehoo, *History of Cumberland Valley*, 1:32; Wayland F. Dunaway, *The Scotch-Irish of Colonial Pennsylvania* (Chapel Hill: University of North Carolina Press, 1944), 58–63; *History of Cumberland and Adams*, 15–16; Guy Soulliard Klett, *Presbyterians in Colonial Pennsylvania* (Philadelphia: University of Pennsylvania Press, 1937), 68–80.

63. For population in 1760, see James T. Lemon, *The Best Poor Man's Country: A Geographical Study of Early Southeastern Pennsylvania* (Baltimore: Johns Hopkins University Press, 1972), figure p. 50; Owen S. Ireland, *Religion, Ethnicity, and Politics: Ratifying the Constitution in Pennsylvania* (University Park: Pennsylvania State University Press, 1995), 211 (quote), see also note 63, 214, where he writes that twenty-seven of the thirty-nine churches in Cumberland County in 1775 were Presbyterian. Other scholars confirm these patterns. Dunaway, *Scotch-Irish of Colonial Pennsylvania*, 59, says that Scots-Irish made up 90 percent of the Cumberland Valley's population until the 1770s; Kerby A.

Miller, Arnold Schrier, Bruce D. Boling, David N. Doyle, eds., *Irish Immigrants in the Land of Canaan: Letters and Memoirs from Colonial and Revolutionary America, 1675–1815* (New York: Oxford University Press, 2003), 146, note that all but a handful of colonists in the Cumberland Valley were of Ulster origins at mid-century. These patterns held for the end of the century: see Thomas L. Purvis, "Patterns of Ethnic Settlement in Late Eighteenth-Century Pennsylvania," *WPHM* 70.2 (1987): 115; he estimates that in 1790 Cumberland County was 29.7 percent Scots-Irish, 14.9 percent Scottish, 10.1 percent Irish, and 25.2 percent English.

64. "List of Lot Applyers"; Tax Rates, Carlisle, 1753, 1768, 1779, 1787, 1795.

65. Liam Riordan, *Many Identities, One Nation: The Revolution and Its Legacy in the Mid-Atlantic* (Philadelphia: University of Pennsylvania Press, 2007), 21 (quote).

66. Patrick Griffin, *The People with No Name: Ireland's Ulster Scots, America's Scots Irish, and the Creation of a British Atlantic World, 1689–1764* (Princeton: Princeton University Press, 2001), chap. 5, esp. 131; Miller, ed., *Irish Immigrants*, 143–47. See also Conway P. Wing, *A History of the First Presbyterian Church of Carlisle, Pennsylvania* (Carlisle, Pa.: Valley Sentinel, 1877), 14–16.

67. Charles C. Sellers, *Dickinson College: A History* (Middletown, Conn.: Wesleyan University Press, 1973), 23–31. For more on Duffield, see Nevin, *Centennial Biography*, 87–91; Schaumann, *History and Genealogy*, 201.

68. See Tax Rates, Carlisle, 1753, 1764, 1779, 1787. See also Dickinson College, "Encyclopedia Dickinsonia, Board of Trustees, Members Index, 1783–2000," http://chronicles.dickinson.edu/encyclo/m/ed_montgomeryJ.htm (19 Sept 2008); Sellers, *Dickinson College*, 27–31; Schaumann, *History and Genealogy*, 214.

69. Sellers, *Dickinson College*, 17–26. For more on Steel, see Nevin, *Centennial Biography*, 71–74; Schaumann, *History and Genealogy*, 219. For the Presbytery's calls to reunite, see "Minutes of the Presbyterian Synod of New York and Philadelphia," 1759, Presbyterian Historical Society, Philadelphia, 353.

70. George Duffield to John Blair, April 20, 1759, as quoted in Sellers, *Dickinson College*, 23–24.

71. Such division was not unusual; see Griffin, *People with No Name*, 143–56.

72. *Charter and Ordinances of the Borough of Carlisle to Which are Prefixed Incidents of the Early History of the Town* (Carlisle, Pa.: Printed at the Herald Office, 1841), 20–21; Donehoo, *History of Cumberland Valley*, 1:454–55; Klett, *Presbyterians in Pennsylvania*, 69–74; Landis, *English Church*, 4–5; Rupp, *History and Topography*, 420–21; William T. Swaim, *Disruptions of the Presbyterian Church and Dickinson College by George Duffield III, 1816–1833* (Philadelphia: Presbyterian Historical Society, 1983), 3, 92–93; Wing, *First Presbyterian Church*, 14–16, 41, 66-70, 88–89. For a copy of the land draft to the Presbyterian Congregation, see "Land Draft," 1766, Misc. Photos of Documents, CCHS, box 38.3.

73. John Armstrong to Richard Peters, as quoted in Rupp, *History and Topography*, 421. For Penn's observations, see John Penn, "John Penn's Journal of a Visit to Reading, Harrisburg, Carlisle, and Lancaster, in 1788," *PMHB* 3.3 (1879): 292.

74. James P. Myers, Jr., "Thomas Barton's Unanimity and Public Spirit (1755): Controversy and Plagiarism on the Pennsylvania Frontier," *PMHB* 119.3 (1995): 232.

75. George Craig, June 16, 1752, "Letters of Rev. Richard Locke and Rev. George Craig, Missionaries in Pennsylvania of the 'Society for Propagating the Gospel in Foreign Parts,' London, 1746–1752," ed. Benjamin Owen *PMHB* 24.4 (1900): 477 (quote). See also St. John's Episcopal Church, *The Spire on the Square* (Carlisle, Pa.: Rector and Wardens of St. John's Episcopal Church, 2002), 6–8.

76. For information on Thomas Barton, see Miller, *Irish Immigrants*, 487–99. See also William A. Hunter, "Thomas Barton and the Forbes Expedition," *PMHB* 95.4 (1971): 431–83; Myers, "Thomas Barton's Unanimity," 225–32; *Spire on Square*, 8–13; Landis, *English Church*, 9–10.

77. Griffin, *People with No Name*, 4–6; Riordan, *Many Identities*, 68–69.

78. *Spire on Square*, 7; Landis, *English Church*, 5–13. Landis (12) says St. John's measured thirty by forty feet. With two stories, that would make it 2,400 square feet in total dimension.

79. Donehoo, *History of Cumberland Valley*, 1:456–59; *History of Cumberland and Adams Counties*, 212; Landis, *English Church*, 4–8; Myers, "Thomas Barton's Unanimity," 225–32; Rupp, *History and Topography*, 421–22. See also St. John's Church, Carlisle, "Vestry Minutes and Accounts, 1795–1829," DCA; Penn Papers, Philadelphia Land Grants, HSP, 7:109, where a 1757 letter from Carlisle church wardens Francis West and Robert Callender offers thanks for Barton's services.

80. Donehoo, *History of Cumberland Valley*, 1:456–57; Rupp, *History and Topography*, 422–23.

81. For the eighteenth-century consumer economy and its connections to communities of the interior, see Timothy H. Breen, "An Empire of Goods: The Anglicization of Colonial America, 1690–1776," *Journal of British Studies* 25.4 (1986): 467–99; Elizabeth A. Perkins, "The Consumer Frontier: Household Consumption in Early Kentucky," *JAH* 78.2 (1991): 486–510; Daniel Thorp, "Doing Business in the Backcountry: Retail Trade in Colonial Rowan County, North Carolina," *WMQ* 3rd ser., 48.3 (1991): 387–408.

82. William Eyre, "Colonel Eyre's Journal of his Trip from New York to Pittsburgh, 1762," ed. Frances Reece *WPHM* 27.1–2 (1944): 40.

83. Tavern Licenses, Loose Papers; Tax Rates, Carlisle, 1764.

84. Peter Thompson, *Rum Punch and Revolution: Taverngoing and Public Life in Eighteenth-Century Philadelphia* (Philadelphia: University of Pennsylvania Press, 1999), 26–27.

85. Schaumann, *Cumberland County Taverns*, 25.

86. Manasseh Cutler, "Journal of Rev. Manasseh Cutler of a Journey from Ipswich, Massachusetts, to the Muskingum, in 1788," in *Life, Journals and Correspondence of Rev. Manasseh Cutler, LL.D.*, ed. William Cutler and Julia Cutler, 2 vols. (Cincinnati: Robert Clarke and Company, 1888), 400 (quote "fat Irishman"); Daniel B. Thorp, "Taverns and Communities: The Case of Rowan County, North Carolina," in *The Southern Colonial Backcountry: Interdisciplinary Perspectives on Frontier Communities*, ed. David Colin Crass (Knoxville: University of Tennessee Press, 1998), 79 (quote "nodes").

87. Oliver Wallace, License Application, July 1751, Tavern Licenses (quotes). See also Schaumann, *Taverns of Cumberland County*, 57; Tax Rates, Carlisle, 1764.

88. Thomas Patton, License Application, July 1762, Tavern Licenses.

89. Wallace, 1751, Tavern Licenses.

90. "Applyers for Lots in Carlisle."

91. Walter Denny, License Application, October 1758, Tavern Licenses (quote). See also Schaumann, *History and Genealogy*, 200.

92. Henry Bouquet to John Forbes, May 25, 1758, ibid., 1:362 (first quote); "Orderly Book of Captain Thomas Hamilton's Company," July 3, 1779, CCHS, Misc. Photos of Documents, box 38.1 (second quote).

93. License Applications of Andrew McIntyre, July 1759; Robert Hammersly, July 1762; John Kennedy, July 1762, Tavern Licenses.

94. Schaumann, *Taverns of Cumberland County*, 62; Will of Andrew McIntyre, February 24, 1761, Will Books, A:17.

95. These words are used frequently in county tavern license applications; see Tavern Licenses.

96. For the importance of roads in the mid-Atlantic interior, see Warren R. Hofstra, *The Planting of New Virginia: Settlement and Landscape in the Shenandoah Valley* (Baltimore: Johns Hopkins University Press, 2004), 1–2, 154–60; Peter Mancall, *Valley of Opportunity: Economic Culture Along the Upper Susquehanna, 1700–1800* (Ithaca: Cornell University Press, 1991), 9, 115–24, 204–8; John F. Walzer, "Transportation in the Philadelphia Trading Area, 1740–1775" (Ph.D. diss., University of Wisconsin, 1968), 147.

97. Griffin, *People With No Name*, 126.

98. Jeffrey D. Kaja, " 'Shewing the Course': Defining the Role of the Public Highway in Early Pennsylvania, 1680–1800" (unpublished paper presented at the McNeil Center for Early American Studies, April 2008), 1–34.

99. Walzer, "Transportation," 43, 146–52; Donehoo, *History of Cumberland Valley*, 1:86–87.

100. Paul A. W. Wallace, *Indians Paths of Pennsylvania* (Harrisburg, Pa.: Pennsylvania Historical and Museum Commission, 1993), 19–21, 38; Walzer, "Transportation," 47.

101. Ibid., 39, 149.

102. Lemon, *Best Poor Man's Country*, 140–41.

103. Inhabitants near North Mountain, Petition, July 1753, Road Petitions.

104. The Divers[e] Inhabitants of East Pennsboro, Petition, July 1753, ibid.

105. Residents of East Pennsboro Township, Petition, January 1774, ibid.

106. The Several Inhabitants of Middleton Township, Petition, January 1769, Road Petitions; The Inhabitants of West Pennsboro, Petition, April 1759, ibid.

107. See, for example, Thomas Evins, Petition, July 1751, Road Petitions.

108. The Inhabitants of Cumberland County, Petition, April 1753, Road Petitions (quote); see also The Inhabitants of Middleton for a road from Matthew Laird's Field to William Moor's Mill, Petition, May 1802, ibid.

109. The Inhabitants of Middleton and West Pennsboro Townships, Petition, 1769, ibid.

110. The Several Inhabitants of Middleton Township, January 1769, ibid.

111. Unidentified Petition, April 1752, ibid.

112. The Sundry Inhabitants of East Pennsboro and Middleton Townships, Petition, January 1758, ibid.

113. John F. Walzer, "Colonial Philadelphia and Its Backcountry," *Winterthur Portfolio* 7 (1972): 167; Walzer, "Transportation," 43; see also John Harris Ledger, 1752–1793, HSP.

114. Walzer, "Colonial Philadelphia," 168.

115. Petition from various inhabitants of Cumberland County, April 1751, Road Petitions.

116. Crist, "John Armstrong," 4; for another example, see Andrew McIntire, Will Book A, 88–89. For York's centrality, see circa 1775 map in Lester J. Cappon, ed., *Atlas of Early American History: The Revolutionary Era, 1760–1790* (Princeton, N.J.: Princeton University Press, 1976), 4. This map shows that by 1775 roads headed out of York in all directions, including three major routes into Maryland.

117. Walzer, "Transportation," 47–49.

118. Robert Hammilton, Petition, October 1752, Road Petitions (quote). For more about Cumberland's mid-century connections to Baltimore, see Clarence P. Gould in "The Economic Causes of the Rise of Baltimore," in *Essays in Colonial History Presented to Charles McLean Andrews by his Students* (New Haven: Yale University Press, 1931), 235–36, 239–41.

119. The Sundry Inhabitants of Middleton and Allen Townships, Petition, January 1771, Road Petitions; Walzer, "Colonial Philadelphia," 168.

120. Walzer, "Transportation," 47–49. Walzer found that although Philadelphia remained an important destination for the sale of York County's agricultural surpluses through the colonial period, Baltimore's markets increased in importance. By 1770, 75 percent of the road petitions submitted to the York county court requested roads that connected in some way to Baltimore. Hofstra, *Planting of New Virginia*, 306–11, also notes the rising impact of Baltimore's markets on the economic activities of the Shenandoah Valley, but does so mostly in a post-revolutionary context.

121. *PG*, November 7, 1751, April 12, 1753.

CHAPTER 3. NEW LINES DRAWN

1. Joseph Rigby to BWM, May 28, 1768, BWM Papers, reel 5.

2. Ibid.

3. Rigby had reason to be scared. Three years earlier, a group of frontiersmen calling themselves the "Black Boys," many of them Scots-Irishmen of Cumberland County, attacked a wagon train sponsored by BWM that was headed to Fort Pitt with arms and liquor destined for trade with Native peoples. See Stephen H. Cutcliffe, "Sideling Hill Affair: The Cumberland County Riots of 1765," *WPHM* 59 (1976): 39–53; Eleanor M. Webster, "Insurrection at Fort Loudon in 1765: Rebellion or Preservation of Peace?" *WPHM* 47 (1964): 125–40.

4. Conrad Weiser to unid., n.d., Weiser Papers, 1:62.

5. W. Fairfax to Gov. James Hamilton, September 14, 1753, *Colonial Records*, 5:657.

For another account of this request, see Richard Peters to Thomas Penn, November 6, 1753, Penn OC, 6:113.

6. For the context of the times, see Daniel K. Richter, *Facing East from Indian Country: A Native History of Early America* (Cambridge, Mass.: Harvard University Press, 2001), 151. For accounts of the conference and its limited outcomes, see Francis Jennings, *Empire of Fortune: Crowns, Colonies and Tribes in the Seven Years War in America* (New York: W. W. Norton, 1988), 54–60; Richard White, *The Middle Ground: Indians, Empires, and Republics in the Great Lakes Region, 1650–1815* (New York: Cambridge University Press, 1991), 235, see also 227–40. See also Charles A. Hanna, *The Wilderness Trail; or, The Ventures and Adventures of Pennsylvania Traders on the Allegheny Path*, 2 vols. (New York: G. P. Putnam's Sons, 1911), 1:111, 227–28, 2:3, 307–8; C. Hale Sipe, *The Indian Wars of Pennsylvania* (Harrisburg, Pa.: Telegraph Press, 1929), 139–44; Albert T. Volwiler, *George Croghan and the Westward Movement, 1741–1782* (Cleveland: Arthur H. Clark Company, 1926), 80–82; Paul A. W. Wallace, *Conrad Weiser, 1696–1760: Friend of Colonist and Mohawk* (Philadelphia: University of Pennsylvania Press, 1945), 344–49; Nicholas B. Wainwright, *George Croghan, Wilderness Diplomat* (Chapel Hill: University of North Carolina Press, 1959), 54–56.

7. For quotes, see *Colonial Records*, 5:675–76. For a transcript of the conference, see 5:666–86. For another firsthand account, see Richard Peters to Thomas Penn, November 6, 1753, Penn OC, 6:113.

8. Peters to Penn, ibid.; *Colonial Records*, 5:680.

9. Peters to Penn, November 6, 1753, Penn OC, 6:113 (quote); see also *Colonial Records*, 5:680–86, see esp. 680, 682. For the conference as a failure, see Jennings, *Empire of Fortune*, 54–60; White, *Middle Ground*, 235. For the Ohio Indians' perspective, see Michael N. McConnell, *A Country Between: The Upper Ohio Valley and Its Peoples, 1724–1774* (Lincoln: University of Nebraska Press, 1992), chap. 5. See also Eric Hinderaker, *Elusive Empires: Constructing Colonialism in the Ohio Valley, 1673–1800* (New York: Cambridge University Press, 1997), 135–40.

10. For Native Americans' motives, see McConnell, *A Country Between*, 89–99, 103–5; Richter, *Facing East*, 164–71, 174–79; Anthony F. C. Wallace, *The Death and Rebirth of the Seneca* (New York: Alfred A. Knopf, 1970), 112. For Hamilton's perplexity, see Peters to Penn, November 6, 1753, Penn OC, 6:113.

11. Peters to Penn, November 6, 1753, Penn OC, 6:113 (quotes "alter place" and "ought to be"); *Colonial Records*, 5:657 (quote "no necessity").

12. *Colonial Records*, 5:658 (quotes). See also Peters to Penn, November 6, 1753, Penn OC, 6:113; James Hamilton to Richard Peters, September 21, 1752, Richard Peters Papers, HSP, 3:71.

13. *Colonial Records*, 5:684.

14. Benjamin Franklin, *The Autobiography of Benjamin Franklin*, ed. Louis P. Masur (Boston: Bedford/St. Martin's Press, 1993), 119–20.

15. Ibid., 119–20 (quotes). According to Richard Peters, the Indians, who "cou[l]d scarce be prevailed on to keep themselves sober during the Treaty," were drunk most of the time they were in Carlisle. See Peters to Penn, November 6, 1753, Penn OC, 6:113;

and November 26, 1753, ibid., 6:133. For another account of Franklin's experience, see Peter C. Mancall, *Deadly Medicine: Indians and Alcohol in Early America* (Ithaca: Cornell University Press, 1995), 11–14.

16. For Callender, see Merri Lou Schaumann, *A History and Genealogy of Carlisle, Cumberland County, Pennsylvania, 1751–1835* (Dover, Pa.: M. L. Schaumann, 1987), 197; Nicholas Wainwright, *The Irvine Story* (Philadelphia: HSP, 1964), 11–12. For his lands, see *PG*, October 31, 1765; for his trading, see Fort Pitt Trading Post Daybook, WPHS; and BWM Papers, particularly various letters discussing him on reel 3. For Duncan, see Dickinson College, "Encyclopedia Dickinsonia, Board of Trustees, Members Index, 1783–2000," http://chronicles.dickinson.edu/encyclo/d/ed_duncanS.htm (24 September 2008); for Duncan's fur trading with BWM, May 14, 1763, BWM Papers, reel 2; October 9, 1766, ibid., reel 3; see also account entry on June 21, 1776, in William West Wastebook #2, West Papers. For Vanlear, see Christopher Van Lear, Christopher Van Lear Daybook, 1767–1783, Winterthur Library, Wilmington, Del., which documents his tavern business and his role as a hauler in the trade; see also Schaumann, *History and Genealogy*, 219–20; Schaumann, *Taverns of Cumberland County, Pennsylvania, 1750–1840* (Carlisle, Pa.: Cumberland County Historical Society, 1994), 29.

17. At least two Carlisle traders, Joseph Spear and William Trent, owned slaves. See Tax Rates, Carlisle, 1765.

18. John McCalister, Indictment, June 1751. See also John Anderson, Indictment, April 1753; Adam Hoops, Indictment, April 1753, Indictments, box 6. For traders' role in keeping Indians drunk during the conference, see Richard Peters to Thomas Penn, November 26, 1753, Penn OC, 6:133. For local traders' negative reputation, see *Pennsylvania Archives 4*, 2:155. For more about liquor sales to Pennsylvania's Indians, see Mancall, *Deadly Medicine*, 14, 23–28, 45–49.

19. Peters to Penn, November 26, 1753, Penn OC, 6:133.

20. Weiser to unid., n.d., Weiser Papers, 1:62.

21. Richard Peters to Thomas Penn, December 14, 1752, Penn OC, 5:313.

22. Jennings, *Empire of Fortune*, 123 (quote). For the war's start, see Fred Anderson, *Crucible of War: The Seven Years' War and the Fate of Empire in British North America, 1754–1766* (New York: Random House, 2000; reprint, Vintage Books, 2001), 109–10; Hinderaker, *Elusive Empires*, 134–44; Louis M. Waddell and Bruce D. Bomberger, *The French and Indian War in Pennsylvania, 1753–1763* (Harrisburg: Pennsylvania Historical and Museum Commission, 1996), 1–31; Matthew C. Ward, *Breaking the Backcountry: The Seven Years' War in Virginia and Pennsylvania, 1754–1765* (Pittsburgh: University of Pittsburgh Press, 2003), chaps. 1–2. For an overview of the Albany Congress and its connection to imperial and provincial politics at mid-century, see Timothy J. Shannon, *Indians and Colonists at the Crossroads of Empire: The Albany Congress of 1754* (Ithaca: Cornell University Press, 2000).

23. The Inhabitants of Cumberland County to Gov. James Hamilton, July 15, 1754, Conarroe Papers, HSP, 10:60 (quote); see also *Colonial Records*, 6:130–31. For the intimate nature of these raids, see Jane T. Merritt, *At the Crossroads: Indians and Empires on a Mid-Atlantic Frontier, 1700–1763* (Chapel Hill: University of North Carolina Press,

2003), chap. 5, esp. 176–85; Peter Silver, *Our Savage Neighbors: How Indian War Transformed Early America* (New York: W. W. Norton, 2008), 60–71; Ward, *Breaking the Backcountry*, 60–70.

24. *Colonial Records*, 7:121.

25. Gen. John Forbes to James Abercromby, April 22, 1758, *Writings of General John Forbes*, Alfred Procter James, ed. (Menasha, Wis.: Collegiate Press, 1938), 69.

26. Maj. Francis Halkett to Col. Henry Bouquet, August 26, 1758, *Bouquet Papers*, 2:428.

27. Report of Benjamin Chew, Alexander Stedman, William West, and Edward Shippen, Jr. to the Governor and Council, April 21, 1756, Penn Papers, Assembly and Provincial Council of Pennsylvania, HSP, 82.

28. *PG*, April 8, 1756 (first quote); Col. Henry Bouquet to Gov. James Hamilton, July 13, 1763, in Thompson, *Two Hundred Years*, 32 (second quote).

29. *PG*, June 2, 1757; see also July 21, 1757.

30. William Trent to Richard Peters, February 15, 1756, *Pennsylvania Archives 1*, 2:575.

31. *PG*, August 7, 1755.

32. Philip Davis and other Inhabitants of Peters Township to Gov. William Denny, 1756, Gratz Papers, case 15, box 18 (quote "relief"); William Rankin, John Armstrong, Nathaniel Wilson, and others of Cumberland County to the Governor of Pennsylvania, November 10, 1755, Provincial Council Records, HSP, case 74, folder 7 (quote "defend"). For the struggles between the proprietary and Quaker parties during the first years of the war, see Richard R. Beeman, *The Varieties of Political Experience in Eighteenth-Century America* (Philadelphia: University of Pennsylvania Press, 2004), chap. 8; Alan Tully, *Forming American Politics: Ideals, Interests, and Institutions in Colonial New York and Pennsylvania* (Baltimore: Johns Hopkins University Press, 1994), 262–75.

33. Draft of letter by Gov. Robert Hunter Morris, n.d. (probably 1755), Gratz Papers, case 15, box 18 (first quote); second quote as quoted in Anderson, *Crucible of War*, 161. These issues were part of the larger struggle within the provincial government to get the Quaker-dominated assembly to allocate money for defense (without taxing proprietary estates) that the governor and proprietor could spend at will—see James H. Hutson, *Pennsylvania Politics, 1746–1770; The Movement for Royal Government and Its Consequences* (Princeton, N.J.: Princeton University Press, 1972), chap. 1. See also Jennings, *Empire of Fortune*, 141–46, 166–68.

34. *Pennsylvania Archives 4*, 2:448.

35. For the fort, see William A. Hunter, *Forts on the Pennsylvania Frontier, 1753–1758* (Lewisburg, Pa.: Wennawoods Publishing, 1999), 436–50; Joseph J. Kelley, *Pennsylvania: The Colonial Years, 1681–1776* (Garden City, N.Y.: Doubleday, 1980), 342; Charles Morse Stotz, *Outposts of the War for Empire: The French and English in Western Pennsylvania: Their Armies, Their Forts, Their People, 1749–1764* (Pittsburgh: Historical Association of Western Pennsylvania, 1985), 109; Thomas G. Tousey, *Military History of Carlisle and Carlisle Barracks* (Richmond, Va.: Dietz Press, 1939), 12–13; Waddell and Bomberger, *French and Indian War*, 15, 17, 86, 366. Although many sources reference this fort, I have

not found a single contemporary account describing it; Waddell and Bomberger (p. 17) even quote from a source who reported there was no fort in Carlisle in 1756. This fort may not ever have been completed. For those who staffed whatever existed, see Robert G. Crist, "John Armstrong: Proprietor's Man" (Ph.D. diss., Pennsylvania State University, 1981), 60.

36. *Pennsylvania Archives 4*, 2:450 (quotes); see also Hunter, *Forts on PA Frontier*, 171.

37. John Armstrong to Governor Denny, December 22, 1756, Gratz Papers, case 15, box 18 (quote). See also *Pennsylvania Archives 4*, 2:448. According to Waddell and Bomberger, *French and Indian War*, 15, although the Governor's request went unmet in 1755–1756 and Pennsylvania's interior was left unprotected after Braddock's defeat, Carlisle was the first town to regain army protection when several companies of Royal Americans arrived there late in 1757. For more about the Carlisle barracks, see Tousey, *Military History of Carlisle*, 10–18; Waddell and Bomberger, 92.

38. *PG*, November 6, 1755 (quotes). See also Crist, "John Armstrong," 65–66; *Pennsylvania Archives 4*, 2:448.

39. *PG*, July 31, 1755 (quotes). See also James P. Myers, Jr., "Pennsylvania's Awakening: The Kittanning Raid of 1756," *PH* 66.3 (1999): 399–403.

40. *PG*, September 23, 1756 (quote). See also Anderson, *Crucible of War*, 162–64; Crist, "John Armstrong," 65–66; Merritt, *At the Crossroads*, 180–84, 198; Myers, "Pennsylvania's Awakening," 403, 407.

41. Crist, "John Armstrong," 60–75. See also Myers, "Pennsylvania's Awakening," 399, 407.

42. Col. James Smith, "An Account of the Remarkable Occurrences in the Life and Travels of Col. James Smith" in Archibald Loudon, *A Selection of Some of the Most Interesting Narratives, of Outrages, Committed by the Indians, in Their Wars, with the White People*, 2 vols. (Carlisle, Pa: A. Loudon, 1808–1811; reprint, New York: Arno Press, 1971), 1:249. For their travel route west, see Myers, "Pennsylvania's Awakening," 405–7.

43. *PG*, September 23, 1756.

44. *PG*, October 7, 1756.

45. *PG*, February 17, 1757. For his reward, see Crist, "John Armstrong," 76; Myers, "Pennsylvania's Awakening," 399.

46. Jennings, *Empire of Fortune*, 200 (quote). For Callender's role, see Myers, "Pennsylvania's Awakening," 407–13. For John Armstrong's account of what happened, see *PG*, September 23, 1756.

47. *PG*, August 7, 1755 (first quote); *PG*, November 6, 1755 (second quote).

48. *PG*, July 2, 1761 (quote). For a similar argument, see Ward, *Breaking the Backcountry*, 73–77.

49. John Florin, *The Advance of Frontier Settlement in Pennsylvania, 1638–1850: A Geographic Interpretation* (University Park: Pennsylvania State University Press, 1977), 11 (quote). For demographic statistics, see Tax Rates, Carlisle, 1753, 1764; see also Judith A. Ridner, "'A Handsomely Improved Place': Economic, Social, and Gender-Role Development in a Backcountry Town, Carlisle, Pennsylvania, 1750-1810," (Ph.D. diss., College of William & Mary, 1994), 79.

50. For the number of troops at Carlisle, see Francis Halkett, "A Sketch of the Troops Under Forbes's Command," Carlisle, July 17, 1758, Forbes Headquarters Papers, reel 2.386. Waddell and Bomberger, *French and Indian War*, 35, note that the 7,000 troops included 2,700 Pennsylvanians under Col. John Armstrong and 2,600 Virginians under Col. George Washington. For more information about Forbes and his expedition, see Niles Anderson, "The General Chooses a Road: The Forbes Campaign of 1758 to Capture Fort Duquesne," *WPHM* 42.2 (1959): 120 note 20, 131; Jennings, *Empire of Fortune*, 374–75.

51. Col. John Stanwix to Gov. Denny, July 18, 1757, *Pennsylvania Archives 1*, 3:220 (quote); see also 3:239, 290.

52. Hugh Mercer to James Burd, May 23, 1759, *Bouquet Papers*, 3:308.

53. For the Forbes Road, see *Colonial Records*, 6:377–78, and 6:401–4. For advertisements for laborers to build the road, see Shippen Papers, HSP, 1:181–85. For more information about the war's transport needs, see Anderson, *Crucible of War*, chaps. 21–23; Jennings, *Empire of Fortune*, 362; Waddell and Bomberger, *French and Indian War*, 35.

54. For laborers, see Robert Callender to Henry Bouquet, June 25, 1758, *Bouquet Papers,* 2:132. For quote, see Henry Bouquet to John Forbes, May 29–30, 1758, ibid., 1:390. See also John Armstrong to Henry Bouquet, April 26, 1759, ibid., 3:260.

55. Bouquet to Forbes, May 25, 1758, ibid., 1:364.

56. Bouquet to Forbes, May 29–30, 1758, ibid., 1:386 (quote); see also Schaumann, *History and Genealogy*, 206.

57. Daniel Clark to Henry Bouquet, May 21, 1759, *Bouquet Papers*, 3:299; John Armstrong to John Stanwix, May 28, 1759, ibid., 2:332; Forbes Headquarters Papers, reel 2.286. For biographical information on these men, see Craig W. Horle, Joseph S. Foster, and Jeffrey L. Scheib, eds., *Lawmaking and Legislators in Pennsylvania, vol. 2, 1710–1756* (Philadelphia: University of Pennsylvania Press, 1997), 1055–62; Schaumann, *History and Genealogy*, 196, 197, 209, 221.

58. Henry Bouquet to John Forbes, June 7, 1758, *Bouquet Papers*, 2:51 (quote). See also Ward, *Breaking the Backcountry*, 76.

59. Bouquet to Forbes, May 25, 1758, *Bouquet Papers*, 1:364 (quote "very glad"); June 11, 1758, 2:73 (quote "No one").

60. "Advertisement for Wagons," ibid., 3:269 (first quote); John Armstrong to Henry Bouquet, January 27, 1759, ibid., 3:85 (second quote). For other references to Carlisle as supply and transport center, see, for example, 1:345; 2:64.

61. Ibid., 2:133 (quote); see also 3:458, 464.

62. Ibid., 2:4 (quote), see also 2:185; 3:458, 464, 542; 4:176–77. For more references, see also Forbes Headquarters Papers, reel 2.367.

63. For hay, see *Bouquet Papers*, 4:144; for horses, see 2:132, 3:429; for wagons, see 2:133. For "spirit of Activity," see Sir John St. Clair to John Forbes, June 30, 1758, Forbes Headquarters Papers, reel 2.340.

64. John Armstrong to Henry Bouquet, June 28, 1758, *Bouquet Papers*, 2:145 (quote "essential service"); see also 2:647 (quote "hardship").

65. Armstrong to Bouquet, September 15, 1758, ibid., 2:511 (quote "unfavorable"); see also 3:18 (quote "timorous").

66. Bouquet to Forbes, May 29–30, 1758, ibid., 1:386.

67. George Stevenson to Henry Bouquet, May 31, 1758, ibid., 1:399. According to Ward, *Breaking the Backcountry*, 82, such fears were warranted as British troops often stole livestock and sometimes plundered civilians.

68. *Bouquet Papers*, 3:401 (quote "wagons"); ibid., 2:105 (other quotes). See also 2:398.

69. Ibid., 3:299 (quote "country people"); 4:61 (quote "grumble").

70. Ibid., 3:106 (first quote); ibid., 3:331 (second quote).

71. Ibid., 1:386 (quote). Ward, *Breaking the Backcountry*, 77–80, notes that the war challenged the authority of backcountry elites who could not compel their neighbors' compliance. In response, some local justices, fearing the wrath of their neighbors, refused to impress supplies.

72. Henry Bouquet to William Denny, July 12, 1759, *Bouquet Papers*, 3:401 (quote); see also 3:360. For a reference to advertisements, see 3:489.

73. Anderson, *Crucible of War*, chap. 28.

74. For Pontiac's Uprising and its effects on Pennsylvania, see Gregory E. Dowd, *A Spirited Resistance: The North American Indian Struggle for Unity, 1745–1815* (Baltimore: Johns Hopkins University Press, 1992), 23–46; Hinderaker, *Elusive Empires*, 144–61; Krista Camenzind, "Violence, Race, and the Paxton Boys," in *Friends and Enemies in Penn's Woods: Indians, Colonists, and the Racial Construction of Pennsylvania*, ed. William Pencak and Daniel Richter (University Park: Pennsylvania State University, 2004), 201–20; Merritt, *At the Crossroads*, 272–82; Richter, *Facing East*, 191–201; Ward, *Breaking the Backcountry*, 220–36; White, *The Middle Ground*, chap. 7.

75. White, *Middle Ground*, 344. Most scholars argue that Indian hating among white colonists was among the most significant and devastating outcomes of Pontiac's Uprising. In the war's aftermath, colonists no longer distinguished among friendly, neutral, and enemy Indians; they despised them all, racializing them as "others." For examples of this interpretation, see Jennings, *Empire of Fortune*, 195; Hinderaker, *Elusive Empires*, 157–61; Merritt, *At the Crossroads*, chap. 8; McConnell, *A Country Between*, 122–24, 190–91; Richter, *Facing East*, 179–82, 206–16; Ward, *Breaking the Backcountry*, 236–40.

76. Hinderaker, *Elusive Empires*, 45.

77. For the "bad Indian," see Merritt, *At the Crossroads*, 274; see also 267, 282, 292. For the "anti-Indian sublime," see Peter Silver, *Our Savage Neighbors: How Indian War Transformed Early America* (New York: W. W. Norton, 2008), 83–85, and chap. 3.

78. Silver, ibid., xxi (quote); Merritt, *At the Crossroads.*, 291–94; Richter, *Facing East*, 206–16.

79. Silver, *Our Savage Neighbors*, xxi (quote); see also xx–xxii, and chap. 4.

80. *PG*, September 9, 1756.

81. Bouquet to Forbes, May 25, 1758, *Bouquet Papers*, 1:361; see also 1:389.

82. Silver, *Our Savage Neighbors*, 99 (quote); see also chap. 4.

83. For the fur and skin trade at mid-century, see Stephen Auth, *The Ten Years War: Indian-White Relations in Pennsylvania, 1755–1765* (New York: Garland Publishing, 1989); Kathryn E. Holland Braund, *Deerskins and Duffels: The Creek Indian Trade with*

Anglo-America, 1685–1815 (Lincoln: University of Nebraska Press, 1993), 42–43, chap. 6; William S. Coker and Thomas D. Watson, *Indian Traders of the Southeastern Spanish Borderlands: Panton, Leslie, and Company and John Forbes and Company, 1783–1847* (Pensacola: University Presses of Florida, 1986); Hinderaker, *Elusive Empires*, 147–52, 162–70, 176–82; Thomas Norton, *The Fur Trade in Colonial New York* (Madison: University of Wisconsin, 1974), 207–15; Stephen H. Cutcliffe, "Indians, Furs, and Empires: The Changing Policies of New York and Pennsylvania, 1674–1768" (Ph.D. diss., Lehigh University, 1976), 249–57; Mancall, *Deadly Medicine*, chap. 2; James H. Merrell, *Into the American Woods: Negotiators on the Pennsylvania Frontier* (New York: W. W. Norton, 1999); Merritt, *At the Crossroads*, 60–86, 237–43, 272–85; Larry B. Nelson, *A Man of Distinction Among Them: Alexander McKee and British-Indian Affairs Along the Ohio Country Frontier, 1754–1799* (Kent, Ohio: Kent State University Press, 1999), 30–31, 40–66; Jack M. Sosin, *Whitehall and the Wilderness: The Middle West in British Colonial Policy* (Lincoln: University of Nebraska Press, 1961); Daniel Usner, Jr., *Indians, Settlers, and Slaves in a Frontier Exchange Economy: The Lower Mississippi Valley Before 1783* (Chapel Hill: University of North Carolina, 1992), chap. 8, esp. 249–52; Waddell and Bomberger, *French and Indian War*, 63; Wainwright, *George Croghan*, 162–63, 208–9; White, *The Middle Ground*, chap. 7. For Indian responses to the new regulations, see McConnell, *A Country Between*, 162; Richter, *Facing East*, chap. 5.

84. For the Friendly Association, Pennsylvania's Commissioners for Indian Affairs, and responses to them, see Hinderaker, *Elusive Empires*, 141–44; see also Historical Society of Pennsylvania, "Minutes of the Friendly Association for Regaining and Preserving Peace with the Indians by Pacific Measures, 1755–1757," http://www.hsp.org/default.aspx?id=385 (29 September 2008); McConnell, *A Country Between*, 149–50; Silver, *Our Savage Neighbors*, 98–100; Waddell and Bomberger, *French and Indian War*, 21, 24, 27–28, 31; Ward, *Breaking the Backcountry*, 191–95; Wainwright, *George Croghan*, 162. For Francis and William West, see *Colonial Records,* 5:761–62; Schaumann, *History and Genealogy*, 221; Hanna, *Wilderness Trail*, 2:342; *Lawmaking and Legislators 2*, 1057–58.

85. James Kenny to Francis West, March 19, 1763, Indian Commissioners Correspondence, HSP. For a similar transaction, see Joseph Morris to Francis West, April 13, 1763, ibid.

86. Francis West to Joseph Morris and other Commissioners for Indian Affairs, November 25, 1763, Indian Commissioners Correspondence, HSP (quote). See also Francis West to William Fisher, May 26, 1763, ibid.

87. Francis West to John Reynall, August 16, 1763, ibid. (quote "in store"). For the various items, see "Inventory of Goods brought from Carlisle to Philadelphia intended for the Pittsburg[h] Trading House," August 22, 1763, Gratz Papers, Indian Affairs, case 14, box 10.

88. For rivalries between the Quaker Friendly Association and independent, or semi-independent Scots-Irish traders led by George Croghan, see McConnell, *A Country Between*, 149–50.

89. Hinderaker, *Elusive Empires*, 166–68. For more on BWM, see also Thomas Doerflinger, *A Vigorous Spirit of Enterprise: Merchants and Economic Development in*

Revolutionary Philadelphia (Chapel Hill: University of North Carolina, 1986), 122–24, 148–51; Carl J. Ekberg, *French Roots in the Illinois Country: The Mississippi Frontier in Colonial Times* (Urbana: University of Illinois Press, 1998), 236–37, 278–79; Nelson, *Man of Distinction*, 52–56; Max Savelle, *George Morgan, Colony Builder* (New York: Columbia University Press, 1932), chaps. 1–2; Volwiler, *George Croghan*, 179, 190–92, 199–201; Wainwright, *George Croghan*, 211–12, 226, 233; Ward, *Breaking the Backcountry*, 191–92; White, *Middle Ground*, chap. 8.

90. For Carlisle as a way station, see Savelle, *George Morgan*, 24; Whitfield J. Bell, Jr., "Carlisle to Pittsburgh: A Gateway to the West," 1750–1815," *PMHB* 35.3 (1952): 157–66.

91. I draw this composite portrait from a number of local sources, including Cumberland County tax rates, deed abstracts, wills, and court records, currently housed at CCHS. Some of my conclusions remain tentative because county records are especially spotty for the 1750s and 1760s, making it difficult to trace these men. Still, it is clear that personal and business connections with Callender and Croghan knit these men together. Irwin, for instance, lived with Callender for a time; Blaine managed and then purchased his mill in the 1770s. Dobson was involved with Croghan in a number of land deals, then became Callender's neighbor when he bought a stone house next door to him in Carlisle in 1767. For more information, see Schaumann, *History and Genealogy*, 195, 201; Gary T. Hawbaker and Clyde L. Groff, *A New Index: Lancaster County Before the Federal Census* (Hershey, Pa.: G. T. Hawbaker, 1982), 3:98; James B. Whisker, ed., *The Bedford County Archives* (Apollo, Pa.: Closson Press, 1985), 1:95–109. For Ephraim Blaine, see especially Harold Keat, *The Cave Hill Miller* (Carlisle, Pa.: Cumberland County Historical Society, 1911); Tousey, *Military History of Carlisle*, 406–7.

92. "Beaver" refers to Big Beaver Creek, a tributary of the Ohio River, where George Croghan established a trading house in the mid 1750s. See Volwiler, *George Croghan*, 34, 296–97.

93. Ephraim Blaine to BWM, August 16, 1766, Society Collection, HSP, Ephraim Blaine folder, 1765–1781.

94. For an idea of the large quantity of pelts agents like Blaine handled, see William West Wastebook #1, West Papers, entries for July 21, 1769; August 12, 1769; and August 26, 1769. During 1769, West got 1,000–2,000 pounds of pelts from his Carlisle contacts in a single month.

95. Ephraim Blaine to BWM, August 16, 1766, Society Collection, HSP (quotes). See also the "Account of Goods and Liquors delivered by the Sundry Contractors for Carriage," 1766, BWM Papers, reel 3, where Ephraim Blaine is credited with delivering numerous bales of an unidentified commodity, boxes of vermillion, and bushels of salt.

96. John Irwin to BWM, October 21, 1765, ibid., reel 4. According to tax rates, which are spotty for the 1760s, BWM owned at least 2,000 acres of land in the county in 1767; see Tax Rates, Cumberland County, 1767. For a reference to the firm's pastureland near Carlisle, see Joseph Rigby to BWM, June 11, 1768, ibid., reel 5. An extant map locates this land along the town's southern border: see Map of Carlisle, 1768, RG-17, Land Office Maps, 73/1:10, PHMC.

97. For the 140 horseloads, see BWM to Joseph Dobson, February 1766, BWM

Papers, reel 1; for the 445 horseloads, see Joseph Dobson to BWM, August 5, 1768, ibid., reel 3. See also Savelle, *George Morgan*, 25.

98. For slaves, see Tax Rates, Carlisle, 1765. For Callender employing his neighbors, see Joseph Dobson to BWM, September 24, 1768, BWM Papers, reel 3.

99. Robert Callender to BWM, December 1, 1762, ibid., reel 2.

100. Joseph Rigby to BWM, May 28, 1768 (quote "Half Barrels") and June 11, 1768, ibid., reel 5 (quote "taken them").

101. John Irwin to BWM, April 14, 1766, ibid., reel 4 (quote). Cash shortages were a chronic problem for BWM. As early as early as 1764 they wrote of how "Our Finances are very low, and even small sums are cautiously granted." See BWM to Robert Callender, August 24, 1764, ibid., reel 1.

102. John Irwin to BWM, April 12, 1766 (quote "Demanding") and April 13, 1766, ibid., reel 4 (quote "putting off"). See also Savelle, *George Morgan*, 18–23.

103. Joseph Dobson to BWM, August 13, 1768, BWM Papers, reel 3.

104. Joseph Dobson to BWM, October 8, 1768, ibid.

105. Joseph Dobson to BWM, October n.d., 1768, ibid., reel 3. Dobson advised his employers that when the cooper arrived, they should discount his bill by an additional £7–8 because of the "bad Keggs that he made Last Spring" and threaten to sue him for damages if he would not settle.

106. Ibid.

107. Joseph Dobson to BWM, November 19, 1768, ibid.

108. Ibid (quotes). See also Dobson to BWM, September 24, 1768, ibid., for how Callender claimed some of Dobson's agents and many of his workers, including a reliable cooper, whom Callender employed to build 150 kegs for the rum he intended to transport west.

109. Joseph Dobson to BWM, November 12, 1768, ibid., reel 3.

110. Evidence suggests that rum was the mainstay of Callender's trade. See Dobson to BWM, November 26, 1768, ibid., where he reported that Callender was about to set off for Fort Chartres with 2,000 gallons of rum. For alcohol's role in postwar trade, see Hinderaker, *Elusive Empires*, 181–82.

111. Joseph Dobson to BWM, November 19, 1768, November 26, 1768, BWM Papers, reel 3.

112. Joseph Dobson to BWM, April 9, 1768, ibid.

113. Joseph Dobson to BWM, November 26, 1768, BWM Papers, reel 3, ibid., (quotes); see also November 19, 1768, ibid.

114. See, for example, Dobson to BWM, April 4, 1768, ibid., in which he talks of sending 102 horseloads of liquor, tobacco, and beaver traps, and April 9, 1768, ibid., in which he asks BWM to send up "your powder and Lead and Knives." See May 11, 1768, ibid., in which he talks of hiding lead in various bundles going west so that if the packhorse train is attacked, the loss will not be so great; and see November 19, 1768, in which he talks of knives being hauled in from Baltimore. Finally, see Joseph Rigby to BWM, June 11, 1768, ibid., reel 5, in which he talks of sending powder and lead west with the troops going to Fort Pitt.

115. For the mood of Carlisle, see Joseph Rigby to BWM, May 28, 1768, BWM Papers, reel 5. For the mounting intercultural tensions of 1768, see Merritt, *At the Crossroads*, chap. 8; Richter, *Facing East*, 210–13; Silver, *Our Savage Neighbors*, chap. 7.

116. Crist, "John Armstrong," 141; Joseph Dobson to BWM, May [n.d.] 1768, May 11, 1758, BWM Papers, reel 3.

117. Dobson to BWM, May [n.d.], 1768, July 22, 1768, ibid.

118. Ibid., April 4, 1768.

119. Ibid., May 11, 1768.

120. Silver, *Our Savage Neighbors*, 210 (quote); see also 191–211.

121. Joseph Dobson to BWM, May 11, 1768, BWM Papers, reel 3.

122. Smith, "An Account," in *Loudon Narratives*, 1:207.

123. Ibid., 1:208. Smith and the Black Boys were correct about this trade; it was technically illegal, but George Croghan, William Johnson's deputy, wanted to have trade goods ready at Fort Pitt when the trade reopened. See Cutcliffe, "Sideling Hill Affair," 45–46.

124. Smith, "An Account," in *Loudon Narratives*, 1:207.

125. Ibid., 1:208. See also Webster, "Insurrection at Loudon," 129–30.

126. Smith, "An Account," in *Loudon Narratives*, 1:209.

127. Ibid., 1:210. See also Cutcliffe, "Sideling Hill Affair," 39–40.

128. Webster, "Insurrection at Loudon," 131 (quote). See also McConnell, *A Country Between*, 243.

129. *PG*, February 28, 1760 (quotes); *Pennsylvania Archives 4*, 3:19–20, 99–100, 142–43.

130. *Pennsylvania Archives 4*, 3:350–51 (quote). See also *PG*, March 24, 1768; Hubertis M. Cummings, *Scots Breed and Susquehanna* (Pittsburgh: University of Pittsburgh Press, 1964), 142–43.

131. Silver, *Our Savage Neighbors*, 154–55.

132. *Pennsylvania Archives 4*, 3:363 (quote). See also Richter, *Facing East*, 213.

133. For the accounts, see John Armstrong to unid. [likely Gov. John Penn], January 29, 1768, Lamberton Scotch-Irish Collection, HSP, 1:80; George Croghan to William Johnson, February 7, 1768, George Croghan Papers, Cadwalader Collection, HSP, 5:30. For Gov. John Penn's desire to punish these men to preserve friendly relations with the Delawares, see *Pennsylvania Archives 4*, 3:362–64.

134. Italicized emphasis mine. *Pennsylvania Archives 4*, 3:350–51 (quote "daring insult"), 363–64, 368–69, 371–76, 387–89, 394–95. For Armstrong's words, see Armstrong to unid. [likely Gov. Penn], January 29, 1768, Lamberton Scotch-Irish Collection, 1:80.

135. For the Black Boys, see John Irwin to BWM, March 21, 1766, BWM Papers, reel 4; see also Joseph Dobson to BWM, April 24, 1768, ibid., reel 3. For Stump, see Dobson to BWM, May [n.d.], 1768, ibid.

136. Joseph Rigby to BWM, May 28, 1768, ibid., reel 5.

137. For Jacobitism in mid-eighteenth-century Ireland, see Eamonn O'Ciardha, *Ireland and the Jacobite Cause, 1685–1766* (Dublin: Four Courts Press, 2002), chap. 7. For Jacobitism in the American context, see Geoffrey Plank, *Rebellion and Savagery: The*

Jacobite Uprising of 1745 and the British Empire (Philadelphia: University of Pennsylvania Press, 2006), chap. 6.

138. Joseph Dobson to BWM, October [n.d.] 1768, BWM Papers, reel 3.

139. Unid. (likely Richard Peters) to the Proprietors, n.d. (though likely 1750), Penn OC, 5:33.

140. Joseph Dobson to BWM, November 19, 1768, BWM Papers, reel 3 (first quote); Dobson to BWM, December 10, 1769, Joseph Dobson Folder, Society Collection, HSP (second quote).

141. Dobson to BWM, November 19, 1768, BWM Papers, reel 3.

CHAPTER 4. WAR AND REVOLUTION

1. John Montgomery to John Hancock, July 14, 1776, Continental Congress Papers, reel 83, 1.185.

2. For Montgomery's assurances, see ibid. For Thompson and his battalion, see Milton E. Flower and Lenore E. Flower, *This Is Carlisle: A History of a Pennsylvania Town* (Harrisburg, Pa.: J. Horace McFarland, 1944), 13. The Irish-born Thompson was a surveyor, entrepreneur, judge, and politician. He was an officer during the Seven Years' War and helped construct the Forbes Road. Like other leading men in Carlisle, he had close ties to fur traders, particularly George Croghan. See Cumberland County Historical Society, "William Thompson: The Forgotten Patriot," http://www.pamidstate.com/cgi-bin/db/list.cgi?eid=6753&Sponsor= (6 October 2008). For the *rage militaire* sweeping Carlisle and other American communities in 1776, see Charles Royster, *A Revolutionary People at War: The Continental Army and American Character, 1775–1783* (Chapel Hill: University of North Carolina Press, 1979, 3rd printing, 1986), chap. 1.

3. John Byers to the Pennsylvania Committee of Safety, March 29, 1776, PA Rev. Gov't, reel 10.414.

4. For nonimportation, see T. H. Breen, *The Marketplace of Revolution: How Consumer Politics Shaped American Independence* (New York: Oxford University Press, 2004), chap. 8. For the fur trade and the interior, see Terry Bouton, *Taming Democracy: "The People," the Founders, and the Struggle over the American Revolution* (New York: Oxford University Press, 2007), 46; Kathryn E. Holland Braund, *Deerskins and Duffels: The Creek Indian Trade with Anglo-America, 1685–1815* (Lincoln: University of Nebraska Press, 1993), chap. 9; William S. Coker and Thomas D. Watson, *Indian Traders of the Southeastern Spanish Borderlands: Panton, Leslie, and Company and John Forbes and Company, 1783–1847* (Pensacola: University Presses of Florida, 1986); Patrick Griffin, *American Leviathan: Empire, Nation, and Revolutionary Frontier* (New York: Hill and Wang, 2007), chaps. 4 and 5.

5. For Carlisle's contributions, see Robert G. Crist, "Cumberland County" in *Beyond Philadelphia: The American Revolution in the Pennsylvania Hinterland*, ed. John B. Frantz and William Pencak (University Park: Pennsylvania State University Press, 1998), 107–32. See also George P. Donehoo, *A History of the Cumberland Valley in Pennsylva-*

nia, 2 vols. (Harrisburg, Pa.: Susquehanna History Association, 1930), 1:439–41; Wayland F. Dunaway, *The Susquehanna Valley in the Revolution* (Wilkes-Barre. Pa.: E. B. Yordy Company, 1927), 6–7, 13–14; Flower and Flower, *This Is Carlisle*, chap. 2; Frederic A. Godcharles, *Chronicles of Central Pennsylvania*, 4 vols. (New York: Lewis Historical Publishing Company, 1944), 1:245, 3:98; John B. B. Trussell, Jr., *The Pennsylvania Line: Regimental Organization and Operations, 1776–1783* (Harrisburg: Pennsylvania Historical and Museum Commission, 1977), chaps. 1 and 8, p. 239.

6. John B. Frantz and William Pencak, "Introduction: Pennsylvania and Its Three Revolutions," in *Beyond Philadelphia: The American Revolution in the Pennsylvania Hinterland*, ed. John B. Frantz and William Pencak (University Park: Pennsylvania State University Press, 1998), ix–xxv, see esp. xix–xxi.

7. Charles Page Smith, *James Wilson, Founding Father, 1742–1798* (Chapel Hill: University of North Carolina Press, 1956), 50 (quote). See also Crist, "Cumberland County," 117–20.

8. "Our Suffering Brethren," in Thompson, *Two Hundred Years*, 49–50.

9. Crist, "Cumberland County," 120 (quote); see also Flower and Flower, *This Is Carlisle*, 12–13; *Pennsylvania Archives 2*, 14:387; Smith, *James Wilson*, 52.

10. William Lyon, Petition, "Appointments File: Political," PA Rev Gov't, reel 33.1526.

11. Flower and Flower, *This Is Carlisle*, 12 (quote). See also "Oath of Allegiance, 1777–78," *Pennsylvania Archives 2*, 14:471–85.

12. Frantz and Pencak, "Introduction," xx.

13. Kerby A. Miller, Arnold Schrier, Bruce D. Boling, David N. Doyle, eds., *Irish Immigrants in the Land of Canaan: Letters and Memoirs from Colonial and Revolutionary America, 1675–1815* (New York: Oxford University Press, 2003), 486 (quote), see also 483–87. See also Joseph S. Foster, *In Pursuit of Equal Liberty: George Bryan and the Revolution in Pennsylvania* (University Park: Pennsylvania State University Press, 1994), chaps. 2–4; Patrick Griffin, *The People with No Name: Ireland's Ulster Scots, America's Scots Irish, and the Creation of a British Atlantic World, 1689–1764* (Princeton, N.J: Princeton University Press, 2001), chaps. 2–3.

14. Crist, "Cumberland County," 118–19. See also Foster, *Pursuit of Equal Liberty*, 49–50; 67–72; Frantz and Pencak, "Introduction," xx; Miller, *Irish Immigrants*, 24–25, 446–47, 476–81.

15. Randall M. Miller and William Pencak, ed., *Pennsylvania: A History of the Commonwealth*, (University Park: Pennsylvania State University Press, 2002), 116; Lorette Treese, *The Storm Gathering: The Penn Family and the American Revolution* (University Park: Pennsylvania State University Press, 1992; reprint, Mechanicsburg, Pa.: Stackpole Books, 2002), 144.

16. Gordon S. Wood, *The Creation of the American Republic, 1776–1787* (Chapel Hill: University of North Carolina Press, 1969; reprint, New York: W. W. Norton, 1972), 227 (quote). For more about the state's radical turn, see also Wayne L. Bockelman and Owen S. Ireland, "The Internal Revolution in Pennsylvania: An Ethnic-Religious Interpretation," *PH* 41.2 (1974): 125–59; Randall M. Miller and William Pencak, eds., *Pennsylvania:*

A History of the Commonwealth (University Park: Pennsylvania State University Press, 2002), 115–23; Richard Alan Ryerson, *The Revolution Is Now Begun: The Radical Committees of Philadelphia, 1765–1776* (Philadelphia: University of Pennsylvania Press, 1978), chaps. 1–2.

17. William Thompson, Petition, November 23, 1778, Continental Congress Papers, reel 178.316 (quote). For the internal revolution's affect on Cumberland County, see Crist, "Cumberland County," 119–22, 126–29.

18. For their political moderation, see Crist, "Cumberland County," 127. For Easton and Allentown, see Liam Riordan, *Many Identities, One Nation: The Revolution and Its Legacy in the Mid-Atlantic* (Philadelphia: University of Pennsylvania Press, 2007), 68–75; see also Francis S. Fox, *Sweet Land of Liberty: The Ordeal of the American Revolution in Northampton County, Pennsylvania* (University Park: Pennsylvania State University Press, 2000), chap. 2. For immigrant leaders' desire to become Americans, see Judith Ridner, "William Irvine and the Complexity of Manhood and Fatherhood in the Pennsylvania Backcountry," *PMHB* 125.1 and 2 (2001): 5–34.

19. Smith, *James Wilson*, 3–116. See also Bouton, *Taming Democracy*, chap. 3.

20. Gertrude Bosler Biddle, *Notable Women of Pennsylvania* (Philadelphia: University of Pennsylvania Press, 1942), 94–96; Nicholas Wainwright, *The Irvine Story* (Philadelphia: HSP, 1964), 2–11. See also Ridner, "Manhood and Fatherhood," 9–14.

21. John Armstrong to James Armstrong, April 30, 1772, Founders Collection, DCA.

22. Wainwright, *Irvine Story*, 2–13.

23. Bouton, *Taming Democracy*, chap. 2, esp. 43–46; Foster, *In Pursuit of Equal Liberty*, 91–95. Frantz and Pencak, "Introduction," xx; O. S. Ireland, "The Crux of Politics: Religion and Party in Pennsylvania, 1778–1789," *WMQ* 3d ser., 62.4 (1985): 453–75; Miller and Pencak, *Pennsylvania: A History*, 121–23.

24. Col. James Smith, "An Account of the Remarkable Occurrences in the Life and Travels of Col. James Smith," in Archibald Loudon, *A Selection of Some of the Most Interesting Narratives, of Outrages, Committed by the Indians, in their Wars, with the White People*, 2 vols. (Carlisle, Pa.: A. Loudon, 1808–1811; reprint, New York: Arno Press, 1971), 1:226–30.

25. Mathew Vanlear, Petition, October 24, 1776, "Appointments File: Military," PA Rev Gov't, reel 32.1561.

26. Frantz and Pencak, "Introduction," xx (quote). See also Gregory T. Knouff, *The Soldiers' Revolution: Pennsylvanians in Arms and the Forging of Early American Identity* (University Park: Pennsylvania State University Press, 2004), chap. 2.

27. "Our Troops Complain," in Thompson, *Two Hundred Years*, 52. Cumberland County residents' prior personal experiences with war contrast markedly with eastern Pennsylvanians' lack of such experiences: see Wayne Bodle, *The Valley Forge Winter: Civilians and Soldiers in War* (University Park: Pennsylvania State University Press, 2002), 23–25.

28. Crist, "Cumberland County," 123–24.

29. Steven Rosswurm, *Arms, Country and Class: The Philadelphia Militia and the "Lower Sort" during the American Revolution* (New Brunswick, N.J.: Rutgers University

Press, 1987; reprint, 1989), 66–67, 77–79. See also Samuel J. Newland, *The Pennsylvania Militia: Defending the Commonwealth and the Nation: 1669–1870* (Annville, Pa.: Pennsylvania National Guard Foundation, 2002), chap. 6.

30. Knouff, *Soldiers' Revolution*, 39–40; Christ, "Cumberland County," 124–26.

31. Flower and Flower, *This Is Carlisle*, 13.

32. Thompson, Petition, November 23, 1778, Continental Congress Papers, reel 178.316–341.

33. Ibid.

34. Pension Application of Henry and Elizabeth McEwen, Pension Applications, reel 1680.W3275; Pension Application of Philip Hornbaker or Baker, ibid., reel 119.27. See also *Pennsylvania Archives 5*, 2:25–29. For more on Thompson's Battalion, see "Journal of Captain William Hendricks," *Pennsylvania Archives 2*, 15:21–58.

35. Miller, *Irish Immigrants*, 262; Charles Patrick Neimeyer, *America Goes to War: A Social History of the Continental Army* (New York: New York University Press, 1996), chap. 2; Wainwright, *The Irvine Story*, 2–11.

36. William Irvine to unid., March 5, 1776, Sol Feinstone Collection, microfilm, DLAR, reel 2.615.

37. William Blakeney, Petition, March 2, 1777, "Appointments File: Military," PA Rev Gov't, reel 31.142 (quote). For O'Hara's record, see O'Hara Pension Application, Pension Applications, reel 1840.BLWT 233–100.

38. Recommendation for James Allen, December 26, 1776, "Appointments File: Military," PA Rev Gov't, reel 31.34.

39. James Irwin, Petition for Clemency, November 20, 1787, "Clemency Files," PA Rev Gov't, reel 39.1357.

40. Brice Smith, Petition for Clemency, February 26, 1787, "Clemency Files," PA Rev Gov't, reel 40.276.

41. Pension Application of John Tate, Pension Applications, reel 2343.S32007.

42. For an important discussion of how service shaped soldiers' identities, see Knouff, *Soldiers' Revolution*, introduction, chap. 2. See also Bouton, *Taming Democracy*, 63; Royster, *Revolutionary People at War*, 87–95.

43. Pension Application of Isaac Thompson, Pension Applications, reel 2375.27.

44. *Journals of Continental Congress*, 3:404 (quote); Crist, "Cumberland County," 129–30; George P. Donehoo, *A History of the Cumberland Valley in Pennsylvania*, 2 vols. (Harrisburg, Pa.: Susquehanna History Association, 1930), 1:440.

45. Crist, "Cumberland County," 129–30. For information on André and Despard, see Judith L. Van Buskirk, *Generous Enemies: Patriots and Loyalists in Revolutionary New York* (Philadelphia: University of Pennsylvania Press, 2002), 92–93.

46. I. Daniel Rupp, *The History and Topography of Dauphin, Cumberland, Franklin, Bedford, Adams, and Perry Counties* (Lancaster, Pa.: Gilbert Hills, 1846), 405–6; Merri Lou Schaumann, *Taverns of Cumberland County, Pennsylvania, 1750–1840* (Carlisle, Pa.: Cumberland County Historical Association, 1994), 43–45.

47. See Van Buskirk, *Generous Enemies*, chap. 3, for a comparative discussion of how

gentlemanly codes of war sometimes conflicted with local and national interests. For details about Carlisle, see Crist, "Cumberland County," 130.

48. As quoted in Schaumann, *Cumberland County Taverns*, 45–46. See also Done-hoo, *History of Cumberland Valley*, 1:440–441; Flower and Flower, *This Is Carlisle*, 14; Rupp, *History and Topography*, 405–6.

49. Cumberland County Committee of Inspection and Observation to Congress, July 14, 1776, Papers of Continental Congress, reel 83, 1.185–86.

50. Crist, "Cumberland County," 128.

51. Ibid., 127–28.

52. John Kearsley to Samuel Postlethwaite, October 21, 1777, Papers of Continental Congress, reel 96, 11.245–46 (quotes). For more about Kearsley, see Knouff, A Soldiers' Revolution, 199; Anne M. Ousterhout, *A State Divided: Opposition in Pennsylvania to the American Revolution* (New York: Greenwood Press, 1987), 112–20.

53. Prisoners at the Carlisle Gaol to the Continental Congress, n.d., Continental Congress Papers, reel 100, 18.117–18.

54. John Montgomery to John Hancock, October 22, 1777, ibid., reel 99.273. For earlier repairs to the jail, see the accounts of Thomas Cannedy and James Ramsey, Postlethwaite Account Book, in the Hamilton Papers, HSP.

55. *Journals of Continental Congress,* 9:840. See also Crist, "Cumberland County," 127–28. Evidence suggests that local officials acted. Two years later, court-appointed examiners found the jail "sufficient for the security of the Prisoners there confined." See Report on the Gaol, April 1779, Cumberland County Court of Quarter Sessions, CCHS, Docket #6.

56. Worthington C. Ford., ed., *Journals of the Continental Congress, 1774–1789*, 34 vols. (Washington D.C.: Government Printing Office, 1908), 6:1044. James Wilson was instrumental in lobbying for Carlisle as a site for this magazine. See Smith, *James Wilson*, 95.

57. David L. Salay, "Arming for War: The Production of War Material in Pennsylvania for the American Armies during the Revolution," (Ph.D. diss., University of Delaware, 1977), iv–v, 116; Thomas G. Tousey, *Military History of Carlisle and Carlisle Barracks* (Richmond, Va.: Dietz Press, 1939), 63–64; Robert K. Wright, Jr., *The Continental Army* (Washington D.C.: Center of Military History, U.S. Army, 1983), 104.

58. Pension Application of Adam Logue, Pension Applications, reel 1579.R6415.

59. Tousey, *Military History of Carlisle*, 96–101.

60. John Wilson and John Montgomery to Richard Peters, November 1777, Carlisle Barracks, Letterbook, 1777–1801, WPHS.

61. Manasseh Cutler, August 3, 1788, "Journal of Rev. Manasseh Cutler of a Journey from Ipswich, Massachusetts to the Muskingum, in 1788," in William P. Cutler and Julia P. Cutler, eds., *Life, Journals and Correspondence of Rev. Manasseh Cutler, LL.D.*, 2 vols. (Cincinnati: Robert Clarke and Company, 1888), 1:401.

62. Salay, "Arming for War," 116.

63. Wright, *Continental Army*, 104. See also Trussell, *Pennsylvania Line*, 226–29; *Pennsylvania Archives 5*, 3:1085–1133.

64. There were disputes about pay, provisions, and rank for the artificers. Officers of the artificer regiment, in particular, complained that they were not treated equally with other officers. See, for example, Continental Congress Papers, reel 175, 1.100–3; reel 157, 2.577.

65. Pension Application of William Ferguson, Pension Applications, reel 966.W2777 (quotes); Trussell, *Pennsylvania Line*, 226–29.

66. As evidence of slowed outward migration during the war, between 1779 and 1782 the town's taxable population held steady at approximately 220 residents, while persistence rates reached a high of 63 percent. See Tax Rates, Carlisle, 1764, 1768, 1779, and 1782. For more information, see Judith A. Ridner, "'A Handsomely Improved Place': Economic, Social, and Gender-Role Development in a Backcountry Town, Carlisle, Pennsylvania, 1750–1810" (Ph.D. diss., College of William & Mary, 1994), 99.

67. Trussell, *Pennsylvania Line*, 228.

68. Pension Application of William Denning, Pension Applications, reel 795.S42150.

69. Pension Application of Isaac Wall, ibid., reel 2478.S40638 (quotes). For more on the activities of the artificers, see Salay, "Arming for War"; Trussell, *Pennsylvania Line*, 226–29; Wright, *Continental Army*, 104. See also Fred A. Berg, ed., *Encyclopedia of Continental Army Units* (Harrisburg, Pa.: Stackpole Books, 1972), 11–12.

70. William Ferguson Pension Application, reel 966.W2777.

71. For Blaine's career, see Tousey, *Military History of Carlisle*, 406–7.

72. Crist, "Cumberland County," 130.

73. John Armstrong to unid., April 12, 1780, "Appointments: Political," PA Rev Gov't, reel 32.627.

74. John Montgomery to Congress, July 14, 1776, Continental Congress Papers, reel 83, 1.185 (quote). For cash scarcity in Pennsylvania and its implications, see Bouton, *Taming Democracy*, 16–30.

75. John Glen, Petition, n.d., "Clemency Files," PA Rev Gov't, reel 40.755.

76. "Bridging the Letort," in Thompson, *Two Hundred Years*, 53.

77. George Stevenson to Congress, July 27, 1776, Continental Congress Papers, reel 83, 1.201–2.

78. John Byers to the Pennsylvania Committee of Safety, March 29, 1776, PA Rev Gov't, reel 10.414 (first quote); Commissioners of Cumberland County to the Pennsylvania Council of Safety, October 18, 1776, ibid., reel 11.32 (second quote).

79. Receipt for repairs by George McGunnegle, September 10, 1776, Nead Papers, HSP, case 36. In 1779, McGunnegle fell into the fourth decile of wealth. See Tax Rates, Carlisle, 1779.

80. For evidence of his work, see the 1776 ledger account of Col. William Irvine, Samuel Postlethwaite Account Book, in the Hamilton Papers, HSP; James Pollock and Samuel Laird to Pennsylvania Council of Safety, October 7, 1776, PA Rev. Gov't, reel 10.1091 (quote). For Cooper's middling status, see Tax Rates, Carlisle, 1779.

81. E. Wayne Carp, *To Starve the Army at Pleasure: Continental Army Administration and American Political Culture, 1775–1783* (Chapel Hill: University of North Carolina Press, 1984), 155–56.

82. Ephraim Blaine was the great-grandfather of Senator James G. Blaine of Maine, nominated for the presidency against Grover Cleveland. See Flower and Flower, *This Is Carlisle*, 19. For the dire state of Blaine's finances by 1781, see Ephraim Blaine to Robert Morris, November 27, 1781, *The Papers of Robert Morris*, ed. John Catanzariti and E. James Ferguson, 7 vols. (Pittsburgh: University of Pittsburgh Press, 1977), 3:295. Blaine asked Morris for assistance as "I am without Money."

83. Postlethwaite Account Book, in the Hamilton Papers, HSP.

84. Ibid.

85. For Postlethwaite at Fort Frederick, see ibid. See also Martha Jane Brazy, *An American Planter: Stephen Duncan of Antebellum Natchez and New York* (Baton Rouge: Louisiana State University Press, 2006), chap. 1; Schaumann, *Taverns of Cumberland County*, 14; Tax Rates, Carlisle, 1779, show Postlethwaite as the thirteenth wealthiest man in town, within the top 10 percent of taxpayers.

86. Orderly Book, 8th Pennsylvania Regiment, July 8–10, 1778, The Draper Manuscript Collection, DLAR, originals at State Historical Society of Wisconsin, reel 96.2NN5-8.

87. Edward Burd to Jasper Yeates, June 28, 1778, Edward Burd Papers, in the Ferdinand J. Dreer Autograph Collection, HSP.

88. John McDowell to Col. David Grier, May 28, 1777, PA Rev Gov't, reel 12.363.

89. Ibid., May 21, 1777, PA Rev Gov't, reel 12.346.

90. For examples of Pennsylvania communities beset by civil-war–like situations during the Revolution, see Bodle, *Valley Forge Winter*, chap. 4; Fox, *Sweet Land of Liberty*, introduction; Riordan, *Many Identities*, chap. 2.

91. For the radical politics Carlisle's leaders reacted to, see Foster, *Pursuit of Equal Liberty*, 91–95; Fox, *Sweet Land of Liberty*, xvi–xviii; Frantz and Pencak, "Introduction," xv–xvii; Ireland, "Crux of Politics," 453–75; Riordan, *Many Identities*, 74–75; Ryerson, *Revolution Now Begun*, 13–14. See also *Pennsylvania Archives 4*, 3:545–46. For the moderate to conservative backlash they were a part of, see Robert L. Brunhouse, *The Counter-Revolution in Pennsylvania, 1776–1790* (Harrisburg, Pa.: Pennsylvania Historical and Museum Commission, 1942), chaps. 4 and 5.

92. Smith, *James Wilson*, 110.

93. As quoted in Crist, "Cumberland County," 126.

94. As quoted in Crist, "Cumberland County," 126; see also Smith, *James Wilson*, 110.

95. As quoted in Smith, ibid.

96. Brunhouse, *Counter-Revolution*, chap. 5.

97. Schaumann, *Taverns of Cumberland County*, 48, 51.

98. "Merchant, Soldier, and Family Man," in Thompson, *Two Hundred Years*, 54–57.

99. John Armstrong to James Wilson, May 26, 1775, Gratz Papers, case 4, box 11.

100. George Stevenson to the Pennsylvania Council of Safety, December 2, 1776, PA Rev Gov't, reel 11.377.

101. John McDowell to Col. David Grier, May 21, 1777, PA Rev. Gov't, reel 12.347.

102. Knouff, *Soldiers' Revolution*, 71–74.

103. George Stevenson to the Pennsylvania Council of Safety, December 29, 1776, PA Rev Gov't, reel 11.643.

104. Stevenson to the Council of Safety, August 17, 1776, ibid., reel 10.909.

105. James Gregory and others to Pres. Thomas Wharton, September 5, 1777, ibid., reel 12.973.

106. John McDowell to Col. David Grier, May 28, 1777, ibid., reel 12.363.

107. Ibid.

108. Lt. Col. William Butler to Joseph Reed, February 28, 1781, *Pennsylvania Archives I*, 8:747.

109. Brig. Gen. William Irvine to President Joseph Reed, July 16, 1781, Irvine Papers, 9:285.

110. John Davis to Ephraim Blaine, February 19, 1779, Ephraim Blaine Papers, Library of Congress, Washington, D.C.

111. John Carothers to Pennsylvania's Executive Council, May 28, 1778, PA Rev Gov't, reel 14.139.

112. Ibid.

113. Residents of Peters Township, Cumberland County, Petition to the Pennsylvania General Assembly, May 14, 1778, Continental Congress Papers, reel 83,1.523 (first quote); Testimony of John Bosley before Justice William Scott of York County, July 1778, ibid., reel 102, 20.279 (second quote).

114. Peter Silver, *Our Savage Neighbors: How Indian War Transformed Early America* (New York: W. W. Norton, 2008), chap. 8, emphasizes Pennsylvanians' desires to fight Indians again, even if they were scared of them. Knouff, *Soldiers' Revolution*, 71–72, challenges these ideas, noting that central Pennsylvanians, seeing themselves as secure, were loathe to fight, even on the frontier.

115. Carothers to Continental Congress, April 24, 1778, Papers of Continental Congress, reel 83, 6.501–2.

116. Bodle, *Valley Forge Winter*, 86–89; Van Buskirk, *Generous Enemies*, intro.—chap. 1.

117. Council of Safety Resolution, n.d., PA Rev Gov't, reel 11.759 (first quote); James Pollock and Samuel Laird to the Pennsylvania Council of Safety, July 25, 1776, ibid., reel 10.844 (second quote).

118. Pollock and Laird, ibid.

119. Cumberland County Committee of Inspection and Observation to the Pennsylvania Council of Safety, December 29, 1776, PA Rev Gov't, reel 11.643 (quote); John Byers to ibid., March 29, 1776, ibid., reel 10.414.

120. James Pollock and Samuel Laird to the Pennsylvania Committee of Safety, February 9, 1776, *Pennsylvania Archives I*, 5:713.

121. Council of Safety Resolution, n.d., PA Rev Gov't, reel 11.759.

122. Cumberland Committee of Inspection and Observation to the Pennsylvania Council of Safety, December 29, 1776, ibid., reel 11.643.

123. Ibid., September 4, 1776, ibid., reel 10.988.

124. Carp, *Starve the Army at Pleasure*, chaps. 2 and 3.

125. Charles Lukens to Samuel Postlethwaite, February 12, 1779, Postlethwaite Papers, in the Hamilton Papers, HSP (quote). In 1778, rations for those at the works were supposed to consist of a generous serving of meat and bread, vegetables, milk, molasses, and a quart of beer or cider. Clearly, the Army could no longer provide these rations by 1779. See Carlisle Barracks, Letterbook, 1777–1801, WPHS.

126. Richard Peters to Congress, October 14, 1780, Continental Congress Papers, reel 159.617 (first two quotes); William Irvine to unid., August 19, 1781, Irvine Papers, 4:97 (quote "odd . . . way").

127. William Irvine to unid., April 10, 1781, ibid., 4:47.

128. Ibid.; unid. to William Irvine, March 11, 1781, ibid., 4:39 (quote).

129. Irvine to unid., August 19, 1781, ibid., 4:97.

130. Peters to Congress, October 14, 1780, Continental Congress Papers, reel 159.617.

131. Richard Peters to William Irvine, March 27, 1781, Irvine Papers, 4:44.

132. Peters to Congress, October 14, 1780, Continental Congress Papers, reel 159.617.

133. John Agnew and Samuel Laird, Order to take Charles Jones and John Perry into custody, April 11, 1781, Postlethwaite Papers, in the Hamilton Papers, HSP.

134. John Perry, Petition, June 5, 1781, "Clemency Files," PA Rev Gov't, reel 37.556. Perry offered to spend the rest of his life in service to the Commonwealth in return for his life. His appeal was not granted; the state issued a death warrant on July 7.

135. Orderly Book, 8th Pennsylvania Regiment, November 6, 1781, Draper Manuscripts, reel 96.2NN196. For Irvine's desire to return to his wife and children at war's end, see William Irvine to Ann Irvine, June 29, 1782, ibid., 6:37; October 4, 1782, ibid., 7:22.

136. Benjamin Lincoln to William Irvine, October 30, 1782, Irvine Papers, 7:39 (first quote); N. Lacassagne to William Irvine, May 15, 1784, ibid., 8:101 (second quote).

137. John Montgomery to Samuel Postlethwaite, August 12, 1782, John Montgomery Papers, CCHS.

138. James Hamilton to John Brown, July 2, 1784, James Hamilton Papers, CCHS.

139. John Armstrong to William Irvine, August 16, 1787, Irvine Papers, 9:84.

CHAPTER 5. STILL IN-BETWEEN

1. DHRC, 671; Milton E. Flower and Lenore E. Flower, This Is Carlisle: A History of a Pennsylvania Town (Harrisburg, Pa.: J. Horace McFarland, 1944), 24.

2. DHRC, 646 (quote); Robert L. Brunhouse, The Counter-Revolution in Pennsylvania, 1776–1790 (Harrisburg, Pa.: Pennsylvania Historical and Museum Commission, 1942), 209.

3. DHRC, 671 (quotes), see also 670–79. For descriptions of the riot, see Saul Cornell, The Other Founders; Anti-Federalism and the Dissenting Tradition in America, 1788–1828 (Chapel Hill: University of North Carolina Press, 1999), 109–10; Cornell, "Aristocracy Assailed: The Ideology of Backcountry Anti-Federalism," JAH 76.4 (1990): 1151–54; Flower and Flower, This Is Carlisle, 24; Owen S. Ireland, Religion, Ethnicity, and

Politics: Ratifying the Constitution in Pennsylvania (University Park: Pennsylvania State University Press, 1995), 130–32; Simon P. Newman, *Parades and the Politics of the Street: Festive Culture in the Early American Republic* (Philadelphia: University of Pennsylvania Press, 1997), 42; David Waldstreicher, *In the Midst of Perpetual Fetes: The Making of American Nationalism, 1776–1820* (Chapel Hill: University of North Carolina Press, 1997), 93–95. For James Armstrong Wilson (apparently no relation to James Wilson), see Mary Jane Seymour, *Lineage Book* (Washington, D.C.: Daughters of the American Revolution, 1896), 310.

4. *DHRC*, 672 (quotes), see also 671–73, 674–78.

5. Cornell, *Other Founders*, 110.

6. For the influence of popular protest and public demonstrations on Pennsylvania and early national political culture, see Terry Bouton, *Taming Democracy: "The People," the Founders, and the Struggle over the American Revolution* (New York: Oxford University Press, 2007), chap. 7; Paul Douglas Newman, *Fries's Rebellion: The Enduring Struggle for the American Revolution* (Philadelphia: University of Pennsylvania Press, 2004), chaps. 1 and 3; Newman, *Parades and the Politics*, chap. 1; Waldstreicher, *Midst of Perpetual Fetes*, chaps. 1 and 2, esp. 93–103.

7. David Duncan to William Irvine, December 12, 1786, Irvine Papers, 9:50 (quote). For more about Pennsylvania's postwar economy and politics, see Bouton, *Taming Democracy*, chap. 4.

8. Tax Rates, Carlisle, 1779, 1787. In 1779, Carlisle taxpayers (224 total) owned 426 livestock (cattle and horses) and forty-two slaves. By 1787, taxpayers (225 total) owned only 407 livestock and thirty-two slaves. For the text of Pennsylvania's Gradual Abolition Law, see Pennsylvania State Archives, Doc Heritage, "An Act for the Gradual Abolition of Slavery, March 1, 1780," http://www.docheritage.state.pa.us/documents/slaveryabolition.asp (31 October 2008).

9. Robert G. Crist, "Cumberland County" in *Beyond Philadelphia: The American Revolution in the Pennsylvania Hinterland*, ed. John B. Frantz and William Pencak (University Park: Pennsylvania State University Press, 1998), 107. See also Brunhouse, *Counter-Revolution*, 114; Flower and Flower, *This Is Carlisle*, 30.

10. Gordon S. Wood, *The Creation of American Republic, 1776–1787* (Chapel Hill: University of North Carolina Press, 1969; reprint, New York: W. W. Norton, 1972), chaps. 10–13.

11. Bouton, *Taming Democracy*, 51–57; Brunhouse, *Counter-Revolution*, 88; Randall M. Miller and William Pencak, eds., *Pennsylvania: A History of the Commonwealth*, (University Park: Pennsylvania State University Press, 2002). *Pennsylvania: A History*, 101–4, 121–51; Wood, *Creation of American Republic*, 83–90, 333–40, 438–53.

12. Brunhouse, *Counter-Revolution*, 120, 221–27; David W. Robson, "College Founding in the New Republic, 1776–1800," *HEQ* 23.3 (1983): 323–25.

13. Benjamin Rush, *Letters of Benjamin Rush*, ed. L.H. Butterfield, 2 vols. (Princeton, N.J.: Princeton University Press, 1951), 1:292 (first quote), 294 (second quote).

14. Rush, *Letters*, 1:292.

15. Brunhouse, *Counter-Revolution*, 77–79; Robson, "College Founding," 323–26; Charles C. Sellers, *Dickinson College: A History* (Middletown, Conn.: Wesleyan University Press, 1973), 28–33.

16. Sellers, ibid., 27, 48–49.

17. Rush and Montgomery were an interesting pair. Montgomery was a former Old Light Presbyterian. Rush was at the beginning of a spiritual transformation that would lead him to Episcopalianism by the late 1780s, but in 1782 he desperately wanted Dickinson College to stand as a bulwark against the theologically liberal College of New Jersey. For information about the two and their goals, see Rush, *Letters*, 1:294; see also David F. Hawke, *Benjamin Rush, Revolutionary Gadfly* (Indianapolis: Bobbs-Merrill, 1971), 234–36, 250–53, 259–61, 283–86; James H. Morgan, *Dickinson College: The History of One Hundred and Fifty Years, 1783–1933* (Carlisle, Pa.: Dickinson College, 1933), 7–8; Sellers, *Dickinson College*, 4, 27–33, 43–49.

18. Brunhouse, *Counter-Revolution*, 121–24.

19. Sellers, *Dickinson College*, 32–33, 52–58.

20. Rush, *Letters*, 1:294–95. He also argued that the college would boost land prices around Carlisle, much as the College of New Jersey had done near Princeton. See ibid., 1:297.

21. *Charter of Dickinson College With its Supplements* (Baltimore: William K. Boyle and Sons, 1874), 3.

22. Ibid., 3.

23. Rush, *Letters*, 1:337 (quotes); see also 1:294–96; Hawke, *Benjamin Rush*, 286. For another Rush critique of the Scots-Irish, see Benjamin Rush, "Dr. Benjamin Rush's Journal of a Trip to Carlisle in 1784," *PMHB* 74.4 (1950), 450–51.

24. Rush, *Letters*, 1:353 (quote "enlightened"), 1:336–37 (other quotes). Franklin College, founded in Lancaster in 1787, targeted Pennsylvania's Germans more specifically. See Robson, "College Founding," 324–27.

25. John Montgomery to Benjamin Franklin, December, 6, 1785, *The Papers of Benjamin Franklin* (CD-ROM version at Library Company of Philadelphia, originals at Yale University), 43:u588.

26. Rush, *Letters*, 1:314 (quote "immense"); 1:316 (quote "key").

27. Brunhouse, *Counter-Revolution*, 140–47; Hawke, *Benjamin Rush*, 285–90; Sellers, *Dickinson College*, 51–62.

28. Rush, *Letters*, 1:335 (quote); Hawke, *Benjamin Rush*, 297, 299–302.

29. Sellers, *Dickinson College*, 6, 58–62. See also Edward W. Biddle, *The Founding and Founders of Dickinson College* (Carlisle, Pa.: n.p., 1920), 3–4.

30. Bouton, *Taming Democracy*, 175; Sellers, *Dickinson College*, 61, 66, 91. The trustees even tried to raise funds in London. See William Bingham to John Montgomery, August 10, 1783, Founders Collection, DCA. For more about the college's precarious finances, see Montgomery to Franklin, December 6, 1785, *Franklin Papers*, 43:u588.

31. For the buildings, see Rush, *Letters*, 1:352. See also Hawke, *Benjamin Rush*, 301; Sellers, *Dickinson College*, 78, 88–91; William Irvine to Robert Magaw, July 28, 1787,

Letters of Delegates to Congress, 1774–1789, ed. Paul H. Smith and Ronald M. Gephart, 26 vols. (Washington, D.C.: Library of Congress, 1996), 24:376. For the curriculum, see Robson, "College Founding," 327–28.

32. Rush, *Letters*, 1:320 (esp. note 6 for Davidson), 1:353. For Ross and Nisbet, see Hawke, *Benjamin Rush*, 296, 301, 307; Sellers, *Dickinson College*, 30, 66, 73. See also David W. Robson, "Enlightening the Wilderness: Charles Nisbet's Failure at Higher Education in Post-Revolutionary Pennsylvania," *HEQ* 37.3 (1997): 273. For more on Nisbet, see *Encyclopedia Dickinsonia*, http://chronicles.dickinson.edu/encyclo/n/ed_nisbetC. htm (10 October 2008).

33. Rush, *Letters*, 1:356 (quote "moving library); 1: 323 (quote "new born"). For Rush's invitation to Nisbet, see 1:315–16.

34. Samuel Miller, *Memoir of the Rev. Charles Nisbet, DD, Late President of Dickinson College, Carlisle* (New York: Robert Carter, 1840), 137 (quote). See also Charles Nisbet to Benjamin Rush, July 18, 1785, Charles Nisbet Papers, Founders Collection, DCA; Hawke, *Benjamin Rush*, 312–14; Robson, "Enlightening the Wilderness," 273–74. For the importance of July 4th celebrations on the political culture of the early republic, see Newman, *Parades and the Politics*, chap. 3; William Pencak, "Introduction: A Historical Perspective," in *Riot and Revelry in Early America*, ed. William Pencak and others (University Park: Pennsylvania State University Press, 2002), 3–20; Waldstreicher, *Midst of Perpetual Fetes*, chap. 1.

35. Rush, *Letters*, 1:357.

36. For "hogpen," see Sellers, *Dickinson College*, 113; see also 73, 86; Rush, *Letters*, 1:373; Hawke, *Benjamin Rush*, 313–14. For Nisbet's side of the story, see Robson, "Enlightening the Wilderness," 273–79.

37. For his resignation, see Charles Nisbet to Benjamin Rush, August 18, 1785, Nisbet Papers, DCA. See also Rev. Robert Davidson, "A Brief State of the College of Carlisle—for publication—given by the Trustees of the Same," 1791, DCA; Rush, *Letters*, 1:323.

38. *Memoir of Nisbet*, 139.

39. Rush, *Letters*, 1:369 (quote "machine"), 376 (quote "insane"). See also 1:373–74; Hawke, *Benjamin Rush*, 314–16. After Nisbet's return to Scotland was delayed, his health and that of his family recovered and he reconsidered his decision, see *Encyclopedia Dickinsonia*, http://chronicles.dickinson.edu/encyclo/n/ed_nisbetC.htm (22 July 2008).

40. Rush, *Letters*, 1:379 (quote); Sellers, *Dickinson College*, 86–87, 91.

41. Davidson, "A Brief State."

42. Rush, *Letters*, 1:350–51.

43. For the newspaper's first issue, see *CG*, August 10, 1785. For Kline, see "George Kline, Pioneer Journalist," Lamberton Prize Essays (Carlisle, Pa.: Cornman Printing Co., 1938), 5; United States, *U.S. Direct Tax of 1798, Tax Lists for the State of Pennsylvania, Sixth District Tax Division* (Washington, D.C.: National Archives Microfilm Publications, M-372), reel 17. For Kline and the other printers and booksellers in town, see *CG*, May 2, 1792; April 8, 1795; September 9, 1795; September 30, 1795; March 14, 1798; March 21, 1798; Tax Rates, Carlisle, 1780s; Merri Lou Schaumann, *A History and Genealogy of*

Carlisle, Cumberland County, Pennsylvania, 1751–1835 (Dover, Pa.: M. L. Schaumann, 1987), 170–74.

44. Flower and Flower, *This is Carlisle*, 30. For the mail stage, see also *CG*, May 14, 1794; May 1, 1799.

45. Abraham Steiner, 1789, in *Thirty Thousand Miles with John Heckewelder*, ed. Paul A. Wallace (Pittsburgh: University of Pittsburgh Press, 1958), 236.

46. Commonwealth of Pennsylvania, *Pennsylvania Septennial Census, 1779–1863*, PHMC, Cumberland County Returns, 1793, 1800; for the 1807 return, see Schaumann, *History and Genealogy*, 170–74. These three censuses identified an average of 409 individuals. Of those, nearly half (48 percent) were craftsmen. For more on these statistics, see Judith A. Ridner, "'A Handsomely Improved Place': Economic, Social, and Gender-Role Development in a Backcountry Town, Carlisle, Pennsylvania, 1750–1810" (Ph.D. diss., College of William & Mary, 1994), 159.

47. *Septennial Census Returns*, 1793, 1800; Schaumann, *History and Genealogy*, 170–74; see also Ridner, "Handsomely Improved Place," 160–63. According to occupational censuses, barkeepers, tavern keepers, merchants, and shopkeepers accounted for an average of just over 11 percent of the town's workforce.

48. Brooke Hunter, "The Prospect of Independent Americans: The Grain Trade and Economic Development during the 1780s," *Explorations in Early American Culture* 5 (2001): 260–87.

49. Anonymous Account Book #1, 1789–1790, in the Hamilton Papers, HSP. This daybook, although from an unidentified Carlisle dry goods merchant and grocer, may have belonged to merchant Joseph Givin, who operated a store in town from approximately 1788 until his death in 1791. My statistics are taken from the first seven months of the book, June–December 1789. For more information on miller Charles McClure, see Tax Rates, Middleton Township, 1795, CCHS. McClure owned five parcels of land totaling 1,388 acres, a grist mill, and saw mill.

50. Le Compte de Colbert Maulevrier, 1794, in Thompson, *Two Hundred Years*, 90.

51. Anonymous Account Book #1, Hamilton Papers, HSP.

52. *CG*, May 21, 1788.

53. Anonymous Account Book #1, in the Hamilton Papers, HSP.

54. Samuel Postlethwaite Ledger, 1760–1778, in Hamilton Papers, HSP. Between 1774 and 1778, 28 percent of his accounts were settled with cash and 38 percent with produce, goods, or services; the rest (34 percent) remained unpaid. By contrast, in Anonymous Account Book #1, in the Hamilton Papers, HSP, between June–December 1789, 24 percent of this merchant's accounts were settled with cash and 58 percent in produce, goods, or services. Thus, a remarkable 82 percent of his accounts were paid.

55. Robert Peebles, Resignation Letter, October 9, 1783, "Appointments: Political," PA Rev Gov't, 33.1907 (quotes). For postwar economic scarcity, see Bouton, *Taming Democracy*, chap. 4.

56. For Carlisle's coopers, see *Septennial Census Returns*, 1793, 1800; for 1807, see Schaumann, *History and Genealogy*, 170–74. Coopers increased from under 1 percent

(seven individuals) to almost 3 percent (eleven individuals) of the town's workforce between 1793 and 1807—see Ridner, "Handsomely Improved Place," 164. See also Hunter, "Prospect of Independent Americans," 275, who discusses how the grain trade fostered the growth of other occupations.

57. For these tradesmen, see *Septennial Census Returns*, 1793, 1800; for 1807, see Schaumann, *History and Genealogy*, 170–74. I include bluedyers, breeches makers, hatters, heel makers, hosiers, reed makers, seamstresses, shoemakers, stocking weavers, tailors, and weavers in this category—see Ridner, "Handsomely Improved Place," 160.

58. *CG*, November 18, 1795 (quote). For the weaving trades in Pennsylvania, see Adrienne Hood, "Organization and Extent of Textile Manufacture in Eighteenth-Century Rural Pennsylvania: A Case Study of Chester County" (Ph.D. diss., University of California, San Diego, 1988).

59. For Gribble, see *CG*, November 25, 1801; see also September 25, 1799. For M'Cann, see ibid., October 19, 1804. For Miller, see ibid., August 31, 1796. For the fulling trade, see Hood, "Organization and Extent of Textile Manufacture," 157–74; Rolla M. Tryon, *Household Manufactures in the United States, 1640–1860* (New York: A. M. Kelley, 1917; reprint 1966), 249.

60. William West Wastebook #1, West Papers, 323–24, 334–35, 339–40, 478.

61. For the purchase of raw cotton and additional cotton and wool cards, see Anonymous Account Book #1, in the Hamilton Papers, HSP; see also John Henry Goeble, Estate Inventory, December 11, 1801, Cumberland County Estate Inventories, CCHS. When Goeble, a merchant, died, there were three pairs of cotton cards listed in the inventory of his store. For M'Bride, see *CG*, November 18, 1795.

62. For a broader discussion of the changes affecting postwar textile production, see Curtis P. Nettels, *The Emergence of a National Economy, 1775–1815* (New York: Holt, Rinehart, and Winston, 1962), 274–77.

63. For Biggs, see *CG*, October 19, 1785, April 19, 1786; for Petrikin, see ibid., September 7, 1785; for Murray, see ibid., April 22, 1795.

64. *CG*, April 22, 1795.

65. For Biggs, see *CG*, October 19, 1785; for Shuler, see ibid., October 4, 1797.

66. For Stuart, see *CG*, November 3, 1790; for M'Cormick, see ibid., August 20, 1788.

67. For women as consumers, see Timothy H. Breen, "An Empire of Goods: The Anglicization of Colonial America, 1690–1776," *Journal of British Studies* 25.4 (1986): 489, 493; Timothy H. Breen, *The Marketplace of Revolution: How Consumer Politics Shaped American Independence* (New York: Oxford University Press, 2004), chap. 6; Elizabeth Perkins, "The Consumer Frontier: Household Consumption in Early Kentucky," *JAH* 78.2 (1991): 495; Barbara Clark Smith, "Food Rioters and the American Revolution," *WMQ* 3rd ser., 51.1 (1994): 3–38.

68. According to *Septennial Census Returns*, between 1793 and 1807 women accounted for an average of nearly 5 percent of Carlisle's workforce; those I have been able to identify represented a range of ages and economic circumstances. For more details, see Ridner, "Handsomely Improved Place," 209–19. Storekeeper/merchant Susannah

Thompson arrived in Carlisle in 1793 as the forty-six-year-old widow of Parson Thompson of Maryland and New Jersey. She soon set up a dry goods and grocery store that retailed largely to women. In 1798, she left the business, selling the contents of her store to another merchant for £638; she died in 1801. See *CG*, April 3, 1793; March 20, 1793; June 26, 1793; June 11, 1794; February 11, 1795; and her obituary March 4, 1801. See also John Oliver Account Book, 1798, HSP, which includes an account of what he "Bought of Susannah Thompson." Tavern keeper Elizabeth Vanlear, another widow, assumed control of her husband Christopher's tavern business upon his death in 1783 and maintained it for several decades. In 1789, a Mrs. Griskey was running a school for "Young Ladies" out of her tavern, suggesting it was a female-friendly place—see *CG*, August 26, 1789. For more about Vanlear and her husband Christopher, see Tavern Licenses, Tax Rates; see also the administrative accounts of Christopher Vanlear's estate, Cumberland County, Orphan's Court, Docket Book #3, CCHS, 1, 12; for his tavern, see Christopher VanLear, VanLear Daybook, 1767–1783, Winterthur Library, Wilmington, Del.

69. *CG*, September 7, 1785 (quote). In "Empire of Goods," 493, Breen notes that in an age when marketing became increasingly aggressive, the "eighteenth-century shopkeeper ignored women at his peril."

70. *CG*, September 7, 1796 (first quote), April 3, 1799 (second quote). Jacob Hendel is regarded as one of the region's finest eighteenth-century artisans. See Milton E. Flower, "The Hendel Brothers," in *Made in Cumberland County: The First Hundred Years, 1750–1850* (Carlisle, Pa.: Cumberland County Historical Association, 1991), 12–15.

71. For Dubuisson, see *CG*, April 13, 1810; for Peticoles, see ibid., June 29, 1796; for Balentine, see ibid., September 5, 1792.

72. Samuel Hay to John Agnew, October 8, 1785, John Agnew Papers, CCHS.

73. My observations are based on *Septennial Census Returns* and advertisements in the *Carlisle Gazette*.

74. For Mattheis, see *CG*, April 1, 1789. For Bullock, see ibid., January 18, 1797; April 11, 1798; November 10, 1802; February 15, 1804; and December 6, 1805. For Graham, see ibid., March 3, 1802; and February 22, 1804. Graham's entrepreneurial activity may be explained by the unexpected death of his wife. As the *Gazette* reported on October 26, 1803, Margaret Graham, his wife, had died in childbirth, leaving "behind her a husband and six small children to bewail her loss."

75. For physicians running apothecary shops, see *CG*, September 12, 1792; November 1, 1805; May 30, 1806; and October 24, 1806. For Holmes, see ibid., November 18, 1789. For Webber, see ibid., August 1, 1787; November 19, 1794; and November 25, 1795. For Moser, see ibid., April 20, 1803. For Bovard, see ibid., May 16, 1792; August 21, 1793; July 7, 1802; and May 8, 1807.

76. For Criswell, see *CG*, May 30, 1798; for Foulke, see ibid., March 26, 1788; for Crouse, see ibid., October 30, 1793.

77. For Hanna, see *CG*, April 25, 1798; and August 10, 1803. For Gray, see ibid., May 26, 1802; and April 5, 1805.

78. Douglass C. North, *The Economic Growth of the United States, 1790–1860* (New York: W. W. Norton and Company, 1961; reprint, 1966), 159; see also Bruce Laurie,

Working People of Philadelphia, 1800–1850 (Philadelphia: Temple University Press, 1980), 15, 20.

79. *CG*, May 30, 1787.

80. Charles Nisbet to Charles Wallace, September 2, 1790, "Dr. Nisbet's Views of American Society," Nisbet Papers, DCA.

81. Bouton, *Taming Democracy*, chap. 9; Jack D. Marietta and G.S. Rowe, *Troubled Experiment: Crime and Justice in Pennsylvania, 1682–1800* (Philadelphia: University of Pennsylvania Press, 2006), chap. 7.

82. Between 1753 and 1764, the town's taxable population had a persistence rate of 44 percent. Between 1768 and 1779, the persistence rate dropped slightly to 41 percent. By contrast, between 1782 and 1795, persistence rates dropped to 33 percent. Although they recovered between 1795 and 1808, when persistence rates returned to 43 percent, these figures suggest that there was a major out-migration in the decade following the war. See Tax Rates, Carlisle, 1750–1810; Ridner, "Handsomely Improved Place," 80.

83. Pension Application of Philip Hornbaker, Pension Applications, reel 119.27.

84. Pension Application of John Tate, ibid., reel 2343.S32007.

85. Pension Applications of Robert Thompson, ibid., reel 2378.S3800; William Alexander, ibid., reel 30.W9697; John Torrence Application, ibid., reel 2400.S6257.

86. Nisbet, "Dr. Nisbet's Views," DCA.

87. Rush, *Letters*, 1:295.

88. *Memoir of Charles Nisbet*, 143 (quotes "torpid state," "private interest," "ruinous practice"); 167 (quotes "new attachment" and "new world").

89. John Armstrong to Benjamin Franklin, December 25, 1787, *Franklin Papers*, 45:u327 (quote); see also *DHRC*, 648–49.

90. Stephen Duncan to William Irvine, October 3, 1787, Irvine Papers, 9:98 (quote); see also Brunhouse, *Counter-Revolution*, 332.

91. Armstrong to Franklin, *Franklin Papers*, 45:u327; *DHRC*, 649.

92. Duncan to Irvine, Irvine Papers, 9:98.

93. Federalists had only 15 percent support in Cumberland County in 1787–1788. See Ireland, *Religion, Ethnicity, and Politics*, 192–96, esp. 195.

94. *DHRC*, 675.

95. Cornell, "Aristocracy Assailed," 1152–55 (includes quote); see also Ireland, *Religion, Ethnicity, and Politics*, 110–12; Bouton, *Taming Democracy*, 176–88.

96. Charles Nisbet to Benjamin Rush, January 30, 1786, Nisbet Papers, DCA.

97. *DHRC*, 672–73 (quotes); Waldstreicher, *Midst of Perpetual Fetes*, 97.

98. John Penn, "John Penn's Journal of a Visit to Reading, Harrisburg, Carlisle, and Lancaster, in 1788," *PMHB* 3.3 (1879): 292 (quote); Bouton, *Taming Democracy*, 185.

99. *DHRC*, 678.

100. Cornell, *The Other Founders*, 116 (quote), see also 114–16; Cornell, "Aristocracy Assailed," 1152, 1160–64; Waldstreicher, *Midst of Perpetual Fetes*, 97.

101. Ireland, *Religion, Ethnicity, and Politics*, 182–86, 211–16.

102. Penn, "John Penn's Journal," 292.

103. *DHRC*, 672 (for quotes); see also 680.

104. Ibid., 672.

105. Ibid., 677; see also Waldstreicher, *Midst of Perpetual Fetes*, 96.

106. Bouton, *Taming Democracy*, 186.

107. John Montgomery to William Irvine, January 9, 1788, Irvine Papers, 9:113.

108. *DHRC*, 678 (quotes); see also Waldstreicher, *Midst of Perpetual Fetes*, 95.

109. *DHRC*, 673–74 (for quotes "vain" and "foolishness"), 681 (for "rabble").

110. Rush, *Letters*, 1:456.

111. Antoine Saugrain de Vigni, July 17, 1788, *Dr. Saugrain's Note-books, 1788*; . . . , ed., Eugene Bliss (Worcester, Mass.: Davis Press, 1909), 20.

112. Nisbet, "Views of America," 83 (quote "Rabble"); *Memoir of Nisbet*, 170–71 (second quote).

113. Waldstreicher, *Midst of Perpetual Fetes*, 98.

114. Rush, *Letters*, 1:456.

115. Ibid.

CHAPTER 6. ADAPTING TO THE NEXT CENTURY

1. F. A. Michaux, "Travels to the West of the Allegheny Mountains . . . in the Year 1802," in *Early Western Travels, 1748–1846*, ed. Reuben Gold Thwaites, 32 vols. (Cleveland: Arthur H. Clark Company, 1904), 3:139 (quote "respectable"); Colonel William Eyre, "Colonel Eyre's Journal of His Trip from New York to Pittsburgh, 1762," ed. Frances R. Reece, *WPHM* 27.1 & 2 (1944): 40 (quote "Stand"); *CG*, December 22, 1802 (quotes "pleasure" and "improving"); Samuel Hay to John Agnew, October 8, 1785, John Agnew Papers, CCHS (quote "flourishing"); James Ford, "To the West on Business in 1804: An Account, with Excerpts from his Journal, of James Ford's Trip to Kentucky in 1804," ed. Bayard Still, *PMHB* 64.1 (1940): 7 (quote "handsome").

2. For Carlisle's size, see United States Census Office, *Return of the Whole Number of Persons Within the Several Districts of the United States: Second Census*, National Archives, Washington, D.C., microfilm. For its rank in the state, see *The Atlas of Pennsylvania*, ed. David J. Cuff and others (Philadelphia: Temple University Press, 1989), 108; James T. Lemon, *The Best Poor Man's Country: A Geographical Study of Early Southeastern Pennsylvania* (Baltimore: Johns Hopkins University Press, 1972), 120–21; Harry M. Tinkcom, *The Republicans and Federalists in Pennsylvania, 1790–1801: A Study in National Stimulus and Local Response* (Harrisburg: Pennsylvania Historical and Museum Commission, 1950), 20.

3. *CG*, December 22, 1802 (quotes "handsome," "spacious"); Rev. Robert Davidson, "A Brief State of the College at Carlisle," 1791, DCA (quote "large"). See also Fortescue Cuming, "Sketches of a Tour to the Western Country . . ." in *Early Western Travels*, 2:48, who offered similar descriptions. For more about Carlisle's infrastructure circa 1800, see George P. Donehoo, *A History of the Cumberland Valley in Pennsylvania*, 2 vols. (Harrisburg, Pa.: Susquehanna History Association, 1930), 1:437–70.

4. I. Daniel Rupp, *The History and Topography of Dauphin, Cumberland, Franklin,*

Bedford, Adams, and Perry Counties (Lancaster, Pa.: Gilbert Hills, 1846), 414–16; Charles C. Sellers, *Dickinson College: A History* (Middletown, Conn.: Wesleyan University Press, 1973), 110–11.

5. For evidence of this boom, see *CG*, December 22, 1800; Cumberland County, Pennsylvania, Commissioner's Minutes, PHMC.

6. *United States Direct Tax of 1798, Tax Lists for the State of Pennsylvania*, Schedules A and B, National Archives, Washington, D.C., microcopy #372, reel 17. According to Paul Douglas Newman, *Fries's Rebellion: The Enduring Struggle for the American Revolution* (Philadelphia: University of Pennsylvania Press, 2004), ix, the 1798 tax was "a levy on lands, dwelling houses, and slaves." Although it assessed dwellings progressively, many farmers opposed it because it favored speculators by assessing cultivated farmland at higher rates than uncultivated land. For more about this tax, see also Lee Soltow, *Distribution of Wealth and Income in the United States in 1798* (Pittsburgh: University of Pittsburgh Press, 1989), chap. 2. According to Soltow, assessed values represented about 85 percent of market value.

7. Theophile Cazenove, *Cazenove Journal 1794: A Record of the Journey of Theophile Cazenove Through New Jersey and Pennsylvania*, ed. Rayner W. Kelsey (Harrisburg, Pa.: Aurand Press, 1922), 56 (quote "neatly"); Manasseh Cutler, August 3, 1788, "Journal of Rev. Manasseh Cutler of a Journey from Ipswich, Massachusetts to the Muskingum, in 1788," in William P. Cutler and Julia P. Cutler, eds., *Life, Journals and Correspondence of Rev. Manasseh Cutler, LL.D.*, 2 vols. (Cincinnati: Robert Clarke and Company, 1888), 1:401 (quote "tolerable"); Benjamin Rush, "Dr. Benjamin Rush's Journal of a Trip to Carlisle in 1784," ed. L. H. Butterfield, *PMHB* 74.4 (1950): 453 (quote "large").

8. My analysis in this chapter draws on a voluminous literature detailing the multiple "revolutions" taking place in the consumer economy and housing between 1750 and 1820. See, for example, Stuart M. Blumin, *The Emergence of the Middle Class: Social Experience in the American City, 1760–1900* (New York: Cambridge University Press, 1989) chaps. 1–2; Richard L. Bushman, *The Refinement of America: Persons, Houses, Cities* (New York: Alfred A. Knopf, 1992; Vintage Books, 1993), chaps. 7–12; Cary Carson, "The Consumer Revolution in Colonial British America: Why Demand?" in *Of Consuming Interests: The Style of Life in the Eighteenth Century*, ed. Cary Carson and others (Charlottesville: University Press of Virginia, 1994), 483–697; Edward Chappell, "Housing a Nation: The Transformation of Living Standards in Early America," in ibid., 167–232; John E. Crowley, "The Sensibility of Comfort," *AHR* 104.3 (1999): 749–82; Bernard L. Herman, *Architecture and Rural Life in Central Delaware, 1700–1900* (Knoxville: University of Tennessee Press, 1987) 84–88, 109–13; Gabrielle M. Lanier and Bernard L. Herman, *Everyday Architecture of the Mid-Atlantic: Looking at Buildings and Landscapes* (Baltimore: Johns Hopkins University Press, 1997) 4–8.

9. Tax Rates, Carlisle, 1779, 1795, 1808. All figures have been rounded to the nearest tenth, thus not all totals equal 100 percent. For more information, see Judith A. Ridner, " 'A Handsomely Improved Place': Economic, Social, and Gender-Role Development in a Backcountry Town, Carlisle, Pennsylvania, 1750–1810" (Ph.D. diss., College of William & Mary, 1994), 374–77.

10. *Direct Tax of 1798*. The data set analyzed here includes all properties from Schedule A (properties with values of $100 or more) as well as those properties from Schedule B that included dwelling houses.

11. For Lancaster, see Jerome H. Wood Jr., *Conestoga Crossroads: Lancaster, Pennsylvania, 1730–1790* (Harrisburg: Pennsylvania Historical and Museum Commission, 1979), 166–73; for Philadelphia, see Billy G. Smith, *The "Lower Sort": Philadelphia's Laboring People, 1750–1800* (Ithaca: Cornell University Press, 1990), 84–91.

12. Carl Lounsbury, "The Structure of Justice: The Courthouses of Colonial Virginia," in *Perspectives in Vernacular Architecture, III*, ed. Thomas Carter and Bernard Herman (Columbia: University of Missouri Press, 1989), 216 (quote). See also Bernard L. Herman, *Town House: Architecture and Material Life in the Early American City, 1780–1830* (Chapel Hill: University of North Carolina Press, 2005), 5, who notes that cities were also sites of tension between "urban disorder and regularity."

13. For the coarseness and simplicity of ordinary housing during the early republic, see Chappell, "Housing a Nation," 167–232; Herman, *Architecture and Rural Life*, 84–88; Camille Wells, "The Planter's Prospect: Houses, Outbuildings, and Rural Landscapes in Eighteenth-Century Virginia," *Winterthur Portfolio* (1993): 1–31.

14. I calculated tenancy figures by comparing the surnames of owners and occupants on the Direct Tax. Of the 298 properties enumerated, 128 (43 percent) were occupied by tenants. See *Direct Tax of 1798*, Schedules A and selections from Schedule B. Of thirty-four identifiable female occupants of the town's houses, ten resided in the twenty-nine lowest-valued properties. By contrast, no women occupied any of the twenty-nine highest-valued structures. Overall, women occupied nineteen of the town's 128 rental properties, accounting for 14 percent of the town's tenant population.

15. Cazenove, *Cazenove Journal 1794*, 62.

16. Pension Application of James Hutton, June 20, 1820, Revolutionary War Pension Applications, 1820–1834, Clerk of Court, Cumberland County, Orphan's Court, loose papers, CCHS (quote); for the value and description of his house, see *Direct Tax of 1798*, Schedule A. Housing conditions among Carlisle's lower sorts resembled those Philadelphia laboring families, see Smith, *"Lower Sort,"* chap. 6.

17. *CG*, August, 1, 1806.

18. Rush, "Dr. Rush's Journal," 451.

19. Ibid; see also note 34. For more on Pollock, see Merri Lou Schaumann, *Taverns of Cumberland County, Pennsylvania, 1750–1840* (Carlisle, Pa.: Cumberland County Historical Society, 1994), 30–32.

20. For Armstrong, see Robert G. Crist, "John Armstrong: Proprietor's Man" (Ph.D. diss., Pennsylvania State University, 1981), 213–24; for Wilson, see Dickinson College, "Encyclopedia Dickinsonia, Board of Trustees, Members Index, 1783–2000," http://chronicles.dickinson.edu/encyclo/w/ed_wilsonJ.htm (12 May 2009); for Montgomery, see ibid., http://chronicles.dickinson.edu/encyclo/m/ed_montgomeryJ.htm (19 Sept 2008); and Merri Lou Schaumann, *A History and Genealogy of Carlisle, Cumberland County, Pennsylvania, 1751–1835* (Dover, Pa.: M. L. Schaumann, 1987), 214. For Irvine, see Kenneth W. Keller, *Rural Politics and the Collapse of Pennsylvania Federalism* (Phila-

delphia: American Philosophical Society, 1982), 29; and Nicholas Wainwright, *The Irvine Story* (Philadelphia: HSP, 1964), 13.

21. John Heckewelder, "Notes of Travel of William Henry, John Heckewelder, John Rothrock, and Christian Clewell, to Gnadenhuetten on the Muskingum, in the Early Summer of 1797," ed. John Jordan, *PMHB* 10.2 (1886): 128.

22. John King to Rev. Robert Davidson, November 25, 1802, Presbyterian Historical Society, Philadelphia, Pennsylvania (first quote); Anonymous, "A Garrison Town in Pennsylvania Fifty Years Ago," n.d., HSP, 3 (second quote). For broader discussions of how early American cultural leaders set themselves apart from their less-privileged neighbors, see Bushman, *Refinement of America*, chap. 12; Carson, "Consumer Revolution," 505–689.

23. Rush, "Dr. Rush's Journal," 452 (quotes). For the family background of Carlisle's leading women, see Gertrude Bosler Biddle, *Notable Women of Pennsylvania* (Philadelphia: University of Pennsylvania Press, 1942). For the many Carlisle families who sent their sons to Dickinson College during the early republic, see George Leffinwell Reed, ed., *Alumni Record: Dickinson College* (Carlisle, Pa.: Dickinson College, 1905), 38–57. Before 1810, 31 percent of the College's graduates came from Cumberland County; see Ridner, "Handsomely Improved Place," 417–20. For discussions of rising class consciousness in America's coastal communities, see Blumin, *Emergence of the Middle Class*, chap. 1; Bushman, *Refinement of America*, 166–69, 231–37; Stephanie G. Wolf, *As Various as Their Land: The Everyday Lives of Eighteenth-Century Americans* (New York: Harper-Collins, 1993), 268–77.

24. For houses as symbolic representations, see Herman, *Town House*, chaps. 1 and 3, esp. p. 2. See also Bushman, *Refinement of America*, chap. 4; Rhys Isaac, *The Transformation of Virginia, 1740–1790* (Chapel Hill: University of North Carolina Press, 1982), chaps. 2 and 4; Susan Mackiewicz, "Philadelphia Flourishing: The Material World of Philadelphians, 1682–1760" (Ph.D. diss., University of Delaware, 1988), 213–15; Kevin M. Sweeney, "High-Style Vernacular: Lifestyles of the Colonial Elite," in *Of Consuming Interests*, 2–5. For Cumberland County particularly, see Nancy Van Dolsen, *Cumberland County: An Architectural Survey* (Carlisle, Pa.: Cumberland County Historical Society, 1990), 2.

25. *Direct Tax of 1798*, Schedule A.

26. Van Dolsen, *Cumberland County: Architectural Survey*, 3 (quote), 76–88. Van Dolsen's chapter on Federal-era Carlisle offers an in-depth analysis of several of Carlisle's extant brick structures. Van Dolsen also offers analysis of the Direct Tax of 1798 (based only on Schedule A, however). Her calculations show that Carlisle's homes had the largest average plan size of any in the county; nearly two-thirds were two stories. In Carlisle, the average plan size was 1,275 square feet. Contrast this with surrounding Middleton Township, where the average plan size was 614 square feet and most were only one or one-half stories; see pp. 3, 77.

27. The *Direct Tax of 1798*, Schedule A, shows that twenty-six of Carlisle's twenty-nine highest-valued properties (the top 10 percent) had separate kitchens. Of those, nineteen were built of stone, four of brick, and three of wood.

28. For the function and social significance of detached kitchens, see Herman, *Architecture and Rural Life*, chap. 2. See also Lanier and Herman, *Everyday Architecture*, 52–59; Wells, "Planter's Prospect," 1–31, esp. 15–16. Despite the state's gradual emancipation law, many Carlisle leading men still held slaves in 1798. According to the census of 1800, twenty of the owners of Carlisle's twenty-nine highest-valued properties in 1798 were slaveholders; nine owned nineteen slaves. See Bureau of the Census, *Return of the Whole Number of Persons Within the Several Districts of the United States: Second Census, Cumberland County, Pennsylvania* (Washington, D.C.: National Archives Microfilm Publication, M-593). For Montgomery's slaves, see Cumberland County Board of Commissioners, "Returns for Negro and Mulatto Slaves," PHMC, reel 5416. In 1780, Montgomery owned eight slaves, five of them women. For Montgomery's kitchen, see *Direct Tax of 1798*, Schedule A.

29. Chappell, "Housing a Nation," 168; Herman, *Town House*, chap. 3.

30. *Direct Tax of 1798*, Schedule A. For brick construction in Carlisle, see Van Dolsen, *Cumberland County: Architectural Survey*, p. 2 and chap. 5. For comparative perspectives, see Herman, *Town House*, 79, who found that approximately one-quarter of Lancaster's town houses were of brick construction in 1798. Easton, by contrast, did not see its first brick dwelling until 1792; see Liam Riordan, *Many Identities, One Nation: The Revolution and Its Legacy in the Mid-Atlantic* (Philadelphia: University of Pennsylvania Press, 2007), 107. For the continued use of stone construction, Lanier and Herman, *Everyday Architecture*, 70–71.

31. Van Dolsen, *Cumberland County: Architectural Survey*, 77–86, see esp. her analysis of the Robert Blaine and Thomas Foster houses.

32. Chappell, "Housing a Nation," 177–78 (quote); see also 183, 189. For the social meaning of brick structures, see also Herman, *Architecture and Rural Life*, 48, 112–13; Lanier and Herman, *Everyday Architecture*, 70–71, 97–99, 127–30; Mackiewicz, "Philadelphia Flourishing," 198–202, 213. For brick construction as an expression of the Federal style, see Wayne Andrews, *Architecture, Ambition, and Americans: A Social History of American Architecture* (New York: Free Press, 1947; rev. ed., 1978), 56–57; James M. Fitch, *American Building: The Forces that Shape It* (Boston: Houghton Mifflin Company, 1947), 25–26; Alan Gowans, *Styles and Types of North American Architecture* (New York: Icon Editions, 1992), 83; Ralph W. Hammett, *Architecture in the United States: A Survey of Architectural Styles Since 1776* (New York: John Wiley and Sons, 1976), 3–4, 10; Talbot Hamlin, *Greek Revival Architecture in America* (New York: Dover Publications, 1944), 3–9, 11–12, 23.

33. For brick makers and factories in Carlisle, see *Cazenove Journal 1794*, 60; Commonwealth of Pennsylvania, *Pennsylvania Septennial Census, 1779–1863*, PHMC, Cumberland County Returns, 1793.

34. For brick's artificiality, see Herman, *Town House*, chap. 3; Lanier and Herman, *Everyday Architecture*, 97–99; Van Dolsen, *Cumberland County: Architectural Survey*, chap. 5.

35. *Direct Tax of 1798*, Schedule B, entry for Abraham Hare. At the time of the 1798 assessment, only the walls had been built on Hare's new home, which measured a more

spacious 21 feet by 31 feet; For John Hunter, see ibid., Schedule A. For Hunter's advertisement for his tavern, see *CG*, November 18, 1801.

36. *Direct Tax of 1798*, Schedule A, entry for James Hamilton. For Hamilton's descriptions of his property, see *CG*, September 10, 1794. For the quote "lofty buildings," see Samuel A. McCoskrey to Dr. William McCoskrey, July 16, 1815, Founders Collection, DCA.

37. Edward Chappell, "Germans and Swiss," in *America's Architectural Roots*, ed. Dell Upton (Washington, D.C.: Preservation Press, 1986), 72 (quote); see also Chappell, "Housing a Nation," 167–232; Mackiewicz, "Philadelphia Flourishing," 5, 198, 213; Van Dolsen, *Cumberland County: Architectural Survey*, 76–88.

38. *CG*, January 29, 1794.

39. *CG*, December 8, 1802 (quotes). For Dickinson's history during this period, see Sellers, *Dickinson College*, 119–26.

40. John Montgomery to John Dickinson, November 20, 1805, Maria Dickinson Logan Family Papers, HSP.

41. Benjamin Henry Latrobe to Hugh Henry Brackenridge, May 18, 1803, in Founders Collection, DCA.

42. John Montgomery to John Dickinson, November 20, 1805, Maria Dickinson Logan Family Papers, HSP.

43. *Direct Tax of 1798*, Schedule A. Stone also remained the preferred construction material in many areas of the mid-Atlantic. See Herman, *Town House*, 21; Lanier and Herman, *Everyday Architecture*, 95.

44. William Irvine to John Rose, May 25, 1794, The Draper Manuscript Collection, DLAR, originals at State Historical Society of Wisconsin, reel 96:197 (quotes "neat" and "large"). In 1794, according to one traveler, "the fine farm of General Erwin [Irvine]," stood some three miles from Carlisle. "He has just had an excellent house built there." See *Cazenove Journal 1794*, 55.

45. Bushman, *Refinement of America*, chaps. 5 and 11; Kenneth W. Keller, *Rural Politics*, 11.

46. "An Act for Erecting the Town of Carlisle . . . into a Borough," passed April 13, 1782, *Statutes at Large*, 11:423–48 (quotes). For the tanners and distillers of northeast Carlisle, see Martha C. Slotten, *From St. James Square to Tannery Row: Carlisle's Old Northeast Side* (Carlisle, Pa.: Friends of the Bosler Free Library, 1982), 2–3. For the poorhouse, see Keller, *Rural Politics*, 11.

47. Charles Nisbet to Mary Turnball, November 8, 1793, June 1, 1799, Charles Nisbet Papers, DCA.

48. *CG*, December 11, 1793.

49. Terry Bouton, *Taming Democracy: "The People," the Founders, and the Struggle over the American Revolution* (New York: Oxford University Press, 2007), 225; Robert L. Brunhouse, *The Counter-Revolution in Pennsylvania, 1776–1790* (Harrisburg: Pennsylvania Historical and Museum Commission, 1942), 221–27; David W. Robson, "College Founding in the New Republic, 1776–1800," *HEQ* 23.3 (1983): 332–35; Sellers, *Dickinson College*, 118.

50. Keller, *Rural Politics*, 18.

51. Bouton, *Taming Democracy*, 219–22; Wainwright, *Irvine Story*, 2-11.

52. Bouton, *Taming Democracy*, 218–19. For histories of the Whiskey Rebellion, see Thomas P. Slaughter, *The Whiskey Rebellion: Frontier Epilogue to the American Revolution* (New York: Oxford University Press, 1986). See also Dorothy Elaine Fennell, "From Rebelliousness to Insurrection: A Social History of the Whiskey Rebellion, 1765–1802" (Ph.D. diss., University of Pittsburgh, 1981).

53. *Pennsylvania Archives 2*, 4:300 (quotes). See also the legal depositions pertaining to the "riot" in the Rawle Family Papers, Series I, The Papers of William Rawle Sr., 1778–1836, HSP, box 5. See also Slaughter, *Whiskey Rebellion*, 206–8.

54. Francis West Gibson, Deposition, Rawle Family Papers, box 5 (quotes); *Pennsylvania Archives 2*, 4:300; Slaughter, *Whiskey Rebellion*, 206–8.

55. Gibson Deposition, Rawle Family Papers, box 5 (quotes). See also the other depositions pertaining to the rebellion in this box, which reinforce Gibson's account. *Pennsylvania Archives 2*, 4:300; Slaughter, *Whiskey Rebellion*, 208.

56. John and Thomas Huling, Anthony Fearer, William Aitken, Francis West Gibson, George Rowan, Joseph Steel, James Dill, Depositions, Rawle Family Papers, box 5, HSP; Slaughter, *Whiskey Rebellion*, 206–12.

57. Scholars disagree on the class dimensions of this rebellion. Slaughter, *Whiskey Rebellion*, chap. 13, downplays class. Bouton, *Taming Democracy*, chap. 10, and Fennell, "From Rebelliousness to Insurrection," 142, by contrast, highlight it.

58. *Pennsylvania Archives 2,* 4:300.

59. Rev. Robert Davidson, *A Sermon on the Freedom and Happiness of the United States* (Philadelphia: Samuel Smith, 1794), 19, 24; Sellers, *Dickinson College*, 118–19; Slaughter, *Whiskey Rebellion*, 212–15.

60. Bouton, *Taming Democracy*, 242; Newman, *Fries's Rebellion*, 157; Slaughter, *Whiskey Rebellion*, 216–21.

61. Soltow, *Distribution of Wealth and Income*, 53, 77–78; *Direct Tax of 1798*, Schedules A and selections from B. According to Soltow, there were marked contrasts in property values between east and west in Pennsylvania.

62. For comparative discussions, see Carson, "Consumer Revolution," 638; Robert J. Gough, "The Philadelphia Economic Elite at the End of the Eighteenth Century," in *Shaping a National Culture: The Philadelphia Experience, 1750–1800*, ed. Catherine E. Hutchins (Winterthur, Del.: Henry Francis duPont Winterthur Museum, 1994), 15–44.

63. William Irvine to Callender Irvine, April 19, 1795, Founders Collection, DCA.

64. James Blaine to Ephraim Blaine, February 25, 1796, Ephraim Blaine Papers, General Correspondence, Library of Congress, Washington, D.C. For more about this trade, see Curtis P. Nettels, *The Emergence of a National Economy, 1775–1815* (New York: Holt, Rinehart, and Winston, 1962), 53–54, 209–16; Daniel H. Usner Jr., *Indians, Settlers, and Slaves in a Frontier Exchange Economy* (Chapel Hill: University of North Carolina Press, 1992), 105–6, 268–75.

65. Thomas Irwin to William Irvine, May 20, 1789, Irvine Papers, 10:28.

66. "Articles of Agreement for partnership between John and Charles Wilkins of

Pittsburgh and William Irvine," September 17, 1790, Irvine Papers, 10:69. Because John Wilkins was a tavern and storekeeper in Carlisle from 1763 to 1783, it is likely that he and Irvine were well acquainted.

67. Thomas Irwin to William Irvine, May 20, 1789, Irvine Papers, 10:28 (quotes). Both men knew that they were violating the spirit of the passports they had been issued. Irwin encouraged his brother to "get a few Familys [sic] to come down in the Boats, with a view of settling in the Natchez district." If he could not find such persons, then "the Boatmen must say when they arrive at the Natchez and this place [New Orleans] that they mean to settle themselves in this country." For more about the Natchez district during the early republic, see Martha Jane Brazy, *An American Planter: Stephen Duncan of Antebellum Natchez and New York* (Baton Rouge: Louisiana State University Press, 2006), 6–8.

68. John Postlethwaite to Samuel Postlethwaite, March 9, 1790, November 29, 1795, Samuel Postlethwaite Papers, CCHS; for the Natchez connection, see Brazy, *American Planter*, 9. See also Anonymous Account Book #3, Carlisle, June 1790–December 1792, 237, 250–53, 300, James Hamilton Papers, HSP.

69. Anonymous Account Book #3, Hamilton Papers, HSP. See "Kentucky Store" shipments, March 30, 1792, p. 237; May 11, 1792, pp. 250–53; October 16, 1792, 300. These three shipments cost this merchant £852; of this, £110 was for transportation costs. According to Warren R. Hofstra, *The Planting of New Virginia: Settlement and Landscape in the Shenandoah Valley* (Baltimore: Johns Hopkins University Press, 2004), 283–85, other towns of the Valley, such as Winchester, Va., saw a similar boom from the opening of Kentucky, but unlike Carlisle, much of it came from supplying settlers on their way west. For information about consumer markets in Kentucky at this time, see Elizabeth A. Perkins, "The Consumer Frontier: Household Consumption in Early Kentucky," *JAH* 78.2 (1991): 486–510; Perkins, *Border Life: Experience and Memory in the Revolutionary Ohio Valley* (Chapel Hill: University of North Carolina Press, 1998), chap. 3.

70. John H. Clun, "March on Pittsburgh, 1794," ed. Herbert Aptheker *PMHB* 71.1 (1947): 65. Clun's remarks referenced Samuel Postlethwaite, the merchant who set up his son with a store in Kentucky.

71. Herman, *Town House*, 80.

72. Blumin, *Emergence of the Middle Class*, 46; Bushman, *Refinement of America*, chap. 8.

73. For quotes, see *CG*, March 25, 1789 (italicized emphasis mine). Hofstra, *Planting of New Virginia*, 300, notes similar blending of work and domestic life in Winchester, Va., where "artisans often attached their shop to an end of their house."

74. *CG*, January 28, 1801 (quotes describing the structure). For floor plan types in the mid-Atlantic, see Lanier and Herman, *Everyday Architecture*, 21–24; Herman, *Town House*, 85–88.

75. *CG*, February 11, 1801.

76. *Direct Tax of 1798*, Schedule A.

77. For the "large and commodious" tavern of Jacob Crever, see *CG*, December 29, 1802; for John Hughes's "convenient" house, see ibid., March 5, 1794. For Lindsey, see

ibid., February 11, 1789. For a discussion of the eighteenth-century meaning of "convenient," see Crowley, "Sensibility of Comfort," 761–62.

78. Cazenove, *Cazenove Journal 1794*, 56 (for the streets); Cutler, *Life, Journals and Correspondence* 1:401 (for the houses).

79. Anonymous, "A Garrison Town in Pennsylvania Fifty Years Ago," n.d., HSP.

80. Keller, *Rural Politics*, 40–48, 62. For a comparative perspective, see Riordon, *Many Identities*, 116–19. Easton's leading men, like those in Carlisle, endorsed the Federalist Ross. But Northampton County voters gave McKean 80 percent of their votes.

INDEX

African Americans, 53, 65, 80, 99, 101, 133,
164, 168, 184, 191, 201. *See also* slaves
Albany Congress, 81
Algonquian, 7, 15
Allegheny mountains, viii *map 1*, 48, 89
Allegheny Path, 16 *map 2*, 30, 68
Allegheny (river), 16 *map 2*, 30, 85
Allentown (Pennsylvania), 1, 35, 118
Alricks, Hermanus, 52
American Revolution, 3, 5, 9, 112–53, 161,
170–77, 198, 207; Carlisle's functions
during, 157; local commitment to, 114–23,
126, 132, 139–48, 182, 203; local conditional support of, 139–48; and the local
economy, 133–39, 149; idea, spirit, or elán
of, 112–13, 115, 123, 141, 146; politics and
political revolution of, 123–24, 132, 139,
154–55; postrevolutionary economy, 149,
163–69; postrevolutionary emigration,
169–71; and Presbyterians, 62; radicalism
of, 117, 139, 154, 173; and the townscape,
124–32; Whiskey protests similar to,
193–95; women and, 166. *See also* artificers regiment
André, John, 125–27
Anglicans: in Carlisle, 60–63; connection to
proprietary authority, 7, 62; ethnicity and
ethnic identity, 7, 95, 97, 101, 136, 206;
churches, 44, 58, 62–64, 177; as founders
of College of Philadelphia, 155; in Ireland,
116; ministers, 62; in early republican
politics, 174; settlement areas, 9, 39; and
Thomas Penn, 24–25, 41. *See also* Barton,
Thomas; St. John's

anti-Constitutionalists, 140. *See also* Republicans
Antifederalists, 151–52, 165, 171–76, 193–94
aristocracy, 116, 152, 173
Armstrong, John: critic of postrevolutionary economy, 149; as Dickinson College
trustee, 157; emigrant from Ireland, 58;
as a Federalist, 171; Kittanning expedition, 85–91, 112; as Major-General of the
Pennsylvania militia, 114; as a New Light
Presbyterian, 60, 155–56; as opponent of
fur traders, 103; participant in the American Revolution, 115, 118–19, 141, 182; proprietors' man, 48, 52, 58–59; slaveholder,
53; and Stump rioters, 107; surveyor, 48;
York county resident, 72. *See also* Kittanning; proprietors' men
army: Forbes's, 81, 89; Braddock's, 83; British, 89–92, 97, 99, 129, 135; Continental
(Carlisle as supply and manufacturing
depot for), 114, 124, 128–35, 144, 147–48,
152–53, 206; Continental (dependence on
British weapons), 129; Continental (guns
of), 135; Continental (men's service in),
115, 119–20, 133, 135, 138, 195; Continental (recruiting efforts of), 141–43;
Continental (staff departments of), 135;
Continental (reliance on local population
for supplies), 133–36, 146, 207; Continental (tensions within), 145; Continental
(units raised in Carlisle and Cumberland
County), 113–14, 122; Continental (vet-
erans of), 151; Continental (wives of officers), 138; federal troops during Whiskey

ACKNOWLEDGMENTS

A project that has taken as long as this one incurs many debts. Where do I begin to offer my thanks? To be sure, the staff at many libraries and archives aided immensely in this work. While researching this book, I spent months at the Cumberland County Historical Society in Carlisle and the Historical Society of Pennsylvania in Philadelphia. The staffs at these libraries offered valuable advice on their collections and leads to sources. I owe special thanks to historian Merri Lou Schaumann at CCHS. Aside from her voluminous work on early Carlisle, from which I draw heavily in this book, she directed me toward several important sources, including the 1751 map of Carlisle that appears in Chapter 1. In addition to those libraries, I spent time working with the sources at Dickinson College's Archives and Special Collections—a gem of a small-college archives—as well as the Pennsylvania State Archives, the Presbyterian Historical Society, and the Library Company of Philadelphia. A research fellowship at the David Library of the American Revolution was also invaluable to my revisions. It was there that I found some of the most provocative materials tucked away in the reels of the Baynton, Wharton, and Morgan Papers. I offer my sincerest thanks to staff at all of these institutions for their assistance.

I also wish to thank the editors at *PMHB* and University of Tennessee Press for permission to republish sections of the article "Relying on the Saucy Men of the Backcountry: Middlemen and the Fur Trade in Pennsylvania," which appeared in *PMHB* 129 (2005): 133–62, and parts of the essay, "Status, Culture, and the Structural World in the Valley of Pennsylvania," which appeared as Chapter 6 in *After the Backcountry: Rural Life in the Great Valley of Virginia, 1800-1900.* ed. Kenneth E. Koons and Warren R. Hofstra (Knoxville: University of Tennessee Press, 2000).

I have numerous other professional debts to honor. As a graduate student, I was generously supported by the History Department at William & Mary and the Philadelphia Center for Early American Studies (now the McNeil Center) at the University of Pennsylvania. I owe my advisor, Jim Whittenburg, and Richard Dunn, then-Director of the Philadelphia Center, many thanks for their support and the hours they put into reading and commenting on a much earlier version of this work. Since completing my degree, the two institutions where I have held faculty appointments—California State University, Northridge and, since 1998, Muhlenberg College—have supported the research and writing of this book with numerous faculty research grants. Equally if not more significant, however, are my history department colleagues at these two institutions. Several of them, including Tom Maddux at Northridge and Dan Wilson at Muhlenberg, read and commented on chapters. I especially appreciate the time they took from their own projects to advise me on mine. Tom Maddux, especially, always had faith in me and this project. I appreciated his support then and still do. I also want to thank my colleagues at these institutions who have become such close friends over the years. My very dear friend and colleague Denise Spooner, with whom I shared an office for a time at Northridge, has been a confidante for many years now. She, perhaps more than anyone else, heard about all of the trials and tribulations of this project—and my life. She took time from her own busy schedule to proofread the manuscript. I know that her sharp editorial eye clarified my prose and I thank her so much for her hard work. But more important, I thank her (and her husband, Joe) for her friendship and the counseling she offered (for free!) over the years that we have known each other. I am sure she must have wondered how a specialist in twentieth-century California came to be reading a manuscript on eighteenth-century Carlisle. But as she knows after teaching at Northridge, anything is possible. At Muhlenberg I have many debts as well. My History Department colleagues, including Anna Adams, Susan Clemens-Bruder, Mark Stein, Tom Cragin, and Gary Jones, offered not just advice and encouragement about my work, but also their friendship. I count myself lucky to be a part of such a great department.

Still other professional colleagues shaped this book in critical ways. Owen S. (Steve) Ireland, William Pencak, and Simon Newman all read this manuscript in very early form. They urged me in their separate ways to speak more to Carlisle's contentious history. This book reflects their insights. Greg Knouff read and commented on my chapters pertaining to the Revolution. I thank him, too, for his worthwhile feedback. My good friends Donna Rilling and Rose Beiler, fellow early Americanists, were also sources of ideas, information, and inspiration. Our lengthy discussions of our work (and academia more generally) over long weekends at one or the other of our houses helped me clarify my interpretations. Last, but certainly not least, are the comments offered by Dan Richter, Bob Lockhart, and the two readers of this manuscript for Penn Press, Paul Douglas Newman and Liam Riordan. Their comments pushed me to sharpen my argument. This is, without question, a better book because of their feedback. As another former Carlisle resident, Dan especially has understood my fascination with Carlisle's tremendously compelling past.

Still, no book project is completed without many personal debts. This is especially true in my case, as I have lived several distinct lives while completing this project. On a light note, old friends like fellow Dickinson alum, Barb Reed, have reappeared in the last few years. Trips to Manhattan with her have been great ways to blow off steam when I felt like I wanted to quit. I thank her for her friendship and generosity. On a more serious note, I also send my sincerest thanks and admiration to Tom Legg, who lived with me and this project for a long time. Although we are no longer together as this comes to fruition, the life we had shapes the way I think about and will remember this project. But life moves on. It is Peter Messer who has been with me as I finish this work. He has been such a pleasant and welcome surprise in my life. Smart, funny, a tenacious debater, and a very good cyclist to boot, he has taken my life in new and unanticipated directions. Having lived with me as I put the finishing touches on this manuscript, he also proved to be a man of infinite patience. I appreciate his smarts, his knowledge of early American history, and, most of all, his companionship. Finally, I am deeply indebted to my family—my brother, Bill, and my parents, Anne and Will Ridner. Although my parents did not live to see the completion of this project—the one they referred to as "my paper"—they nonetheless always supported their headstrong and often high-strung daughter. This book is dedicated to them.